Europe and the Decline of Social Democracy in Britain

From Attlee to Brexit

Adrian Williamson

THE BOYDELL PRESS

First published 2019
The Boydell Press, Woodbridge

ISBN 978 1 78327 443 7

The Boydell Press is an imprint of Boydell & Brewer Ltd
PO Box 9, Woodbridge, Suffolk IP12 3DF, UK
and of Boydell & Brewer Inc.
668 Mt Hope Avenue, Rochester, NY 14620–2731, USA
website: www.boydellandbrewer.com

A CIP catalogue record for this book is available
from the British Library

The publisher has no responsibility for the continued existence or accuracy of URLs for external or third-party internet websites referred to in this book, and does not guarantee that any content on such websites is, or will remain, accurate or appropriate

This publication is printed on acid-free paper

MIX
Paper from
responsible sources
FSC® C013056
www.fsc.org

Printed and bound in Great Britain by
TJ International Ltd, Padstow, Cornwall

Contents

Tables

Graph

Preface

This book has grown out of a paper, of the same title, that I gave at the Annual Conference of the Economic History Society at Royal Holloway, University of London, on 1 April 2017. Some might think that this was an appropriate date to discuss Brexit, and the events of the intervening months have not necessarily dispelled that impression.

Anyone who takes an interest in British politics or history will have realised that 23 June 2016, when the United Kingdom narrowly voted to leave the European Union, represented an important turning point in the country's post-war history. For some this was a moment of liberation, as the nation finally shook off the European yoke. For others, it was a catastrophe, a dark mixture of nativism and nostalgia for a non-existent past. Certainly, the referendum exposed divisions within British society: friends fell out and families were at war, at least verbally. The atmosphere was quite unlike a general election where, usually, both winners and losers shrug their shoulders and look forward to another contest a few years hence.

This book is an attempt to understand what has led us, as a nation, to this point. I am old enough to remember the UK's accession in 1973, and the previous referendum in 1975, although I did not then have a vote. Over the course of my adult lifetime, the British (or, at least, the 52% who supported Brexit) have moved from engagement with Europe to semi-detachment, and then to outright hostility. This book is an attempt to understand that process.

I am very grateful to Boydell & Brewer for their support in relation to this project. It has been a fascinating exercise to seek to unravel the sequence of events that led to 23 June 2016. It has been all the more intriguing to do so while those events have continued to unfold, with the May government conducting protracted negotiations with their European counterparts and British politicians of all sorts seeking to make sense of the people's verdict. I have, in general, entered into a self-denying ordinance to end my account in June 2016. Subsequent developments will, no doubt, be the subject of much scholarly endeavour in due course: but that must await some form of denouement.

Abbreviations

AES	Alternative Economic Strategy
BBC	British Broadcasting Corporation
BIE	Britain in Europe
BNP	British National Party
CAP	Common Agricultural Policy
CBI	Confederation of British Industry
DEA	Department of Economic Affairs
ECJ	European Court of Justice
EEC	European Economic Community
EFTA	European Free Trade Association
EMS	European Monetary System
EMU	Economic and Monetary Union
ERM	Exchange Rate Mechanism (of the EMS)
EU	European Union
FCO	Foreign and Commonwealth Office
GDP/GNP	Gross Domestic/National Product
HC Deb	House of Commons Debates
IEA	Institute of Economic Affairs
LCE	Labour Committee for Europe
LCMSC	Labour Common Market Safeguards Campaign
MEP	Member of European Parliament

MP	Member of Parliament
NEB	National Enterprise Board
NEC	National Executive Committee (of the Labour Party)
NEDC	National Economic Development Council
NRC	National Referendum Campaign
ONS	Office for National Statistics
PLP	Parliamentary Labour Party
PPS	Parliamentary Private Secretary
SDP	Social Democratic Party
SEA	Single European Act
TGWU	Transport and General Workers' Union
TUC	Trades Union Congress
UK	United Kingdom
UKIP	UK Independence Party
VAT	Value Added Tax

Introduction

The British Government and the British people have been through a searching debate during the last few years on the subject of their relations with Europe. The result of the debate has been our present application. It was a decision arrived at, not on any narrow or short-term grounds, but as a result of a thorough assessment over a considerable period of the needs of our own country, of Europe, and of the free world as a whole. We recognise it as a great decision, a turning point in our history.

(Edward Heath, address given 9 August 1961)[1]

The British people have voted to leave the European Union and their will must be respected. ... I was absolutely clear about my belief that Britain is stronger, safer and better off inside the European Union ... but the British people have made a very clear decision to take a different path.

(David Cameron, resignation speech, 24 June 2016)[2]

Independence Day

In the hit 1996 film *Independence Day*, people converge in the Nevada desert in the aftermath of a worldwide attack by an extra-terrestrial race. The events of 23 June 2016 were a little less dramatic than this in Britain, but only a little. The polls closed at 10pm at the end of only the third-ever nationwide referendum. It had been an acrimonious and divisive campaign, a far cry from the previous European referendum of 1975. There was no exit poll and so there was little immediate excitement. A YouGov opinion poll suggested Remain were on course for a 52%/48% victory. At 10.15pm, Nigel Farage, the leading figure in the 'unofficial' Leave.Eu camp, appeared to concede defeat. The pound soared to $1.50, its strongest performance in 2016.

The results, when they came, presented a somewhat different story. Just after midnight, the first significant voting figures were announced: a narrow win in Newcastle for Remain and a big victory for Leave in Sunderland. The pound fell by nearly 4.7%, greater than the Black Wednesday crash in 1992. More votes were counted; by 4am, Leave was well ahead, with a lead of 500,000 votes. At this point, Farage, surrounded by cheering supporters, claimed victory:

> Dare to dream that the dawn is breaking on an independent United Kingdom. This, if the predictions now are right, this will be a victory for real people, a victory for ordinary people, a victory for decent people. We have fought against the multinationals, we have fought against the big merchant banks, we have fought against big politics, we have fought against lies, corruption and deceit … we will have done it without having to fight, without a single bullet being fired. … Let June 23 go down in our history as our independence day.[3]

These were chilling words for the Remain camp, not least because a Brexit supporter had murdered one of their number, Jo Cox MP, during the campaign. At 4.40am, David Dimbleby announced on the BBC that Leave had won. The pound was by now in free fall, eventually dropping by 10% to $1.33, a thirty-one-year low and the biggest one-day plunge ever seen. The FTSE 100 fell more than 7% within minutes of the markets opening. When the votes were all counted, Leave had secured 51.9% (17,410,742) to 48.1% for Remain (16,141,241).[4]

At 8.23am, the Prime Minister, David Cameron, announced his intention to resign: it was necessary for someone else 'to be the captain that steers our country to its next destination'. A few minutes later, Mark Carney, Governor of the Bank of England, sought to calm financial markets by saying that the Bank would take any measures needed to secure economic and financial stability. Carney looked a little panicked, but, unlike the Chancellor, George Osborne, who had apparently gone into hiding, he was at least willing to face the cameras.[5]

The government was, therefore, in some disarray. Labour, the official Opposition, was in little better shape. Over the weekend of 25 and 26 June, a series of Shadow Cabinet members resigned in protest at what they claimed had been the lukewarm support that their leader, Jeremy Corbyn, had offered the Remain cause. On the following Tuesday, Labour MPs passed a motion of no confidence in Corbyn by a majority of 172 to 40.[6]

This was, therefore, a calamitous blow to the leadership of the British state. The government had worked hard for a Remain vote, and Cameron and Osborne were in the forefront of this effort. Their political careers were over, and it would be necessary for others to seek to rebuild the government. Labour had been generally of the same mind and was equally devastated by the result. Those politicians who would survive the referendum were faced with a series of difficult challenges. There had, after all, never been a previous national referendum that had mandated change, and so these were uncharted waters. Could the Conservatives identify within their ranks plausible candidates for senior ministerial roles who had Leave credentials? If not, could Remain supporters take on those roles and implement a Brexit in which they did not believe? Was there available 'a Europe of sovereign nation states, trading together', as Farage suggested in his victory speech? If not, on what terms might the UK be able to trade with the EU? How was the UK to stay united in circumstances where London, Scotland and Northern Ireland had voted decisively for Remain, against the wider trend?

The argument of this book

This book will not attempt to answer these questions (which remain unresolved at the time of writing) but will rather seek to explore how and why the events of June 2016 occurred. Why did Britain change from a country which, in 1961, and following a great debate, had made 'a great decision' to go into Europe to a nation that was determined in 2016 to get 'my country back'? How did the commitment in 1961 to take 'a great opportunity for new advances together' turn into what has been described as the 'hysteria, hatred, savage emotions, and the sinister monster of exclusionary, ethnic nationalism' of the 2016 referendum? Of course, not everyone in 1961 supported entry, and the politicians then arguing for this course were not required to submit to the rough and tumble of a referendum. Nor, equally, did everyone in 2016 wish to 'take back control'. However, the direction of travel was clear enough.[7]

As will be considered further in Chapter 7, there has been no shortage of instant analysis of these questions. Not surprisingly, explanations have tended to concentrate on the events in the period running up to the referendum: political miscalculations by Cameron; the defection of Boris Johnson; the rise of UKIP; the misuse of personal data; public discontent over immigration, and so on. The aim of this book is to look at matters in a somewhat longer perspective and to suggest that the Brexit decision stems from changes in British political culture that date back considerably further. In short, the UK was once a social democracy, and, therefore, it made perfect sense to join a Europe that marched to a social democratic beat. But since the 1980s, Britain has ceased to be a social democracy and has taken the course of neoliberalism (or Thatcherism). In so deciding, the country has, increasingly, moved away from the EEC/EU and, in particular, from 'Social Europe', the concept that a market system needs to be complemented by extensive measures to promote social solidarity.[8]

What, then, do I mean by social democracy? I do not suggest that domestic policy was ever constrained by any very rigid ideology. The term 'social democracy' has had many meanings over the years, but I equate this very approximately to the policies pursued by British governments, especially Labour governments, from the 1940s to the 1970s. These policies included: an explicit commitment to full employment as a central goal of macro-economic strategy; egalitarian and redistributive approaches to taxation and public spending; strong trade unions, with a substantial role in both industrial and political affairs; a mixed economy, with utilities held in public ownership; comprehensive education; the welfare state; and a substantial public rented housing sector.

To describe this programme as social democratic requires a number of qualifications. For one thing, British politicians of the Centre Left, let alone the Centre Right, did not operate within tight ideological constraints, a point returned to in Chapter 1. Moreover, British social democracy had much in common not only with European social democracy but also with the forms of Christian Democracy practised on the Continent for much of the post-war period. There were differences with Europe as well, not least because the UK was not a Catholic, and scarcely a Christian, country during this period. Nonetheless, for all its untidiness and incoherence, 'social democratic' remains an apt description of the loose bundle of policies adopted by UK governments before the advent of neoliberalism. In that sense, I am using 'social democracy' as a convenient shorthand for the policy mix generally adopted before 1979.

That this version of social democracy collapsed in the late 1970s, and has not subsequently revived, seems indisputable. British governments since 1979 have all operated within a Thatcherite framework: full employment has vanished as a political objective; privatisation, deregulation and outsourcing have been followed with almost religious fervour; the trade unions have been 'tamed'. Public provision has declined and, in the case of housing, all but disappeared. Above all, the UK has become a much less equal society and, in this respect, has taken a markedly different course from most European countries.

What has this to do with British commitment, or lack of it, to the EEC? I suggest that the period of the UK's most enthusiastic engagement with Europe coincided with the high tide of domestic social democracy. Between the early 1960s and the mid-1980s, it was the social democratic centre – that is to say, the Labour Right and the Tory Left – who were the best friends to the EEC. In this period, those who opposed membership were mainly to be found on the Left, who wished to move forward to a much more full-blooded version of socialism. They thought, probably rightly, that EEC rules would obstruct the socialised, planned economy they wished to develop. Opposition on the Right was confined to a Powellite rump, who argued for a fundamentalist form of free-market nationalism. However, most Conservatives were content to make their peace, at least to some degree, with the prevailing social democratic order. In any event, the EEC appeared to provide a solid safeguard against further progress towards socialism, for precisely the reasons the Left feared.

In this analysis, the crucial year for the UK's relationship with the EEC is not 2016, but 1988. In that year, the Right began to turn against Europe and the Centre Left began to see the virtues of membership. With Thatcherism now in the ascendant, Conservatives became increasingly anxious that Social Europe, and EU rules that sought to regulate capitalism, might become a fetter upon their domestic objectives. Socialism was no longer a threat, and British Tories needed no support from Brussels against their domestic opponents. At the same time, the Labour Movement, despairing of achieving a domestic political breakthrough, began to perceive the EU as an external ally against the internal excesses of Thatcherism. At this stage, Labour, although moving rightwards, was still a thoroughly social democratic party.

There, roughly, matters stood for the next twenty years. 'Euroscepticism' became more and more the norm on the Conservative side. Tory aficionados of Europe were thin on the ground. Labour, and its union allies, settled into a general acceptance of membership, albeit with limited enthusiasm for developments towards European unity such as the Euro. In domestic policy, however, the UK had fewer and fewer genuine social democrats. On the Conservative side, Thatcherism was an unquestioned orthodoxy. Repeated electoral failure after 1997 did not give rise to any great policy reappraisal. The 'near socialism' of the Macmillan and Heath eras was regarded with contempt. New Labour dominated the scene on the Centre Left after 1994 and treated Old Labour egalitarianism with similar disdain. The Liberal Democrats absorbed their former social democratic allies and then took the path of economic liberalism.

There matters stood when the financial crisis struck in 2008/9. The effect of the crisis, as with the oil shock of the 1970s, was to shake up the political system and send politicians and voters scurrying to the Left and Right. On the Left, New Labour, which had put most of its eggs in the City basket, ran out of ideas and lost power. The Labour Party swung to the Left, at first gently and then more sharply. After 2015, the Corbyn–McDonnell leadership urged a socialist approach, which had been little heard since the 1980s. The new leadership were also, relevantly in this context, veteran Eurosceptics. The Eurosceptic Right of the Tory Party saw the opportunity to press for, and get, a referendum on membership.

At the same time, austerity dominated domestic policy, with the strong support of the Conservatives and Liberal Democrats. The pre-2015 leadership of Labour was unable to decide whether it was for or against austerity, but Corbyn had a clear anti-austerity message. Austerity served to expose the cracks in British society, which had been concealed, at least to some extent, by the financially based boom that had sustained the economy prior to the crash. The nationalist Right, in particular UKIP, skilfully exploited these fissures. The 2016 referendum, in contrast to the exercise in 1975, revealed deep divisions in British society, between young and old, and rich and poor, and sharp regional variations, especially between London and the rest of England. By 2016 there were few English political leaders willing to stand up for social democracy, and fewer still who would couple this with wholehearted support for Europe.

To put these arguments in some initial context, I next set out a brief chronology of events in the period covered by this book, and then summarise what follows in the substantive chapters.

A brief chronology

The aftermath of the Second World War gave rise to the need to rebuild shattered economies and societies. In Britain, this took the form of a social democratic policy framework, pursued energetically by the Labour government of Clement Attlee (1945–51) and the Conservative governments of 1951 to 1964, in particular that led by Harold Macmillan (1957–63). In Europe, an important aspect of reconstruction was the formation in 1951 of the European Coal and Steel Community by the original six states (France, West Germany, the Benelux nations and Italy). In 1957, the six signed the Treaty of Rome, which established the European Economic Community (EEC). The Treaty aimed to create a common market in goods and services, set up a customs union and provide for free movement of capital and labour.

Britain did not, initially, seek to join the EEC and, indeed, was instrumental in the creation in 1960 of the rival European Free Trade Association (EFTA). However, in 1961, the Macmillan government, with Edward Heath as chief negotiator, applied for membership of the EEC. The French President, Charles de Gaulle, vetoed this application in 1963. Despite this rebuff, British government policy generally favoured membership, while domestic programmes remained broadly social democratic. The Labour government of Harold Wilson renewed the application in 1966/7, and once more encountered a French veto.

The departure of de Gaulle in 1969 opened the door to British admission. The Conservative government of 1970–4, with Heath now Prime Minister, successfully negotiated membership, and Britain, Denmark and Ireland joined the EEC in 1973. The British honeymoon was, however, quite short. The Labour government of 1974–9, with Wilson once more Prime Minister, won the 1974 general elections on a platform of renegotiating membership, and then putting the results to the people in a referendum. Following those renegotiations, a referendum was held in 1975, in which the vote to remain was 2 to 1 in favour.

The 1970s proved a turbulent period in British politics. The rise in oil prices in 1973/4, and the subsequent recession, caused many to question the post-war policy model, as inflation and unemployment rose sharply and simultaneously. The Left, led by Tony Benn, developed the Alternative Economic Strategy (AES). The AES, which, inter alia, required import controls, was incompatible with EEC membership, and from the early 1970s onwards, the Left and the unions were hostile to continued membership. The Left dominated Labour after its election defeat in 1979, and withdrawal from the EEC remained party policy until the late 1980s.

The Right agreed that the post-war model was broken, but they proposed a rather different solution, which has been widely characterised as Thatcherism or neoliberalism. This involved the conquest of inflation through monetary discipline, the abandonment of the full employment commitment to which both parties had subscribed since the war, and widespread privatisation of nationalised industries and social housing. Margaret Thatcher deposed Heath as Tory leader in 1975, and became Prime Minister in 1979. Her government (1979–90), and that of her successor, John Major (1990–7), enthusiastically pursued these neoliberal policies.

Meanwhile, the EEC had been developing. In 1979, the European Monetary System (EMS) introduced the European currency unit (Ecu) and the exchange rate mechanism (ERM). All EEC members joined the ERM except the UK. Greece (1981) and Spain and Portugal (1986) became EEC members. In 1987, the Single European Act entered into force (SEA). The SEA sought to complete the work begun by the Treaty of Rome in order to create a single market. The Thatcher government was a keen supporter of the SEA, but Thatcher insisted that the UK remain outside the ERM, despite strong Treasury and Foreign Office pressure to join. In terms of domestic policy, the 1980s were a bruising period for the British Left. Labour lost the elections of 1983 and 1987, with the Conservatives securing 100-plus majorities on both occasions. The unions were defeated in a series of high-profile strikes. In this context, the appointment of Jacques Delors, a French Socialist, as president of the European Commission in 1985, became significant. Delors was an evangelist for the single market. However, he argued that this economic development had to be matched by increased European integration and EEC-driven social development (Social Europe).

Delors became something of a hero to the demoralised British Left, receiving a rapturous reception at the 1988 TUC Conference. But, at the same time, he, and Social Europe, came to be seen by many British

Conservatives as a threat. Thatcher, in a speech at Bruges (also in 1988), denounced Social Europe and made clear her intention that Brussels should not be allowed to undo the changes that her government had implemented since 1979. However, although the Right remained strong in Britain, Thatcher's own position was weakening by the late 1980s. Against her wishes, the UK finally joined the ERM in October 1990. Despite this concession, in November 1990 the Conservatives replaced her with Major, who was thought likely to provide a more emollient form of Thatcherism. Major succeeded in reviving Tory fortunes and the party narrowly won the 1992 general election.

This electoral success did not, however, make for smooth political sailing. In 1991, the Maastricht Treaty on European Union was signed. This brought the EU into existence, paved the way for monetary union and included a Social Chapter. Major signed the treaty, but secured a British opt-out on both monetary union and the Social Chapter. He appeared, at first, to have party support for his approach. However, on 16 September 1992 ('Black Wednesday'), the government was forced to withdraw the pound from the ERM after it was unable to keep it above its agreed lower limit.

Black Wednesday irretrievably damaged the credibility of the Major government. ERM membership had been central to his economic programme, and, without it, the government appeared rudderless. This policy failure emboldened Conservative opponents of the UK's involvement with the EU, and during 1992/3 the 'Maastricht rebels' in the Commons engaged in frequent revolts on crucial votes. The government came close to defeat on a number of occasions. The Major government limped on until the 1997 general election, when it suffered overwhelming defeat to Labour.

Since 1994, Labour had moved sharply rightwards under the 'New Labour' leadership of Tony Blair. In domestic terms, New Labour accepted most of the Thatcherite legacy and, in certain respects, such as the Private Finance Initiative (PFI), even extended it. In relation to Europe, New Labour struck a more positive note than the

Conservatives had managed in the later Thatcher and Major eras. The Blair (1997–2007) and Brown (2007–10) governments had no great difficulty in securing parliamentary consent to the Amsterdam Treaty (1997) and the Treaty of Lisbon (2007), which extended the process begun at Maastricht. Labour also supported enlargement to the East, with ten countries joining in 2004 and two more in 2007, mainly former Soviet bloc states.

However, the principal business of the EU in the New Labour period was the creation (in 1999) and implementation thereafter of the single currency, the Euro. This was the culmination of the process of monetary union, which had begun in 1979 and had moved forward at Maastricht. In due course, the Euro became the official currency of 19 of the 28 EU member states. Despite much agonising, and Blair's personal support, the UK did not join.

New Labour won the general elections of 1997, 2001 and 2005, and, for the Conservatives, the 1997–2007 period was the mirror image of Labour's agonies in the 1980s. The party tried a series of leaders (William Hague, 1997–2001; Iain Duncan Smith, 2001–3; Michael Howard, 2003–5). All were strongly Eurosceptic – Duncan Smith had been a Maastricht rebel – but none had much electoral appeal. The party also appeared to have moved out of the political mainstream, socially conservative at a time when New Labour had a broadly popular liberal agenda, and stridently Eurosceptic despite the fact that many voters appeared to have little interest in European policy. In 2005, following its third successive defeat, the party turned to David Cameron as leader. He offered a modernising platform, coming to terms with social change and downplaying the significance of Europe.

Until 2008, New Labour, whether through luck or judgement, enjoyed ten years of economic growth. The financial crisis of that year saw the luck run out. The economy experienced a deep recession in 2008/9, and the public finances plunged into deficit. As in 1992, the government struggled to recover its credibility following an economic crisis. Labour lost the 2010 general election, but the Conservatives did not achieve an overall majority, despite Cameron's modernisation programme. The party, therefore, entered into a coalition with the Liberal Democrats. The two parties, at least at leadership level, were close ideologically, being committed to a mix of economic and social liberalism.

The consequences of the financial crisis dominated British politics between 2008 and 2015. Broadly speaking, there were two alternative solutions on offer to restore the public finances. The Brown government in effect adopted a neo-Keynesian approach from 2008 until 2010, seeking to grow its way out of the crisis through deficit financing. The Conservatives, with the strong support of the Liberal Democrats, argued for 'austerity', i.e. deep cuts in public spending. This was the policy pursued by the Coalition between 2010 and 2015. It proved more successful electorally for the Conservatives than for the Liberal Democrats. The Tories won a small overall majority at the 2015 general election, but the Liberal Democrats were rewarded for their unstinting support for austerity with almost complete annihilation.

There had, since at least the early 1990s, been a Europhobic fringe in British politics, small parties who campaigned on the single issue of British membership of the EU/EEC. However, until the financial crisis, these groups were little more than political gadflies. From 2008 onwards, however, UKIP and Farage began to emerge as serious political contenders, albeit with little parliamentary representation. The effects of austerity, and increasing public concern over immigration, especially from the recent accession states, saw UKIP's support surge in the polls. In 2013, Cameron felt compelled to offer an in/out referendum on EU membership, partly in a bid to dampen down the UKIP threat and partly to placate Eurosceptics in his own party. This was the Conservative position at the 2015 election, and Cameron's government then legislated for the referendum.

Chapter summaries

Chapter 1 seeks to describe the policy framework that existed in Britain in the post-war period from 1945 until the mid-1970s. This was both an economic Golden Age and an era in which the social democratic system was in full flower. Full employment, secured through interventionist industrial and demand management strategies, was a key policy goal and was consistently achieved. The trade unions had, as a result, a very strong position, and governments, both Labour and Tory, were obliged to bargain with them. Social policy was egalitarian. The state intervened actively, building large numbers of houses for rent and developing a network of comprehensive schools. Governments also adopted a redistributive approach to taxation. These policies were underpinned, at least to some extent, by 'democratic socialist' thinkers, such as R.H. Tawney and Tony Crosland, who believed that it was a central function of the state to promote increased equality. In consequence of these policies, the Britain of the 1970s was the most equal it had ever been. However, the oil price shock of 1973/4, and the subsequent economic crisis, put huge strain on this framework. Waiting in the wings were the Thatcherites, who had never subscribed to these ideas. After 1979, Britain took a very different course. Full employment ceased to be a policy goal, and joblessness increased to levels not seen since the 1930s. The Thatcherites had little time for interventionist industrial and demand management strategies, believing that the proper function of government was to create the conditions for economic growth and then leave matters to the market. The trade unions were marginalised industrially and politically. Large numbers of council houses were sold off, and very little social housing was built. The comprehensive ideal in education receded. The state's role changed significantly, from provider to procurer. In short, as Martin Daunton puts it, Britain changed 'from an opportunity state to an enterprise society', in which 'the pursuit of incentives at the cost of social integration became possible'. Since 1979, a much less equal society has emerged, and Britain, together with other English-speaking countries, has taken a very different approach to social solidarity than that pursued in continental Europe. The crisis of the mid-1970s had exposed a fundamental divide in British society as to whether the country should persist with the post-war model or should turn to the Right, or, as some were urging, the Left. After 1979, the UK moved decisively to the Right and away from the social democratic approach, which it had pursued until 1979, and which remained largely intact in continental Europe.[9]

Chapter 2 attempts to contextualise Britain's attempts to join the EEC between 1960 and 1973. The UK's dealings with the EEC in this period consisted of two failed attempts to join (1961–3 and 1966–7), followed by a successful application after 1970, which culminated in accession in 1973. In this process, the British people were not deceived, as Brexiteers were to claim in 2016. On the contrary, it was made clear that joining the EEC entailed far more than participation in a Common Market. Examining the arguments of the key exponents of entry, one can see that concerns about sovereignty were dealt with in a detailed and sophisticated manner. The chapter focuses on three such figures in particular: Harold Macmillan, whose government made the first application in 1961–3; Edward Heath, chief negotiator in that application and then Prime Minister during the 1970–3 process; and Roy Jenkins, whose support was critical to the success of the Heath government's application. These were not the only pro-European voices in this period, but they were certainly among the most persuasive. Their point of view was typical of the more enthusiastic British advocates of entry. These arguments went well beyond claims of economic advantage, important though these were. The UK was setting out with the Europeans upon a collective journey with a considerable economic and social element. Britain would become part of a United Europe, and such integration would involve changes in the UK's sovereignty, but this was not a loss, but a pooling, of sovereignty. Crucially, the politicians who put forward this case most ardently were also those who were striving the hardest to uphold the social democratic model. They saw no contradiction between these objectives. As Heath told the

Commons in the decisive debate of October 1971, this was, after all, a shared enterprise, for 'surely we must consider the consequences of staying out … we should be denying to Europe, also – let us look outside these shores for a moment – its full potential, its opportunities of developing economically and politically'.[10]

Chapter 3 seeks to explain the balance of opinion in this same period between those who favoured entry and the dissenters of Left and Right. The leadership in each main political party was committed to EEC membership, albeit this commitment was often framed in qualified terms. Ranged against the respective leaderships were the Left of the Labour Movement and the Powellite Right of the Conservative Party. The ground on which both Left and Right chose to take their stand was sovereignty. The Left had always been suspicious of the EEC, believing it to be a capitalist club. These suspicions became more pronounced as the Left, from the late 1960s onwards, began to develop a detailed critique of the economic policies of the 1964–70 government. That government, they argued, had been overwhelmed by short-term difficulties and had, therefore, failed to pursue socialist policies with sufficient vigour. The answer was to develop a much more coherent economic strategy, based on socialist planning and controls on capital and imports. Labour should march purposefully towards the promised land of full socialism, rather than settling for the soggy social democratic compromise that the party had offered in the 1960s. The rules and structures of the EEC stood in the way of these policies. Britain should not, therefore, join, or remain within, the EEC. The Left opposed Heath's application for membership, and then campaigned in 1974 and 1975 to leave. For the Right, the position was more complex. The free trade and free movement aspects of the EEC looked attractive to many Conservatives: the Treaty of Rome would not prevent them from pursuing the domestic economic policies they favoured and might inhibit a Labour government, particularly one of the Left, from carrying out a fully socialist programme. On the Right, Enoch Powell, by 1968 semi-detached from the Conservative Party, was a relatively lone voice in opposing membership. His case was couched almost entirely in terms of sovereignty, but his crusade against the EEC formed part of his wider campaign against much that had characterised post-war British government policy. Indeed, those who opposed British membership in this period tended to be at the fringes of mainstream politics and to reject the prevailing social democratic model. The Left believed that social democracy did not go far enough, as the 1964–70 experience had shown, and that it was necessary to move on towards socialism. The Powellite Right rejected both socialism and social democracy, and argued for something much closer to the Thatcherism that would prevail after 1979. The forces of the antis were, therefore, marginal. However, considerations of party management persuaded the Labour leadership, most of whose party activists were on the Left, and opposed to the EEC, that it was necessary to resolve the issue finally through a referendum, an idea first promoted by Tony Benn in the early 1970s.

Chapter 4 discusses the 1975 referendum, when the UK voted, by a 2 to 1 majority, to stay in the EEC, and its aftermath. On the face of it, this was an upbeat time for the UK's involvement with the EEC. The British people were offered the opportunity to leave on two occasions (at the referendum and the 1983 general election), and unequivocally rejected these opportunities. After a little delay, direct elections were held to the European Parliament. The governing parties, both Labour from 1975 to 1979, and the Conservatives from 1979 to 1983, had reasonably tranquil relationships with Europe, although Britain stood aloof from the principal European development of the time, the EMS. However, at the same time as Britain was deepening its commitment to the EEC, the post-war social democratic model was collapsing. Margaret Thatcher became Leader of the Conservative Party, and led her party in a very different direction. By 1983 both her star, and that of the creed to which she gave her name, were in the ascendant within the Conservative Party and more generally. Labour moved leftwards after 1979. The Bennite Left regarded the EEC as an obstacle to its domestic policies, and so the party, despite the result of the referendum, committed itself to withdrawal. The high point of the Left's influence was between 1981 and 1983: Labour's disastrous showing at the general election of the latter year, and the emphatic rejection of withdrawal that this entailed, pushed the Left to the margins of the party for the next thirty years. The mainstream, Thatcherite Right had not yet come to view the EEC as a fetter upon its domestic policies. However, the fact that both main parties had embraced the extremes of the political spectrum meant that this was a fragile era for the post-war model and the values of social democracy. Social democracy was not quite dead, however. The Social Democratic Party (SDP) had emerged as its unrepentant defenders. The SDP continued to maintain that the post-war model remained the correct path and that this required, among other things, unwavering dedication to Europe. The Centre, which dominated the Yes campaign in the referendum, was, however, by 1983 imperilled in both main parties.

Chapter 5 considers the evolution of Conservative policy on Europe between 1983 and 2005. At the beginning of this period, the Tories remained enthusiastic about Europe. Thatcherism was becoming established but had not yet swept all before it. By 2005, the party was overwhelmingly Eurosceptic. Indeed, Euroscepticism virtually defined the Conservative Party. Thatcherism was completely dominant within the party: there were very few Conservatives left who were prepared to raise any fundamental doubts about the path the party had taken since 1975. These changes occurred in a number of phases. From 1983 to 1987, Thatcherism was dominant domestically. However, at this stage, most Conservatives did not see any conflict between their domestic policies and a Europe that they took to be moving in a free-market direction. Indeed, Thatcher, and her party, were strong supporters of the single market. The period from 1987 to 1990 spanned the third successive Tory general election victory to the fall of Thatcher and saw Conservative opinion begin to turn against Europe. Thatcher's Bruges speech of 1988 encapsulated the view that the EEC and, in particular, Social Europe were now becoming a fetter upon domestic neoliberal policy rather than a bulwark against socialism. Between 1990 and 1997, the

Conservatives remained in office but were intensely split over Europe between pragmatic Eurosceptics and fundamentalist Europhobes. Bitter divisions over the Maastricht Treaty, and the UK's ignominious exit from the ERM, reinforced the position of the latter. Finally, after the party's landslide defeat to New Labour in 1997, the Conservatives kept moving ever further to the Right. The party became increasingly Europhobic and obsessed with European issues.

Chapter 6 describes the journey the Labour Party made in this same period. However, Labour's direction of travel was quite the opposite. In 1983 Labour had fought, and lost disastrously, a general election on a left-wing platform, which included an unambiguous commitment to withdraw from the EC. This defeat prompted Labour to move steadily to the Right, or, more accurately, back to a traditional social democratic position, after 1983. In keeping with this, the party embraced EEC membership, at first hesitantly, and then more enthusiastically. However, as with the Conservatives, 1988 was a crucial turning point. The visit of Jacques Delors to the TUC Conference was not quite comparable to Lenin arriving at the Finland station in 1917, but, from the perspective of the Labour Movement's attitude to Europe, it was not far short. Following industrial and electoral defeats in 1985 and 1987, the EEC appeared to offer the only viable protection against domestic Thatcherism. Labour retained this broadly pro-European stance consistently after 1988. However, in domestic policy, the rise of New Labour after 1994 saw the party move away from its social democratic roots. Policy accommodated, rather than challenged, Thatcherism and the right-wing press. In European terms, this placed considerable restrictions upon the substance of what New Labour could achieve in office after 1997. In particular, the Blair government did not sign up to the single currency and was keen to keep its distance from other developments in Europe, especially Social Europe.

Chapter 7 deals with the decade between the 2005 general election and the 2016 referendum. A great deal happened in this short period. Flushed with a third successive election victory, and sustained economic growth, Labour appeared invincible in 2005. However, hubris soon turned to nemesis. The financial crisis of 2008 destroyed New Labour's reputation for economic competence and delivered a substantial blow to the British economy. In this context, New Labour's defeat at the 2010 general election appeared inevitable. What followed was a coalition government between Conservatives and Liberal Democrats, who were closely aligned ideologically and who both strongly supported the austerity policies introduced after 2010. The financial crisis, and austerity, undermined the credibility of the neoliberal, 'third way' centre of British politics. The crisis also exposed large divisions in British society between rich and poor, North and South, and young and old. Labour, after 2015, moved sharply Left and began to embrace policies that had not seen the light of day since the 1980s. The populist right, in the shape of UKIP and some elements of the Conservative Party, were equally disdainful of New Labour, albeit for very different reasons. The Right made effective appeals to those most affected by the crash and austerity. In parallel with this, the new Conservative leadership of Cameron and Osborne, although anxious to stop 'banging on about Europe', felt constrained to offer Conservative Eurosceptics a referendum on British membership of the EU. When the referendum came in 2016, the centrist, social democratic forces that had been so effective in 1975 were in poor shape. There were no social democrats left in the Conservative Party and very few among the Liberal Democrats. Labour now had socialist leaders, who were also veteran Eurosceptics. The referendum campaign was ugly and divisive. Leave secured a narrow victory with a skilfully created coalition of the 'left behind' and those who had never accepted the neoliberal settlement. Without the stoutly social democratic framework that had brought the UK into Europe in 1973, and kept it there in 1975, the pro-European case lacked sufficient robustness to fight off the forces ranged against it.

1 The Rise and Fall of British Social Democracy, 1945–2016

The social revolution which we are peacefully bringing about must be established not merely in institutions but in the hearts of men and women. I look forward to the continuance of the spirit of enthusiasm, idealism, and self-sacrifice which has brought us thus far. It will carry us further on our journey to freedom.

(Clement Attlee, 19 May 1948)[1]

Who is society? There is no such thing! There are individual men and women and there are families and no government can do anything except through people and people look to themselves first … there is no such thing as society.

(Margaret Thatcher, 23 September 1987)[2]

Introduction

In June 2014, at the start of the fifth year of the Clegg–Cameron coalition, the celebrated playwright Alan Bennett gave a sermon at King's College Chapel, Cambridge. Bennett, as he pointed out, had been 'educated at the expense of the state, both at school and university'. After a grammar school education in Leeds, he had gone on to Oxford and then become a star of the 1960s satire boom. In a sense Bennett's life story had embodied the social democratic system that had held sway in the UK from 1945 onwards. But since the 1980s, things had changed, and not for the better:

without ever having been particularly left wing, [he was] happy never to have trod that dreary safari from left to right … there has been so little that has happened to England since the 1980s that I have been happy about or felt able to endorse. One has only to stand still to become a radical.

This chapter seeks to outline the system that made Bennett and his ilk, and the changes that have occurred since the 1980s.[3]

Bennett's sermon highlighted some of the key policy changes that the nation as a whole experienced since the 1980s: the declining role of the state; increasing inequality; heightened class divisions. In this chapter, a sketch will be offered of the UK as a social democracy in the period from the 1940s to the late 1970s, together with some brief observations on the neoliberalism that increasingly usurped that system thereafter. For shorthand, the post-1979 approach will, generally, be referred to as 'Thatcherism', a mix of policies that sharply departed from those pursued in the earlier period. This shorthand is, of course, a simplification in two respects. Firstly, not all the politicians who governed Britain after 1979 were fully paid-up Thatcherites (although most of them were). Secondly, the Thatcherite revolution left largely untouched some aspects of the pre-1979 world, most notably the National Health Service and state pensions. However, the direction of travel of the 'dreary safari from left to right' was clear enough, these two qualifications notwithstanding. As Thatcher's political soulmate Ronald Reagan put it in his inaugural address in 1981: 'In this present crisis, government is not the solution to our problem; government is the problem.' Such anti-state rhetoric had little appeal to the Left and Centre in the UK or Europe, and, even on the Right, mainstream European Christian Democrats had much more time for the state than did Thatcher or Reagan.[4]

This is not the place to embark on the familiar debate on whether the UK was or was not subject to a 'post-war consensus' or 'post-war settlement'. There is an extensive literature on this question. As Paul Addison put it in *The Road to 1945*, wartime discussions had led, by the 1950s, to 'a species of consensus in which a Labour party led by social democrats competed against a Conservative party led by "One Nation" Tories. For the present author's taste, these arguments smack too much of the suggestion that there was some form of agreement between all the key actors in British society or that there was some permanent resolution of pre-war differences. Of course, there was no such agreement or settlement, in the sense of a permanent resolution of policy differences. Even in the 1950s and 1960s, one could find plenty of people – from both Left and Right – who were deeply unhappy with the direction of policy. For present purposes, it is sufficient to note that between 1945 and the mid-1970s policy had a distinctly social democratic hue, and that this period coincided with the UK's most enthusiastic engagement with the EEC. This post-war period, the so-called 'Golden Age', was also a time of strong and sustained economic growth throughout the Western world, an era that ended with the oil crisis of 1973 and the 1973–5 recession.[5]

It is, equally, no part of this argument to suggest that there was a social democratic blueprint to which policymakers rigorously adhered. There are texts from which one could cull some of the ideas that underpinned the social democratic era, but policy was made ad hoc and responsively. Indeed, some initiatives, such as Prices and Incomes Policy, even though they were often resorted to, had no clear ideological moorings. Tony Benn once astutely observed that 'The Labour party has never been a socialist party, although there have always been socialists in it – a bit like Christians in the Church of England.' The same might be said of social democrats within both main parties in the post-war period. Neither party was an unequivocally social democratic party: Labour because there were 'socialists in it' and the Conservatives because, to adapt Benn, there were a good many capitalists in it. But there were social democrats in both parties, that is to say politicians who were content to pursue the loose bundle of policies described above, and they were very influential for much of this period.[6]

This chapter, therefore, examines in turn the main policies that were pursued in the post-war period: full employment, secured through interventionist industrial and demand management strategies; the acceptance of strong trade unions, with whom governments were obliged to bargain; the quest for social solidarity in housing and schooling; an active state; a redistributive approach to taxation. There is then a discussion of the egalitarian outcomes that these policies achieved, and the much less equal society that has since emerged. Finally, I examine the crisis of the 1970s, which led to the abandonment of many of these policies in the Thatcher period, together with the question of whether, in truth, social democratic Britain was based upon any coherent ideology.

The full employment commitment

Mass unemployment was the great scourge of the inter-war years. Between 1921 and 1939, the proportion of insured workers unemployed varied between 9.7% and 22.1%. This had devastating social consequences, and it left a lasting political legacy: Never Again. At the time, however, the solutions urged by Keynes and others, which necessarily required government activism, made little political headway. Winston Churchill, delivering his budget speech in 1929, expressed the conventional view:

> for the purpose of curing unemployment the results [of public spending are] … so meagre as to lend considerable colour to the orthodox Treasury doctrine which has steadfastly held that, whatever might be the political or social advantages, very little additional employment and no permanent additional employment can in fact and as a general rule be created by State borrowing and State expenditure.[7]

Rearmament, and then the war, put paid to this problem in the short term, but the wartime coalition (with Churchill now Prime Minster) took a very different view of the role of government in tackling unemployment. The celebrated 1944 White Paper on Employment Policy, drafted by William Beveridge, committed the government to 'accept as one of their primary aims and responsibilities the maintenance of a high and stable level of employment after the war'. Beveridge regarded

3% unemployment as equivalent to full employment, so that 'the labour market should always be a seller's market rather than a buyer's market'. Between the war and the mid-1970s, this target was generally achieved.[8]

The full employment commitment had important consequences for government policymaking as a whole. Since government was responsible for the level of employment, it was obliged to manage demand with this in mind. When other policy objectives clashed with the commitment, they were made to yield to it. For example, in 1958, Macmillan saw his entire Treasury team resign over their refusal to approve reflationary increases in public spending. He was not unduly concerned about this 'little local difficulty'. Between 1958 and 1964, policy developed in accordance with the 'Middle Way', which Macmillan had promoted since the 1930s. Full employment was the key objective, to be secured by planning for a 'growth target of 4 per cent a year'. Reginald Maudling, appointed Chancellor in 1962, understood that his task was to secure expansion and avoid the waste of resources that Macmillan had witnessed in pre-war Stockton (where he had been MP until losing his seat in 1945).[9]

Full employment was generally, and quite easily, achieved until the 1970s. In this environment, it is not surprising that, when unemployment reached the unprecedented post-war figure of 1 million in January 1972, there were furious scenes in the Commons and elsewhere. Within days, Heath and his senior officials had secretly agreed a package of reflationary measures and a more interventionist industrial policy. The government promptly took steps to increase demand, the 'Dash for Growth'. The Chancellor, Anthony Barber, in his 1972 Budget Statement spoke of 'the high growth of output which I intend to sustain … as an integral part of the general management of demand'. This was a far cry from Churchill's approach in 1929, and the consequences were dramatic: for the first quarter of 1973 alone, the growth rate exceeded 5%.[10]

More generally, governments took the view that it was their duty to plan the economy, an undertaking that would certainly have been anathema to the pre-war Treasury. Planning had, in fact, had its supporters before the war. Labour had argued for a planned economy. Many non-socialists agreed. In particular, Harold Macmillan, then out of favour with his party, advocated 'planned capitalism', with a National Investment Board, Economic Council and government commitment to full employment.[11]

The Attlee government adopted a highly interventionist industrial policy. The coal, electricity, gas, inland transport, and steel industries were nationalised. The government instituted 'a period of economic planning unique in British peacetime history'. Under the Conservative governments of 1951 to 1964, most nationalised industries remained in public ownership. Until the early 1960s, there was less enthusiasm for planning. However, in 1961, Macmillan's government began to practise what he had preached, establishing new machinery for national planning, including a national growth target. The National Economic Development Council (NEDC) was established to 'improve the general economic performance of the country ... promote expansion on a sound basis'.[12]

In 1964, Labour called for a modernising National Plan: 'the community must ... take charge of its own destiny and no longer be ruled by market forces beyond its control'. In 1965, the government announced an ambitious plan to achieve 25% growth over the next five years. The Industrial Reorganisation Corporation was charged with promoting industrial modernisation and eliminating inefficiency. Government also enthusiastically supported technical change, especially through the Ministry of Technology. However, in the event, the growth rate (2.6%) was less than that required by the National Plan (3.8%) and less even than that achieved in the 'wasted' 1950s (2.9%). Nonetheless, in the 1960s, planning for growth seemed to many well-informed people an obviously sensible approach and one that chimed with the methods adopted in other advanced economies.[13]

The 1964–70 government may have been the high watermark of interventionist policies, but subsequent governments took a similar line in substance, although framed in less confident terms. The Heath government, having initially flirted with a policy of allowing 'lame ducks' to go to the wall, soon changed course. In 1971, it nationalised Rolls-Royce, which was on the brink of failure. The government also gave support to Upper Clyde Shipbuilders and other struggling companies. The Industry Act 1972 provided for financial assistance for industry in assisted areas, with general powers for selective financial assistance, and set up the Industrial Development Advisory Board to aid these operations. The Labour government of 1974–9, having itself considered a much more radically interventionist approach, in the event pursued policies that were very similar to those of the Heath era. The 'Industrial Strategy' was central to government policy. Government provided financial assistance to failing companies, including Chrysler and Ferranti, in accordance with the 1972 Act, but otherwise had limited involvement in the private sector. Labour pursued an activist regional policy, establishing the Scottish and Welsh Development Agencies.[14]

Governments of both parties, with varying levels of zeal and success, found that the pursuit of full employment necessarily drew them very closely into the management of the economy. It was not just a matter of stimulating aggregate demand, important though that was. It was also necessary to keep a close eye on industry: ideally driving forward the industries of the future, in practice often propping up the industries of the past. Moreover, of course, the government had a large hand in industry itself. The 'mixed economy' included a substantial number of nationalised industries, essentially those that had been brought into public ownership by the Attlee government (and one or two more, such as shipbuilding).

However, this was not the end of the government's responsibilities. In 1944, Beveridge had been concerned that, in this new environment, 'action taken by the government to maintain employment will be fruitless unless wages and prices are kept reasonably stable ... it is the duty of both sides of industry to consider together all possible means of ... avoiding a rise in prices'. The key was to ensure that wages rose in line with improvements in productivity. What if 'both sides of industry' did not see the obvious good sense of this linkage, and inflation resulted?[15]

The answer from the authorities was, for most of the 1960s and 1970s, wage restraint, often buttressed by statutory controls. Such controls were thought necessary if full employment was to be maintained. They would also, it was argued, produce a fairer society and a more harmonious workplace. Although there were brief attempts at a wages policy in 1948–50 and 1956–7, the 1960s saw the first real attempt by governments to control prices and incomes. Macmillan embarked in 1961 on Prices and Incomes Policy 'not (as) an instrument of deflation but a weapon for more rapid growth'. Through the voluntary co-operation of both sides of industry, incomes should rise in line with the long-term rate of growth. Such a wages policy coincided with a widespread view on both Left and Right that wages, and economic development generally, could no longer be left to the caprice of the marketplace.[16]

In 1964 the employers and unions entered into a 'Joint Statement' with the new Labour government as part of the National Plan. It committed the parties 'to raise productivity and efficiency so that real national output can increase, and to keep increases in wages … in line with this increase'. A pay 'norm' of 3.5% was stipulated, in line with the growth target. The National Board for Prices and Incomes was established in 1965 to support this process. All this would have been music to the ears of Beveridge, had he still been alive: a government, wholly committed to full employment and rapid growth, had induced both sides of industry to agree that wages should rise in accordance with improvements in productivity. The Secretary of State for Economic Affairs (George Brown) invited the Commons to agree 'that the sense of national purpose and the spirit of mutual confidence reflected in this agreement are most exciting'.[17]

In the event, the spirit of mutual confidence did not last very long. Wages rose faster than productivity. A balance of payments crisis and a run on the pound ensued in 1966. Wilson's government reacted with a pay freeze, followed by a series of rounds of pay restraint. From this point onwards, governments of both parties found Prices and Incomes Policy – and the containment of inflation generally – a subject of particular difficulty.[18]

The Heath government, in its turn, having ruled out such a policy at the 1970 election, in the event introduced very comprehensive statutory controls in 1972. The process by which this occurred neatly illuminated the pressures upon policymakers who were seeking to adhere to the full employment commitment in a period of rising inflation. The government sought to persuade the 'industrial partners', business and the trades unions, in the form of the CBI and the TUC, to accept voluntary restraint on pay and prices in exchange for its own commitment to reflation. This culminated in lengthy tripartite discussions in the autumn of 1972, at which the government put forward proposals for 'faster growth in national output and incomes and moderation in the rate of cost and price inflation'. In November 1972, the tripartite talks collapsed. The government then introduced statutory controls over wages, prices and dividends: they could either 'revert to the previous policy of seeking to challenge inflationary claims one by one … or … operate through … massive deflation. … Ministers did not really think it was practicable to fight on without statutory backing.'[19]

Labour, surveying this chaotic scene and mindful of its own travails in the 1960s, went into the 1974 election offering a 'Social Contract', whereby the unions would offer voluntary restraint in exchange for a major increase in the 'social wage', substantial redistribution of wealth, and controls on prices and dividends. However, by the summer of 1975, wage settlements were running at 26%. The government and the TUC therefore agreed a flat rate pay policy of £6 per week. Between 1976 and 1979, the revised Social Contract continued with a series of pay guidelines. Inflation fell from a peak in 1975 of 24% to 8% in 1978. However, the policy, and the agreement with the unions, collapsed during the 'Winter of Discontent' of 1978–9.[20]

The governments of the 1960s and 1970s, therefore, sought to secure full employment and growth above all. This was the central object of policy. To deal with inflation these governments, often breaking their initial promises, were drawn into pay and prices policy. The contrast with the policies adopted during the Thatcher era was very stark. As

Nigel Lawson (Chancellor from 1983 to 1989, at a time when Thatcherism was in the ascendant in every respect) put it in his 1984 Mais lecture:

> The conventional post-War wisdom was that unemployment was a consequence of inadequate economic growth, and economic growth was to be secured by *macro*-economic policy – the fiscal stimulus of an enlarged Budget deficit, with monetary policy (to the extent that it could be said to exist at all) on the whole passively following fiscal policy. Inflation, by contrast, was increasingly seen as a matter to be dealt with by *micro*-economic policy – the panoply of controls and subsidies associated with the era of incomes policy. The conclusion on which the present Government's economic policy is based is that there is indeed a proper distinction between the objectives of macro-economic and micro-economic policy, and a need to be concerned with both of them. But the proper role of each is precisely the opposite of that assigned to it by the conventional post-War wisdom. It is the conquest of inflation, and not the pursuit of growth and employment, which is or should be the objective of macro-economic policy. And it is the creation of conditions conducive to growth and employment, and not the suppression of price rises, which is or should be the objective of micro-economic policy.[21]

What did this mean in practice? After 1979, the full employment commitment was unceremoniously abandoned. Perhaps to their surprise, governments found that they could survive, and prosper politically, with unemployment rates above 10%. Thus, the Conservatives secured large majorities in the 1983 and 1987 general elections, despite unemployment rates of 12% and 10.5% respectively. National plans and growth targets likewise disappeared from the policy agenda. It was for governments to create the conditions for economic growth through supply side reforms, but it was for the market to deliver such growth. Likewise, an activist industrial policy was, at least until the financial crisis of 2007–9, anathema to post-1979 governments. As Peter Mandelson (who was Business Secretary under New Labour) put it in 2009, '[a modern industrial strategy] isn't us picking winners as happened too often in the 1970s, when more often the losers were picking us'. And no government in the Thatcherite era even considered a pay and prices regime: as Lawson made clear, the answer to inflation was monetary discipline, not deals with the unions or statutory controls.[22]

Bargaining with the workforce: the role of strong trade unions

By contrast with the Thatcherite period, the era of full employment gave workers considerable negotiating strength. In a seller's market for labour, employees sought, and often obtained, constant improvements in their pay and conditions. This environment, in turn, made the trade unions, the collective expression of workforce power, highly influential both industrially and politically.

The post-war period was a Golden Age for the unions, as it was for the economy generally. Membership increased from 8.6 million in 1946 to a peak of 12.6 million in 1979, and from 43% to 53% density within the workforce. The unions recruited successfully in traditionally weak sectors: participation expanded among women, and in 'white collar' occupations like insurance and finance. The unions proved effective in protecting the living standards of their members. Wages increased substantially in real terms, at the expense of profits.[23]

Governments of both parties necessarily treated the unions with considerable respect. Indeed, the period from 1945 to the early 1970s was also the Golden Age of Voluntarism, what the great legal scholar Otto Kahn-Freund described as 'the retreat of the law from industrial relations and of industrial relations from the law'. This retreat, of course, was very much to the advantage of the unions, since they could press home their bargaining advantage untrammelled by the courts. The Conservatives pursued this course between 1945 and 1964. In 1947, indeed, one Mass Observer in eight had believed the Labour Party's new Worker's Charter to be the work of the Communist Party. In government after 1951, they took the line that the state should be neutral in industrial affairs. Conservative ministers were on good terms with the unions. Tom O'Brien of the TUC thought that Sir Walter Monckton, minister from 1951 to 1955, 'left the Ministry of Labour a better place than he found it'; his successor John Hare (1960–3) saw his role as being to 'smooth the relationships between employers and unions'. Indeed, in this period, relations were so cordial that Arthur Deakin of the TGWU was to say in 1953: 'I believe Sir Walter Monckton has given us a square deal and we have been able to do things that were difficult under our own people.'[24]

The unions also exercised extensive political influence. Relations between Labour politicians and trade union leaders, in particular, were close, especially during the difficult economic times of the 1970s. Thus, the TUC–Labour liaison committee met monthly, with attendance by all the senior figures on both sides. Denis Healey, Chancellor from 1974 to 1979, assured his union colleagues that 'the Labour party and the TUC depended on each other'. In exchange, the 1960s and 1970s saw a significant body of pro-union legislation to support individual workers and collective bargaining. Furthermore, the unions worked closely even with natural foes. The TUC and the CBI often agreed on the need to help manufacturing industry. There was continuous dialogue even with the Conservatives. In short, it seemed that, by the late 1970s, the unions had acquired considerable influence – industrial, political, institutional – which they were unlikely to lose.[25]

After 1979, things were very different. During the 1980s and 1990s Conservative governments passed numerous (anti-) union laws. Legislation curtailed rights to strike and to picket. Union funds were 'placed at the mercy of the law'. Membership declined sharply from 53% density in 1979 to 34% in 1991, and the decline continued thereafter. By 2017, the figure was about 23%, and in much of the private sector unions were almost unknown. The unions had negligible political influence, even under the 1997–2010 Labour government. The rate of strikes fell sharply and, save in certain sectors, industrial action was no longer a viable prospect. The high level of unemployment for much of this period, and the increasing casualisation of labour, did much to reduce union militancy. In short, argued the labour historian Alastair Reid, from 1979 onwards 'there was a growing feeling among almost all shades of political opinion that it was somehow demeaning to have to take so much account of the views of ordinary working people'.[26]

Social solidarity: housing and schooling

Two key components of the social democratic era were public housing and comprehensive schools. Social housing, it was thought, should be affordable, widely available and of good quality. Secondary education should not only be available free to all, but should seek to educate together the managers and workers of the future.

Anyone who has been to Welwyn Garden City, or walked past a Peabody Estate in London, will appreciate that concern over the housing of the less well-off had begun well before the Second World War. However, the period between 1945 and 1979 witnessed a major attempt to solve the housing problems of the working classes. As Aneurin Bevan, Minister for Health and Housing in the Attlee government, told the Commons in 1945:

> We propose to start to solve, first, the housing difficulties of the lower income groups. In other words, we propose to lay the main emphasis of our programme upon building houses to let. That means that we shall ask local authorities to be the main instruments for the housing programme. ... The architectural composition to which we could look with delight must have much more variety in design, and, therefore, I am going to encourage the housing authorities in their lay-outs to make provision for building some houses also for the higher income groups at higher rents. ... The full life should see the unfolding of a multi coloured panorama before the eyes of every citizen every day. Therefore, I hope that local authorities will arrange their schemes in this fashion.[27]

Bevan's statement encapsulated many of the themes of post-war housing policy. In the next three decades, there ensued a huge council house-building programme, including substantial slum clearance exercises. By 1979, 5.5 million homes were rented from local authorities (32% of all households). In the decade from 1969 to 1979 alone, 1.2 million such homes were constructed. In some areas, council housing predominated to an extraordinary extent. In Tower Hamlets, in London's East End, 82% of the population were renting from the council in 1979. The Becontree Estate in Dagenham, begun by the London County Council before the war, was 'the largest Council Housing Estate in the world'. The early tenants regarded the estate as 'Like Heaven with the Gate Open'. Indeed, at this time, Dagenham was said to be 'probably the most solidly working class district in the world'.[28]

In parallel with the construction of houses by local authorities, the Attlee government also initiated the New Towns, to which poorly housed families could move from the cities. For example, Harlow was designated as a New Town in 1946, and the 1952 'Masterplan' aimed for an eventual population of 80,000, a figure achieved by 1974. Some 76% of the population rented their homes from the Council or the Development Corporation. By the mid-1970s, the New Town project had been under way for thirty years. Not all the original aspirations had been fulfilled, but the journalist Jason Cowley, who grew up there then, recalled 'a vibrant place, with Utopian yearnings'. The principal designer of the New Town, Sir Frederick Gibberd, actually lived there, and told the local paper that he was happy to pay his rates since 'in Harlow more was spent per head of population on the arts than in any other town in the country'.[29]

Images of Utopia, even of Heaven itself, recurred when discussing these new houses, but not everyone saw things in such a rosy light. Indeed, a Thatcherite academic, Alice Coleman, put Utopia on trial and found it wanting. She cited, critically, a crusading architect who had proclaimed 'the role of architecture as a weapon of social reform … the coming Utopia … heaven on earth'. For Coleman, 'Utopia is not automatically synonymous with progress, and much of our planned housing is proving to be retrograde – the scene of many kinds of social malaise.'

Her solution was that housing should be 'genuinely returned to the free market, with unfettered responsiveness to people's needs'.[30]

This in essence was the policy initiated by the Thatcher government in 1979, and faithfully pursued by governments of both parties thereafter. Neoliberals saw social housing as an offence against 'the efficient and beneficent operations of the free market'. After 1979, therefore, the Conservative government embarked upon a massive sale of council houses, by far the largest of the privatisations. By 1997, 1.8 million houses had been sold, and the proportion of households in council accommodation had fallen to 20%. Two additional, less widely advertised policies, which served to diminish the role of public housing still further, accompanied this sell-off. Firstly, 'there was no pretence that new council housing was to be built to replace homes lost to the market'. In 1978/9, 79,000 new council houses were built, but by 1996/7 this figure had fallen to 400. Secondly, the sales tended to be of the better stock and to the more affluent tenants. In consequence, public housing was no longer seen as 'a multi coloured panorama' for the benefit of a large slice of the community but rather as grim residual accommodation for those at the bottom of society.[31]

The nation's schooling underwent a similar journey. The 1944 Education Act had made secondary education universal, but the system was not equal. At 11, pupils either proceeded to an academic, selective grammar school or to a less academic secondary modern. This separation prompted Tony Crosland to write in 1956 that 'the school system in Britain remains the most divisive, unjust, and wasteful of all the aspects of social inequality'. Or, as the journalist Hunter Davies recalled of his own experience in post-war Carlisle, 'Everyone knew that those who failed the eleven-plus and went to the sec mod were doomed to be second-class citizens, not just educationally but socially and economically ... at eleven years old, you had already failed the first big hurdle in life.'[32]

The proposed solution to this educational apartheid was a system of comprehensive schools, whereby all pupils, regardless of ability or

social background, would be educated within the same secondary institutions. This idea began to take root during the 1950s: by 1962, there
were 152 such schools. In this era, local authorities enjoyed considerable
autonomy in educational matters and large cities, in particular London,
took full advantage of this freedom. However, it was the coming of the
1964 Labour government that saw the drive to comprehensivisation
really get under way. In 1965, Crosland, now Education Secretary, told
his wife that 'if it's the last thing I do, I'm going to destroy every fucking
grammar school in England'.[33]

This commitment, in somewhat more tactful language, found expression in Circular 10/65, which requested local authorities to submit plans
for reorganising secondary education in their areas on comprehensive
lines: it was the government's intention 'to end selection at eleven plus
and to eliminate separatism in secondary education'. Thereafter, things
changed swiftly: between 1965 and 1973, the proportion of secondary school students in comprehensive schools rose from 8% to 48%.
Although the Heath government replaced 10/65 with another Circular
(10/70) expressed rather less definitely, the drive towards comprehensivisation continued apace under Margaret Thatcher, Education Secretary from 1970 to 1974. As her official biographer observed, 'she found
herself presiding over a vast change of educational structure whose
underlying egalitarian principles she did not support, but which she
was powerless to reverse'.[34]

What were these 'egalitarian principles'? The core idea was that
these new schools should offer equality of opportunity for pupils from
all backgrounds and of all abilities. They 'transcended the divisions of
the selective system and pointed the way to a general transformation
… a new concept of the nature and function of secondary education'.
In this new era, the private schools, the subject of Bennett's ire in his
2014 sermon, were also somewhat beleaguered. In 1973, Roy Hattersley,
Labour's Shadow Education spokesman, pledged that Labour would
eventually abolish private education altogether. Political pressures
apart, British society was moving away from its previous domination by

the private sector: symbolically, state-educated meritocrats like Wilson and Heath (and Bennett himself) seemed to be usurping the public schoolboys.[35]

It cannot, however, be said that the views of Labour egalitarians like Crosland and Hattersley enjoyed universal support across the political spectrum, even during the heady days of the 1960s and 1970s. There were Conservatives, such as Edward Boyle, Education Minister and then Shadow Education minister in the 1960s, who believed that the new system 'was gaining considerable political momentum', but there were many within the party who were strong supporters of the grammar schools. After 1979, certainly, Thatcher did not repeat what she believed were her errors of the 1970–4 period. The remaining grammar schools gained a reprieve, which proved to be permanent. The first Thatcher government indicated its commitment to the private sector through the Assisted Places Scheme, whereby less well-off pupils gained a private education at public expense.[36]

These privatising tendencies continued under the Major, New Labour and Coalition governments. In February 2001, Blair introduced a Green Paper outlining plans for a radical reform of secondary schools if Labour won the next general election, with businesses to take over the running of weak state schools: the time had come to move on to a 'post comprehensive' era. As Alastair Campbell, Blair's spokesman, put it, 'the day of the bog-standard comprehensive school is over'. From 2002, these new 'Academies' began to open their doors. The Coalition greatly expanded this programme, and also embarked on a 'free schools' scheme. Meanwhile, the remaining grammar schools, and the private schools, sailed serenely onwards, with most politicians viewing them benevolently.[37]

The 'egalitarian principles' of the 1960s and 1970s had not fared well in the 1980s and beyond. Most secondary pupils continued to attend ostensibly non-selective state schools, but the comprehensive ideal now had few political friends. Researchers identified evidence that comprehensivisation had both improved standards and reduced the effect of social class on attainment, but this received little political attention. By contrast, 'independent and grammar schools ... continued to enjoy enormous privileges and advantages where entry to universities and the higher professions was concerned'. By the end of the New Labour era in 2010, the process of maximising equal opportunity in schooling had ended and indeed reversed. The symbolism now was of David Cameron and Nick Clegg in the Rose Garden at No. 10, unapologetic public schoolboys both: their government would enthusiastically promote academies and free schools. Michael Gove, Education Secretary from 2010 to 2014, dedicated himself to marginalising 'The Blob – the network of educational gurus in and around our universities' who operated 'from a classical Marxist perspective', and were 'in thrall to Sixties ideologies'.[38]

The role of the state: taxing and spending

Until the mid-1970s, British governments tended to regard public spending as a generally good thing. Government expenditure on goods and services rose rapidly in the 1960s and early 1970s. The political parties competed to show who could achieve the largest increases, especially in health, social services and education. For example, in 1972 and 1973, under the Heath government, the increase in spending was greater than any year bar one in the 1960s, itself a period of rapid increase. This process ended with the economic crisis of the mid-1970s. There were large spending cuts from 1975 onwards under Labour, from 1979 to 1983 under the Conservatives, and through the austerity policies of the Coalition after 2010.[39]

Nonetheless, the state did not fade away. Public spending continued to grow in real terms throughout the Thatcher years and subsequently. The proportion of GDP taken by all government spending hovered around 40%, the percentage tending to rise in recessions and fall in periods of expansion. The footprint of British government spending, at about 40%, was, by 2015, unremarkable by international standards.

The UK spent somewhat more than 'small state' economies, such as the US and Australia (30–35%), and less than many European countries who placed greater emphasis on welfare (France, Sweden and Denmark devoted about 50–55%).[40]

If the size of the state did not markedly change, its role certainly did. In the post-war period, the state itself undertook substantial tasks. Central government directly ran organisations like prisons, and, at arm's length, directed the operations of a large number of nationalised industries. Local government, likewise, maintained its large housing stock through Direct Labour Organisations. After 1979, and, even more so, after 1997, this delivery model changed significantly. Government, both locally and nationally, became a procurer, rather than a provider, of services. As far as possible, the provision was outsourced to private companies. These companies delivered services such as prisons and council house maintenance through complex, long-term contracts with government bodies. In the Thatcher era, utilities such as gas, electricity and telecoms were privatised. Thereafter, privatisation went further, extending even in due course to the Royal Mail. The positive state gave way to the regulatory state. The key players in this new state were accountants and auditors, whose role was to hold to account financially both the procurers and the providers of services. Certainly, in twenty-first-century Britain, few people seemed to agree with the Labour politician Douglas Jay's well-known observation after the war that 'the Gentleman in Whitehall is usually right'.[41]

Although the total share of GDP taken by government did not change radically throughout the post-war period, the way in which governments financed their activities, and the social objectives of taxation, altered very significantly. The overall trends were in favour of indirect and payroll taxes, and away from direct taxation. The system also became much less redistributive in intention, and concern over the unfair capital shares of the rich diminished.

The post-war system relied heavily upon income tax and super-tax to fund government spending. In 1950, these taxes accounted for 41% of total government revenue. The standard rate of income tax was 45%. The Conservative governments of 1951–64 were characterised by 'continual movement and little change'. Indeed by 1962, these two taxes accounted for an increased share of the Exchequer's receipts (46%). After 1979, by contrast, governments, and particularly Conservative governments, placed increasing reliance on indirect and payroll taxes. Above all, VAT was the Tory tax of choice: doubled in 1979 (from 8% to 15%), increased again in 1991/2 to 17.5%, and twice raised by the 2010–15 coalition. By 2016/17, the proportion of government revenue from income tax had fallen to 25%, whereas national insurance contributions accounted for 18% and VAT for 17%.[42]

The post-war system was also highly redistributive. The Attlee government imposed marginal tax rates as high as 98%. Again, the Conservative governments of the 1950s made little change in this respect. A married man with two children earning £10,000 at 1947 prices (equivalent to about £370,000 in 2017) paid about 66% in income and surtax under Labour but saw this rise to 69% under the Conservatives. Macmillan was unsympathetic to complaints from the better-off, remarking 'I am always hearing about the Middle Classes. What is it they really want? Can you put it down on a sheet of notepaper, and then I will see whether we can give it to them.' This indifference to the plight of the wealthy was typical of the times. Eisenhower's Republican Administration in the US legislated in 1954 for a progressive income tax, with rates up to 91% on very high earnings. The traditional arguments against such tax rates, that they would reduce incentives and inhibit economic activity, cut little ice in the Golden Age.[43]

In opposition from 1964 to 1970, the Conservatives agonised over taxation, and ultimately proposed a reduction in marginal rates, which they implemented in the 1970–4 government. However, the change was itself quite modest: the top rate of income tax fell only to 75%, and the 1974–9 Labour government reversed the changes so that the highest rates were 83% on earned income and 98% on investment receipts. These changes were clearly couched in the language of redistribution,

Healey (as Shadow Chancellor in 1973) telling the Labour conference with some relish that 'there are going to be howls of anguish from the 80,000 people who are rich enough to pay over 75% [tax] on the last slice of their income'.[44]

Again, the divergence after 1979 is stark. In that year, the top rate of income tax was reduced to 60%. In 1988, Nigel Lawson, as Chancellor, announced the abolition of all rates of income tax over 40%. Since then the highest rate has never exceeded 50%, and then only for a brief period. The 1988 budget was an important symbolic moment. Lawson, as he sought to proclaim his great reform, was constantly interrupted by a left-wing Labour MP. 'Grave disorder having arisen in the House', the Speaker was compelled to suspend the sitting for ten minutes. Very high earners did well out of these changes. A taxpayer with an income of £1 million (2014) would have been liable to pay 75% in 1973/4 and 83% in 1978/9 on large tranches of that income but after 1988 was obliged to pay no more than 40%. The change was greater still for a person with a large investment income who was no longer subject to the 15% investment income surcharge, which Lawson had also abolished in 1984.[45]

So much for the fruit: what about the tree, i.e. capital? The Attlee government had targeted inheritances, with a rate of 80% applicable to estates over £21,500 in 1950 (about £700,000 in 2017). Death duties accounted for 5% of revenue, and again the position did not alter very much under the Conservatives (4% in 1962/3). The problem, of course, with death duties was that the government had to wait patiently for the rich to die, and they were able to avoid much of the sting by well-timed disposals in their lifetime. Attention therefore turned to taxing capital. For example, in a 1951 pamphlet, *Fair Shares for the Rich*, Roy Jenkins proposed a capital levy of 50% on sums between £20,000 and £30,000, rising to 95% over £100,000 (£600,000 to £900,000 and £3 million in 2017 terms).[46]

The Conservatives investigated a Wealth Tax in some detail in the 1960s, before deciding that it was politically unacceptable. Even so, inequality was a live issue for the Tories of the 1960s. Keith Joseph, later to emerge as Mrs Thatcher's ideological mentor, expressed concern at the Selsdon Conference of 1970 that the top 1% of earners would benefit unduly from the (quite modest) income tax reforms that the party was then proposing: 'he had been attracted by an early form of the tax package where the regressive redistribution could be balanced by a wealth tax'. Labour did not share the Tory squeamishness about capital taxes on the rich and announced in 1974, once back in government, 'a determined attack on the maldistribution of wealth'. This would include a Wealth Tax and a Capital Transfer Tax. The government also set up a Royal Commission on the subject. In the event, the 1974–9 government was waylaid by economic and other crises, and little happened on the capital taxation front.[47]

It was, however, striking, that in the mid-1970s a British government could consider that 'the maldistribution of wealth' was so severe as to require a Royal Commission. As it turned out, this was to be a time of peak equality in the UK: see below. After 1979, the country became steadily more unequal. However, certainly until the financial crisis of 2008, this rising tide of inequality disappeared as a political issue. Capital taxes also became of marginal budgetary importance: by 2016/17, inheritance tax accounted for just 0.7% of government revenue, with a further 1.0% from capital gains tax (introduced by the 1964–70 Labour government).[48]

Equality and inequality

The combined effect of policy (housing, taxation, full employment) and circumstances (strong trade unions, steady economic growth) made the Britain of the mid-1970s a country of unprecedented egalitarianism. This was particularly striking in terms of income. Wage earners obtained continual real improvements in their remuneration. These improvements were secured at the expense of capital: between the 1950s and the 1970s, the share of national wealth taken by profits fell, and the portion for wages rose, by about 12%. At the same time, the share taken by the best-off fell steadily. In 1937, the top 1% took 16.6% of all income.

By 1974, this had declined to 6.1%. There had been a long steady fall in the relative incomes of the rich throughout the twentieth century, but there were also 'distinct periods of equalisation, notably during the two world wars, from 1946–1957 and from 1965–1972'. Very high earners had felt the squeeze: the top 0.1% received 10% of national income in 1910, but only about 2% in 1980.[49]

What was true of income was likewise true in respect of wealth and other indices. The wealth share of the top 1% dropped dramatically from the early part of the twentieth century, from 70% in 1910 to 15% in 1975. Life expectancy at birth improved substantially over the same period (from the age of 52 to 69 for men and from 55 to 77 for women). While, of course, there remained lifestyle inequalities, the gross disparities of the Victorian era seemed to have receded. In the UK, at the beginning of the Thatcher period, the vast majority of the population (66%) could properly be regarded as neither rich nor poor.[50]

These trends have not continued, indeed have reversed very substantially since the 1970s. The weakened position of the trade unions, high levels of unemployment, and the casualisation of labour have enabled capital to regain its share of national income at the expense of wage earners. For most of the 1960s and 1970s the UK wage share was between 58% and 61% of GDP. Between 1981 and 2010, this figure has oscillated between 52% and 56%. As shown in Table 1.1, the UK's performance in this respect has been striking in international terms.

The rich in the UK have, over the same period, done very well for themselves. As of 2012, the richest 1% were taking about 14% of all income, more than double the 1978 share, and almost back to pre-war levels. A.B. Atkinson, a leading analyst of these data, observed in 2002 that 'since 1979, we have seen a reversal, with shares of the top income groups returning to their position of fifty years earlier. The equalisation of the post-war period has been lost'. Again, the position as to wealth shares was similar: 'with the 1980s, the downward trend in top shares came to an end and went into reverse': by 2015, the top 1% were holding about 20% of the nation's wealth.[51]

Table 1.1 Wage share in 10 advanced economies, 1970–2007 (percentages)

Country	Wage share 1970	Wage share 2007	Change
Australia	60	53	−7.1
UK	65	60	−5.3
Sweden	66	61	−4.9
Canada	59	55	−3.8
Germany	59	55	−3.7
USA	64	60	−3.1
France	56	57	+0.9
Finland	55	56	+1.0
Denmark	59	65	+6.1
Japan	41	49	+8.2[52]

These changes had important social and political implications. The gap between rich and poor was increasingly evident, especially in London: the proportion of wealthy and poor people in London increased between 1980 and 2010 from 15% to 27% and 20% to 36% respectively. The middle was squeezed from 65% to 37%. Inequality (and the austerity policies of the coalition) appeared to have a detrimental impact on health. After 2011, the rate of increase in life expectancy, which had been steady for decades, slowed for both males and females. On the day of the Brexit referendum in 2016, an increase in death rates in England and Wales of 9% was announced by the ONS (2015 compared to 2014). This increase, according to the geographer Danny Dorling, was 'huge' and 'unprecedented'.[53]

The UK, once a relatively egalitarian society, has become notably unequal by the standards of large European countries. The comparison with France, in particular, is marked. About 56% of the French GDP is devoted to government spending, compared with 42% in the UK. France has not experienced a Thatcherite revolution. But it has, however, seen life expectancy rise more rapidly than in the UK or the US, and the top 1% have seen their income share fall since 1960. Graph 1.1 illustrates the considerable divergence in inequality between the UK and other comparable EU countries.

Graph 1.1 Income ratio of best-off/worst-off households, 2015[54]

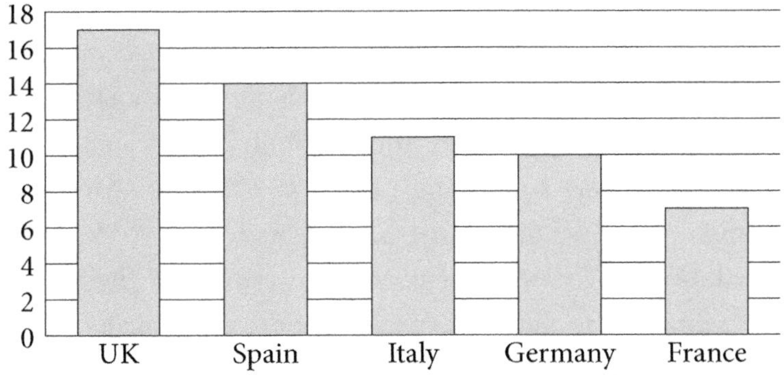

Adapted from Danny Dorling, *Peak Inequality: Britain's Ticking Time Bomb* (Bristol, Policy Press/Bristol University Press, 2018).

Indeed, since the early 1980s, there has been another Great Divergence, but this time between Europe and the English-speaking world. Throughout the Western world, there was a steady decline in income inequality from 1900 onwards, with a very similar pattern in both Continental and Anglo-Saxon economies. Since the rise of neoliberalism in the latter, income inequality has increased sharply in English-speaking countries, including the UK. In Continental Europe, there has been no real change. According to Atkinson and Piketty, writing just before the 2008 crash, 'most striking is what did not happen [in Europe]: there has not been a U-shaped pattern over the twentieth century'. The Anglo-Saxon U-shaped trend was markedly similar in the UK, the US, Canada and Australia.

This Great Divergence in due course mapped onto the arguments for leaving the EU. The advocates of Brexit did not, of course, praise increased inequality per se, but they did suggest that 'this is an opportunity to renew our strong relationships with Commonwealth and Anglosphere countries' who, not coincidentally, embraced such inegalitarianism most fervently.[55]

Things fall apart

It is no part of the present argument to suggest that the UK had achieved some form of Paradise prior to the rise of Thatcherism. In the field of sexual politics, for example, pre-1979 Britain left much to be desired. For much of the post-war period male homosexuals faced criminal sanctions. Even after partial decriminalisation in 1967, social ostracism persisted. There was a shocking lack of concern over 'domestic violence', and sexual assaults against women. As Jeffrey Weeks has rightly observed, despite the wave of permissive reform in the 1960s many matters remained, to the modern eye, 'prior to the rebirth of feminism, outside the bounds of intelligibility'.[56]

However, even in areas where the pre-1979 system had stood on more solid ground, tensions had begun to appear. As we have seen, a cornerstone of this system had been the voluntarist arrangement with the unions, coupled, at least in the case of Labour, with a relationship of close interdependence between government and workers. By the late 1960s, relations between the political and industrial wings of the Labour Movement had become strained. The Wilson government, therefore, brought forward in 1969 the *In Place of Strife* proposals for cooling-off periods and strike ballots, with a view to curbing unofficial industrial action. The unions resisted and the government backed off. The Heath government sought to go further in this direction with the Industrial Relations Act 1971. This met with determined union resistance and the Act proved unworkable. Industrial disputes nonetheless dominated the life of the Heath government. There were, for example, two national miners' strikes.[57]

These attempts at legislative interference in the industrial arena were a symptom of a wider problem. Governments struggled to find a suitable balance in their relations with the unions. Nowhere was this truer than in the area of pay policy. As we have seen, the political parties tended to disavow prices and incomes policy in principle, but to adopt them in practice. For example, Labour had foresworn a traditional pay policy at the 1974 elections, but then implemented one in the summer of 1975 in the face of 'a massive bear attack on sterling'. The TUC reluctantly agreed, but they complained that they 'were being invited to negotiate at pistol point'. Joe Haines, Harold Wilson's press secretary, thought that the efforts of the Treasury and the Bank of England to impose a compulsory incomes policy were a 'civilian coup against the Government'. This excitable language did not suggest that a pay policy was a recipe for harmony, and so it proved. The various pay norms held until 1978, but then collapsed acrimoniously during the 'Winter of Discontent' of 1978/9.[58]

The travails of 1970s governments over pay policy, and their relations with the unions, did not happen in a vacuum. For most of the Golden Age, it had been easy enough to deliver both modest inflation and low unemployment, with the occasional tweak on the tiller if one measure or the other seemed to be moving upwards. A view had emerged, indeed, that the 'Phillips curve' offered a secure equilibrium between inflation and unemployment. However, even before the oil price shock of 1973/4, unemployment and inflation had begun to rise at the same time. After that shock, the rate of inflation shot upwards, reaching 25% in 1975. Throughout the 1970s and early 1980s, inflation in the UK was both very high and considerably worse than in other European countries. For example, in 1976, the rate was 15.8% in Britain, 9.9 % in France and only 4.2% in Germany. At the same time, unemployment exceeded 1 million, hovering at around 5%: the full employment target of 3% proved hard to achieve.[59]

This phenomenon of 'stagflation' – high inflation, rising unemployment and indifferent growth – led to a degree of pessimism, even among Labour politicians. Jim Callaghan told the Labour conference in 1976 that 'we used to think that you could spend your way out of a recession.

… I tell you in all candour that that option no longer exists, and that in so far as it ever did exist, it only worked on each occasion since the war by injecting a bigger dose of inflation into the economy, followed by a higher level of unemployment as the next step.' Denis Healey, Callaghan's Chancellor, had become sceptical about the effectiveness of Keynesian methods of demand management.[60]

One needs to be careful, however, in attributing to the political leaders of the 1970s too settled a view as to the continuing achievability of full employment and economic growth. After all, the oil shock was a massive blow to the Western economy as a whole, but by the end of the 1970s, inflation was falling, and unemployment, although high by post-war standards, seemed to be manageable. After all, the Conservatives fought and won the 1979 election on the slogan 'Labour isn't working', the implication being that they could sharply reduce a jobless total then standing at 1 million. In the event, such a figure seemed for a long time after 1979 to be a remarkable achievement, not a sign of failure. Indeed, by 2017, Conservative ministers were trumpeting an unemployment rate of 4.4% as the lowest since the 1970s, as if that had been an idyllic era (albeit that the way the rate is measured has changed so much in the interim that the figures cannot sensibly be compared). It may be that Callaghan's pronouncement demonstrated only that 'you should not let your son-in-law write your speeches'.[61]

The reference in that speech to 'spend[ing] your way out of a recession' was partly a matter of party management, since the government had embarked upon a number of rounds of spending cuts. The 'social contract' had been premised upon union co-operation in exchange for generous social provision. The recession of 1973–5 had plunged the public finances into deficit. The government responded not only with cuts, but a broader assertion that the ratio of public expenditure to gross domestic product had become unsustainable. At the end of 1976, the government entered into a Letter of Intent with the International Monetary Fund, which required 'a continuing and substantial reduction over the next few years in the share of the resources required for the public sector'.[62]

The post-war system was, therefore, tottering by the mid-1970s, but it was not yet out of business. The British economy had taken a pounding from the rise in oil prices, but many on the Labour Right (and Tory Left) continued to believe that it was possible to maintain high levels of employment and public spending. Crosland, for example, agreed to the 1976 cuts only with the greatest reluctance. Others took a different approach, and the 1970s crisis offered them an opportunity to promulgate views they had long held. Since 1955, the Institute of Economic Affairs (IEA) had been disseminating free-market ideas, advocating a substantially unplanned economy, with lower taxes and less public spending. The state could not promote growth through demand management or industrial strategies: only competition in the free market could achieve economic progress. Government should be 'limited to services that cannot be organised by spontaneous contract in the market'.[63]

These arguments began to gain traction on the Tory Right, in particular following the fall of the Heath government in 1974. As inflation rapidly increased, Keith Joseph argued, in a series of speeches in 1974, that governments should completely change their policy focus. The cause of inflation was not wages negotiated by unions (to which Prices and Incomes Policy was wrongly thought to the answer) but governmental monetary indiscipline. Governments should concentrate on sound money and otherwise leave it to the market to promote growth. There were 'limits to the good which Government can do to help the economy, but no limits to the harm'. Inequality, far from being a bad thing, was a necessary spur to entrepreneurial activity. Thatcher became leader of the Conservative Party in 1975 with Joseph's support and adopted these arguments, albeit that many Conservatives were hostile to, or sceptical of, such propositions.[64]

Was there a social democratic ideology?

Did this system have any overriding body of ideas that held it together? It will be suggested here that there were certain beliefs to which, broadly speaking, British social democrats subscribed: in a phrase, that it was the duty of politicians and the state to strive for increased, but not absolute, equality of opportunity and outcome. Or, as the economist Arthur Lewis put it in 1949, 'socialism is about equality. A passion for equality is the one thing that links all socialists; on all others they are divided.' Before descending into the detail behind this shorthand summary, several immediate caveats should be entered.[65]

For one thing, try as one might, it is not possible to construct a theoretical structure that can coherently accommodate all those who contributed to the post-war social democratic system. After all, we have identified among our social democratic leaders Macmillan and Eisenhower, both essentially conservative, and both, coincidentally, proponents of the Middle Way. But even a more rigorous thinker, like Crosland, disavowed any 'vulgar fallacy that some ideal society can be said to exist'. On the contrary, 'the ultimate objective lies wrapped in complete uncertainty'. Moreover, 'complete uncertainty' was a reasonable description for some of the policy initiatives to which governments returned time and again in the social democratic era, such as planning and Prices and Incomes Policy.[66]

Secondly, there is a danger of seeing the writings of leading social democratic thinkers as providing sacred texts from which policy later flowed. But the connection between text and policy was often tenuous at best. Take *The Future of Socialism*, Crosland's great work of 1956. In truth, Crosland might as well have called his book *Does Socialism have a Future?* The book was, after all, written after Labour had been defeated in a second successive election in 1955, in which Crosland lost his own seat. Things did not get any better after 1956. In 1959 Labour lost again. The social democrats clustered around Hugh Gaitskell, including Crosland himself, feared that the party might never win again, or that, to have any chance of doing so, it would have to abandon any hint of a socialist programme. After all, it was inherent in the need for 'revisionism' that something needed revising.[67]

Thirdly, the success of the post-war system had many fathers (the sexist language being appropriate, since this was a very masculine endeavour). One could trace much of what happened after 1945 to the deliberations in the 1930s of left of centre economists such as Hugh Dalton, Jay and James Meade. These economists were, in turn, heavily influenced by Keynes who was himself a Liberal, and who, in turn, had considerable impact on the thinking of progressive Conservatives like Macmillan and Boothby.[68]

Having entered those qualifications, one can nonetheless identify certain themes that recurred in the works of influential social democrats (by which I mean, broadly, writers on the Left who were not Marxists), and which featured in the policies of post-war Labour governments prior to 1979. These ideas were also important in setting the policy framework within which Conservative governments could operate, albeit that the debt was less openly acknowledged. This was, not least, because most of these social democrats referred to their approach as 'democratic socialism', a creed to which even the most progressive Tory could scarcely subscribe.

That there were some intellectual underpinnings to British post-war social democracy is not to derogate from the broad point made in the Introduction that the policies adopted by UK governments before 1979 were a loose bundle rather than an ideological straitjacket. Ideas do inform political debate, but the relationship between writing and action is opaque and indirect. What one can say, however, is that there was a significant body of social democratic literature, which spelled out the arguments for increased equality and which was influential upon politicians of the Centre-Left. Conservative politicians on the Centre-Right had, at least, to operate within a framework that gave considerable weight to such egalitarianism.

For example, the work of the great economic historian R.H. Tawney (1880–1962) 'was appropriated and sanctified by the Labour Party' and 'exerted substantial influence on revisionist thought'. It was also a 'prescient guide to the intentions and achievements of the Labour Governments after 1945'. A core message in Tawney's work was that equal opportunity was not enough. It was necessary to have 'not only … an open road, but … an equal start'. Equality, or, at least, reduced inequality, must be achieved within a democratic context, but it would also entail 'the extension of democracy from the sphere of government and law to that of economic life'. And for Tawney, unlike the Reaganite and Thatcherite neoliberals, the state was, in large measure, 'the solution to our problems':

> We must spend, not less, but more on education, health, housing, and the establishment of security against the contingencies of life. We do not intend, therefore, to yield to the clamour for reduced taxation, but to maintain it and to use its proceeds for purposes essential to the general welfare.[69]

Tawney's arguments were rooted in his strong Christian faith. His most recent biographer notes that an important work, *Equality*, 'burns with indignation' and writes of his 'passionate moralism'. For a younger generation of social democratic thinkers, who came to prominence in the 1930s, the specifics of economic policy were equally important, in particular planning. This was, of course, a time of economic crisis and one in which democratic values were, internationally, under attack from Left and Right. The 1930s economists therefore needed to explain how the economy could work better under a democratic socialist government and why the answers to the crisis proposed by the Marxist Left were wrong. Rather than embrace Marxism, they contended, it was possible to combine Tawney's moralism with the economic theories of Keynes. Thereby, argues Ben Jackson, 'equality could be reconciled with, and indeed enhance, economic efficiency'. Prominent figures in this set included Dalton, Hugh Gaitskell and Jay (all subsequently to serve as Labour ministers), together with academics such as Meade. Their case was briskly confident: in Jay's words, 'the case for socialism is mainly economic and it rests on fact'.[70]

A key influence was Evan Durbin (1906–1948), who died after serving for only three years as a Labour MP. Durbin's arguments were intended to set out a 'moderate' case for democratic socialism in answer to what he felt to be the seductive but wrong-headed case advanced by the Marxists. Durbin's work, despite his early death, continued to be significant, and Gaitskell, in particular, remained under his influence, giving copies of his work to Soviet visitors. The case advanced, although 'moderate', was not anodyne. Durbin's anger over injustice was similar to Tawney's. In his most important book, *The Politics of Democratic Socialism*, he asserted that 'we have, in this country, much of which to be ashamed. The distribution of income is nowhere less equal. The grip of a class system … is extraordinarily strong.' The solution was social justice, and the means to this end was 'a planned economy, centrally controlled in order to pursue expansionist and egalitarian policies'.[71]

Durbin and his colleagues were economists, but scholars of other disciplines were also instrumental in devising the mix of policies that were developed during and after the war. The sociologists loosely grouped around Richard Titmuss (1907–1973), Professor of Social Administration at the LSE from 1950 until his death, were, according to Jackson, 'extremely influential on Labour's social policy in the 1950s and 60s'. Their work highlighted the importance of the politics of welfare and, in particular, the plight of *The Poor and the Poorest* (the title of a well-publicised 1965 study of poverty by two of Titmuss's disciples, Abel-Smith and Townsend).[72]

In this survey of social democratic thinking, pride of place should, however, be reserved for the work of Tony Crosland (1918–1977). Crosland was not only an important theoretician of social democracy but also, as we have seen, a significant ministerial practitioner. His most celebrated work, *The Future of Socialism*, published in 1956, attracted hyperbole at the time and subsequently. Kenneth Morgan, a distinguished historian of Labour politics, observed in 2011 that 'there has been no significant statement of socialist doctrine in this country – perhaps in any country – since Crosland in the mid-1950s'. Crosland's biographer claimed that from 1956 until his death, Crosland was the 'acknowledged high priest of "revisionism"', a mixture of neo-Keynesian economics and progressive social reform. What then did this great theoretical work seek to argue?[73]

In a sense, *The Future of Socialism* was a negative undertaking. The Labour Party of the 1950s was bitterly divided between the Bevanite socialist Left and the Gaitskellite revisionist Right, and it was Crosland's aim to dismantle the arguments of the former. He sought to show that the ownership of the means of production – the focus of Clause IV of the party's constitution – was now immaterial. Capitalism as it had been known in the nineteenth century had ceased to exist. It followed that 'a steadily extending chain of State monopolies [was] wholly irrelevant to socialism'. For his troubles, Crosland was excoriated in *Tribune*, the house magazine of the Bevanite Left, although Richard Crossman, a prominent Bevanite, grudgingly acknowledged that his ideas were 'diabolically and cunningly left wing'.[74]

However, this was not to say that, for Crosland, there was no role for the State and no way forward for Labour. What was clear was that 'in Britain equality of opportunity and social mobility … are not enough'. Although it was pointless to speculate upon how equal society should ultimately be, there was no doubt that it should be much more equal, with 'large egalitarian changes in our educational system, the distribution of property … social manners and style of life, and the location of power within industry'. Governments should pursue these objectives through, among other things, a 'concerted attack on the misdistribution of wealth' (which Crosland took to be far more troubling than income inequality). And there were so many important calls upon the resources of a Labour government that the party should be as keen as, if not keener than, the Tories to promote rapid economic growth. This was, therefore, the case for socialism as equality, within a mixed, and still largely capitalist economy.[75]

In the Golden Age, social liberalism came a poor second to social justice in British society. But, to be fair, the social democratic intellectuals did rage against 'socially-imposed restrictions on the individual's private life and liberty'. For Crosland, it was necessary that 'there should always run a trace of the anarchist and the libertarian, and not too much of the prig and the prude' in the blood of the socialist. Jenkins defined social democracy as a commitment that combined individual freedom and social justice. Such permissive sentiments were certainly present within social democratic thinking, therefore, albeit often drowned out by other economic and social concerns. Certainly, for this generation of social democrats, unlike the puritanical Webbs, 'total abstinence and a good filing system are not now the right signposts to the socialist Utopia'.[76]

Social democrats often appeared somewhat earnest, with their concerns over equality, planning and poverty, but there was still something of the spirit of William Morris about them. In the drab 1950s, Crosland sought 'to make Britain a more colourful and civilised country to live in':

> We need not only higher exports and old-age pensions, but more open-air cafés, brighter and gayer streets at night, later closing hours for public houses, more local repertory theatres, better and more hospitable hoteliers and restaurateurs, brighter and cleaner eating-houses, more riverside cafés, more pleasure gardens on the Battersea model, more murals and pictures in public places, better designs for furniture and pottery and women's clothes, statues in the centre of new housing-estates, better-designed new street lamps and telephone kiosks, and so on ad *infinitum*.[77]

Crosland's work in the mid-1950s was the culmination of much that had gone before. It was highly influential upon a generation of social democrats within and outside Labour: in 1976, Edward Boyle called *The Future of Socialism* 'the most impressive contribution by any politician to serious thinking on politics/economics/social science since the war'. Yet it would be wrong to end this brief survey on anything other than a melancholy note. When Crosland died in 1977, social democracy in Britain was faltering. By 1981, when a number of his friends and admirers assembled a volume of essays in his memory, it was in headlong retreat. The values for which Crosland had argued, such as the central place of equality, the need for high public spending, and the idea that 'only the best was good enough for his Grimsby constituents', were now firmly out of fashion. His former special adviser, David Lipsey, asked despairingly 'why, in the Britain of the 1980s, do the comers against Crosland's castle seem so numerous and the defenders so dispirited?'[78]

The 'comers' kept coming and the defenders remained dispirited. 'Crosland's castle' was so prominent, in large part, because of the flatness of the surrounding landscape. The ideals of egalitarianism seemed omnipresent prior to 1979, and almost wholly absent thereafter, with a brief flicker of interest in the wake of the financial crisis. Certainly, the New Labour era did little to revive interest in arguments for social democracy. Morgan is surely right to accuse the Blair/Brown leadership of producing 'verbiage of extreme vacuity' and relying, in the so-called Third Way, upon a 'mélange of generalities'.[79]

Conclusions

An ideological tent big enough to accommodate Eisenhower and Bevan was not likely to be a very intellectually rigorous place. In truth, the postwar order embraced a series of policies that had only limited coherence. This is likely to be the case in any democratic society. After all, Thatcherism has survived a number of reverses and contradictions. The notion that one could conquer inflation through monetary means alone did not long survive contact with reality. The attitude of Thatcherite governments to 'industrial strategy' has varied from hostility to enthusiasm.

However, the British people were, from 1945 to 1979, largely spared what Roy Jenkins would call, in his Dimbleby lecture of the latter year, 'queasy rides on the ideological big-dipper'. Policy change was, in truth, quite limited, despite numerous changes of government and personnel. Of course, there are those who argue that the British economy would have benefited from a stiff dose of Thatcherism long before the 1980s. As will be seen in subsequent chapters, there was no shortage of voices urging radical change, whether back to a much more free-market system or forward to socialism. However, those holding the levers of power did not take much notice of such arguments. After all, the system delivered, or appeared to be delivering, economic growth coupled with social cohesion. From 1979 onwards, however, this system was largely dismantled. The real contrast in British politics is not, in truth, between the parties but between pre-1979 social democracy and post-1979 Thatcherism.[80]

As we shall see, the great arguments over Europe mapped, imperfectly but unmistakeably, this fundamental issue of whether the UK should persist with the social democratic model or should turn to the Left or Right. Most of those who argued strongly for continuity in domestic policy were the most enthusiastic for engagement with the EU. Those who sought a radical break with the post-war system were much more likely to be in the 'anti' camp. And it is perhaps no coincidence that the 1971–5 period, in which the UK made and then affirmed its European vows, was also a time when Britain was the most equal society it had ever been. In the 1970s, the post-war system was both at its apogee, in the sense that egalitarianism was in the ascendant, and approaching a decisive crisis, as the economic storm clouds gathered.

2 A European Love Affair, 1960–1973?

It breaks my heart to see what is happening in our country today. A terrible strike is being carried on by the best men in the world. They beat the Kaiser's army and they beat Hitler's army. They never gave in. … Then there is the growing division … in our comparatively prosperous society between the South and the North and Midlands, which are ailing. This cannot be allowed to continue.

Earl of Stockton, formerly Harold Macmillan,
maiden speech in House of Lords, 13 November 1984[1]

My passion in politics was for Europe. … I was converted to 'the European ideal' by Roy Jenkins. … It was a cause which Harold Macmillan embraced, and which Ted Heath consummated: it has been left to others to neglect it.

Julian Critchley MP, Tory 'Wet', 1986[2]

Introduction

The rise of Euroscepticism, and the intense emotions that accompanied it, raise the question: how and why did the UK become entwined with Europe in the first place? The Eurosceptic answer to this, of course, is that the British people were lied to in the 1970s. They were led to believe that membership of the EEC amounted to no more than participation in a Common Market, but without any diminution of British sovereignty. Only later did it dawn on the voters that they had inadvertently signed up to a project which would create a European superstate and would leave the UK as a mere province of an over-mighty Brussels. As Nigel Farage put it in 2016, discussing accession in 1973 and the referendum in 1975:

> The British establishment knew it was giving away its decision-making powers. It would not admit this in public and it was prepared to be highly duplicitous in covering it up. I believe most British people would say the British establishment lied. I believe most British people would be right.[3]

This argument – and Farage was by no means alone in advancing it – is a curious one. For one thing, the sovereignty argument was made, as we shall see in Chapters 3 and 4, loud and long by the opponents of entry. The fact that this was more than a Common Market was obvious as soon as the UK joined, if it had not been obvious before. As Lord Denning (Master of the Rolls and one of the few judges, then or subsequently, with a prominent public profile) pointed out in 1974, European Law was 'like an incoming tide … it cannot be held back'. Indeed, as a recent and thorough study of the earlier referendum observes, there was an 'extensive and sophisticated discussion of sovereignty in 1975'. The purpose of this chapter is not, therefore, to deny that there were many British politicians and voters who were wary of the EEC for exactly the reasons deployed by Farage in 2016. Rather it is to explore the extent to which other political leaders made the case which, according to Brexit orthodoxy, was 'covered up', and what motivated them to put forward those arguments.[4]

As appears below, the UK's formal engagement with the EEC in this period consisted of two failed attempts to join (1961–3 and 1966–7), followed by a successful campaign after 1970, which culminated in accession in 1973. These efforts to join were conducted successively by the 1957–63 Conservative government of Harold Macmillan, with Heath the key minister; the 1964–70 Labour government of Harold Wilson, in which Roy Jenkins served as Home Secretary and Chancellor; and finally, the Conservative government of 1970–4, with Heath now Prime Minister. Throughout there was a chorus of disapproval from dissenters within and outside the two main parties, with the issue much more ago-nising for Labour than for the Conservatives.

This chapter, therefore, concentrates upon the arguments that the advocates of entry made: in particular, Macmillan, Heath and Jenkins. The selection of the first two is self-explanatory. Jenkins perhaps requires a little more elucidation. In the 1960s and 1970s, there were at least four strands of Labour opinion, only one of them strongly pro-EEC. For the Left, the EEC was a capitalist club, which would seek to stop a Labour government from carrying out its socialist policies. The nationalist Right, such as Gaitskell, Jay and Shore, were also hostile: the UK did not need to sell its birthright of political independence and links to the Commonwealth for a mess of European pottage. Many other senior figures did 'not feel enthusiastic' about the EEC (not least because of the divisiveness of the issue for the party) but tended, in the end, to sup-port membership. Wilson, Callaghan, Healey and Crosland were all of this view. Standing apart from these other factions were the Jenkinsites: they saw 'Europe' as the central issue in British politics, upon which they were prepared to split and, ultimately, leave Labour. From the early 1960s onwards, Jenkins was an enthusiastic proponent of British mem-bership. Crucially, in 1971, the Jenkinsites defied a three-line whip to support the Heath government's application for membership.[5]

Macmillan, Heath and Jenkins were not the only pro-European voices in this period, but they were certainly among the most influential, and their arguments were typical of those that the more enthusiastic British advocates of entry advanced. Of course, they said, membership would bring economic advantages. But this was not a purely transactional arrangement. The UK was to embark with the Europeans upon a joint venture, with a significant social component. This process of integra-tion would involve changes in the UK's sovereignty, but this was not a loss, but a pooling of sovereignty. This was a case, therefore, that went far beyond a 'Common Market'. And it was no coincidence that this argument was put forward most enthusiastically by politicians who were seeking to uphold the social democratic system.[6]

This chapter considers in turn the positions on Europe of Macmillanite Conservatives, Jenkinsites within Labour and the Heathmen. Before doing so, it is first helpful to summarise the three attempts of the UK to join the EEC in the years between 1961 and 1973.

Non, Non – and Oui at last, 1961–1973

Before examining this story, it is worth just considering whether any British politician in the 1960s and 1970s could seriously have thought that membership was simply a matter of joining a free trade area, but without any reduction of British sovereignty or corresponding obligations. After all, if that was indeed the European offer, it was surely too good to be true. Who would wish to say no to free access to these large and swiftly expanding European markets if there were no associated disadvantages or restrictions of any kind? Certainly, the reactionary fringe, for example the Monday Club in the Tory Party, were deeply unhappy with the post-war free trading order that the hated Americans had devised. They were suspicious of multinational companies, who were pressing for a large, open European market. However, this was a very marginal position: most British politicians, Left, Right and Centre, subscribed to the principle of free trade.[7]

A cursory perusal of the Treaty of Rome, the instrument that had created the Community in 1957, would have disabused such politicians of any illusion that this was to be a deliciously one-sided bargain from which only the UK would benefit. After all, the very first words of the Treaty proclaimed that the signatories were

> DETERMINED to lay the foundations of an ever-closer union among the peoples of Europe, RESOLVED to ensure the economic and social progress of their countries by common action to eliminate the barriers which divide Europe.

And how was this progress to be achieved? The Treaty made this clear by articles 117 and 118:

Member States agree upon the need to promote improved working conditions and an improved standard of living for workers, so as to make
possible their harmonisation while the improvement is being maintained. They believe that such a development will ensue not only from
the functioning of the common market, which will favour the harmonisation of social systems, but also from the procedures provided for
in this Treaty and from the approximation of provisions laid down by
law, regulation or administrative action ... the Commission shall have
the task of promoting close co-operation between Member States in the
social field.

Indeed, the features of the EEC/EU to which Eurosceptics were to
return time and again in 2016 were clear from the outset: the approximation of the laws of Member States (article 3(h)); freedom of movement
for workers (articles 48 to 51); the role of the Court of Justice (articles
164 to 188). And if there were any doubts about how this fitted together,
the Court had dispelled them long before the UK joined the EEC:

By contrast with ordinary international treaties, the EEC Treaty has created its own legal system which, on the entry into force of the
Treaty, became an integral part of the legal systems of the Member States and which their courts are bound to apply. By creating
a Community of unlimited duration, having its own institutions,
its own personality, its own legal capacity and capacity of representation on the international plane and, more particularly, real
powers stemming from a limitation of sovereignty or a transfer
of powers from the States to the Community, the Member States
have limited their sovereign rights, albeit within limited fields,
and have thus created a body of law which binds both their na-
tionals and themselves.[8]

Moreover, not many people observing British efforts to join the
EEC could really have thought that the UK was able to dictate terms
to Europe. The initial response to the formation of the EEC had been

to establish EFTA with the 'outer seven' as a competing free trade area. However, this left Britain as part of a free trade area with a population of 89 million (including its own 51m), but outside the EEC's tariff walls and population of 170m. This looked like an increasingly unattractive option as time went by. Between 1958 and 1972, GNP per head grew 178% in West Germany, 185% in France and 180% in Italy, but only 140% in Britain.[9]

This is the background of the three attempts that British governments made to join the EEC between 1961 and 1973. One other aspect of the context is worth emphasising. Since the UK had not joined at the outset in 1957, there was no question of a British government simply joining without more ado. There had to be a formal application, and then negotiations. Since any such negotiations were, in principle, open-ended, it was always a little difficult for opponents of membership to resist the mere commencement of negotiations. After all, if one pointed to a potentially unattractive aspect of the EEC (such as the Common Agricultural Policy), there was a ready answer available to the applicant government, namely that this was a matter for discussion in the negotiations. The fact that such discussions might end unsatisfactorily for the UK was possible, but it was not a given and it was scarcely a reason not to embark on negotiations at all.

The first such set of negotiations took place from 1961 to 1963 under Macmillan's government, with Heath as chief negotiator and Jenkins as the most prominent of the thirty or so Labour MPs who actively supported membership. This process ended in failure when General de Gaulle vetoed the application in January 1963, following lengthy and detailed discussions. It is, therefore, a moot point what the attitude of government, people and parliament would have been to such final settlement as Heath might have recommended, although the official history suggests that by mid-1962 the Cabinet had concluded that there was no 'convincing alternative to membership'.[10]

In this process, there was careful consideration, at an official and political level, of the implications of the treaties for sovereignty, and the obvious conclusions were drawn. For example, Lord Kilmuir, the Lord Chancellor, advised Heath in December 1960 that accession would involve a serious surrender of sovereignty and the supremacy in some fields of European over English Law. Eurosceptics would, many years later, seize upon such advice as 'chilling evidence' of Heath's 'lies'. At the time, these conclusions did not become a matter of wider public debate, not least because of the ultimate breakdown of the negotiations. However, for anyone following the matter closely, those implications were fairly spelt out. For example, Lord Home, the Foreign Secretary, told the Lords in August 1961 (just after the launch of the application) that:

> the Treaty of Rome would involve considerable derogation of sovereignty. Let me say also that the field in which there could be surrender of sovereignty is clearly defined and restricted to economic matters … within this restricted field, derogations of sovereignty will be different in kind from any contract into which we have entered before. It is well that people should realise that, although I cannot forecast whether these derogations would be substantial or whether in any particular case the derogation of sovereignty would act against us or for us.[11]

There the matter rested until 1966. In October of that year, the Wilson government agreed that he and George Brown should make a series of exploratory visits to European capitals with a view to a renewed application. Following this process, the government announced the following May that it would be making a formal application for membership. Negotiations then proceeded until 27 November 1967 when, in the words of the official history, 'categorically and contemptuously de Gaulle dismissed Britain's application'.[12]

During these Cabinet discussions, and the ensuing negotiations, the implications for sovereignty were, once more, both appreciated and explained. Lord Gardiner, the Lord Chancellor, told his colleagues in April 1967 that 'the major political aspects related to the extent to which our entry into the E.E.C. would involve a loss of sovereignty. Some loss would admittedly be involved but this was true in respect of every international treaty … the issue was therefore one of degree, not of principle.' Likewise, Wilson told a press conference in February 1967 that 'when you use the phrase "surrender of sovereignty" I want to make it quite plain that this emotive phrase … has never been one that has frightened me … a progressive surrender of sovereignty is a mark of an advancing civilisation.' And the government's 1967 White Paper made clear that 'the constitutional innovation would lie in the acceptance in advance as part of the law of the United Kingdom of provisions to be made in the future by instruments issued by the Community institutions – a situation for which there is no precedent in this country'. Moreover, the antis in the Cabinet made the point that:

> there was a difference of principle in the extent of the restriction on our sovereignty imposed by entry into the EEC on the one hand and the signing of other international treaties on the other hand … if we were to become a member of the EEC however there would be a progressive limitation of our national sovereignty through the legislation which the Community was empowered to pass and we should, therefore, not know at the time of entry how extensive the restrictions on our sovereignty would subsequently prove to be.[13]

The second veto put the UK's application on ice, but able to be revived once the General at last retired in 1969. The Heath government pursued the application vigorously after it had won the 1970 general election, culminating in Geoffrey Rippon, the chief negotiator, securing 'most satisfactory terms' in June 1971. Not without some difficulty, the government obtained the agreement of Parliament to the European Communities Act 1972, which gave effect in UK law to the relevant European treaties. The UK finally acceded in January 1973. The chief architect of the 1972 Act was another Geoffrey (Howe), then Solicitor-General. He too agonised over the question of sovereignty, as had his Conservative and Labour legal predecessors Kilmuir and Gardiner. He made clear (as did the Act) that Community law would take precedence over UK law. He concluded that this was in accordance with constitutional principle, for 'the very sovereignty of Parliament entitled that body to manage or deploy that sovereignty, on behalf of the British people, in partnership with other nations on such terms as Parliament itself might decide'. In so doing, he, in effect, endorsed the view taken by the Labour government in 1967, namely that European laws 'would derive their force under the law of the United Kingdom from the original enactment passed by Parliament'.[14]

That being the chronology and process whereby Britain applied to join the EEC, we turn now to consider the case that the promoters of entry made in this period.

Macmillan

Harold Macmillan was, in many ways, uniquely well placed to assess the potential advantages of membership in a wider historical context. He had a long apprenticeship before he became Prime Minister in 1957. Born in 1894, he had served in the First World War, and been seriously wounded. During the Second World War, he was minister resident at allied forces headquarters in Algiers. Although a Conservative, he was between the two wars often at odds with his own party over both foreign policy (as an opponent of appeasement) and domestic policy (as an advocate of measures to reduce unemployment). After 1945, Macmillan, who had lost his seat in the Labour landslide of that year, was prominent among those Tories who argued for an accommodation with the new, post-war order. For example, he was Minister for Housing in Churchill's final administration of 1951–5, during which period the government achieved the target of building of 300,000 houses a year.[15]

In the 1930s, Macmillan was, to a large extent, in the wilderness politically, but he could be said to have astutely anticipated much of the policy approach adopted by post-war governments. His theoretical contribution, *The Middle Way*, published in 1938, argued for a form of highly managed capitalism, in which the state would be responsible for 'guiding capital investment into the correct channels', the trade unions would have a key role in 'preserving working-class freedom and seeking to develop industrial democracy', and there would be a minimum wage. Although the 'Tory back (and front) benches growled distrustfully' on its publication, *The Middle Way* therefore explored a number of themes to which post-war governments would turn. In a sense it was as much a guide to British social democracy as *The Future of Socialism*.[16]

That Macmillan, and his governments, embraced a form of social democracy seems clear enough. It is more debatable as to how keen he, and they, were on the European ideals enshrined in the Treaty of Rome. On the one hand, as early as the 1940s, Macmillan was speaking 'with a fervour ... about his belief in the European idea'. In Churchill's last government, he was one of the leading 'Europeans' in an administration of which the most senior members were unenthusiastic, especially Churchill himself and Eden, the Foreign Secretary. On the other hand, a careful study of the Macmillan government's approach to Europe has questioned whether he 'actually believe[d] in anything'. Whatever the truth of Macmillan's real beliefs, two things are, it will be suggested, apparent about the approach of his government to the European question. The first is that there was, from 1960 onwards, a real turn towards Europe. The second is that this was explained, boldly and unapologetically, in terms which were not merely those of economic pragmatism, but which fitted neatly into the broader approach of the Macmillan government to social questions.[17]

Certainly, the turn towards Europe was slow in coming. In May 1955, Eden, the newly elected Prime Minister, appointed Macmillan Foreign Secretary. His attitude to the 1955 Messina conference, which took place a month later, and which in effect gave birth to the EEC, was lukewarm. In November 1955, the Economic Policy Committee, not the full Cabinet, decided not to join the new organisation, with neither Eden nor Macmillan attending the meeting. During 1956 and 1957, the government therefore developed 'Plan G', for the EFTA 7 nations as a rival free trade area. However, this arrangement was unsatisfactory: Britain was part of a limited free trade area, but stood outside the EEC's much larger and more prosperous area.[18]

In the late 1950s, government thinking developed and changed. At the end of 1957, Macmillan told Heath (already regarded as a strong pro-European) that the isolationist tendencies in the Tory Party represented 'a stultifying policy'. By 1960, Macmillan was, according to a recent biography, 'convinced that closer European economic association for Britain was not only inevitable, but desirable'. Thereafter, things moved quickly. In April 1960, Sir Frank Lee (Joint Permanent Secretary to the Treasury) prepared a memorandum on membership for the Chancellor, which Macmillan asked to see, and which provided 'the definitive document that was to set Britain on a new course, not only in terms of trade, but also in terms of Britain's political role and outlook'. In July of that year, the government was reshuffled, with promotions for known 'Europeanists'. In particular, Macmillan appointed Heath as Lord Privy Seal, with special responsibility for European matters.[19]

There could be little doubt how this would all end, but various steps had to be taken before the government could actually apply for membership. In February 1961, Heath announced that Britain was contemplating 'a fundamental change of principle' in its approach to the EEC. Nonetheless, it was necessary to consult widely with the Commonwealth, then often regarded as the UK's principal trading and cultural partner. The support of the Kennedy Administration in the USA was obtained. Macmillan strove to ensure that he had wide backing in the Cabinet, the parliamentary party and the press. Ultimately, in July 1961, the Cabinet resolved 'that a formal application for accession to the Treaty of Rome should be made without delay in order that negotiations might be opened with the Community'. As has been rightly observed, however, 'to a remarkable extent the decision to apply for British membership was made by Macmillan alone. He had, of course, to take the Cabinet with him but it was he who led and the rest who followed' (albeit that the official history argues that the Cabinet had rather more influence than this would suggest, but the parts of leader and followers seems clear enough).[20]

In explaining this decision to the Commons, Macmillan dealt head-on with both the social and the sovereignty issues, which he considered intertwined:

> the social implications of the Treaty, such things as movements of population, equal pay and all the rest. At present, the countries of the Six are only beginning what we might call the harmonisation of their social policies. There are very different circumstances in the various countries and, naturally, each one must take into account its own circumstances. So if we joined at a formative stage, as it were, we should be able to bring our own ideas into the common pool with, I hope, mutual benefit. … These apprehensions about the social implications of joining the Treaty are really aspects of a wider constitutional anxiety about what has often been called 'sovereignty' … every treaty limits a nation's freedom of action to some extent. Even before the First World War there were certain international conventions to which we bound ourselves. Before the Second World War they grew in character and affected both political and social questions, like the conventions agreed at the International Labour Organisation. Since the war this tendency has grown and our freedom of action is obviously affected by our obligations in N.A.T.O., W.E.U., O.E.E.C. and all the rest. … Here again, unless we are in the negotiations, unless we can bring our influence to bear, we shall not be able to play our part in deciding the future structure of Europe. It may be, as I have said, that we shall find that our essential needs cannot be met, but if they can I do not feel that there is anything on the constitutional side of which we need be in fear and which cannot be resolved to our satisfaction.[21]

In October, Heath, reported to his colleagues the text of his opening statement to the existing Member States a few days earlier:

> We now desire to become full, whole-hearted and active members of
> the European Community ... we are ready to accept without qualifica-
> tion the objectives laid down in Articles 2 and 3 of the Treaty of Rome,
> and to play a full part in the institution of the Community. ... It will
> certainly not be our aim to slow down the pace of development of the
> Community ... the habit of working together, once formed, will mean,
> not a slowing down, but a continued advance and the development of
> closer unity.[22]

During 1961 and 1962, the government was engaged in delicate negotiations to secure membership. It had to balance a number of domestic
and international interests of its own, as well as seeking to persuade
the Six and, in particular the French, that it was in their interests for
the UK to join. Could the British 'put forward a formula for 6s and
7s wh[ich] both Commonwealth and British agriculture will wear' (6
being the EEC and 7 EFTA)? Could Macmillan win over a 'hostile and
jealous' de Gaulle? At the same time, the Conservatives had to keep a
close eye on the media and their own activists. With the exception of
the Beaverbrook titles, the press were broadly sympathetic, although
needing careful attention; for example, Macmillan spent time ensur-
ing the support of Cecil King, the Chairman of the (pro-European but
Labour supporting) *Mirror* Newspapers. Party members, too, proved
surprisingly easy to rally, with an overwhelming vote in favour of entry
at the Conservative conference of October 1961.[23]

Macmillan nonetheless took no chances with the activists, and published a pamphlet so as to influence debate at the 1962 conference. In
this, he did not shrink from accepting the logical concomitant of membership, namely that:

> It is sometimes alleged that we would lose all our national identity by
> joining the European Community and become what Mr Gaitskell con-
> temptuously described the other day as a mere 'province' of Europe. It is
> true, of course, that political unity is the central aim of these European

countries and we would naturally accept that ultimate goal. But the effects on our position of joining Europe have been much exaggerated by the critics.

Accession to the Treaty of Rome would not involve a one-sided surrender of 'sovereignty' on our part, but a pooling of sovereignty by all concerned, mainly in economic and social fields. In renouncing some of our own sovereignty we would receive in return a share of the sovereignty renounced by other members.[24]

When Macmillan made what proved to be his final conference speech as party leader in 1962, he devoted almost the entirety of his text to the European negotiations. There were a number of striking features of his arguments. The first was that, although there was much said about the economic benefits of membership, the rhetorical context was much more wide-ranging:

The European movement has caught the imagination of the young; it has transcended party politics and national barriers. Its impact has not been limited to economic affairs. ... We in Britain cannot stand aside from all this. Although in the latter part of the nineteenth century and the first half of this century, we have sometimes tried to ignore the Continent, we have never really been able to insulate ourselves from what happens only twenty miles away...

The instrument of coalition, of alliance, is one which we have always used in war. In peace perhaps we have used it less; but anyone who looks honestly at the history of the first half of this century cannot help feeling that the prospects of peace might have been better if we had played in peacetime as large a part in the affairs of Europe as we – and our Commonwealth partners too – have in war. For this hesitation we have paid a heavy price. Is not that, perhaps the lesson learned from the battlefields we remember, and the comrades we mourn? ... we must welcome the determination of our neighbours in Europe to seek to bury for good their age-old conflicts.

The second feature of note was that Macmillan did not unduly spare the sensitivities of his audience of Tory activists, whose 'massive vote you gave on Thursday shows that the party is solidly behind us in these efforts', but whose ranks contained a good many Little Englanders. It was, said Macmillan, 'nonsense' for Gaitskell to 'prattle about our being reduced to the status of Texas or California' (as he had done at the previous week's Labour Conference). Of course, 'going in must involve some pooling of national freedom of action'. The UK would 'agree to the rules of the club', but that was as nothing compared to the

> far more formidable and far-reaching NATO on the defence side. Remember that under the terms of the NATO Treaty, we are pledged to go to the aid of any one of fourteen other countries if they are attacked. In terms of the totality of modern war, this is indeed a tremendous pledge. It may not involve our formal sovereignty, but it does involve our physical survival.

Finally, Macmillan drew an explicit comparison between the economic benefits of membership and the interventionist industrial policies his government was pursuing domestically:

> If we go in, we shall have wider economic opportunities. We shall be part of, and have free access to, a home market of 250 million people instead of 50 million people ... how do all these changes affect us here at home? Well, one thing is clear. In or out of Europe, we shall have to live in a world of increasing competition. If there is one thing more than anything else that has struck me in your debates, it is the way you all recognise that, inside or outside Europe, this country has got to be prepared for change. It is a job for us all over the next decade – for Government, employers, trade unions and the general public – it is our job to see that change is brought about not only with efficiency but with humanity as well. We are all more or less planners today. I was a planner thirty years ago when it was not quite so fashionable. The real difficulty about planning is not the concept but the execution. ... During

the last year, the Government have taken two important forward steps in planning – 'Nicky', the National Incomes Commission, to ensure that rates of reward are both fair and in step with what we produce; and 'Neddy', the National Economic Development Council, to help us produce more, and produce more efficiently, by keeping our plans in line with our resources and by removing obstacles to growth.[25]

These rhetorical efforts proved effective. The conference rejected a Eurosceptic motion, with 'only 50 or so out of 400 voting for it'. De Gaulle proved less easy to persuade. Not for nothing had he been given the codename of Ramrod during the war, suitable for one who had 'all the rigidity of a poker without its occasional warmth'. In January 1963, he vetoed the British application: for Macmillan, this 'was a devastating blow'. For unrelated reasons, Macmillan resigned as Prime Minister later that year, and the Conservatives lost the 1964 general election. For the time being, the UK's involvement with the EEC was at an end. This had been, to this point, very much a Conservative venture and one to which Macmillan had given his all. The failure of the application was 'the end of the world' and 'all our policies at home and abroad are in ruins'.[26]

The negotiations of 1961–3, although abortive, were nonetheless illustrative of a number of themes that would recur in later years. The first was the dog that did not bark and, indeed, scarcely growled: the Conservative Eurosceptics. When the government presented the Commons with its proposal to commence negotiations in August 1961, fewer than two dozen Tories abstained, a mixture of 'earnest Imperialists' and disgruntled ex-ministers whom Macmillan had sacked. As noted above, the party conference was easy enough to convince. Yet Edward Boyle (a progressive, pro-European Tory) was surely right to give the following warning to Macmillan, although he was perhaps thirty years ahead of his time:

I don't see how the Conservative Party can avoid some sort of split on this issue. But the example of Balfour after 1903 surely suggests that the attempt to avoid any split, on some hotly contentious issue, may simply result in a far greater and more damaging one (and in electoral disaster).[27]

The second key theme to emerge from this period was that there was, embryonically, an anti-European alliance of Left and Right in Britain, but it was one that had not really been able to rally its forces. Macmillan had skilfully secured the unanimous agreement of his Cabinet to the application before exposing it to public gaze, having 'encouraged everyone to speak and [having] made no attempt to bring my colleagues to a premature conclusion'. Potential opponents were therefore presented with a fait accompli: the Anti-Common Market League was not formed until August 1961, after Macmillan's statement to the Commons.[28]

However, although tactically outmanoeuvred on this occasion, the anti-EEC forces had not gone away. There was, Macmillan noted in his diary, a 'new alliance between the extreme Right and the extreme Left'. The position was confused in that Gaitskell had, in October 1962, seemingly 'thrown himself into the arms of the men he has been fighting for three years, and has abandoned the friends on whose loyalty he has depended' (in his 'thousand years of history' speech, as to which see Chapter 3). Yet, as Macmillan also noted, there was no doubt that the Left were 'violently anti'. The Right, although marginalised in the Conservative Party of the early 1960s, held similarly strong opinions, albeit for different reasons. The *Express* was on this issue 'violent to a degree hardly believable', as it would be once more in 2016. And Macmillan was warned (and again there are shades here of 2016) of 'the trouble which the "sovereignty" argument was going to cause in the party. It is being put about that I am determined to abandon the Queen and promote a federal Europe at the expense of the national identity'.[29]

Finally, this episode had shown that the most steadfast friends of the UK's application were the progressive Left of the Conservative Party and the social democratic Right of the Labour Party. Macmillan had himself conducted operations with considerable dexterity. However shallow his underlying commitment may have been, he had taken the country to the brink of membership. The failure of the application had been beyond his control: everything that he could influence (party, Commonwealth, Commons), he had adroitly managed. Heath, his European negotiator, had made a thorough job of convincing the Europeans of the UK's bona fides. Both had made clear, domestically and internationally, that this was very much more than an economic bargain. The position of most of those on the Labour Right, Gaitskell's defection notwithstanding, was supportive and similarly expressed. Macmillan noted in particular a 'luminous speech' on Europe by Jenkins in June 1961, and that he had made 'the most significant speech of the debate' when the Commons discussed the government's proposals in August 1961.[30]

The Jenkinsites

In formal terms, Labour's contribution to the UK's accession to the EEC in 1973 was quite limited. Of the three attempts at membership, only one (1966–7) took place under a Labour government. The final and successful application of 1971–2 was pursued by a Conservative government, and, in the main, fiercely opposed by the Labour Movement (see Chapter 3). Nonetheless, it is well arguable that Britain would never have become a member of the EEC at all had it not been for the support of a small but dedicated band of pro-Europeans on the Right of the party, of whom Jenkins was the most conspicuous. He and his followers were the crucial components of this element of the party, albeit that there were others who played a role, notably George Brown. Such sentiments were by no means universal on the Right of the party. Some, like Jay and Shore, were hostile to the EEC. More were cautious or indifferent, regarding the unity of the party as more significant than this issue: Callaghan, Healey and Crosland, for example, fell into this category. Such hostility, caution or indifference had a substantial pedigree on the Centre and Right of the party. The giants of the 1945–51 government, such as Attlee and Bevin, were proud British/English nationalists, keen to promote co-operation within the Anglosphere and suspicious of notions of European unity.[31]

What then motivated the Jenkinsites? Their leader was born in 1920 into the Labour purple. His father was a Welsh miner, who was imprisoned during the general strike in 1926, and was later a Labour MP and PPS to Attlee. Despite this heritage, Jenkins, who was himself a Labour MP from 1948 to 1976, pursued political interests that were idiosyncratic within the Labour Movement. A noted libertarian, Jenkins was a reforming Home Secretary from 1965 to 1967 and 1974 to 1976, overseeing what many felt were overdue reforms to the law on abortion and homosexuality, and enacting anti-discrimination legislation in respect of race and gender. However, his central passion was Europe and, in the words of a recent biography, 'he played a role second only to Edward Heath in taking Britain belatedly into the European Community'. This role in due course took him to the fringes of, and then out of, the Labour Movement into which he had been born.[32]

Jenkins was an early adopter of the European cause. Like Macmillan and Heath, his early life was dominated by war in Europe. The Munich by-election took place in his first term at Oxford; after graduation, he served in the Army during the war. These experiences clearly influenced his thinking: by the later 1950s he was to be found disdaining EFTA as 'a foolish attempt to organise a weak periphery against a strong core', and warning against the UK 'living sullenly in the past'. By the early 1960s, he was deputy chairman of the cross-party Common Market Campaign and Chairman of the Labour Committee for Europe (LCE). His approach was dismissive of the UK 'self-righteously trying to preserve our little corner of sovereignty'. While stressing the economic and political advantages of membership, Jenkins sought also to persuade his comrades that there was a Labour case for entry: 'if we could have an economic plan working as effectively as the French, that would be a very great step towards social and economic progress in this country'. He told the 1961 Labour Conference that nothing in the Treaty of Rome would prevent a British government from further nationalisation.[33]

One key strand in Jenkins's arguments was that Labour needed to look outwards to Europe, and 'recognise that Britain's power in the world is inevitably diminished, and that we must change with it, and then we can best achieve our objects in the future by co-operating with our power equals in the world, and by doing it with enthusiasm'. One difficulty in this regard was that the leader, Gaitskell, to whom Jenkins was close politically and personally, was unpersuaded of this case, despite Jenkins's best efforts. Indeed, Gaitskell's 'thousand years of history' speech in October 1962 was a grave disappointment to the Labour pro-Europeans. Brown saved the day. In what his biographer thought 'the finest moment in [his] entire political career', Brown wound up the conference debate by 'stating the case for going into Europe'. He was then deputy leader of the party and a Gaitskellite: unlike his leader, Brown was convinced of the need to 'build one Europe with leadership and full participation from Britain'.[34]

January 1963 was a depressing time for the Labour Right in general and the pro-Europeans in particular. De Gaulle vetoed the UK's application. Gaitskell died suddenly. In the ensuing leadership contest, Harold Wilson (broadly on the Left and with little known enthusiasm for the EEC) defeated Brown and Callaghan. Nonetheless, the pro-Europeans stuck to the aim that Jenkins had set out in October 1962, namely 'to show that there is a substantial body in the Labour movement that still believes that one can get into the Common Market on reasonable terms'. To that end, LCE, under Jenkins's chairmanship, urged Labour to work for 'a radical Europe ... in concert ... with our continental allies of the Left'. In particular, it was argued that social welfare, industrial training and the like were better in Europe than in the UK so that there was nothing to fear from the EEC. On the contrary, 'Britain is no longer the "welfare state" it was once called, and now has much to learn from other countries'.[35]

By the summer of 1964, the Conservative government (now with Alec Douglas-Home as PM) was faltering. LCE urged Labour 'to have far-ranging and clear-cut policies towards Europe'. For the pro-Europeans, a Labour government was welcome not only in itself, but also in that it would dispel the impression that their support for Tory attempts to join the EEC indicated a more general lack of socialist enthusiasm. A Labour government could devise its own European policy. LCE was an increasingly influential group within the party, with 56 MPs and 20 Ministers in the 1964–6 Parliament.[36]

Having won the 1964 and 1966 general elections, the Labour government indeed attempted to devise its own European policy, which, to no one's great surprise, turned out to be a revival of the British application for membership. The party nonetheless remained divided. Genuine pro-European beliefs inevitably criss-crossed with baser political considerations. Wilson, ever prone to paranoia, was obsessed by the idea that the Common Marketeers were ganging up on him. Many senior ministers hid behind mantras such as not being 'prepared to go into Europe except very much on the right terms'. Even so, in 1967 government and Commons resolved to apply, only to be met once more with a de Gaulle veto. Jenkins played little part in this, apparently believing the enterprise to be hopeless while 'Ramrod' remained in office.[37]

Indeed, the hero of the pro-European hour was Brown, who served as secretary of state for economic affairs from October 1964 until August 1966, and then as foreign secretary until March 1968, when he resigned from the government. In the latter role, Brown recommended to the critical Cabinet meeting in April 1967 that:

> for economic and political reasons … the United Kingdom should make a clear application now to negotiate for early membership of the Community; that our essential interests should be set out in a statement to Parliament; but that the Government should not stipulate conditions at the time of their application which would commit them, before negotiations had taken place, on the terms which they would be willing to accept at the end of the day.[38]

In the heady days of 1967, such enthusiasm spread beyond the confines of the Labour Right. Eric Heffer, very much on the Left, supported entry at a PLP meeting on the basis that 'the Common Market was not socialist but it offered a vision of a socialist Europe': he was embarrassed to be congratulated by Jenkins. Brown took his case to the party conference in October 1967, securing (in the eyes of Barbara Castle) 'a walk-over on the Common Market'. Even after the French veto, Brown was 'fighting like a tiger' in Cabinet for the British application to remain on the table.[39]

The application was, therefore, available to be revived once de Gaulle resigned in 1969, and Labour entered the 1970 election with a commitment to negotiate entry, but in a more favourable European climate. Unhappily for Labour, the domestic weather had turned chilly, and the Conservatives won the election. As the Heath government conducted the negotiations, Labour's tensions boiled over. Jenkins was at the heart of these debates (Brown having by now lost his seat).

This Labour turmoil is described in more detail in Chapter 3, and the intention of what follows is to locate, ideologically, the case that the Labour pro-Europeans were making in this period. By the early 1970s, the Jenkinsites and the pro-Europeans were essentially interchangeable. Jenkins sought, necessarily, to advance a case that went beyond the obviously unattractive course of supporting a Tory government, even one pursuing a path that Labour had itself embarked upon. His arguments, in addition to emphasising the broad political and economic advantages of entry, sought to secure the social democratic high ground. Thus, in April 1971, the pro-Europeans organised a statement of welcome for Britain from a dozen continental socialist leaders. In July, he told the PLP that 'socialism in one country' was 'not a policy'; the party could not simply 'pull up the drawbridge and revolutionise the fortress'. As Jenkins pointed out to the Commons, if the UK wanted a social democratic future, that would necessitate entry into the EEC, not detachment from it:

> If we believe that we are different in a qualitative sense, that we have a
> different and separate rôle in the world, that we can remain as semi-

detached from Europe as can the Americans, then I fear that at the end of the day the real difference will turn out to be that the countries of the Community have gone way ahead, have adjusted themselves both more realistically and more imaginatively to both the harshness and the opportunity of the modern world and that they have achieved more than we have done in influence, standard of living, social services and in help for developing areas too, and that we have increasingly been left behind.[40]

Matters came to a head in the critical Commons vote on the principle of entry on 28 October 1971. The government allowed its MPs a free vote. Labour imposed a three-line whip, which Jenkins and 68 other Labour MPs defied by supporting the government. Twenty more abstained; 33 Tories voted with Labour. The upshot was a pro-European majority of 112, but one only secured by Labour votes. The Jenkinsites, still bound by collective responsibility and therefore unable to speak in the debate, nonetheless proved decisive. If they had obeyed the whip, it is likely that the government would have lost the vote and the UK's application would have fallen, and the government itself with it.[41]

These events left permanent scars upon the party. Jenkins resigned as Deputy Leader in April 1972, a post he had held since Brown's departure in 1970. His supporters behaved like a party within a party, determined to 'punish' dissenters like Crosland, who had abstained in October 1971. Jenkins now seemed uneasy in a working-class party, on the day of the crucial vote lunching at Brook's club and dining at Lockett's. As Crosland observed to his wife, 'Roy has come actually to dislike socialism. … It is Roy's misfortune that because of his father, he is in the wrong Party. As a Liberal or Conservative, he might make a very good Leader.' He was never to lead Labour. Although returning as Home Secretary in 1974, still possessing 'a substantial, gallant and militant body of troops behind me', there were not enough to secure better than third place in the contest to succeed Wilson in 1976.[42]

Indeed, 1971 foreshadowed the break-up of the Labour Right, which was to come to full fruition a decade later: see Chapter 6. On the one hand, Jenkins was by now out of sympathy with many Labour policies, not just those of the Left but even the Wilson/Callaghan/Healey version of Labourism. On the other hand, many MPs on the Right of the party had voted against the government in 1971. They did so, claiming to be 'the true heirs of Hugh Gaitskell' not only because they could not accept the Tory terms for entry but also because they 'believed that membership ... is not for Britain compatible with the ideals of social democracy'. How true was this claim?[43]

Political manoeuvring apart, there did remain a compelling case that EEC membership was not only 'compatible with the ideals of social democracy' but essential to preserve those ideals. After all, it was the enthusiastic European Brown who had presided over the National Plan from 1964 to 1966, believing that 'any modern society must ... plan the way ahead'. And as Jenkins told the Commons in 1972:

> we must aim to make the Community at least as much concerned with the use of wealth as with its creation. Not nearly enough attention has yet been given to the distribution of wealth, between individual countries, between regions and different groups, or to the problems of amenity and environment...
>
> We can hardly complain that the Community has not enough social responsibility and refuse to influence it in the right direction. We can hardly complain that it is a league of capitalists and prevent the Socialist group, by our abstention, from being the largest group within the Community. ... Where, if we turn our backs – and I am addressing this side of the House – on European social democracy, do we expect to find our friends in the future?[44]

Indeed, in 1978 (by which time the skies were darkening and the neoliberals were at the gates), Jenkins argued in a lecture that it was necessary to move more rapidly towards European unity in order to preserve social democracy in Europe. The post-war period had been

'characterised above all by the triumph of social democracy': all EEC
Member States were mixed economies, practised economic planning
and had welfare states. To buttress this, it was necessary for the Community to become more interventionist and to advance the 'redistribution of resources in favour of the weaker regions and disadvantaged
social groups'. This argument, albeit perhaps conveniently blurring
a few political distinctions in Europe (were Adenauer and de Gaulle
really social democrats?), nonetheless perfectly illustrated the comfortable three-legged stool on which British pro-Europeans sat: domestic
social democracy, EEC membership and enthusiasm for the continental
political model.[45]

Heath and the Heathmen

Edward Heath, born in 1916 in modest circumstances, was, in Conservative terms, very much a new man, a grammar school-educated
meritocrat. His personal formation could not have been more appropriate for a politician whose career would be dominated by Europe.
He was at Oxford from 1935 to 1939, during which time he travelled in
Spain during the Civil War and Nazi Germany. In Spain, he supported
the Republicans against Franco and met Jack Jones, then a Republican
volunteer and subsequently General Secretary of the TGWU. In the
famous Munich by-election of 1938, Heath supported the anti-appease-
ment Master of Balliol, Lindsay, against the Conservative candidate
Hogg: Macmillan spoke to a well-attended Lindsay rally.[46]

Once elected to the Commons in 1950, Heath made clear in his
maiden speech where his priorities would lie, urging support for the
Schuman Plan for a single European market in coal and steel, the fore-
runner of the EEC:

> We on this side of the House feel that, by standing aside from the dis-
> cussions, we may be taking a very great risk with our economy in the
> coming years – a very great risk indeed ... after the First World War we

all thought it would be extremely easy to secure peace and prosperity in Europe. After the Second World War we all realised that it was going to be extremely difficult; and it will be extremely difficult to make a plan of this kind succeed. ... I appeal tonight to the Government ... go into the Schuman Plan to develop Europe and to co-ordinate it in the way suggested.[47]

Heath rose steadily through the Tory ranks during the 1950s, and by 1959 was Minister of Labour. His approach to that role chimed with the voluntarist spirit of the times. On leaving the Ministry, Vic Feather (Deputy General Secretary of the TUC, and later General Secretary) congratulated him for having 'so quickly won the respect and confidence of the unions ... from one hot spot to another!' The new hot spot was his appointment as Lord Privy Seal in July 1960, effectively as Foreign Secretary in the Commons (Home performing this role in the Lords). In this capacity, he conducted the negotiations for the UK's first application to join the EEC. As a biographer observed, 'even when the negotiations failed he remained indelibly established in the public mind as "Mr Europe", the undisputed leader of the growing movement in British public life that was determined to take Britain into the Common Market sooner or later'. That failure left him 'frozen into profound depression'.[48]

Heath was conscious from the start that this was a 'primarily political' enterprise, and that, as a European Commissioner advised him, the EEC was 'only a stage on the road to a wider political union'. He did not hide these political realities from his party or the Commons, telling the former that 'the unity of Europe is not complete without us' and the latter that 'our presence would undoubtedly ... contribute towards the balanced development of the Community ... we should use all our strength and energy to find a solution to the problem of a closer relationship between ourselves and our partners and the [EEC].'[49]

Although Heath was virtually monolingual, he displayed considerable facility at 'speaking European' in this period. On formally presenting the UK's application in October 1961, he told the Six that this was 'a great decision, a turning point in our history'. Amid the depression arising from de Gaulle's veto in 1963, he nonetheless ended the negotiations on a rousing note:

> We in Britain are not going to turn our backs on the mainland of Europe or on the countries of the Community. We are a part of Europe: by geography, tradition, history, culture and civilisation. We shall continue to work with all our friends in Europe for the true unity and strength of this continent.[50]

After 1964, Heath, who became Conservative Leader in 1965, was largely a spectator as Labour considered and then pursued the second UK application for membership. As with Jenkins, Heath did not think it necessary to expend great political capital upon a venture that was doomed to failure while de Gaulle remained in office. Even so, both Heath personally and the party he led were strongly supportive. A three-line whip by both main parties saw the Commons approve the application by 488 votes to 62, with only 21 Tories defying the whip. Indeed, in the 1960s, the Conservative Party as a whole had an enthusiasm for Europe that now seems unimaginable. For example, Nigel Lawson, later a prominent Eurosceptic, argued that membership would bring economic benefits, introducing 'the cold douche of competition'. Even Nicholas Ridley, who, in 1990 would have to resign from Thatcher's Cabinet after complaining that the EMS was 'a German racket designed to take over the whole of Europe', then favoured 'a United States of Europe': it was 'essential for the economic survival of our people that we adopt a more federalist route'.[51]

Heath shared these views at the time: unlike Lawson, Ridley and others, he did not later abandon them. Indeed, as with Macmillan, he was quite prepared to confront his own activists with the realities of EEC membership, telling his party conference in 1966:

The Community is moving apace to its final state. It will be in that final state by the time that any British Government will be able to negotiate with it.

Certain fundamental facts follow from this which the British Government today must recognise and they are these, that they or any other member who wishes to join will have to accept the European Economic Community as it is for itself. The time has long passed, to my regret, when any member could expect to influence the Community from its outside in its basic beliefs and its basic organisation. So, the British Government must recognise that there are some things on which there can be negotiations and others which have got to be accepted; and that includes the Treaty of Rome, the Common Tariff, the agricultural policy, and the institutions.[52]

Furthermore, anyone who listened carefully to what Heath was saying in Opposition should have had little doubt not only that any government led by him would seek to revive the UK's application but also as to the wide-ranging basis of this undertaking. In a series of lectures delivered at Harvard in March 1967, Heath laid out this basis. Sovereignty would be pooled, for 'Britain can best achieve her purpose in the modern world as a member of a larger grouping'. The expression 'Common Market' was misleading: 'this organisation is much more than a Market. It is a Community. Its members live and work together as such.' And it was a Community en route to economic union, whereupon 'a new range of subjects which are the essence of politics, for example the form of taxation or the level of social security, will be added to those already taken by the Community as a whole'.

Most strikingly, Heath made the point that Labour had shifted its position because, in the past, they had not wished to enter 'what was, and what they believed as it turned out correctly, was going to be fundamentally a Christian Democratic Europe and not a Socialist Democratic one'. This observation requires some exegesis, and it is perhaps central to the UK's agonies over Europe in the ensuing half-century.

In the 1960s, many progressive Conservatives in the Macmillan and Heath moulds were supportive of policies such as industrial planning and the encouragement of a strong trade union movement, which were the norm in Christian Democratic Europe. There was likewise much in Christian Democratic Europe that the Jenkinsites could accept. It was, primarily, the Labour Left, aspiring as they did to move on a fully socialist society, who feared the potential inhibitions that the EEC might impose upon that ambition.[53]

As the 1970 general election beckoned, there were two relevant developments. The first was that, in 1968, Heath dismissed Enoch Powell from the Shadow Cabinet. Thereafter, Powell was Heath's bitter opponent, and the anti-EEC forces in the Tory party had a powerful champion. The second was that in 1969, de Gaulle resigned. His successor, Pompidou, was well known to Heath and appeared likely to be more amenable to a British application. The party's formal position at the election was that it would seek to negotiate acceptable terms for entry, but it seemed probable that it would recommend entry. Indeed, within a few days of its victory in June 1970, ministers had set off to Brussels to reopen negotiations. There was a pleasing symmetry on the British side, in that the key ministers (Heath himself and Home, once more Foreign Secretary and in overall charge of the negotiations) had been intimately involved in the UK's first attempt to join. The talks proceeded relatively smoothly, and in July 1971 the government announced that it would seek to join.[54]

Charming the Europeans was one thing. But what of obtaining domestic approval? There were, of course, a number of constituencies to consider: the party; public opinion; and parliament. The first two presented comparatively little difficulty. Heath demanded and won a card vote at the 1971 party conference by a margin of 8 to 1, despite a powerful speech against entry from Powell. Public opinion was fragile, with, for example, the antis 12% ahead in October 1971. Heath, in a speech in Paris in May 1970, had stated that 'it was in the interest of the Community that its enlargement should take place with the full-hearted consent of the Parliament and peoples of the new member countries', and there were some on the Conservative side who argued for a referendum once the terms of entry were known. However, Heath had made it clear in the same speech that it was for Parliament to 'approve a settlement', and he never seriously considered a referendum (although the suggestion that a referendum had been promised and then withheld was to 'taunt and haunt' Heath thereafter).[55]

Parliament was another matter. Given Labour's position, and the Powellite minority on the Tory benches, considerable finesse was required. Conservative MPs were given a free vote. The motion on 28 October 1971 was 'carefully framed in consultation with the Jenkinsites to draw the maximum possible support'. Even so, 39 Conservatives voted against the government. Without the Jenkinsites, Heath would have lost. Even then, the progress of the detailed legislation through the Commons was fraught with difficulty. On Second Reading, in February 1972, the government had a majority of only 8, despite treating the vote as one of confidence: 15 Tory MPs voted against and a further 5 abstained.[56]

However tricky the politics (and it should be remembered that the government had other problems: Heath came to the House to salvage the vote in February 1972 straight from talks aimed at settling a national miners' strike), there was nothing timid about the vision of Europe on offer. The White Paper published in July 1971 at the end of negotiations spoke boldly of the UK 'join[ing] in building a strong Europe on the foundations which the Six have laid; or we choose to stand aside from this great enterprise'. When he wound up for the Government on 28 October 1971, at the end of the great debate on the principle of entry, Heath put it in this way:

> if this House so decides tonight, it will become just as much our Community as their Community. We shall be partners, we shall be cooperating, and we shall be trying to find common solutions to common problems of all the members of an enlarged Community. ... It is right

that there should have been so much discussion of sovereignty. I would put it very simply. If sovereignty exists to be used and to be of value, it must be effective. We have to make a judgment whether this is the most advantageous way of using our country's sovereignty. Sovereignty belongs to all of us, and to make that judgment we must look at the way in which the Community has actually worked during these last 12 years. In joining we are making a commitment which involves our sovereignty, but we are also gaining an opportunity. We are making a commitment to the Community as it exists tonight, if the House so decides. We are gaining an opportunity to influence its decisions in the future ... to be there as a member of the Community, in my view, would be an effective use of our contribution of sovereignty. ... I want Britain as a member of a Europe which is united politically, and which will enjoy lasting peace and the greater security which would ensue ... when this House endorses this Motion many millions of people right across the world will rejoice that we have taken our rightful place in a truly United Europe.[57]

There is every indication that Heath meant what he said. In January 1972, Heath signed the Accession Treaty in Brussels, in a ceremony attended by Macmillan and Brown. Afterwards, Heath told the BBC of his 'great vision of a united Europe, vying with the superpowers to enable the 250 million people of Europe to speak with one voice and to influence international affairs'. In this vein, he attended a summit in October 1972 (before the UK's formal accession the following January) in which he sought to secure the creation of a European Regional Development Fund. A few days earlier, he had told the Conservative conference of the 'deep and satisfying challenge to carry on the work of world building in which Britain in the past has played so great a part'.[58]

There seems little reason to dispute the verdict of biographers and fellow politicians alike that it was Heath's first priority and overarching achievement to take the UK into the EEC. As Jim Prior, a Cabinet colleague, recalled: 'Ted's great ambition was that Britain should take her rightful place in the European Community. ... Ted had the sheer determination to find the answers and overcome all the difficulties.' John Campbell observes, that 'his purpose was to realign the country's sense of identity irrevocably towards Europe'. Heath was not anti-American or dismissive of the Commonwealth, but, in his view, these relationships had to yield to the new European focus. The Europeans had to come first. Thus, when Henry Kissinger, the US National Security Adviser, proclaimed that 1973 was to be the 'Year of Europe', Heath's reaction ('we didn't want a "Year of Europe"') was almost as disdainful as Pompidou's ('for Europeans, every year is the year of Europe').[59]

Although Heath did not always spell this out, this turn towards Europe had important ramifications domestically as well as internationally. The UK would be irreversibly committed to the sort of modified capitalism pursued by the Six nationally and by the EEC corporately, the 'Christian Democratic Europe' of which he had spoken in 1967. For example, economic and monetary union would enable Europe to 'stand up to the economic might of the United States', advised the Bank of England in 1972, but on the footing that 'all the basic instruments of national economic management … would ultimately be handed over to the central federal authorities'. Of course, in 1972, modified capitalism à la Europe looked a good bet for a British politician of the Centre-Right. The British version of capitalism was performing less well than the European variety. And the alternative to modified capitalism did not look like a more fundamentalist American-style capitalism, but the socialism then advocated by the Labour Left.[60]

Conclusions

During and after the 2016 referendum, the supporters of Brexit tirelessly invoked 'the British people'. These stout yeomen (and, as it turned out, most of those doing the invoking were men) were, so it was said, solidly opposed to the EU and all its continental ways.

It would be hard to argue that 'the British people' unreservedly took the EEC to their hearts in the 1960s and 1970s, still less that they did so after a full evaluation of the arguments relating to sovereignty. Indeed, public opinion on Europe was somewhat fickle. There was, certainly, real enthusiasm at the very start of the period discussed in this chapter. In 1959, 54% of Gallup respondents thought that 'it would be a good idea' for the UK to apply to join the Common Market. This level of support remained steady until about the summer of 1962, when the figure dropped to 36%. Thereafter, and, in particular, after the twin rebuffs of 1963 and 1967, opinion grew steadily less favourable. In April 1970, a Gallup poll found only 19% of voters favouring entry, with more than half those polled rejecting the idea of even talking to the Europeans. This was, therefore, an elite project. Not every high-profile pro-European was a Balliol man (or, like two of our three champions of entry, a future Chancellor of Oxford), but the pool of enthusiasts for the EEC was not very wide or deep. Hugo Young, in his magisterial study of the subject, is surely right to say that 'of one feature there could be no doubt throughout the period: the high proportion of the people who found themselves unable to share the fascination of the politicians with this subject'.[61]

However, Young is, perhaps, a little harsh in accusing those politicians of a 'pinched, apologetic stance' on the European issue. There were, as we have seen, real enthusiasts for the EEC among the political elite, and they did not hide that enthusiasm from their colleagues or the electorate. This zeal was based upon a full understanding of the implications for sovereignty of membership of the EEC, an understanding that was fully shared with the voters – or, at least, those voters who paid attention to the relatively intricate debates about the pooling of sovereignty in the interests of wider economic and social progress. Indeed, the true European believers tended also to be those most fully embedded in the British social democratic state as it had developed during this period.

If, therefore, most British people would by 2016 join Farage in saying that the British establishment had lied to them in the 1960s and 1970s, they would be misremembering the debates that had taken place. One should also bear in mind the difficulties under which the political leaders of the day had to operate, ever fearful of party disunity or public hostility. And, of course, consideration of Europe did not take place in a sealed environment. Events occurred, and problems piled up, regardless of the state of European negotiations. For example, in October 1966, the Cabinet had agreed to meet at Chequers on a Saturday to thrash out these issues. The previous day, 144 people, including 116 children, had died when a coal tip collapsed at Aberfan, and Wilson reached Chequers at 2.30am on the Saturday, straight from a visit to the disaster.[62]

As will be seen in Chapter 3, the three attempts at joining the EEC took place to a mounting chorus of disapproval from those who did not accept the idea of membership at all, let alone subscribe to the more expansive vision put forward by Jenkins and Heath in particular. The antis laid out the contrary arguments fully and with passion. Some, like Gaitskell (who was, on this issue, a Powellite *avant la lettre*), took surprising positions. Most did not. Macmillan may have been a little hyperbolic in perceiving a 'new alliance between the extreme Right and the extreme Left', but he was not far off in seeing this debate as to some extent a proxy war between the defenders of the British social democratic state and its enemies. Those defenders saw no contradiction between their support for that state domestically and the need to achieve further integration with the EEC. On the contrary, the policy overlaps between British social democracy and continental Christian and social democracy seemed to make a perfect fit.

3 The Voices of Dissent, 1960–1973

If the British people are herded into a federation against their will, the whole fabric of our society will be threatened. First, we shall find ourselves governed by laws we did not make and cannot change. Second, we shall find ourselves taxed by people we did not elect and cannot remove. Third, we shall find ourselves locked in to economic policies that may harm us and cannot be altered because they were devised to meet the needs of others. Fourth, we shall be governed by European bureaucrats elected by no one for whom Ministers are only needed as a rubber stamp.

(Tony Benn, 17 March 1972)[1]

The supreme right of the Commons to tax, legislate and call the executive to account has already been ceded. In the next Parliament will be completed the absorption of Britain into the new European State as one province along with others. ... There is just the little matter of securing for all this, before it is irrecoverable and irreversible, what used to be considered as manifestly indispensable – the full-hearted consent of the British people.

(Enoch Powell, 9 June 1973)[2]

Introduction

In April 1969, Richard Crossman noted in his diary that 'to get in now is somewhat a point of honour for poor, battered Britain who has been on the doorstep for six years'.[3] The UK was to remain battered, or, at least, on the doorstep, for a further four years. And yet, after all this toil and trouble, the British embarked upon an in/out referendum within two years of accession. How and why did this striking volte-face come about? This chapter seeks to provide an understanding of sources of opposition to membership.

The principal explanation is concerned with sovereignty. Although there were exceptions – supporters or opponents of membership who took their stand on anomalous or idiosyncratic bases – the core of the opposition to the EEC was the assertion that the UK would, by joining, cease to be a fully independent state. This in turn invites the question: sovereign to do what? Sovereignty would scarcely seem an overwhelming objection if one wanted to pursue domestic policies that aligned closely with those permitted or required by the EEC. At the heart of the sovereignty arguments, there necessarily lay alternative visions of how the UK should change as a nation state, visions that were radically at odds with the prevailing consensus. The arguments over EEC membership were, in some sense, a substitute for these domestic disagreements. It was not surprising, therefore, that the arguments against membership were led by the Labour Left and the Powellite Right.

As we have seen, the forces urging the UK towards entry were most vocal on the social democratic Right of the Labour Party and the progressive mainstream of the Conservative Party, under the leadership of Macmillan and Heath. The Labour Left were deeply, and increasingly, mistrustful of those like Roy Jenkins, who urged upon his colleagues the need 'to build with fellow European socialists … a society based upon the ideals and values of our inheritance within the framework of European supranational institutions'. The Tory Right, at least in its Powellite incarnation, was vehemently opposed to such progressivism, and did not wish 'to go forward with [Heath] in the building of a new Europe'.[4]

Of course, political calculation and studied ambiguity were also part of the picture. Thus, one could find Crossman confiding in April 1970 that 'Barbara [Castle] and I are willing to try but not on terms that are too high'. Vague formulations such as this offered politicians of all kinds cover for whatever conclusions they wished to draw. After all, who could really disagree with the proposition that the UK should join if acceptable terms were offered but stay out on the basis of unacceptable terms, the criteria for acceptability always satisfyingly elusive?[5]

Likewise, especially on the Labour side and particularly during the Heath government's efforts to join in 1970–4, there were always pressing political reasons to find grounds for opposing entry. After all, why should a Labour opposition help out a Conservative government, assailed on all sides by domestic problems, to pursue membership? Why attract the wrath of many in the constituencies and the unions, who were firmly 'anti', in support of a project that might prove unpopular with the wider electorate in any event? Such considerations serve to explain how it was that many leading Labour figures on the Centre and Right of the party found themselves cautiously in favour from 1964 to 1970, firmly against from 1970 to 1974, and once more in favour after 1974. This seems a fair summary of the tortured, often opportunistic, positioning of figures such as Wilson, Callaghan and Healey.

Moreover, and not only on the Labour Centre Right, one could see base political and personal motivations at work. Powell, who was, at one time, a supporter of membership, seemed at least partly inspired to change his mind by his hatred of Heath, who had dismissed him from the Shadow Cabinet in 1968 following the 'Rivers of Blood' speech on immigration. The idealism of Jenkins on the European issue was matched by his zeal, and that of his strongly committed supporters, to advance his claims to lead the party in place of Wilson.[6]

Having entered those caveats, it is clear that the most consistent theme of the 'antis' of Left and Right was the issue of sovereignty. But what lay behind this? On the face of it, the leading opponents of the EEC were united only in their desire to tear down the established order. What they wished to put in its place, however, was very different. For the Powellite Right, the version of capitalism on offer from the mainstream Conservative Party was a poor substitute for the sort of free-market fundamentalism they favoured. The Left had no time for capitalism, whether softened by social democracy or otherwise. They wished to move forward to socialism, whereby the state took control of the 'commanding heights' of industry.

However, and curiously, Left and Right often seemed to find common cause, and not only on the European issue. The leading spokesmen for the anti-EEC case, Powell, Benn and Michael Foot, had much in common. In a time when the art of oratory was in decline and public meetings on the wane, the Commons filled when they spoke and halls were overflowing to hear them. Their personal relations were close. From the 1950s onwards the Benns and Powells dined together, and Powell thought their friendship 'as genuine and pleasant as it was possible to achieve in politics'. After 1968, when 'Rivers of Blood' had made Powell a pariah to many, the Foots would entertain the Powells to dinner in Hampstead. Foot defended his friend to comrades on the Left who claimed that he was racist.[7]

These areas of agreement went beyond dinner party pleasantries, surprising though these were. The anti-marketeers agreed, in an almost mystical way, upon the irreplaceable centrality of the House of Commons. In 1969, Foot and Powell combined to defeat the Labour government's Lords Reform Bill. Benn regarded them then as 'Conservatives of Left and Right'. Yet within two years, in the great debates over entry, Benn was to

> plead with the House … to recognise that parliamentary democracy is a very fragile thing indeed. … If ever this House were to create a situation in which people thought that it no longer reflected their power ultimately to decide, I believe that parliamentary democracy, which hangs by a gossamer thread, could easily fall to the ground.

He was rewarded the next day with a congratulatory note from Powell, who said that he had agreed with 90% of the speech.[8]

The Left against the EEC

To understand why the Labour Left was to play a leading part in the campaign for, and conduct of, the 1975 referendum, one needs to go back a little in time. From 1951 onwards, the Labour Party had experienced bitter divisions between, broadly, the Bevanite Left and the Gaitskellite Right over both domestic and foreign policy. The Left favoured an extension of the public ownership and interventionist economic policies of the Attlee government, and, in foreign affairs, a non-nuclear defence policy, much more distant from the United States. The Right urged an accommodation with both capitalism and the Americans. Leading figures on the Left included Foot, Barbara Castle, Crossman and Ian Mikardo and, to some extent, Wilson himself. George Brown, Jenkins, Crosland, Jay and others represented the Right.

When the European question reached the agenda in the early 1960s (after Bevan's death), the Labour factions lined up essentially along these Left/Right lines. There were exceptions: Jay, for example, was both a partisan Gaitskellite and a convinced anti-European, and, as we shall see, Gaitskell was, in the end, to oppose the EEC after much agonising. For many on the Left, however, the issue was fundamentally a simple one. Of course, there were minutiae to consider and possible economic and other advantages to ponder, but the Treaty of Rome was essentially a capitalist conception, intended to give maximum freedom to capital. As Alf Lomas, later to be leader of the Labour MEPs, put it in 1970, the Common Market was 'founded by businessmen … run by businessmen in the interests of businessmen'. For the Labour Right, the EEC represented exactly the sort of measured accommodation with capitalism that they advocated in the domestic sphere, and it allowed Labour to work towards 'a radical Europe … in concert with our Continental allies of the Left'. Those allies, notably the German SPD, had of course already accepted the need for such an accommodation.[9]

This was roughly the state of play when Gaitskell mounted the platform to address the Labour Conference in October 1962. In the hall, the majority of constituency and union delegates were opposed to entry. From 1962 until at least the late 1980s, most activists remained suspicious of the EEC, essentially for the reasons put forward by Lomas. Gaitskell dismayed the Right and delighted the Left, whose 'wild applause … rolled on and on for an "unparalleled" eighty-eight seconds'. As his wife remarked, 'all the wrong people are cheering'. They were cheering an emphatic denunciation of British membership:

> We must be clear about this: it does mean, if this is the idea, the end of Britain as an independent European state. I make no apology for repeating it. It means the end of a thousand years of history. You may say 'Let it end' but, my goodness, it is a decision that needs a little care and thought. And it does mean the end of the Commonwealth. How can one really seriously suppose that if the mother country, the centre of the Commonwealth, is a province of Europe (which is what federation means) it could continue to exist as the mother country of a series of independent nations? It is sheer nonsense.[10]

Gaitskell died unexpectedly in January 1963. In the ensuing leadership election, Wilson defeated Brown, broadly a victory for the Left. Labour won the 1964 election with an ambitious programme for economic transformation. To illustrate its desire to break free of the orthodox constraints of the Treasury, which had hamstrung past Labour governments, a new Department of Economic Affairs (DEA) was created under Brown. This formed part of an ambitious 'National Plan' to achieve 25% growth over five years. These high hopes were largely frustrated. The promised growth did not materialise and wages rose faster than productivity. A balance of payments crisis and a run on the pound ensued in 1966. Wilson's government reacted with a pay freeze, followed by a series of rounds of pay restraint. In 1967, the government was forced to devalue the pound. Jenkins replaced Callaghan as Chancellor and pursued orthodox and deflationary polices thereafter. The DEA was dissolved in 1969. The squeeze on pay brought the government into conflict with its supposed allies in the unions.

These and other developments gave rise to considerable discontent on the Left. The world was, in any event, being turned upside down with the rise of the New Left, *Les événements de mai 1968* and protests over the Vietnam War. Against this background the conventional, Parliamentary Left began in the late 1960s to develop a wide-ranging critique of the Wilson government. Broadly speaking, this went as follows. Wilson had inherited an economy that was failing after thirteen years of Tory misrule. The response should have been to use this crisis as the occasion for implementing, not abandoning, socialism. Instead, the government had embraced deflationary orthodoxy and had sought to manage the crisis by suppressing the living standards of the working class. Why had it done this? Partly because the government had lacked a coherent economic and industrial policy, and partly because of the gulf between the leadership and the rank and file. What was needed instead was a party committed to socialist policies and leaders who would stick by, rather than depart from, manifesto commitments.

At the same time as the 1964–70 government was being battered by economic and other storms, it was moving, slowly and crab-like, towards seeking accession to the EEC. The 1964 manifesto was scathing about the recent Tory attempts to join. Although the document referred vaguely to 'seek[ing] to achieve closer links with our European neighbours', it affirmed in suitably Gaitskellite terms Labour's conviction 'that the first responsibility of a British Government is still to the Commonwealth'. In reality, however, there were strong pressures pushing Labour, once elected, towards entry. The Gaitskellite Right, although mourning their lost leader, constantly urged on Wilson the case for entry. Brown, for example, was 'hell-bent on getting us in'. The Left was, as we shall see, still opposed, but potential support for membership went well beyond the Right. For Benn, then a Cabinet minister and not yet fully aligned with the Left, the choice was between becoming an American protectorate and joining the Six, as a precursor to a wider European federation. Wilson himself recognised that 'the difficulties of staying outside Europe and surviving as an independent power are very great compared with entering on the right conditions'. What emerged was a formula that sought to ensure party unity, while allowing sufficient room for manoeuvre: 'yes to entry, but only on the right terms'.[11]

The 1966 manifesto edged cautiously towards Euro-enthusiasm, while remaining suitably vague and aspirational:

> Labour believes that Britain, in consultation with her E.F.T.A. partners, should be ready to enter the European Economic Community, provided essential British and Commonwealth interests are safeguarded. ... Labour believes that close contact with Europe – joint industrial ventures, scientific co-operation, political and cultural links – can produce among the 'Six' that understanding of Britain's position which is necessary to a wider European unity.[12]

What followed was a curious political and diplomatic dance. In truth, the leadership (Wilson, Brown, Michael Stewart [Foreign Secretary 1965–6, and first Secretary for Economic Affairs 1966–7]) were determined to secure entry, but could not express unqualified enthusiasm for this course for reasons of party management. The Jenkinsites, whose fortunes rose with their leader, felt the same way but had less inclination to conceal their emotions. The Left remained opposed, but, given their internationalist traditions, and the claimed economic advantages of joining, tended, at least at Cabinet level, to rely on practical objections.

Thus, in May 1966, one could find Brown assuring the National Executive Committee (NEC) of the party that 'the question isn't about our getting into this Europe. The issue is whether we should get into a new transformed organization or stay outside it.' This claim – that the British could marry and then tame a wayward European husband – was to recur down the years. So also was the suggestion that the UK could secure such advantageous and special terms that entry was the only sensible course. In this vein, the Cabinet agreed at a special meeting on Europe in October 1966 that Wilson and Brown should visit the Six to carry out a 'probe', i.e. to see if such terms were indeed on offer. Benn concluded that this charade would see the UK in the Common Market by 1970 (a correct prediction in substance, if not as to timing).[13]

Wilson and Brown duly carried out their European tour, and reported back to the Cabinet in March 1967. The discussion centred on the details rather than the principle. At the end of April, the Cabinet convened at Chequers for an all-day meeting to decide whether to apply. The discussion was wide-ranging. The possible disadvantages in relation to agriculture, the Commonwealth, the balance of payments and the like were ventilated. In the end, the Cabinet voted by 13 to 8 to support an unconditional application for entry. For Benn, then in favour, the time had come 'to cut Queen Victoria's umbilical cord'.[14]

When Wilson made the case for entry to the Commons on 8 May 1967, he did so in qualified terms, rehearsing at length the potential drawbacks of membership: the effects on agriculture; relations with the Commonwealth; the economic risks. His conclusion was less a call to arms than an acceptance that entry was unavoidable:

> These applications will be made from strength, in a spirit of resolve, not as one who seeks favours, resolved … let no one think – as too many people in Britain and in Europe five years ago tended to think – that there is no other course for Britain except entry. Britain is called today to make a choice, and it is a choice between alternatives. We are choosing here not the only possible or available course. It is not a question of 'Europe or bust', as Europe perhaps believed five years ago. We are choosing the right course, the best course, for Britain, and for Europe. There is no question of Britain's power to survive and develop outside the Communities, though no one will be in any doubt about the determination that would be needed, the efforts our people would have to make – and indeed the sacrifices of cherished industrial attitudes – to keep Britain among the world leaders, if the opportunity were to be missed of the wider economic grouping...[15]

Wilson had little difficulty in commanding the support of the House, which voted by 488 to 62 in favour of the government's position. The front benches of each party were united in support of entry, despite some private misgivings. The small band of dissenters was, in the main, the Labour Left and the nationalist Tory Right (albeit that they were not then joined by Powell, still bound by the constraints of collective responsibility as a member of the Shadow Cabinet).

However, anyone who believed that the argument was won forever was in error. The huge majority for entry was illusory. The Left were unreconciled. There was nothing new about this. When the NEC reviewed the draft manifesto in March 1966, 'the only actual disagreement' was over the proposed commitment that Britain 'should be ready to enter' the EEC. The Left (Castle, Mikardo and others, including Benn on this occasion) voted against this pledge but were outvoted. At the Chequers meeting in April 1967, Castle declared that she 'remained and had always been against entry'. Crossman, whose position was more equivocal at this stage, shrewdly summarised the Left's argument for staying out:

> Today Barbara made a tremendous speech saying that entry would transform our socialism and make us abandon all our plans. In a sense she is completely right. If anybody wanted … Britain to be a socialist offshore island, entry to the Market would mean the abandonment of that ideal.[16]

When the Commons deliberated, Castle and Crossman were, of course, like Powell, obliged to vote with the government. Others on the Left, however, were not so constrained, and Foot and Mikardo led the opposition forces. Foot touched in his speech upon the usual matters of detail – agriculture, the balance of payments, trade with the Commonwealth – but his real case against joining was more fundamental. The first strand of this case was that, in the end, the capitalist EEC would not permit the UK to pursue socialist polices domestically. In short, although Foot did not put it in quite this dramatic fashion, entry meant the permanent abandonment of the economic policies that the Left wished to implement:

we are told that we must be prepared to sign the Treaty of Rome to prove our good faith. But if we look at individual items in the Treaty, the Common Marketeers say 'You can throw away all that. You do not have to look at the details in the contract.' The right hon. Gentleman [Wilson] said that he looked at these matters pragmatically. So they do in Europe. We are all pragmatists now. Unhappily, we cannot say, as Sir William Harcourt said long ago, that we are all Socialists now.

The Prime Minister and all of those of the Labour Party who now sit on the Government Front Bench claimed in 1962 that one of their objections to the Treaty of Rome was that it prevented the kind of planning in which they believed. We want a detailed account of why they consider that position has changed. … It will not be possible for a Government which goes into Europe to decree that our own industrialists, or less still, industrialists from elsewhere, shall go to those development areas. We can give the inducement but we shall not be able to maintain the negative procedures in future. That is a fierce blow at the whole of the regional development plans.

The second, closely associated, issue was the democratic case against the EEC. Membership would pass power from Foot's beloved Commons to a remote and unaccountable European bureaucracy, for

we should have to accept the decrees of the Community on a whole vast range of matters covering our economic affairs … part of the price [for entry] – no one can deny it – is a diminution in the power of this House of Commons to control our own economic affairs. … If we get there I hope that we shall try to introduce some democracy into the whole apparatus. But there is precious little democracy in their set-up at present.

Was the nation of the Levellers and Oliver Cromwell to be reduced to this?[17]

The Left lost the vote by a crushing margin in 1967, and the entry process continued until later that year de Gaulle once more vetoed Britain's application to join the Common Market. However, the desire on the Left for 'Britain to be a socialist offshore island' did not go away and as soon as the issue arose again, these arguments would likewise re-emerge. It was also noticeable that the 1967 Noes included a number of MPs with a strong following among Labour activists. For example, Frank Allaun was a leading member of the NEC from 1967 until 1983; Norman Atkinson was party treasurer from 1976 until 1981; Mikardo served on the NEC from 1950 to 1959 and 1960 to 1978. These NEC positions were influential in formulating party policy and were selected by the rank and file in the party and the unions.[18]

After the veto, the European issue did not go away but, for a time, it became a less intense preoccupation on the Left. Interest in government circles revived with the departure of de Gaulle in 1969. However, as already noted, the Left's frustrations focused more strongly on perceived failures in domestic policy. Certain things were apparent and unchanging. The leadership remained determined to pursue a fresh application and, indeed, the party's 1970 manifesto committed a Labour government to the UK's application, which would 'be pressed with determination with the purpose of joining an enlarged community provided that British and essential Commonwealth interests can be safeguarded'.[19]

The Left was, if anything, becoming more hostile to the project. After all, a key criticism of the Wilson government was that it had been swept off course by the failures of capitalism. What was required instead was a socialist government, which would take on capitalism. As Castle noted during the 1967 party conference, 'the real case against going in is that, if we do, we shall be hampered in being interventionist – and, if conference has voted for anything this year, it is for interventionism'. The ranks of the Left against the EEC were swelling. For example, Eric Heffer, who had voted for entry in 1967, had concluded by 1970 that the price required would be too high.[20]

There were also some new factors emerging in the debate within the Left. Increasingly, they were concerned about the rise of multinational firms and their role in thwarting the policies of a Labour government. This introduced a new aspect to the arguments over Europe: perhaps,

Benn mused in April 1970, 'if we have to have some sort of organisation to control international companies, the Common Market is probably the right one'. Benn was not, at this stage, irrevocably tied either to the Left or to the anti-EEC case. There was, however, here the glimmerings of an idea, which others would later develop, that Britain should seek to be a socialist onshore entity, exercising economic control through pooling sovereignty within the Common Market rather than asserting it outside.[21]

Benn's fertile mind was at work in other areas as well. By 1969, as discussed below, Powell had begun his journey into Tory exile, which included a dramatic volte-face on the European issue. Public opinion was at best equivocal. It was also extremely erratic: between 1961 and 1973, the balance of feeling on membership varied between plus 45% and minus 42% (pro less anti). Many in the Labour Movement were sceptical or hostile to membership. Perhaps, suggested Healey, it would be better to let Powell split the Tory Party rather than to force the issue and create such a division within Labour? Benn's solution to this dilemma was to let the people decide. He therefore began to float the idea of a referendum, much to the distaste of the leadership. This had several advantages. The people's verdict, delivered in a referendum, could not be wrong and would have to be accepted on all sides as final. It provided a neat solution for parties who were divided internally on this issue much more profoundly than on most other economic and foreign policy issues. And it offered a convenient way forward for Benn himself, who was 'not opposed in principle' to membership and was also beginning to court the Left, but thought the matter must be resolved by the electorate rather than the politicians.[22]

Labour lost the 1970 election and then embarked on a period of introspection over the failures of the Wilson government. This introspection soon turned to something approaching civil war over Europe. In relation to policy generally, two themes stood out. The first was that a future Labour government should respect the primacy of conference decisions on policy, as, it was suggested, the 1964–70 government had failed to do. The second was the development by the NEC of a radically new industrial policy, largely devised by Stuart Holland, then a young academic. This called for extensive further nationalisation, compulsory planning agreements with private companies, and a state holding company to oversee the industrial strategy (eventually called the National Enterprise Board). *Labour's Programme 1973* included a proposal for a new Industry Act to give effect to these ideas.[23]

Despite the party's official position at the 1970 election, anti-EEC sentiment was also building in the party. At the October 1970 conference, a card vote came within 94,000 votes, out of approximately 6 million cast, of reversing the party's position on membership. At the same time, an opinion poll showed that only 22% of Labour voters favoured entry. In November 1970, Benn called publicly for a referendum, of which Callaghan remarked that this might 'be launching a little rubber life-raft of which we will all be glad in a year's time'. Benn's own position was complex: he favoured entry and was 'a long-term federalist', but thought that the party's position must respect conference decisions and public opinion, for otherwise there would be 'a major crisis in the Party and maybe break the party system'. Hence, the referendum was 'the key issue'.[24]

During the course of 1971, a Great Debate took place in the party and the country as the Heath government edged towards membership. Some positions did not much change. The Jenkinsites remained committed to the EEC, and pursued this course so relentlessly that many thought them 'a Party within a Party', more committed to Europe and Jenkins than to advancing socialism or defeating the Tories. Foot and the Left were equally opposed to the 'rich man's club', which would strip a British government of its powers of economic management. Activists in the party and the unions largely agreed with this analysis. The Tories favoured the EEC because it would produce 'the weakened, anaemic and controlled brand of trade unionism' they favoured. The Jenkinsites, such as Dick Taverne (an MP deselected by his local party), 'live[s] on a different plane to what we do ... we live different lives'.[25]

More worryingly for the pro-market cause, the leadership shifted its position to one of 'no entry on Tory terms'. In May 1971, Callaghan, always a reliable weathervane, spoke out against membership, referring Gaitskell-like to 'the language of Chaucer, Shakespeare and Milton'. For the leadership, this position served to keep the party together and oppose the Conservative government, while leaving the door open to entry at some later stage on better terms. At a Special Conference in July 1971, Wilson hinted strongly that the party would not support the conditions of entry negotiated by the government. Neil Kinnock, then a young and ambitious backbencher, and later Leader of the Party, was in tune with much party opinion when he said that 'because I want to see the Tories beaten, and because I am willing to use any weapon to beat them, I am against E.E.C. entry on these terms at this time'. In September, the TUC General Council voted against entry 'on the terms negotiated'. In October, the party conference voted 5 to 1 to support the NEC's position to the same effect. Callaghan called on 'all members of the Party [to] join hands on this issue and accept the verdict of the Party'.[26]

Not everyone joined hands. Within the Parliamentary Labour Party (PLP), there was more support for accepting Heath's terms, but the PLP voted 2 to 1 nonetheless to accept the NEC line and impose a three-line whip to this effect. The crucial debate in the Commons took place in late October 1971 on the principle of entry. Heath secured a majority of 112, but suffered a substantial rebellion on his own side and was saved by 69 Jenkinsite Labour MPs who voted with the government in defiance of the whip and party policy. The atmosphere was 'terribly tense … [with] rumours of people fighting'. The party within a party had saved a Tory government. These events would not be forgotten or forgiven on either side. As another Jenkins (Hugh, a left-winger and long-term opponent of entry) put it in the debate:

> In the very long term it is possible that the Community may evolve into a more socially orientated body, but its present purpose is to preserve

the acquisitive society and perhaps to extend its life beyond its natural length. It boils down to this. If one is prepared to settle for welfare capitalism with more capitalism than welfare, one may be able to force oneself into the Lobbies with the Tories on Thursday. But those who do that should, I think, be limited to those who feel that they can do so with the support of their constituency parties. On such a count, would all the fingers of one hand be needed to number them?[27]

During the passage of the European Communities Bill in the remainder of 1971 and 1972, the Jenkinsites mainly voted against the government, albeit reluctantly. However, this obedience to the whip did not mean that unity had been restored. On the contrary, party opinion fell into at least three largely irreconcilable factions: unrepentant Jenkinsites; the Left, who were determined to get Britain out; and the leadership, who saw increasing attractions in the 'little rubber life-raft'.

From 1971 onwards, the Jenkinsites became ever more of a party within a party. They felt betrayed by erstwhile colleagues on the Right of the party, like Crosland and Healey, who, they thought, had behaved treasonably over Europe. Of the former, for example, who had toed the line in the October vote, they said 'he's behaved like a shit and we must punish him'. More generally, one could see the first signs of a potential realignment of British politics. Benn thought that Jenkins's group perhaps 'represented a new political party under the surface'. The party system might break up and re-form into a Powellite right, a pro-European Centre party and an anti-EEC Left.[28]

The Left, if anything, hardened its line. At the 1972 party conference, almost all the speakers were anti-EEC. Conference approved a report from the NEC recommending that the UK should only remain in on the basis of a renegotiation and a referendum. However, a motion was also passed that membership could only be acceptable if there were 'no limitation on the freedom of a Labour government to carry out economic plans, regional development, extension of the public sector, control of capital movement and the preservation of the power of the

British Parliament over its legislation'. These conditions were, of course, essentially incompatible with continued membership. By 1973, Benn and others were moving towards a position that involved an incoming Labour government boycotting all the instructions of the EEC and ceasing all payments.[29]

Acknowledging these tensions, the leadership of the party moved rapidly towards advocating a referendum. In March and April 1972, the Shadow Cabinet and the PLP, in each case narrowly, voted to support a referendum. A few days after the latter vote, the Commons defeated by 284 to 235 a referendum amendment to the Bill introduced by a Tory anti-marketeer, Neil Marten. Supporters of the amendment included Benn, speaking on behalf of the Opposition, who made a powerful speech in favour of the principle that the British people should have the final say. In June 1972, Wilson himself came out for the referendum. While these manoeuvres offered some prospect of a way forward for Labour, party unity proved elusive. Jenkins resigned as deputy leader in April 1972 in protest at the Shadow Cabinet's decision to support a referendum, taking with him a number of pro-marketeers.[30]

In February 1974, Labour therefore faced the electorate with a manifesto that proposed that if and only if there were 'a successful renegotiation and the expressed approval of the majority of the British people, then we shall be ready to play our full part in developing a new and wider Europe'. Some of the items identified for renegotiation were, at first sight, capable of being dealt with, such as the Common Agricultural Policy and the Budget. However, others seemed to go the heart of a fundamental incompatibility between the aspirations of the Left and the realities of the treaties:

> The retention by PARLIAMENT of those powers over the British economy needed to pursue effective regional, industrial and fiscal policies. Equally we need an agreement on capital movements which protects our balance of payments and full employment policies. The economic interests of the COMMONWEALTH and the DEVELOPING COUN-

TRIES must be better safeguarded. This involves securing continued access to the British market…[31]

Labour won this election narrowly and embarked on the promised renegotiation. It did so in very challenging circumstances. The Conservative government had ended in economic chaos and industrial conflict. The oil shock of 1973/4 had produced a deep recession. Inflation was rising rapidly (and would reach 25% by 1975), due in part to the lax monetary policies of the Heath government. The public finances were under substantial strain. There had been a large number of strikes from 1970 to 1974, culminating in the national coal strike that had precipitated the election. In these unpromising circumstances, Labour's manifesto, the product of the policy review in opposition, committed the party to 'bring about a fundamental and irreversible shift in the balance of power and wealth in favour of working people and their families'.

This ambitious programme included the agenda that Stuart Holland had devised: a National Enterprise Board (NEB), with powers and funds to invest in industry; compulsory planning agreements with large companies; further nationalisation. Benn became Industry Secretary, with Heffer as his Minister of State, in 1974. However, Benn's was a lone voice within government. His Permanent Secretary, Sir Antony Part, asked at their first meeting whether he could possibly be serious about this programme. Wilson and Healey assured the CBI that they were 'determined to follow practical policies to overcome our economic problems … [with a] full commitment to a healthy private sector'. The Industry Act 1975 therefore gave effect to a much-reduced form of these policies. The NEB received limited funds. Planning agreements were to be voluntary, not compulsory.[32]

However, it soon became apparent that Benn and Heffer were not only isolated within government but also seeking to implement policies that involved potential collision with the rules of the EEC. For example, Benn was advocating regional polices which, he argued, required either that the European Commission agree not to enforce those rules or that there be amendments to the treaties. When civil servants advised that public support for British Leyland required Commission approval, Benn asked them to 'put on record my view that membership of the E.E.C. – with its unacceptable interference in our national interest – requires us to seek to mislead them'. By April 1975, Heffer had had enough, denouncing the Common Market in a Commons speech. Wilson sacked him immediately.[33]

At the same time, the government was seeking to deal with the mounting economic crisis, which it had inherited. From 1975 onwards, this involved large public spending cuts. Healey, the Chancellor, told the Commons that his 1975 measures required that 'public expenditure must be firmly contained for several years to come … an absolute reduction in the real level of public spending'. Within Cabinet, Benn compared the situation to 1931, when a Labour government had accepted similar deflationary advice in the midst of economic crisis and the party had split.[34]

The Left therefore developed an Alternative Economic Strategy (AES). This required physical controls on imports and capital outflows. Such an approach, of necessity, was irreconcilable with EEC membership. The leading advocate of the AES within government was Benn, although he met with little success in persuading his colleagues of the merits of this course. The Left was, therefore, rapidly losing ground on economic policy. Moreover, it was becoming increasingly clear that it was a necessary condition for the implementation of the AES and the Left's industrial policy that the UK escape the clutches of the EEC. Was the Common Market 'a life-raft', as its supporters maintained or the means by which 'we were being tossed into the deep in a straitjacket', as the Left feared?[35]

It was soon apparent that the leadership (Wilson, Callaghan [as Foreign secretary, in charge of the renegotiation] and Healey) were determined to stay in the EEC and marginalise the Left. Wilson and Callaghan began from the premise that they sought to renegotiate within the existing treaties. By June 1974, the negotiations had progressed such that there was a short list of remaining contentious issues, and Callaghan was talking of when, not if, matters were 'put right'. Labour's manifesto for the October 1974 election said little other than that the outcome of the 'tough negotiations' would be put to a referendum. Safely re-elected, in December 1974, Wilson met the leaders of France and West Germany, and told them that he was likely to be able to recommend the new terms to the British people. The terms were then settled at a summit in Paris later that month. At a two-day Cabinet meeting in March Callaghan outlined his view, item by item, that the conditions outlined in the February manifesto had been achieved. The Cabinet agreed by 16 votes to 7 to recommend the new terms.[36]

The Left, most of the constituency activists and many in the unions were unhappy with the negotiations, which did not seem to them to address the central question of economic self-determination. At the party conference in November 1974, resolutions were passed seeking 'complete safeguards' on issues such as public ownership and capital movement. During the Christmas break Benn circulated a letter arguing that membership removed 'democratic rights which are at the heart of parliamentary democracy'. In January, it was agreed that dissenting ministers would have the right to differ from the government line during the referendum campaign, when it took place. At the March Cabinet meeting, Foot inveighed against the 'alien system' of the EEC, which would move the seat of power to a permanent coalition in Brussels and curtail the powers of Parliament. Benn likewise suggested that continued membership would be to abandon parliamentary democracy and 'destroy the whole basis on which the Labour movement was founded'.[37]

The Left had been outmanoeuvred and marginalised within government, but within the party as a whole it was another matter. On 26 March 1975, 18 members of the NEC (out of a total of 29), including Benn, Castle, Foot and Mikardo, supported a motion that asserted that the new terms 'fall very short of the renegotiation objectives' set by the manifesto and would deny the UK 'the right of democratic self-government'. In the Commons on 9 April, the government motion to endorse these terms passed by 396 to 170, but with heavy reliance on Tory support. Of Labour MPs only 137 backed the motion, with 145 against and 33 not voting. A special conference at the end of that month voted by 2 to 1 against continued membership, in accordance with the recommendation of the NEC.[38]

On the face of it, therefore, the social democratic Right, the pro-Europeans, had seen off the anti-European Left. However, in two important respects, this conclusion requires tempering. The first is that the victory for the 'yes' camp was grudging. The government was committed to staying in, but the PLP and the broader movement remained hostile to membership. The commitment of the leadership was half-hearted, Wilson telling the April 1975 Special Conference that his was a reluctant yes, for he had 'never emotionally been a Europe man'. The renegotiation had in some ways made the divide starker. It was hard now for anyone in the movement to shelter behind a mantra such as 'yes on the right terms'. The renegotiated terms were the only ones available. Progress on the minutiae of the CAP or the budget did not address concerns about the right of the UK to govern itself or, in the words of the NEC motion of April 1975, 'to pursue policies designed to ensure full employment'.

Nor were the Jenkinsites altogether content with the outcome. Jenkins was 'profoundly unhappy' with the decision to have a referendum at all, which might, of course, produce the wrong result. Moreover, it was clear that enthusiasts for the EEC were a distinct minority within the PLP and almost an endangered species in the wider movement. After all, Wilson and Callaghan had only secured limited support with the full weight of government at their disposal and upon a highly qualified basis. Certainly, surveying the scene in 1975, it was hard for the Jenkinsites to believe that there was much appetite within the movement 'to build with fellow European socialists … a society based upon the ideals and values of our inheritance within the framework of European supranational institutions', as Jenkins had urged in 1963.[39]

The second caveat is that 'the Left' did not all think as one. Some of the intellectuals on the New Left were somewhat scornful of the 'social chauvinism' of the Left within Labour. EEC membership, they argued, could allow more effective action against capitalism, not less. Such Marxist thinking had little influence within the wider movement (and none at all inside the PLP or government). However, Holland, who was more persuasive and who had devised much of the new industrial strategy, made a number of important points in his writings, which rather undercut the simplistic notion that membership would hamstring a socialist UK government. Might not entry facilitate 'coping with the multi-national company's challenge to a Labour government's freedom of economic management'? Whatever the treaties might say, 'a determined national government can play the E.E.C. game very much as it likes', and there were elements within the Commission sympathetic to interventionism. Most interestingly, the European Left, operating within the EEC, was devising and implementing strategies for planning and reflation, from which the British Labour Movement could learn.[40]

Of course, so far as the pro-Europeans were concerned, a victory was a victory, and provided the referendum could be won, the issue of membership would be settled once and for all. Dissenting pro-EEC voices on the Left made little headway in 1975, and Holland eventually fell into line, accepting that the 'so-called common market … tends to neutralise political power and disintegrate national economic and social structures'. However, this muffled dissent on the Left and uneasiness on the Jenkinsite Right suggested that the referendum might not settle very much. In due course, the Jenkinsites were to form their own political party, as Benn had predicted, with a strongly pro-European programme. By 1988, the Labour Movement would give a hero's welcome to Jacques Delors, one of Holland's 1976 collaborators, and by then President of the European Commission.[41]

Powellism: resistance on the Right

Between 1968 and 1975, Powell and Powellism represented essentially the only plausible opposition on the Right of British politics to EEC membership. When pollsters asked electors in 1975 to identify leading 'no' advocates, 92% mentioned Powell, more than any other figure of Left or Right. The only other right-wingers noted were Ian Paisley (83%) and Neil Marten (11%). The Ulster demagogue was never likely to embrace a Treaty of Rome, but his sway outside his own community was limited and most of those polled said that they disliked him. Marten was a longstanding anti-European, but his public profile was minimal and his career never rose above the rank of Minister of State at the Foreign Office from 1979 to 1983. As Castle noted, he may have been 'a pleasant chap' but there was little prospect of 'getting much drive behind our plans under their leadership'.[42]

On the Right it was, therefore, Powell or nothing. As explained below, Powell had developed a distinctive creed of free-market nationalism from the 1960s onwards; he was also a rare British politician in that he enjoyed a substantial personal following. Why then was the Right so committed to the EEC, and Powell so out of step?

To understand this one needs to begin by remembering that, in this era, there were relatively few functioning European democracies with a whole-hearted commitment to capitalism. Most of these were already EEC members. Many of the current EU membership were part of the Soviet bloc (such as Bulgaria, the Czech Republic, Hungary and Poland) or emerging from dictatorship (Greece, Portugal and Spain). It was natural for Conservatives, who were firmly anti-Soviet and anti-socialist, to wish to make alliances with countries who were broadly similarly aligned.

There were prominent Conservatives who shared much of Powell's free-market zeal (such as Geoffrey Howe and Keith Joseph), but they tended to see the EEC as a bulwark, rather than an obstruction, to such ideas. After all, the Treaty of Rome embodied free-market principles:

that was why the Left disliked it. The Commission might be able to prevent 'socialist planning' and nationalisation, which the Left sought to
implement and which the Conservatives strongly opposed. Moreover,
the EEC was likely to insist on economic policy changes that Conservatives, certainly of a free-market bent, favoured, such as the relaxation of
exchange controls. In contrast socialists sought 'a Berlin wall of financial controls' behind which they could implement a planned economy.[43]

More generally, many Conservatives looked enviously at the economies of Western Europe. They did things differently there, and much
better. The Bundesbank had an anti-inflationary zeal that the British
authorities lacked. German trade unions were far more co-operative
than their British counterparts. Mrs Thatcher (by no means a Ger-
manophile) concluded when she first met Helmut Schmidt, the SPD
Chancellor, in 1975 that 'he was a good deal less socialist than some
members of my own Shadow cabinet'. All in all, most Conservatives
seemed to think that membership of the EEC would allow some of
these virtues to filter through to the UK. Of course, as Powell and Holland both pointed out in their own way, it might be possible to emulate
good European practice outside the EEC, but this was too subtle a point
for most Conservatives.[44]

This mainstream Conservative commitment to the EEC provided
considerable room on the Right for Powellism to flourish. There was
also a lack of sensible competition. However much people disliked
Powell, they had to recognise his intellect and rhetorical skill. The same
could not be said for many other anti-marketeers, who tended to put
their case in a repellent fashion. The Anti Common Market League
sneered that Heath was 'a middle-aged bachelor and occasional choir-
master', under the influence of bankers who had 'recently come from
the Continent'. Keep Britain Out stoked fears of 'immigrants from the
Continent admitted without restriction'. Some saw 'another Popish plot
by Catholic Europe to undermine Protestant England'.[45]

In the 1960s and, even more so, in the 1970s, Powell stood outside the
Tory mainstream, indeed, sought to challenge much of what passed for

Conservative received wisdom. Before he began to carve out a distinctive position on Europe, he had already broken with much of the party over economic policy and immigration.

Powell was, on any view, a difficult colleague. He resigned from a junior ministerial post at the Treasury in 1958 over the issues of inflation and public spending, was reinstated as Minister of Health in 1960 and resigned again in 1963 in protest at Home's elevation to the Premiership. He thereafter repudiated the economic policies of the Macmillan and Home governments. His starting point on economic matters was fundamentalist: 'often when I am kneeling down in church, I think to myself how much we should thank God ... for the gift of capitalism'.[46]

From this premise, various important conclusions flowed. The pound should float freely. Governments or, certainly, Tory governments, should escape from 'the limbo of semi-socialism ... which has been our consensus system'. There should be lower taxes and more disciplined government spending. The answer to inflation was governmental self-control, not Prices and Incomes Policy, which was 'nonsense in massive doses'. It was necessary to let 'price – genuine, competitive, market price – tell us the truth'. The UK should dismantle the whole edifice of Boards, National Plans and Neddies, all of which deployed 'the powers of government to ... bully people into trying to fulfil the mistaken forecasts of the planners'. The nationalised industries should rejoin the private sector. The trade unions should lose their statutory immunities. In short, Powell (who had resigned from his government in 1958) was a sort of anti-Macmillan, opposed to almost every aspect of the policy approach adopted in the 1957–63 period.[47]

Much of this was very much a preview of what was to become orthodox Thatcherite or New Labour thinking. But at a time when governments of both parties struggled to manage the balance of payments and to persuade or coerce the unions towards wage restraint, these views were jarring. Even more controversial were Powell's views on race. In April 1968, he delivered a notorious speech in Birmingham that appeared to foresee or even incite violence on account of post-war immigration by 'piccaninnies'. Powell was 'filled with foreboding; like the Roman, I seem to see "the River Tiber foaming with much blood"'. Heath, who had defeated Powell for the leadership in 1965, sacked him from the Shadow Cabinet the next day. The effect of the speech was sensational. Powell was condemned by most senior politicians, but attracted considerable public support. Trade unionists marched to the Commons from the docks and Smithfield meat market in his support. Powell's ministerial career was finished. He drifted away from the Tory Party, eventually leaving in 1974 to join the Ulster Unionists.[48]

By 1968, therefore, Powell had developed a very different economic approach to that advocated by either main party and had made himself infamous over immigration. He had, in fact, hit upon the two issues that were to underpin the 2016 Leave campaign: the need for a 'freer' (i.e. less regulated) economy and less immigration. However, by that stage, Powell had shown little interest in the anti-EEC case. This was perhaps not surprising. The EEC, as many Conservatives, believed, provided protection against socialism. It certainly did not oblige a member state to embrace the interventionist policies, against which Powell railed, and positively discouraged at least some of them. Nor was free movement, in 1968, much of a concern to those alarmed about immigration. This panic centred upon the 'three and a half million Commonwealth immigrants and their descendants' who, according to Powell, would be living in the UK by the 1980s. These immigrants, of course, would not be prosperous white Europeans from the Six, for whom the UK of the time might not have seemed much of a prospect, but 'coloured' arrivals from the Caribbean or the Indian subcontinent.

Indeed, until 1969, Powell was a quite orthodox Conservative when it came to Europe. In 1962, he supported the government's application, explaining afterwards that he 'didn't raise dissent because at that stage it was presented as free trade exercise' (a refrain heard again in the run-up to the 2016 referendum from other born-again Eurosceptics). In 1965, Powell co-drafted a pamphlet setting out the arguments for entry, which contained a plea for the 'full economic, military and political union of the free states of Europe'. A 1969 collection of speeches, covering the period from 1963 to 1968, had little to say on Europe. Such material as it did contain pointed out that the Common Market represented a fast-growing trading area from which the UK was excluded. At this stage, it was left to a very limited group on the Right of the party to raise the sovereignty issue; Marten argued that the Common Market only made sense if the UK was to 'become a state in the United States of Europe'.[49]

In 1969, Powell, by now a pariah to many in British politics, embarked on a radical change of position on Europe. In speeches at Clacton and Smethwick, he acknowledged that 'a looser form or free-trade area' would be acceptable, but 'we do not need to be tied up with anybody'. Moreover, 'the disastrous results that were predicted from our exclusion have not presented themselves'. Pro-Common Market Tories attacked him; Marten welcomed his conversion. Powell's motivation was, no doubt, mixed. However, opportunism was surely part of the picture. There remained, certainly among Conservative activists, Eurosceptic sentiment, however much the leadership might seek to ignore it. At the 1969 Tory conference, speakers denounced the fact that 'we bow and scrape to be allowed to join the unholy alliance ... in the process sacrificing our most treasured possessions – our independence'. The presentiments of 2016 were unmistakable, even down to Powell's choice of Clacton to make his démarche, the seat where UKIP would secure their first MP in 2014.[50]

In 1970, the Conservatives faced the electorate with a manifesto that promised that 'If we can negotiate the right terms, we believe that it would be in the long-term interest of the British people for Britain to join the European Economic Community. ... Our sole commitment is to negotiate; no more, no less.' As with Labour, the argument was essentially circular: if suitable terms were available, it would be right to join. Powell published his own dissenting manifesto in which he promised to 'do my utmost to make sure we never do [join]'. By 1970, Powell was increasingly developing the sovereignty argument in very similar terms to Foot and Benn. As he told the Commons:

the Common Market is ... to be a unit which increasingly has common monetary, economic and social policies. ... Are not social policies, growth targets, unemployment, development and taxation the very stuff of politics, about which we in this House argue day and night? Are they not the subjects about which we compare our differing opinions and objects before the electors, seeking to bring them to our point of view? This is what politics is about, what this House is about, what the electoral system of the country is about...[51]

Powell played a full part in the Great Debate of 1971. He spoke all over the country. In September 1971 he published a book setting out his case against membership. The argument was overwhelmingly about sovereignty, for 'the economic case is neutral at best'. He explained his change of mind on the basis that it was now 'clear that the Community would be something quite different from a free trade area and something to which Britain could not belong'. As Brexiteers were to argue in 2016, the UK could embrace 'a looser form of free trade area'. At the 1971 party conference, Powell wound up for the antis. Echoing Gaitskell, he did not 'believe that this nation, which has maintained and defended its independence for a thousand years, will now submit to see it merged or lost'. In the event, Heath demanded and won a card vote by a margin of 8 to 1. For a party whose leaders had traditionally taken the view that they would rather take advice from their valet than from the Conservative Party conference, this was a bold step.[52]

In the Commons, Powell voted with the 39 Tory MPs who disobeyed the whip. He told a journalist at the time that if a Conservative government took the UK into Europe, he could not then stand for election as a Conservative. His objections to entry boiled down to two points. The first was sovereignty, the 'unprecedented act of renunciation which th[e] House is called upon to make'. The second was that such a step could only come about if there were 'our full-hearted consent', which was transparently lacking. Powell thereafter continued to vote against the Bill as it made its way through the House, on one occasion seeing the government's majority reduced to eight.[53]

By the time of the February 1974 election Powell had made good on his threat to stand down as a Conservative; he did not contest the election. Instead he addressed large public meetings, in effect urging voters to vote Labour since this was 'the first and last election at which the British people will be given the opportunity to decide whether their country is to remain a democratic nation'. Labour would, at least, offer the chance of the electorate having its say on the renegotiated terms. By the summer of that year, Powell had been absorbed into the mainstream anti-EEC movement, sharing a platform with Jack Jones.[54]

The Powellite position certainly enjoyed some public support. Public opinion was fragile on the issue. In early 1971, detailed polling showed limited enthusiasm for entry. Although there were thought to be potential economic advantages in the long term in joining, this was a finely balanced view among those polled. The disadvantages, however, were all too apparent: short-term economic pain; loss of sovereignty, with 69% concerned that the UK 'won't be able to decide her own future'. A majority thought the UK would be better off out (56% to 25%, the rest non-committal). Powell tapped into this mood. A contemporary study (not altogether sympathetic) referred to his 'enormous popular support' and noted that 'his ability to fill a hall was unrivalled in British politics between 1968 and 1974'. In Powell's native West Midlands, the swing from Conservative to Labour between 1970 and 1974 was about 12%, much higher than the 2% national swing.[55]

The problem for anti-marketeers on the Right was that, Powell apart, their resources were very limited. As is explored in the next chapter, business and the media, as well as the overwhelming bulk of the Conservative machine, were strongly in favour of getting in and staying in. *The Spectator* (one of the few publications on the Right to maintain a consistent line over the decades) warned of an 'irrevocable step … towards a European state'. However, this was a small-circulation publication, and its arguments suffered from hyperbole. Heath and his supporters were not just wrong: they were 'dishonest and fraudulent', seeking 'another disastrous accommodation with Europe' comparable to Munich.[56]

The other major problem for antis on the Right was that most free-market Conservatives thought that there was a good degree of synergy between their overall policy of encouraging competition, and entry into a well-functioning European market system. Membership of the EEC would have a powerfully Darwinian effect since 'free movement of labour and capital would open up the closed nature … of British industrial life; the increased competition from Europe would force businesses to wake up or go under'. On occasion, one could find Powell seeking to confront this economic case for entry. Might not it be bad for British business to see 'policy determined increasingly by the views and interests of the continental countries of Western Europe'? It was 'manifest folly' for the UK to 'tie herself to the Continent and loosen her ties with the open sea'. However, the great bulk of Powell's case related to sovereignty, not economics.[57]

Conclusions

There were significant internal divides on both Left and Right on Europe. However, it was clear that the leadership in each main political party was committed to seeking to join the EEC, albeit that this commitment was often framed in qualified terms. The custodians of the post-war accommodation between the political parties were equally the guardians of the UK's proposed accommodation with the EEC.

Ranged against the respective leaderships were the Left of the Labour Movement and the Powellite Right. The ground on which both Left and Right chose to take their stand was sovereignty. Both essentially agreed on the need to escape 'the limbo of semi-socialism … which has been our consensus system'. For the Left, the way forward was to march purposefully towards the promised land of full socialism. The rules and structures of the EEC stood in the way of this ambition, and so it was obvious that most on the Left would not wish to become subject to those rules.

For the Right, the position was more nuanced. The free trade and free movement aspects of the EEC looked attractive, at least to an economic liberal like Powell. It was, therefore, difficult for the antis on the Right to claim that leaving the Common Market would 'cement our status as a great trading nation', as Liam Fox suggested in 2017. Here and there, one could see hints about the undesirability of 'a single government whose policies determined every aspect of economic life', but the economic dangers were a long way down the hierarchy of problems. The core argument was, therefore, that membership would undermine sovereignty. However, given the lack of tension between the principles of the EEC and the policies which a British Conservative government, even one of a relatively free-market disposition, might wish to pursue, such concerns had limited salience on the Right.[58]

To resolve these intra-party conflicts, Benn appreciated at an early stage that the conventional means of debates and votes in the Commons would not suffice. How could electors express their views on this issue if both main parties would, in the end, whip their members to deliver the necessary legislation? Powell and others later took up this argument that there was an illusory choice between parties. There were, however, a number of problems with the sovereignty arguments and with the proposed referendum as a means to resolve them. If, as Powell maintained, and as Benn and Foot also argued (but with less deference to the monarch), the question was whether the UK was to 'continue to be governed by the Queen in Parliament', why should this be settled not by Parliament but by a plebiscite? Moreover, what exactly was this sovereignty to be exercised to do? The Left, at least, were clear on this: an economic and industrial strategy that was at odds with the Treaty of Rome. But what did the Right want to do which the EEC would prohibit? This was wholly unclear. And did the Queen in Parliament support the Left's alternative strategy?[59]

With hindsight, there were some quite fundamental difficulties with the prospectus that Benn, Foot and Powell were laying out. For one thing, if it were really the case that EEC membership would spell the end of British parliamentary democracy, how could those who took that view be content with the result of a referendum unless it went in their favour? More fundamentally still, was it right that the UK possessed sovereignty over its affairs that could be kept secure outside the EEC? This looked like a rather naïve assumption in a globalising world. The UK had not, for example, been to able exercise much sovereignty over the decision of the Nixon administration to abandon the Bretton Woods settlement in 1971 or the huge increase in oil prices imposed by the OPEC bloc in 1973. Pro-Europeans tended to focus on the perceived economic benefits of membership. However, the dissenters of Left and Right had done enough to put the sovereignty issue on the table and to require it to be resolved by a referendum. How, if at all, would the referendum resolve the issue?

4 The Referendum and its Aftermath, 1975–1983

For all the talk of a 'great debate' it was really a contest between David and Goliath, which Goliath won. The substantial issues often went by default.

(Margaret Thatcher, 1995)

It was like David and Goliath, only Goliath won.

(Alf Lomas, 2000)[1]

Introduction

The antis had asked for a referendum. When they got it, they suffered a crushing defeat, which, in the main, they accepted with reasonable grace. However, as the above quotations suggest, they felt it was not a fair fight. In many respects, this was a justifiable complaint. Certainly, despite the 2 to 1 margin of the result, the referendum settled somewhat less than at first appeared. The Left could not, in the end, accept defeat: for them enduring the EEC meant giving up on socialism, something they would not do. For the antis on the Right, 1975 seemed to be the end of the road. For a dozen years thereafter, most Conservatives remained strongly pro-European, until the tide began to turn in the late 1980s. In this chapter, I explore how the referendum was won and lost, and then consider the subsequent response of the victors and the vanquished.

The period from 1975 to 1983, in addition to being an important turning point for European policy, saw the post-war social democratic model fracture and then disintegrate. On the Right, Thatcherism, after a difficult start, was in the ascendant by 1983 both within the Conservative Party and more widely. Labour moved sharply Left after 1979. The Centre, which dominated the Yes campaign in the referendum, was by 1983 endangered in both main parties. The Left regarded the EEC as an obstacle to its domestic policies. The Right had not yet come to this conclusion.

The Referendum

The antis were not so much defeated as crushed. Not only did Yes secure 67% of the vote, but its triumph was virtually uniform across the UK, in all regions, classes and age groups. The Noes had struggled and failed to counter four interlocking forces, all dedicated to securing a vote to stay in. The first, and perhaps the most important, was the government itself. Then there was the well-financed, but separate, organisation of Britain in Europe (BIE), the umbrella group running the campaign for a Yes vote. Thirdly, the Conservative Party put its weight firmly behind BIE's efforts. Finally, the media, in particular the press, was relentlessly supportive of the Yes campaign, and dealt brutally with the antis.[2]

The movement in public opinion, as tracked by the opinion polls, was testament to the decisive influence of the lead given by government. Most voters, of course, did not feel strongly either way and did not follow political developments closely. However, there was certainly no great enthusiasm for membership. Between February 1970 and May 1972, supporters of entry varied between 16% and 43% of those polled, with between 41% and 66% against. When the UK acceded in January 1973, a slim majority favoured membership (51% to 49%), but by October 1974 60% believed that Britain had been wrong to join. The crucial factor, which then changed minds, was the course of the renegotiations. In January 1975, in a Gallup poll 57% favoured withdrawal, but 71% would have voted to stay in 'if the government were to renegotiate the terms and strongly urge that Britain stay in'. Once the government had concluded the renegotiations and recommended that the UK stay in on the new terms, opinion changed swiftly and decisively. Polling in March and April 1975 showed a 2 to 1 majority for 'Yes': the results were both consistent and immovable, exactly predicting the outcome of the vote in June 1975.[3]

The government – and, in particular Wilson and Callaghan – played a clever hand in support of their position that, on balance and on the basis of the new terms, the country should stick with the status quo, rather than make a leap in the dark. Wilson, in an unprecedented departure from the principle of collective responsibility, permitted 'ministers who do not agree with the Government's recommendation in favour of continued membership of the European Community … in the unique circumstances of the referendum … [to be] free to advocate a different view during the referendum campaign in the country'. These ministers, led by Benn, Castle and Foot were, essentially, the Left within the government.[4]

Generally, the leadership preserved a serene neutrality, mindful no doubt of the fact that after the referendum was over it would be necessary to work with the Dissenting Ministers and a largely anti-EEC party. Callaghan told Robin Day that he was not pressing one case or the other, but was simply 'trying to present the facts as I see them'. Wilson kept a low profile, preparing his own speeches 'to demonstrate that he was not in the hands of the so-called "Euro-fanatics"'.[5]

However, the serenity was deceptive. Tactically, it was clearly better for Wilson and Callaghan to steer clear of the enthusiasts of BIE. They had both wavered on the European issue; it seemed obvious, therefore, that 'the hesitant could best be won not by partisans but by other hesitants'. The government nonetheless needed to make sure it won. The campaign was masterminded by a specially established Referendum Unit, which met each day in the Foreign Office under the chairmanship of Callaghan or a junior minister. The Referendum Act 1975 prescribed the form of the ballot paper in the following terms:

> The Government have announced the results of the renegotiation of the
> United Kingdom's terms of membership of the European Community.
> DO YOU THINK THAT THE UNITED KINGDOM SHOULD STAY
> IN THE EUROPEAN COMMUNITY (THE COMMON MARKET)?

This formula emphasised that a 'Yes' vote was a vote for the status quo;
used the familiar wording of the Common Market; and drew attention
to the government's (in its view, successful) renegotiation.[6]

The government also distributed a leaflet to every household setting out its case for a 'Yes' vote. This summarised, in positive terms, the
results of the renegotiation. The sovereignty arguments were dealt with
reassuringly. The benefits of staying in were contrasted with the risks
of being 'outside … on our own'. These risks to trade and jobs would
be real for British 'outsiders looking in'. Above all, voters should trust
their experienced leaders, whose judgement, all things considered, was
to remain:

> We do not pretend … that we got everything we wanted in those negoti-
> ations. But we did get big and significant improvement on the previous
> terms … these better terms can give Britain a New Deal In Europe. …
> The Government have made THEIR choice. They believe that the new
> terms of membership are good enough for us to carry on INSIDE the
> community. Their advice is to vote for staying in…[7]

BIE was much closer to 'Euro-fanatic' in its approach. It certainly
included leading figures who might answer to that description. It was an
extremely well-funded organisation, with total resources of about £2m
(c. £16m in 2016 money), and headquarters in Old Park Lane supplied
by Alistair McAlpine, a wealthy Conservative businessman. BIE also
had the support of the pre-existing European Movement. The great and
the good rallied to the European cause, with celebrities like Graham
Greene and Lew Grade enlisted. The Establishment, however defined,
put its shoulder to the 'Yes' wheel, with every living former PM and
Foreign Secretary pledged in support. As a Tory No, Richard Body later

complained 'the extremists were "No"; all the "nice people" were "Yes", and were safe'. Or as Jenkins wisecracked, the leaders of BIE looked like 'well-fed men who had done well out of the Common Agricultural Policy'. This prosperity allowed BIE to spend large sums on advertising, with sports and TV stars advocating a Yes vote. Other advertising complemented this material during the campaign, attacking Benn for his nationalisation policies.[8]

As the McAlpine connection suggests, business was very keen to secure a Yes vote: 95% of chief executives wanted to stay in. Companies wished to retain tariff-free access to expanding European markets. Blue-chip companies such as Vickers, ICI and Shell made large donations to BIE. Their directors made their views known to their staff: for example, the Chairman of GKN, also a large donor to BIE, told his staff that a No vote would 'torpedo' the company.[9]

BIE was, like the Chairman of GKN, quite willing to deploy scare tactics. These were of two kinds. The first was to warn against walking out of Europe into an unknown future. According to Christopher Soames (then a EEC Commissioner), it was 'damned cold outside'. As Jenkins put it, for Britain to leave Europe would be to retire into 'an old people's home for fading nations'. As he noted, 'I do not think it would be a very comfortable old people's home. I do not like the look of some of the prospective wardens.' The second tactic was to suggest, more or less subtly, that the antis were dangerous extremists. After all, the Soviets and British Communists were strong supporters of exit. As Reg Prentice, a right-wing Labour Minister, cautioned, 'the people who would lead us out of the market ... with one or two honourable exceptions ... belong to the way-out factions'.[10]

There were difficulties for BIE being over-ready to denounce their opponents as extremists. After all, a sizeable minority of the Cabinet, and much of the Labour Movement, was campaigning for a No vote. What emerged as a more plausible approach was to emphasise that the Yes forces represented an informal coalition of all that was good and sensible in the Centre ground of British politics, and that the Yes campaigns showed how well these forces could co-operate. There was an eerie echo here of the warning of the antis that the EEC was a 'coalition government that we cannot change'.

Coalition was very much in the air in the UK in the mid-1970s. The oil price shock of 1973, the industrial troubles of the Heath government and rising inflation had led to calls for men of good sense to come together in the national interest (there were few women then in contention for such roles). These arguments had very nearly come to fruition in the inconclusive outcome of the February 1974 election. The Conservatives secured more votes than Labour but fewer seats, and neither party had an overall majority. Heath then sought to interest the Liberal Leader, Jeremy Thorpe, in a pact, but nothing came of this. By 1975, Labour was in power with a tiny majority. The atmosphere of crisis had not gone away. During the referendum campaign itself, the Environment Secretary, Tony Crosland, informed local authorities that 'the party is over' (i.e. there was no more money). *The Times* reported that inflation was running at an annual rate exceeding 30%.[11]

It was, therefore, no accident that BIE relied heavily upon senior politicians from precisely that Centre ground which seemed to offer fertile territory for coalition-building. The most prominent figures were Jenkins, Heath and Thorpe, politicians from three different parties but whose ideas and attitudes were very similar. Jenkins, according to his biographer, 'played an almost Prime Ministerial part. Only Heath was as prominent.' Jenkins found the experience of sharing platforms with moderate Tories and Liberals liberating, often travelling with William Whitelaw, deputy leader of the Conservative Party. In particular, Jenkins formed a high opinion of David Steel, who would in later years become leader of the Liberal Party and take his party into pacts with both Labour and the SDP. Heath led the Tory forces in the campaign, and was 'rapturously received' by large crowds. Margaret Thatcher, who had deposed Heath as Tory leader in February 1975, was 'marginalised'. Heath, too, relished sharing all-party platforms. Thorpe, the third of the 'big three', was equally at home in this environment: 'at times, it almost seemed as if the "government of national unity" for which he had called the previous years had come to pass'.[12]

The all-party enthusiasm occasionally became a little too much. Just before the vote, Prentice, claiming that it had been a 'refreshing experience' to work together, urged that 'we must not lose this spirit of unity after June 5'. However, the spirit of unity was fragile, as the fate of the most prominent BIE speakers demonstrated. In 1976, when Wilson resigned, Jenkins stood for the leadership of the Labour Party, and came third in a field of six. The victor, Callaghan, declined to offer him the post he coveted as Foreign Secretary, in part because the Left would not accept 'an ardent pro-Marketeer conducting a love-in with Europe'. Jenkins then left British politics for the European Commission (albeit that there was to be a second Act in this political life, as leader of the SDP). Heath remained in the Commons for another 26 years, but in a state of 'internal exile', out of sympathy with his increasingly monetarist and Eurosceptic party. As his ODNB entry remarks, 'the European referendum campaign of 1975 provided the last happy episode in Heath's political career'. Prentice, already under pressure from the Left in his own constituency, resigned from the Labour Party and crossed the floor to join the Conservative opposition in October 1977. Thorpe's fall from grace was the most spectacular of all. His political career ended in disgrace, when he was tried (and acquitted) at the Old Bailey on charges of conspiracy to murder, in 1979.[13]

What, then, of sovereignty? How true is it, as Brexiteers were to complain, that the real implications of membership were concealed from the electorate? BIE also distributed a leaflet to every household (so that the leaflet balance was 2 to 1). This emphasised the practical advantages of membership for jobs, food and prosperity. It set out the bleak nature of the alleged alternatives, such as 'controls and rationing' or becoming 'a Communist Britain – part of the Soviet bloc'. Significantly, there were numerous encouraging statements from Heath, Jenkins, Whitelaw and others, emphasising the 'catastrophe' that would befall the UK were it 'to shuffle off into the dusty wings of history'. This all chimed with the advice that BIE were receiving from their pollsters. Most voters were not fiercely attached to one side or the other: the EEC was of limited interest to many electors. BIE's best points were that the electorate was prepared to trust well-known leaders in preference to the wilder figures prominent on the No side. Voters preferred the devil they knew to the risks of exit: an unenthusiastic embrace of the view that 'now we are in, we should stay in.'[14]

BIE's literature dealt briefly, and soothingly, with questions of sovereignty. The Queen's position was unaffected, as was 'English Common Law' (this was a stretch; as Lord Denning had pointed out, EEC Law was 'like an incoming tide'). Most BIE speakers preferred not to dwell on these issues, concentrating on 'the vaguely defined goal of European unity'. Heath, however, told the Oxford Union, in a televised debate just before the poll, that he was 'absolutely prepared to make a sacrifice of national sovereignty to the well-being of the community'. Indeed, Heath sought to challenge 'the myth that in the modern world Britain can survive alone'. Rather, he argued:

> We are an outward-looking nation with great reserves of energy. The European Community presents us with the opportunity to channel our experience and skill towards great and constructive causes … these are noble objectives. They can only be achieved by Britain inside the European Community. It is this which gives us the opportunity in the modern world to fulfil ourselves as a nation.[15]

The notion of British exceptionalism was to feature very strongly in 2016, but it had little impact in 1975. Robert Worcester, of the polling company MORI, advised BIE that prices were the key issue, with sovereignty not at a significant level. The campaign should not 'scatter your shots: let the opposition talk about sovereignty/independence, Britain's role in the world, defence, etc.'[16]

The third strand in the Yes campaign was the Conservative Party itself. In November 1974, the party set up a group to co-ordinate the Tory effort in the referendum, under the direction of the deputy chairman. Seminars were held across the country. The party, then still a mass membership organisation, was 'able to provide a formidable array of constituency workers to help in the constituencies'. Conservatives nationally played a prominent part in the Yes campaign. They saw this as an exercise to get the Tory vote out: if this could be achieved, there would be a positive result. The psephological analysis of the result seems to bear this out.[17]

There were good political reasons for this endeavour. The Conservatives had, of course, just taken the UK into the EEC. Thereafter, the Conservatives identified themselves as *the* party of Europe. By 1973, virtually all MPs were members of the Conservative Group for Europe. This group was the dominant force in the European Movement. Party propaganda suggested that the Conservatives, the party of Europe, would work towards a 'strong free Europe' and 'a Conservative Europe', whereas the Labour attitude was 'negative'.[18]

The European effort also coincided neatly with domestic concerns. It did not escape the attention of the Conservatives that the leading figures in the No organisation were mainly left-wingers and trade union leaders, just the sort of people that the Tories warned against domestically. There were, of course, few drawbacks for the Tories to suggest that those who wanted the UK to leave were pursuing a far-Left strategy, supported by the Soviets (alleged Russian influence in support of a Leave vote being an element of continuity between 1975 and 2016). Likewise, it could be pointed out that Bennites who argued for import controls wanted the UK to leave the EEC 'in order to have a better chance of turning the country into a socialist siege economy with rigid controls'. The tiny band of Conservative antis objected to these smear tactics, but could do nothing to restrain them. As Colin Kidd has recently observed, 'in 1975 anti-EEC sentiment was a minority pursuit on the right. After all, it seemed perverse to oppose something the Labour left demonised'.[19]

The position of the new Leader was of little significance at the time, but was, perhaps, an indication of problems to come. Thatcher had asked Heath to lead the Tory campaign in the referendum, but he refused. Within days of her elevation to the leadership in February 1975, rumours were circulating that she was anti-Europe. During the referendum campaign, *The Sun* (which catered to a key demographic for both the Yes campaign and the Tories) complained that she had 'mysteriously disappeared'. Once the result was in, the *New Statesman* thought she had been 'invisible … inaudible … a "lukewarm marketeer"'.[20]

Thatcher was, admittedly, in a difficult political position. She had no foreign policy experience. She had become leader just before the referendum, deposing the former PM who had secured entry and established the Conservatives as the party of Europe. Her victory represented a 'peasants' revolt', against the establishment of her own party, but the establishment was still well represented in the Shadow Cabinet and party organisation. As she said, when launching the Conservative Group for Europe's referendum campaign, 'it's with some temerity that the pupil speaks before the master, because you know more about it than any of the rest of us'. This was the first public appearance together of Heath and Thatcher since her election as leader, making the situation doubly awkward. Even so, there were, even in 1975, some slight hints that Thatcher took a different view of European issues from her predecessor. Although she dutifully played her part in the campaign, making speeches and writing articles, there was suspicion, even in the Tory press, of 'Margaret's silence'. This 'silence' was to find echoes in 2016 in the similar allegations made against Jeremy Corbyn, another new Leader of the Opposition with little support in the higher echelons of his party.[21]

The final component of the Yes campaign was, in effect, the press, which, with the (very marginal) exception of *The Morning Star*, was massively supportive of staying in. Some antis thought that the broadcasters were equally biased, Benn noting that the BBC was 'a hotbed of pro-Market people' (another refrain that would be heard in 2016). However, this was a minority view. Marten, Chairman of the National

Referendum Campaign (NRC), 'had no grievance against the broadcasters though he had against the press'. He had good reason for this.[22]

Before exploring that grievance, it is worth noting that the press barrage seems to have made little difference to the result. By March 1975, most voters appear to have made up their minds on the basis of the terms recommended by the government. The Yes campaign made little headway thereafter and even fell back in the last few days. Moreover, the result was so overwhelming that press bias can hardly explain the scale of the defeat.

The press was, nonetheless, a real force in 1975. The 'big five' newspapers had a combined circulation of more than 13 million people. Given that their readership was between two and three times this figure, it is likely that almost all 40 million voters read a paper daily. The coverage of these papers, both editorially and in terms of news, was strongly pro-EEC. The smaller-circulation papers (*The Guardian*, *The Times* and *Financial Times*) had a combined circulation of less than 1 million. Although also very pro-EEC, their influence was less and their readership was, in any event, largely drawn from middle-class voters who were strongly inclined to vote Yes in any event.[23]

The Daily Mirror (circulation 4 million and broadly allied to Labour) had no doubt in its position: 'YES to a future in which we play a leading and prosperous role as part of a Great Western Europe.' It had no truck with 'The Minister of Fear', Tony Benn, for his claim that membership had cost 500,000 jobs. By contrast, its longstanding columnist Marje Proops posed reassuringly with the 'two main reasons why I shall vote YES', her grandchildren.

The Sun (circulation 3.4 million, with wide working-class dissemination and still on its journey from Labour to uber-Thatcherism) took a similar line, attacking Benn and Powell, and the day before the referendum advising its readers thus:

> the whole history of our nation … is a history of absorbing, and profiting by … European influences … what have citizen Benn and Brigadier

Enoch and the Communist Party and the racist National Front got in common?... They are frustrated. They are bitter. They are demagogues.[24]

The Daily Express (circulation of 2.8 million and a strongly 'working-class Tory' base) was 'for the Market'. However, given its imperialist background, the paper of Beaverbrook was perhaps less than inspiring in its message that 'the most sensible vote is a Yes vote'. Its rationale for this recommendation was that this was so due to 'the tide of fear: that we now have no other role to play, no other trading system to live in, no other credibility to keep us in funds'.

The Daily Mail (1.7 million, much more middle-class but also Tory) was happy to join in the press attacks on Benn for 'scare-mongering at its most brazen'. It, too, pointed to the risks of exit, but offered a more positive vision of staying in. This would give the UK 'the power to direct and influence our own future'. In contrast to much of the press in 2016, it poured scorn on the option of 'splendid isolation' and reassured its readers that 'political union is not much of a live issue now'.[25]

The Daily Telegraph (1.3 million) was, in 1975, the High Tory voice of the suburbs. Its coverage was more thoughtful, and it embraced some of the wider issues such as defence, and 'the chance of giving the extreme Left a massive rebuff' that the referendum offered. The paper called for 'a massive "Yes"' but also explored the wider issues in ways in which the other outlets did not. In particular, there was some acceptance that 'the undoubted benefits' of the trading arrangements which the UK now had with the EEC might form part of 'the road ahead [towards] a Europe able to govern itself'.[26]

Nonetheless, there are grounds for scepticism about the claims of No supporters that a hostile press denied them victory. Despite the editorial commitments of the papers, room was found for dissenting views. For example, *The Daily Express* printed personal articles by leading antis, including the trade union leader Clive Jenkins, Powell and Benn. Furthermore, the antis in fact drove some of the biggest stories during the campaign. On the eve of the vote, Edward Du Cann, Chairman of the

1922 Committee, suggested that many Conservatives harboured mis-givings about the Market. The press were critical of this intervention, but still noted that it was causing 'turmoil at Tory HQ'. Moreover, the biggest single issue of the campaign was Benn's claim that membership had cost 500,000 jobs. The press, although critical of Benn for having 'created the most fraudulent scare of the whole campaign', gave the story substantial and persistent coverage. The jobs question forced BIE on to the defensive, and they did not devise any comparable theme of their own to dominate the debate.[27]

In any event, the referendum did not dominate the press. Most of the papers devoted a maximum of a page per day to the campaign, with occasional front pages, comment or editorials. There was far more coverage of sport in all the papers than there was of European issues. Celebrity news likewise gained much more space than the campaign. On 27 May 1975, eight days before the vote, the *Mirror*, *Mail* and *Express* filled their front pages with stories about misfortunes that had befallen Frank Sinatra and Evel Knievel, an American stunt performer. There was also plenty of room for sensational and human-interest stories: snow in June; a 'child branded in the house of sex'; a lost city found in the jungle; a 'baboon in heart link with baby'.[28]

Some of the shortcomings in the press coverage may have been because the referendum lacked the compelling narrative to which press and politicians were accustomed as part of a general election. The role of the press was usually clear: support their party and attack their oppo-nents. But who was the enemy here? For the Tory press, in particular, this was a challenge. They sought to create an atmosphere of crisis, for which they blamed the Labour government and the unions, in relation to mounting inflation and widespread strikes. However, it was then necessary to come to the aid of the government, or, at least, its leading figures, because they were advocating a Yes vote. For much of the press, the referendum was therefore something of a distraction from the really urgent business of attacking the government and the unions. The press essentially believed that the UK was in the midst of an emergency that the EEC could not solve. However, the institutions of the EEC could at least serve to contain the real enemies of freedom, the Left and the unions.[29]

The No campaign was a very different proposition from the well-heeled and smoothly organised BIE outfit. It was like comparing 'a racing car to a bicycle'. In January 1975, the NRC was formed as an umbrella body, bringing together two existing anti-EEC organisations, the Common Market Safeguards Campaign and Get Britain Out. As was noted after the referendum, this was 'a far more disparate army than the pro-Marketeers and they were sadly lacking in money, facilities and … professionalism'. The NRC raised only £9,000, with only one business and one union donation exceeding £100. Marten was selected as Chairman, because he was essentially the only available and acceptable non-Labour figure. Rather than lavish facilities in Park Lane, the NRC had two rooms off the Strand, run by his daughter. These organisational issues were compounded by the fact that the two most prominent figures in the No camp, Powell and Benn, provoked negative responses from many voters. Some Tories were suspicious of Powell as a turncoat. Benn was the subject, as we have seen, of a relentless press barrage. All in all, as Castle noted 'the professionalism of the pro-Market campaign' stood in marked contrast with a campaign 'run by idealistic and very charming youngsters with no money and long hair'.[30]

More fundamentally, the NRC had an inherent conflict in their ranks in that they were seeking to bring together the Left and the Right. Jenkins, Thorpe and Heath, albeit in different parties, appeared to agree on most issues, and not merely the EEC. This smoothly presented united front gave Yes spokespersons a considerable advantage in the debates, at least as framed by the media. When Heath and Thorpe took on Castle and Shore at the Oxford Union, the former 'wiped the floor with us' (according to Castle), and Heath received a standing ovation. The No camp had a much less united front. Even within the Labour camp, there was limited common ground. Were they Churchillian free traders (Jay, Shore) or seeking to build socialism in 'fortress Britain', like the advocates of the AES? And what common ground could there be between any variety of Labour view and the Tory Right, let alone the National Front? At local level, this looked very much like a 'left-wing campaign' in which dissident Conservative activists struggled to feel comfortable. They may not have been much reassured by the fact that senior Tories like Heath and Lord Hailsham were proclaiming that a No vote might well open the door to Communism. Likewise, any nervous Labour people might have taken fright to see Heath and Prentice stand-ing shoulder to shoulder as they attacked the Left. And the Dissenting Ministers, when proposing their plan for 'orderly withdrawal', did not explain how the Labour government could survive in circumstances where its leading members had urged a Yes vote after a renegotiation it had itself carried out. Might not this lead to '1931 all over again', as Wilson warned, with a 'pro-Market coalition' and a Labour Party split asunder?[31]

That said, the referendum did, for all these manifest difficulties, allow David to secure some victories over Goliath. As the press coverage illus-trated, Benn's case that membership had cost 500,000 jobs was the issue that did most to bring the campaign to life. It was also a theme that put the 'well-fed men' of BIE on the defensive and potentially had traction with the working-class voters who were most sceptical about the EEC in any event. Moreover, the experience of fighting for a No vote was exhilarating for the Left in the Labour Movement, who had free rein, as they did not in a general election. Large public meetings were held that brought together MPs and union leaders. Most of the big unions supported a No vote, as did the wider Left. The Left felt, with some justification, that they were in a battle for their core principles against the British state, the European Commission and even the CIA.[32]

In a sense, also, the NRC had the best tunes, even if they lacked the right amplifying equipment. At Labour's Special Conference in April, Foot made 'a brilliant speech ... quoting Aneurin Bevan and ... the Putney Debates of 1647'. He said 'to our great country "Don't be afraid of those who tell us we cannot run our own affairs"'. Likewise, Powell warned the British people that they needed to listen to the EEC's stated intention to become a political union, such that the UK would be a mere 'province of the new superstate'. The NRC's literature, although giving full weight to the bread and butter issues of food, jobs and trade, did confront the sovereignty issue head-on:

> The real aim of the Market is, of course, to become one single country in which Britain would be reduced to a mere province. ... Unless you want to be ruled more and more by a Continental Parliament in which Britain would be in a small minority, you should vote NO.[33]

Despite the overwhelming margin of victory and the euphoria of the press and the political establishment, the referendum had not really settled the European issue. In the short term, most in the NRC had to accept defeat with dignity. They had had 'a very big message from the British people', Benn acknowledged. This was, said Marten, 'the wish of the British people'. However, although the battle had been decisively lost, the war would continue.[34]

So far as the Left were concerned, and however tortuous their position might become in having demanded and then lost a referendum, the central problem had not gone away. The EEC made their socialist project impossible, or so they believed. As Tony Benn had told the Cabinet at the key meeting in March 1975:

> The real case for entry has never been spelled out, which is that there should be a fully federal Europe in which we become a province. It hasn't been spelled out because people would never accept it. We are at the moment on the federal escalator ... going towards a federal objective we do not wish to reach. In practice, Britain will be governed by a European coalition government that we cannot change, dedicated to a capitalist or market economy theology.[35]

If that were so – and Brexiteers in 2016 would express very similar fears in very similar language, the last eight words excepted – how could a socialist in good conscience give up the fight, however a referendum might turn out? After all, if the Left (or anyone else) lost a general election, that was not, usually, the signal to abandon one's ideals or accept the correctness of the programme of the winning party. Moreover, the 'agreement to differ' among Ministers was all very well, but some differences seemed unbridgeable. During the campaign, Jenkins said that he found it 'increasingly difficult to take Mr Benn seriously as an economics minister' (in reference to Benn's jobs claim). When one looks now at the debate between these two leading figures on the Left and Right of the Labour Party, it is hard to see how they could both long remain in the party into which they had been born: their fathers had both been Labour MPs. Their disagreements went far beyond the ostensibly narrow question posed by the referendum.[36]

Moreover, the experience of 1975, in which party discipline largely broke down and politicians saw both the advantages and drawbacks of co-operation with those whom they generally opposed, suggested that this constitutional novelty might not have seen its last outing. As *The Daily Express* noted in May 1975, 'If Mr. Wilson can go for a referendum to solve the Labour Party's internal difficulties, others will do the same.' Not every prophecy made in 1975 may have stood the test of time, but this one was strikingly accurate.[37]

This co-operation gave pointers for the future, but not, perhaps, entirely those that the protagonists were expecting. Not everyone in the upper reaches of BIE suffered the same melancholy fate as Thorpe. The BIE message was, of course, larger than its spokesmen, and the clarion call of the Radical Centre was to be heard once more in the 1980s, as Jenkins returned to British politics and Heath poured scorn on Thatcherism. However, there was a worm in the bud, feeding on the damask cheek of pro-EEC sentiment. It was true, as Jenkins pointed out, that the voters had 'listened to the people they were used to following'. But were not these exactly the people who had, according to the Right of the Tory Party, presided over Britain's post-war failure and its slow surrender to socialism? Was this a farewell tour for the Centre?[38]

The deepest problems lay ahead for Labour in the short term, and not only in seeking to reconcile the views of irreconcilable senior figures. For the Conservatives, the result meant that they had 'secured an impressive victory and ha[d] a new base for its European policy'. Their voters (by 85% to 15%) had voted Yes, far the highest proportion of any political party. With a few minor exceptions, Tory MPs had supported the party's position, and the constituency activists seemed happy enough. For Labour the position was very different. The party went into the referendum divided at the top. There was also a significant split between the leadership and the wider Labour Movement.

The referendum had done little to heal these divisions. It had, in addition, exposed differences among Labour voters. These voters split roughly 50/50. Moreover, while the Yes vote was overwhelming everywhere, the best indication for a No vote was class: C2 and DE voters were much less pro-European than ABC1 voters. The former groups were, of course, those from whom the Labour core vote was traditionally drawn. Moreover, the margin of victory served to mask an underlying lack of enthusiasm for the wider European project. For example, a detailed attitudinal survey carried out in 1974, before the conclusion of the renegotiations, revealed that only 3% of those asked identified as 'pro market'; 63% thought membership would give us less say in our own affairs; 40% believed that Commonwealth countries were 'better friends to Britain than Western Europe will ever be'. More than a quarter thought that 'we have wrongly linked up with some of our oldest enemies'. These sentiments, which would recur very strongly in 2016, and which were much more prevalent among manual workers, inevitably raise the question that some sceptics over referenda had been asking: did a vote one way or the other really disclose the 'will of the people'?[39]

So far as the Tory Right were concerned, the European issue appeared now to be resolved. Any doubts could be put to one side in the glow of victory and party unity. However, Powell still had many admirers on the Right, and he had not given up the fight, telling Benn the day after the vote that 'the great political education is only just beginning'. His point was that 'the vast majority of those voting had no notion that they were saying yes or no to Britain continuing as a nation at all'. In years to come, it would become an article of faith for the resurgent Powellite Right that the voters had been misled in 1975 by a Europhile establishment. These appeasers, in their desperation to merge the UK into a European superstate, had withheld the true implications of EEC membership from the people. This was at best a half-truth, and the NRC had put the sovereignty issue forcefully before the electorate. But Powell had advanced the germ of an idea, which would grow once there were more Powellites to advance it.[40]

The Right, 1975–1983

Between 1975 and 1979, the Conservatives reappraised many aspects of domestic policy. After the election victory in May 1979, the Thatcher government began the process of dismantling the post-war social democratic model. It adopted as its principal tool for combating inflation the newly fashionable doctrine of 'monetarism', with very mixed results. Unemployment ceased to be a central policy-making priority and the number of jobless rose towards the previously unthinkable figure of 3 million. Significant tax changes were enacted, particularly big tax cuts for higher earners and as to the balance between direct and indirect taxation. The 'right to buy' was established.

However, until 1982 at the earliest, Thatcher was not in full command of her party, and Thatcherism was not yet a dominant force. In 1981, there were prolonged riots at Toxteth, Brixton and elsewhere. The Conservative Party was bitterly divided throughout the first term between 'wets' and 'dries' on economic policy. Some aspects of what was to become known as 'Thatcherism', such as privatisation and the marginalisation of the trade unions, did not much feature.

In relation to European policy, there was, overall, little change. It was as if the momentum of the Heath years continued for a time after his leadership had come to a juddering halt in all other respects. The party continued to proclaim itself the party of Europe. It was instrumental in the formation of a new Alliance of the Centre Right in Europe, the European Democratic Union, which was founded in 1978. Consistently with this approach, the Party strongly supported the introduction of direct elections for MEPs. The Conservatives contrasted their own enthusiasm for these elections with Labour's 'delay and obstruction': the first direct elections were not held until June 1979, following a lengthy and convoluted process in which the Labour government had sought to obtain Parliamentary agreement for the applicable voting system. Obviously, this additional democratic mandate could only afford more legitimacy to 'Europe', as Powell pointed out. There was, for this reason, limited enthusiasm for direct elections on the Labour side. When the elections were held, they were a triumph for the Tories, winning 60 out of 78 seats and 51% of the vote.[41]

Indeed, while in opposition from 1974 to 1979, the Conservatives became, if anything, even more Europhile. In particular, the party saw the German CDU as 'our natural colleagues in the European venture', in the words of Chris Patten, the pro-European, Roman Catholic, director of the Conservative Research Department at this time. Moreover, such sentiment was not confined to Patten's wing of the party. In 1974, Keith Joseph, a keen admirer of Erhard and the Ordoliberals, decided to create 'The Institute for a Social Market Economy', which eventually became the Centre for Policy Studies. As Leader of the Opposition, Thatcher was in regular contact with Helmut Kohl, the CDU leader. Her PPS went so far as to suggest that the party change its name to 'The National Democratic Conservative Party', since this 'would allow a gradual transition to National Democrats and this abbreviation would gain more ready usage in Europe'. The concern was that the existing name gave the 'erroneous' impression to Centre Right Europeans that the Tories were 'insufficiently "Christian" and excessively "Conservative" (i.e. reactionary in their terms)'.[42]

In government, the principal European focus of the 1979–83 term was upon a budget rebate for the UK, an issue that had formed part of the Wilson/Callaghan renegotiations. Thatcher's initial approach to the issue, at the June 1979 Strasbourg summit, was low-key and even 'communautaire'. However, by the Dublin Council of November 1979, her attitude had become more combative, dismissing the European offer of a rebate of £350m as 'a third of a loaf', the 'loaf' being the £1bn she had demanded. By this stage, the Cabinet had agreed that 'it was a major objective of policy to secure a satisfactory settlement of the budget question'. In the event, Thatcher's Foreign Office team (Lord Carrington and Sir Ian Gilmour) reached a three-year settlement with their European counterparts in May 1980. Carrington and Gilmour were both 'wets' (i.e. Tories of the *ancien régime* who were highly critical of the government's economic policies) who would soon leave the government. Thatcher was unenthusiastic: according to Gilmour, 'to her, the grievance was more valuable than its removal'. Nonetheless, the Cabinet endorsed the deal.[43]

In general, Euroscepticism was a very peripheral concern on the Right in this period, with the exception of Powell and a small number of irreconcilables on the Tory benches. However, there were, at the least, some straws in the wind. Even in 1979, Thatcher was, privately, 'more and more disillusioned with the E.E.C.'. In public, she asserted that she would not 'play Sister Bountiful to the Community'. Her language at the Dublin council was far from 'communautaire', telling the press that:

> We are not asking for a penny piece of Community money for Britain. What we are asking is for a very large amount of our own money back. … Broadly speaking, for every £2 we contribute we get £1 back. That leaves us with a net contribution of £1,000 million next year to the Community and rising in the future. It is that £1,000 million on which we started to negotiate, because we want the greater part back. But it is not asking the Community for money; it is asking the Community to have our own money back.[44]

This concept of getting 'our own money back' would loom large in 2016, albeit in the context of departure rather than negotiation.

However, even in this period, there was the potential for the UK's relationship with the EEC to sour further. For one thing, public opinion remained lukewarm at best. At the time of the Dublin council, most of those polled supported Thatcher's defiance, and 53% thought 'we should get out'. By the following year, more than thirty Tory MPs were members of the Conservative European Reform Group, whose prospectus called for 'fundamental reform of the Common Market ... based on the partnership of nation-states' and 'the reassertion of the power of national Parliaments over the institutions of the Community'. The hostility was not all one-way. Following a dispute over agricultural prices, in May 1982 President Mitterrand of France, and his Foreign Minister, both suggested that it might be better if the UK ceased to be a full member and instead acquired a 'special status': an idea that was to resurface, on the British side, in and after 2016.[45]

Perhaps the most significant issue in the long run was one that received little public attention, the ostensibly arcane question of whether the UK should join the Exchange Rate Mechanism (ERM). In 1977 Roy Jenkins, by now President of the Commission, had sought to revive the idea of monetary union. One of the arguments that he deployed in favour of this proposal was that 'monetary union stands on offer as a vehicle for European political integration ... the successful creation of a European monetary union would take Europe over a political threshold'. Self-evidently, Economic and Monetary Union (EMU) raised an important issue of principle, since it involved a nation state giving up one of its most important prerogatives, the right to issue and manage its own currency.[46]

In July 1978, at Bremen, the European Council instructed the Finance Ministers to draw up a detailed 'scheme for the creation of ... closer monetary co-operation ... leading to a zone of monetary stability in Europe'. In December 1978, at Brussels, the Council agreed to establish the EMS. Britain alone did not join. Each currency was allocated a central rate, expressed in terms of the ECU, from which it was only allowed to deviate by a specified percentage. The EMS came into operation in

March 1979. Once more, the UK was standing aloof from developments in Europe.[47]

The official Tory line on EMU was enthusiastic. The senior Tories who were, at this time, constructing a 'dry' economic policy, such as Howe, the Shadow Chancellor, and Lawson (later Chancellor himself), favoured joining. Howe recorded the consensus in a note to Thatcher of 31 October 1978:

> We should pronounce in favour of the EMS – not as ... ideal ... but ... to be welcomed for providing greater currency stability and encouraging convergence of economic policies. The political case for this conclusion is a strong one: the alternative means surrendering the direction of the E.E.C. and its policies to the Franco-German high table.[48]

When the Commons debated the matter in November 1978, Howe rejected a floating exchange rate, in favour of 'a set of rules applying nationally as well as internationally.' What was required was 'the discipline that the EMS would impose ... tighter control of public spending, a commitment to currency stability', in preference to 'socialist illusions or nationalist myths'. In December 1978, the government confirmed that the UK would not be joining. The Conservatives described this as 'a sad day for Europe and for Britain. ... The Prime Minister ... is evidently content to see us relegated to the Community's Second Division.'[49]

The Tory Manifesto for the 1979 European elections contained a commitment to join the system. In the event, the first Thatcher government did not take the matter further forward, for various short-term reasons. Its deliberations were largely technical and high-level, so that there was little public or party interest in the question. However, this was in due course to form a central and divisive issue for the second and third Thatcher governments and for the Major government of 1990 to 1997.[50]

These divisions had been ventilated in 1978/9, but not much exposed to public gaze. Some Shadow Ministers were hostile to the proposal. John Biffen, a close associate of Powell, told Thatcher that the Bremen proposals would lead to 'a demand for full monetary union and the cessation of the United Kingdom as a national monetary agency'. Her own views were similar: she told Biffen that 'the fundamentals worry me greatly'. 'The fundamentals' did receive some airing, since Powell pointed out in his speeches that 'currency alignment ... is [EMU], and [EMU] *is* political union' and that 'a common currency meant common government'.[51]

The Left, 1975–1983

Before the referendum, Lord Elwyn-Jones, the Lord Chancellor, had been concerned that Wilson was 'near to resignation', in despair at the difficulties of keeping his warring tribe together, and that this 'could be a disaster for social democracy'. In the event, Wilson managed to steer the government through the referendum and did not resign for another year. However, the 'disaster for social democracy' ensued in any event, as Wilson, Callaghan and Healey tried and failed to keep afloat the ideas of Keynesian social democracy in very challenging times.[52]

These challenges drove the government away from most of the ambitious plans that had been developed in Opposition and, to some extent, from the whole trend of post-war policy on taxation and spending. In 1974, Labour had campaigned for the Social Contract, whereby the unions would offer voluntary restraint in exchange for a major increase in the 'social wage' and substantial redistribution of wealth, and controls on prices and dividends.[53]

By the time of the referendum, wage settlements were running at 26%. The government and the TUC therefore agreed a flat rate 'voluntary' pay policy of £6 per week. Increases in the 'social wage' fell victim to pressures on public spending: the 1976 White Paper condemned the rising ratio of public expenditure and the associated tax burden. This presaged substantial further cuts in public spending in July 1976, and, again, in December 1976. At the end of 1976, the government entered into an agreement with the IMF, which required continuing spending reductions.[54]

The Left were relegated to the very margins of the government, partly through these changes in policy and partly owing to their devastating defeat in the referendum. Even before the referendum, Benn had complained that 'the Tories now think that Wilson, Healey and Callaghan are doing their work so well that they don't want a coalition government'. Things did not get any better thereafter. On the Monday after the referendum, Wilson demoted Benn from the Industry Department. The Left's industrial policies perished with him. The Left also tried, in vain, to deflect Callaghan and Healey from the policy of spending cuts and wage restraint during the IMF crisis of late 1976, urging instead the adoption of the AES. 'Within government, the Left was on the defensive on all fronts.'[55]

The Left's position on the EEC was less easy to articulate than on domestic policy. On the latter, the argument was straightforward. The party had developed in opposition a radical economic challenge to capitalism and won two elections on that basis. In the face of a crisis of capitalism, the government had immediately retreated and embraced Treasury orthodoxy. On Europe, on the other hand, the Left had demanded, fought and lost the referendum. Other than to emulate Brecht's ironic suggestion that they should dismiss the people and appoint a new one, the democratic way forward was unclear. Was the Left unwilling to take Yes for an Answer, in the words of Roger Broad?[56]

The answer, it soon emerged, was that this was the line which most on the Left would indeed take. The problem was that they continued to 'loathe the Common Market'. Within a few months of the referendum, the Dissenting Ministers were grumbling about the proposed introduction of European passports (another issue that would re-emerge in 2016). Castle complained that 'we [would] continue on our relentless way to European uniformity'. This issue was largely emotional and symbolic, but Benn, more generally, told his colleagues that 'the Treaty of Rome is hostile to what the Labour Party believes in, and we will be chewing over these issues ... for a hundred years'. Benn's collaborator on the left, Stuart Holland, sought to make the case that Labour could pursue its regional and industrial policies within the confines of the Treaty and that the EEC could provide a vehicle to control the multinationals, but this was a minority view on the Left.[57]

The Left took its stand in this period on two principal issues: direct elections to the European Assembly and EMU. Clive Jenkins, who had expressed himself defiant following the referendum defeat, spoke out against these twin dangers at the TUC Conference in September 1975. The government published a Green Paper on direct elections in February 1976. The antis argued that such elections were 'not sanctioned by the Referendum Result'; the party conference in September 1976 endorsed, by 2 to 1, a NEC recommendation opposing such elections, on the grounds that they would pave the way to a superstate. In the event, the government published a White Paper in April 1977 offering three possible electoral systems for these elections. The ensuing Bill eventually passed the Commons in December 1977, on the basis of single-member constituencies and 'first past the post'. However, on the Second Reading, the government had allowed a free vote in which six Cabinet ministers, 26 other ministers and 92 Labour MPs voted against the Bill, albeit that it passed by 394 votes to 147 with Tory support. There was even talk of Labour boycotting the elections when they were eventually held, an option which, the party's General Secretary warned, could lead to 'the most serious split the party has ever known' (which would be saying something).[58]

EMU was an equally divisive issue in principle, although the leadership did not press this issue. There were good practical reasons to keep the UK out of the system, as the previously enthusiastic Conservatives themselves discovered in due course: the influx of North Sea oil meant that it would have been necessary to intervene in the EMS to keep sterling's value down, which might have proved inflationary. However, most of the wider Labour Movement was hostile to the principle of EMU. Benn called in Cabinet 'for a British "non" of Gaullist clarity and resonance'. The NEC voted by 2 to 1 against EMS, and the 1978 party conference supported this position overwhelmingly. Many Labour MPs were hostile, believing that the EMS would see 'the Cabinet reduced to the status of a pressure group on most central economic issues'.[59]

These skirmishes, on matters that must have seemed of peripheral interest to most electors, were evidence that much of the Labour Movement did not accept that the referendum had settled anything at all. As early as November 1975, the Labour Common Market Safeguards Campaign (LCMSC) identified seven key aims. Some, such as the evergreen call for reform of the CAP, were arguably compatible with continued membership. However, objections to, for example, free movement of capital and VAT harmonisation went to the heart of the UK's engagement with the EEC. These sentiments were shared beyond the confines of the LCMSC. The party conferences of 1977 and 1978 passed, by large margins, resolutions that were, in substance, incompatible with continued membership. Resolutions were tabled, but not passed, which called for a second referendum or withdrawal. Many of the larger unions backed the calls for fundamental reform of the UK's relationship with the EEC.[60]

The leadership, broadly, was able to keep the senior echelons of the party acquiescent in a policy of pragmatic, but unenthusiastic, continued membership. With the departure of Jenkins to Europe, the pro-EEC zealots in the party lacked a figurehead, although some remained in senior posts. The Dissenting Ministers necessarily became less vocal in the light of the referendum result, although still able to express this dissent in the free vote on direct elections. Benn remained an unrepentant anti, in tune with the wider Movement but scarcely tolerated by many of his colleagues. He complained that he 'was a member of the first British Government in history to be informed that it was behaving illegally by a court whose ruling you could not alter by changing the law in the House of Commons'. At a special Cabinet meeting to discuss Europe, the 'tension was electric' when Benn announced his intention 'to restore to the British people the power to govern themselves'.[61]

This tension came to the surface during preparations for the 1979 general election, when Callaghan vetoed a proposal to include a commitment to withdrawal in the manifesto. Even so, the final text offered the British people

> the prospect of bringing about fundamental and much-needed reform to the E.E.C. ... [by] develop[ing] a Europe which is democratic and socialist, and where the interests of the people are placed above the interests of national and multinational capitalist groups, but within which each country must be able to realize its own economic and social objectives, under the sovereignty of its own Parliament and people.

The British people were unmoved, since the Common Market scarcely 'impinged on British consciousness during the election'. Voters who were still paying attention a month later (not very many, the turnout being 32%) would have noticed that Labour's manifesto for the European direct elections threatened withdrawal if the EEC was not fundamentally reformed. This represented a victory for the anti-European Left.[62]

Were the Left, and their supporters in the wider Labour Movement, simply bad losers? Having demanded and lost the referendum, should they not have accepted defeat? The problem for the Left was that, in a sense, the EEC was a sideshow to their central aims of achieving a socialist Britain, but it was a sideshow that was liable to ruin the main event. For example, the party at its 1976 conference had overwhelmingly adopted *Labour's Programme 1976*, which committed the party to the AES and an interventionist industrial policy, and proposed seeking derogations from the UK's EEC obligations to bring this about. The LCMSC urged that the Commons should have restored to it the power to decide whether or not any EEC regulations should apply to the UK, and that the Treaty of Rome should be amended to curtail the Commission's powers. There should be 'express recognition to the rights of the member states to pursue their own economic, industrial and regional policies'. This was all a little disingenuous. The truth was that it was simply not possible to implement the sort of socialist strategy the Left had in mind without contravening the EEC's founding statutes. For 'safeguards' one had to read withdrawal, and one had also to impute to the much-invoked British people an enthusiasm for the AES and associated industrial policy that had not been evident in 1975 or subsequently. If this was a lie, however, it was a lie that the Left had to live if it was to survive at all.[63]

The Callaghan government remained in office until May 1979, and, even in the autumn of 1978, appeared to have reasonable prospects of winning a general election. However, the winter of 1978/9 saw the collapse of the government's pay policy, and widespread industrial action, during the 'Winter of Discontent'. These events enabled the Conservatives, and Thatcher in particular, to construct a powerful challenge to the existing order. In March 1979, the government lost a vote of confidence in the Commons, and in May the Conservatives won the election decisively.[64]

The Thatcher government then embarked on its monetarist counter-revolution. For the Labour Movement, and the Left in particular, this was a time to regroup in opposition and for not a little retribution. The same leaders (Wilson, Callaghan, Healey) had dominated this government as they had the 1964–70 administration. In each case, the party had developed ambitious policies in opposition, and these had fallen away as the governments struggled to deal with economic crises. Shortly after the 1979 defeat, a group of left-wing MPs and intellectuals published a collection entitled *What Went Wrong*. This encapsulated the Left's disillusion with Labour's record: as the editor, Ken Coates, noted 'as it began, so it ends. The decade from 1970 to 1979, entered, and left, to the sounds of a Labour Government falling.' And why was this so? There were two core complaints. First of all, the government had abandoned any pretence of socialism in its economic policies: retreating from Keynesianism in relation to public spending, forsaking full employment and neutralising the industrial strategy so carefully developed in opposition. Secondly, the leadership had simply ignored party policy, as agreed by the NEC and at Conference. For example, Callaghan had vetoed the inclusion of a proposal to abolish the House of Lords in the 1979 manifesto, although this had received overwhelming support at conference.[65]

The Left did not wish to see this unhappy history repeated. It therefore embarked on a constitutional campaign to reform the structures of the party. The essence of this campaign was the proposition that a future Labour government would implement party policy, provided that the leadership was made properly accountable to the wider party. The chosen methods to achieve this objective were the compulsory reselection of MPs and the control of the manifesto by the NEC (adopted at the 1979 conference) and a new method of electing the leader, an electoral college composed of MPs, unions and members (approved at a special conference in January 1981). Previously, the MPs alone had chosen the leader. Shortly before this change took effect, Callaghan resigned and was replaced as leader by Foot, elected under the old system.

Foot was the party's most left-wing leader since the 1930s, and a longstanding opponent of the EEC. However, the driving force behind the reforms was Benn, who used the new system to challenge Healey for the deputy leadership in 1981. Benn lost narrowly after a lengthy and bitter contest. Between 1979 and 1983, the Left consolidated the party's economic policy, largely along the lines already developed in previous periods of opposition: full employment; import controls; an industrial strategy based on planning and public ownership. Labour's Keynesian and reflationary strategy was in sharp contrast to the policies being pursued by the Thatcher government.[66]

These developments in the fields of party structure and economic policy had a number of other effects. One was that a number of Jenkinsite MPs left Labour and formed the SDP. European policy was an important, but not the only, *casus belli* for these defectors. The emergence of the SDP, its policies and its approach to Europe are an important part of this story, and will be returned to below. Another consequence was that the Left sought to move Labour away from its traditional foreign policy stance. In the 1960s, many in the Labour Movement had become disillusioned with the Wilson government's 'unethical foreign policy'.

After 1979, the Left steered the party in a new direction, as party conferences adopted a programme of unilateral nuclear disarmament and the removal of American military bases. This programme was anathema to those contemplating defection. It also indicated a major shift in axis away from Atlanticism.[67]

Despite the recent defeat of the No campaign, the path to a policy of withdrawal was wide open. Quite apart from the rise of the Left, and the recriminations over the Wilson and Callaghan governments, there was deep hostility to the EEC in many parts of the Labour Movement. Most of the activists were of this view, but even among those seeking the leadership after Callaghan's departure, three of the four candidates (Shore, Silkin and Foot) were veteran antis.[68]

The party's formal conversion to withdrawal had, therefore, an air of inevitability about it, and it did not take long to materialise. There were some moves in this direction in 1979, although constitutional issues drew more attention. However, at the party's 1980 conference, a resolution demanding withdrawal was carried by 5 million votes to 2 million: 'a fantastic victory', according to Benn. David Owen, Foreign Secretary from 1977 to 1979, and shortly to depart for the SDP, argued for a further referendum, but Shore suggested that this was unnecessary provided withdrawal was clearly identified in a general election manifesto. His language was impassioned: 'We are going to have to … fight if we are going to restore to Britain and the British people its own power over its own future … [Entry to the EEC was] a rape of the British people and their rights and constitution.'[69]

During 1981 and 1982, the party fleshed out its proposals. The NEC adopted a 12-month timetable for withdrawal in July 1981. Conference endorsed this the following September. Foot appointed Heffer as the party's European spokesman. Despite the strongly anti-EEC drift in policy, and the wide support for this approach within the wider movement, there remained a number of uncertainties. Foot, as leader, showed surprisingly little interest in foreign affairs, concentrating instead on the difficult task of keeping his fractious party together. Relations with

European socialists were strained. It was not obvious how Heffer's vision of 'a socialist Europe standing independent and neutral between the two great powers' might be achieved. Even Foot, and other veteran antis like Castle (by now leader of the Labour MEPs), appeared to suggest that somehow withdrawal could be combined with some continued relationship or that the rules of the EEC could be eased to accommodate Labour's programme.[70]

However, these sentiments were peripheral to the main trends in party policy. This rested on two planks. The first was the essential incompatibility between the party's socialist policies and the constraints imposed by the EEC. The second was that there was no need for another referendum. After all, the last one had been swayed by 'a Tory, media and big business campaign which was extremely successful in misleading the electorate'. To vote Labour was to vote against the EEC, since the party's approach to 'trade planning, selective aid for industry ... the direction of investment and capital flows ... [was] in conflict with either the letter or the practice of the Treaty of Rome'.[71]

Thus prepared, Labour offered a radical socialist manifesto at the 1983 election. The European element lacked any trace of ambiguity, with no mention of further referenda or renegotiations. The Tories, and their press allies, attacked Labour relentlessly for their supposed extremism, and suggested that withdrawal would put jobs at risk by scaring away foreign investors. In party terms, however, the manifesto was the logical culmination of the debates that had been going on in the party since at least 1970:

> The next Labour government, committed to radical, socialist policies for reviving the British economy, is bound to find continued membership a most serious obstacle to the fulfilment of those policies. In particular the rules of the Treaty of Rome are bound to conflict with our strategy for economic growth and full employment, our proposals on industrial policy and for increasing trade, and our need to restore exchange controls and to regulate direct overseas investment. ... For

all these reasons, British withdrawal from the Community is the right policy for Britain – to be completed well within the lifetime of the parliament.[72]

The result, too, lacked ambiguity. Labour suffered a catastrophic defeat, and was very nearly pushed into third place by the Liberal/SDP Alliance, as the table shows. 1983 was a watershed year. Thatcher acquired an overall majority of 144. The Left, who had devised the programme, would not enjoy the same influence in Labour circles for another thirty years.

Party	Votes	Seats	Change	UK vote share (%)
Conservative	13,012,316	397	+58	42.4
Labour	8,456,934	209	–60	27.6
Liberal/SDP	7,780,949	23	+12	25.4
Others	1,420,938	21	+5	4.6

What then of the SDP? It was evident to all concerned that, once the 1979 election had been lost, there would be turmoil within the Labour Party, and turmoil duly ensued. The Right of the party responded to these developments in various ways, but it soon became apparent that the Jenkinsites would find it difficult to remain within the party. In November 1979, Jenkins, then still president of the European Commission, delivered the Dimbleby lecture. In this he deplored the fractious state of British politics and called for a 'new grouping'. Jenkins was also at this stage exploring potential links with the Liberal Party, for whom he clearly felt more affinity than for many of his old Labour colleagues.

At the same time, Shirley Williams, Bill Rodgers and David Owen (who had all held Cabinet office under Callaghan) were expressing discontent with the direction of Labour policy. The so-called 'Gang of Three' issued a joint statement in June 1980 and an open letter in August of that year. Taken together, these documents raised, in coded terms, the possible creation of a new party. These developments took on further momentum when Foot defeated Healey for the leadership of the Labour Party in November 1980: many right-wing Labour MPs were 'appalled'. In January 1981, the 'Gang of Four' (Jenkins and the Gang of Three) issued the Limehouse Declaration and set up the Council for Social Democracy. The SDP was formally launched in March, with a number of Labour MPs defecting to the new party.

The next year, until March 1982, was an *annus mirabilis* for the new party. The prevailing political climate was favourable. For the first six months, Labour was locked in bitter internal struggle as Benn and Healey contested the deputy leadership. The Thatcher government was subject to its own travails, both internal and external. The SDP took full advantage of these opportunities, scoring remarkable by-election victories at Crosby for Williams and Hillhead for Jenkins.

It was obvious that there was not room for two competing centrist parties, and the SDP therefore entered into an 'Alliance' with the Liberals, ratified by the latter's conference in September 1981. The Alliance fought the June 1983 election, with Jenkins as 'Prime Minister Designate'. It secured an impressive vote share, but relatively few seats (see above). Many of the defectors lost their seats. The hoped-for realignment of the centre had not quite taken place, and the Conservatives, aided by the patriotic fervour that flowed from the Falklands War of 1982, very substantially improved their position from the dark days of 1981 (and indeed in comparison to 1979).[73]

What did the SDP believe in? How did a party founded by the leader of the Jenkinsites approach the European question, and how did that approach relate to the remainder of its policies? E.H.H. Green, a leading scholar of Thatcherism, recalled that 'in 1982 a leading intellectual in the SDP, tongue firmly in cheek, informed this author that "We want the policies that failed before"'. Even removing tongue from cheek, there was an element of truth in this *aperçu*. The SDP's leaders had been in power, on and off, from 1964 to 1979. They were, in the main, unapologetic about the policies that they had pursued: not those that had been promised or attempted or considered, but those that had in fact been deployed.[74]

Their break with Labour arose principally from three matters. The first was the rise of the Left, and, in particular, the constitutional changes that the Left promoted after 1979, which served to marginalise the Right of the party. The second was the trend in the party away from close relations with the USA, and in the direction of unilateralism. The SDP's founders had been Gaitskellites before they were Jenkinsites, and they would fight, fight and fight again to defend the UK's commitment to NATO and nuclear defence. And, of course, there was Europe. The Gang of Four had all been longstanding supporters of the EEC and they had voted with the Heath government in October 1971. Indeed, when the Gang of Three made their first intervention in June 1980, the subject matter was Europe: they condemned any decision to leave as 'irresponsible, opportunistic and short-sighted'. With a note of menace, they concluded that 'there are some of us who will not accept a choice between socialism and Europe. We will choose them both.'

As the reference to 'socialism' suggests, the SDP was, these three crucial matters apart, generally comfortable with the record of what would eventually come to be known as 'Old Labour'. In his Dimbleby lecture, Jenkins had protested against the 'queasy rides on the ideological big dipper' that the two main parties were offering. In practice, this amounted to a plea to carry on with, rather than to rip up, the post-war model. This found natural resonance with the Liberals who, for example, supported incomes policy and suggested that the boundary between the public and private sectors should remain unchanged. The Liberals had, after all, entered into a pact in 1977 to keep the Callaghan government in power, much to the disgust of Hayek: 'a party that keeps a socialist government in power clearly has lost all title to the name "Liberal".'[75]

The Alliance naturally, in the words of its 1983 manifesto, proclaimed that it was 'wholly committed to continuing UK membership of the

European Community'. Indeed, it embraced further developments within the EEC, such as the UK becoming a full member of the EMS. For the Alliance, the Europeans had lessons to teach the British. There could be less 'divisive industrial relations', if we emulated 'our European partners [who] have long traditions of participation and co-operation backed by legislation'. However, this Europeanism sat within a broader approach of commending much of what the UK had itself achieved since the war and could continue to achieve if it jumped off the big dipper.

The SDP and its members, unsurprisingly, supported the mixed economy, full employment and Keynesian economic management. They thought, in the words of the Limehouse declaration, that 'our economy needs a healthy public sector and a healthy private sector without frequent frontier changes'. The 1983 manifesto was both a trip down memory lane and also a portent of what Corbyn's Labour Party would offer to the British people more than thirty years later:

> We propose a carefully devised and costed jobs programme aimed at re-ducing unemployment by 1 million over two years. … The Programme has three points:
>
>> Fiscal and Financial Policies for Growth
>>
>> Direct Action to provide jobs
>>
>> An Incomes Strategy that will stick…
>
> We must get away from the incessant and damaging warfare over the ownership of industry and switch the emphasis to how well it performs. Thus we will retain the present position of British Aerospace but will not privatise British Telecom's main network nor sell off British Air-ways…
>
> We propose a steady expansion of local Council and housing asso-ciation building programmes.

Conclusions

In one sense, this period was a very positive one for the UK's involvement with the EEC. The British people were offered the opportunity to leave on two occasions and turned these opportunities down resoundingly. After a little delay, direct elections were held. The governing parties, both Labour from 1975 to 1979 and the Conservatives from 1979 to 1983, seemed happy enough with the UK's position, despite some skirmishing over the budget. The Left, the principal advocates of departure, were very much in retreat: symbolically, Benn even lost his own seat in 1983. It is, however, worth noting that Britain refused to participate in the principal European development of this era, the EMS.

This was, however, a fragile, even terminal, era for the post-war model and the values of social democracy. Labour had moved left and the Conservatives rightwards: both parties seemed reluctant to embrace the policies on which they had stood in the 1950s and 1960s. Thatcherism, which had endured many problems after 1979, now seemed triumphant. Social democracy was not quite dead. The SDP had emerged as its unrepentant champions. There remained many social democrats within Labour: even at the 1983 election, the leading Labour figures (such as Healey, Hattersley and Shore) were ex-ministers from the Right of the party. Labour as a whole remained committed to Keynesianism and full employment. It was the SDP, however, who presented to the electorate, in its purest form, the idea that the path pursued since 1945 remained the correct path and that this required, among other things, unswerving commitment to Europe.

Few would have predicted in 1983 that a Tory government would eventually attempt to lead the UK out of the EEC. It was less hard to foresee that a Thatcher government, having put its domestic and international enemies to the sword, might next turn its attention to what remained of the social democratic model. That there might be a conflict between this enterprise and the UK's engagement with Europe was not self-evident. Indeed, most Conservatives, and the Tory press, continued to regard opposition to membership as the preserve of the dangerous socialist Left. It was, perhaps, only *The Spectator* that seemed to see the

> profound and very real division between those who favour an eventual goal of [EMU] ... as a penultimate step to European federation, and those who, even if they accept the Community and British membership, would wish to see it as a free trade area ... within which member states' currencies must float freely if those states are to operate sound monetary policies.[76]

What was more obvious by 1983, however, was that the British model of social democracy was in headlong retreat. This model may never have been notable for its ideological coherence, but its advocates had pursued this path doggedly since 1945. Now there were many within the Labour and Conservative Parties who thought that a fresh approach was required. The Liberal/SDP Alliance urged 'the policies that failed before', but they had themselves failed to make the necessary breakthrough at the 1983 election.

5 The Tories Turn Against Europe, 1983–2005

We have not successfully rolled back the frontiers of the state in Britain, only to see them re-imposed at a European level with a European super-state exercising a new dominance from Brussels.

(Margaret Thatcher, September 1988)[1]

[Eurosceptic Tories] think that Europe is their secret electoral weapon, despite an abundance of evidence that it is their curse.

(Michael Portillo, June 2004)[2]

Introduction

In 1983, the Conservatives remained the party of Europe, almost without exception dedicated to continued and deepened membership. Indeed, it was the Tories who fought and won the election of that year in defence of that idea and in opposition to a Labour Party determined to take the UK out of the EEC. Within a decade, the Tories had become a party defined by violent disagreement over Europe. The term 'Eurosceptic' was in common use and was synonymous with a substantial body of Conservative opinion. How did this change come about?

The explanation lies within the tension to which Thatcher referred in her Bruges speech, quoted above. Thatcherism had, by 1988, conquered almost all in the domestic sphere. British social democracy was in tatters. Thatcher's concern was that the UK's involvement within the EEC might partially reverse this process. In expressing this concern in 1988,

Thatcher was relatively isolated within her party, and this isolation contributed to her downfall in 1990. However, within a few years this view had gained ground, and by the mid-1990s it was the pro-Europeans, such as Kenneth Clarke and Michael Heseltine, who were isolated. Euroscepticism became the default Conservative position.

To understand these developments, the period from 1983 to 2005 can usefully be divided into four sub-periods. The first is from 1983 to 1987, during which the UK under Thatcher appeared to move in a pro-European direction. The second runs from 1987 to 1990, when Thatcher and her most loyal lieutenants turned against Europe. The third period is from the fall of Thatcher in 1990 to the emphatic defeat of the Conservatives in 1997, a time when the party became increasingly defined by its hostile, and bitterly divided, attitude to Europe. Finally, from 1997 onwards, the Tories became the party not of Europe but of Euroscepticism.

To put these developments in context, it is necessary, however, first to understand the economic and social creed that dominated British political life in the 1980s and to which Thatcher gave her name.

Thatcherism

Few historians would deny that the Conservative election victory in 1979 represented a turning point in British post-war politics. There was 'a watershed in post-war economic policy in which the post-war consensus … broke down, full employment ceased to be the overriding object of policy, and control of inflation became the abiding preoccupation'. Although, this change began to develop before 1979, the Thatcher governments pursued this policy (often labelled 'monetarism') with vigour. In practice, monetarism meant high interest rates and a strong pound, both intended to exert downward pressure on inflation. Prices and incomes policy, a staple governmental tool for economic management, disappeared. Indeed, the whole notion of tripartism between government, industry and the unions vanished. As Keith Joseph, Thatcher's intellectual guide, put it, 'governments can't direct the economy in a free society … what governments … should do is to create conditions in which business flourishes.'[3]

Both the specific tools of policy, such as high interest rates, and the general ambition that governments should withdraw from economic dirigisme, contributed to the high level of unemployment that persisted through the 1980s and beyond. Low inflation was the central aim. Full employment ceased to be a goal of policy at all. Table 5.1 illustrates this and shows, further, how this policy mix persisted into the New Labour years after 1997.

Table 5.1 UK unemployment/inflation rate (average for selected years)[4]

Year	Unemployment %	Inflation %
1964	1.7	4.8
1969	2.5	4.7
1974	2.6	19.1
1979	5.7	17.2
1984	11.5	4.6
1989	6.3	5.4
1994	9.4	2.1
1999	6.2	1.2
2004	4.8	1.6

The state was, therefore, no longer directing the economy or seeking to achieve full employment. However, as the Bruges speech made clear, the aim of Thatcherism was to cut the state down to size in other respects. The Conservative governments of 1979 to 1997 carried out a huge programme of privatisation, selling back into private ownership most of the 'commanding heights' that the Attlee government had nationalised. Telecoms, gas, electricity, the railways and the mines were all denationalised. However, the most significant privatisation of all was probably the sale of council housing under the policy of 'Right to Buy', introduced in 1980. Between 1980 and 2007, there were 2.5 million right-to-buy sales, and by the latter year, there were only about 2.6m council dwellings left in the UK. The proportion of local authority tenants fell from 29% to 10%.[5]

These changes were important economically, but they were intended to, and did, have a major social effect as well. Workers in privatised industries, and former tenants who owned their own homes, were, it was thought, much more likely to be supportive of a culture of enterprise. If there were any doubt on this score, the Thatcher governments also sought to encourage this culture with tax reforms. These reforms placed much more of the fiscal burden on indirect taxes, especially VAT, and aimed to improve incentives. Table 5.2 shows how the changes in relation to marginal rates of taxation were particularly striking.

Table 5.2 Highest marginal rates of income tax, 1973–2015, selected years[6]

Year	Rate	IIS	Total
1973/4	75%	15%	90%
1974/5	83%	15%	98%
1979/80	60%	15%	75%
1984/5	60%	–	60%
1988/9	40%	–	40%
1998/9	40%	–	40%
2010/11	50%	–	50%
2013/14	45%	–	45%

Incentives for individuals were a central tenet of Thatcherism, but, by the same token, collective action, especially by the trade unions, was strongly discouraged. Legislation curtailed union rights very sharply. In Robert Taylor's assessment (and that of many others) the unions were 'tamed'. The Thatcher government took on the miners in a bitter, year-long dispute in 1984/5. The miners were defeated, and, thereafter, successful large-scale disputes were a rarity.[7]

Thatcherism had its limits. There were some in her entourage, in particular the free-market zealots of the IEA, who advocated a massive reduction in the size of the state. This would have involved the withdrawal of government from public provision of health services, pensions and even education. Although there is evidence that Thatcher personally had sympathy for some of these ideas, Conservative governments made little but gestures in this direction. As a result, total outturn public spending for fiscal 1978/79 was £371bn (at 2015 prices), but this rose to £421bn by 1989/90 (and £742bn by 2014/15).[8]

The state rolled on, rather than being rolled back. As Nigel Lawson was obliged to accept, 'the Conservative Governments of 1979–92 cannot claim to have reduced the burden of tax as a proportion of GDP … the tax take was in fact a couple of percentage points higher in 1991–92 than it had been in 1978–79, the previous Labour Government's last year'. Lawson found this 'understandably disappointing'; he might have added that this was particularly so given the windfall benefits that the Thatcher/Major governments enjoyed of North Sea oil, privatisation receipts and council house sales.[9]

There are two important things to note about this near total triumph of Thatcherism (a more apt term in many ways than neoliberalism: a nineteenth-century liberal would scarcely have warmed to the size and role of the state under Thatcher). The first is that New Labour very largely accepted this direction of policy after 1997. The second is that Thatcherism was, or, at least, became, uncontroversial within the Conservative Party.

The point about New Labour, of course, was that they were not Old Labour. New Labour did not, therefore, embrace a full employment commitment, or reintroduce the very high marginal tax rates of the post-war period, or renationalise the utilities, or restrict the right to buy. Above all, Labour, after 1997, kept a very marked distance from the unions, who had, of course, given birth to the party in the first place. As John Monks (General Secretary of the TUC from 1993 until 2003) recalled:

> After [Blair had] been elected Leader of the Labour Party after the death of John Smith, '94, he came into the office and said 'Is this the TUC's trophy room?' I said 'What do you mean, "trophy room"?' He said 'I'm looking around for the heads of Wilson, Heath and Callaghan, and you're not going to get my head on the wall.' I said 'Congratulations on getting elected.'[10]

As far as the Conservatives were concerned, there were aspects of Thatcherism that caused disquiet, especially in the first term and particularly in relation to monetarism and the high levels of unemployment that flowed from it. Conservative politicians from earlier generations thought that the Thatcher governments had abandoned the previous Tory commitment to 'the post-war economic and social consensus in which the basic goal of economic policy was full employment'. Heath complained that 'the complacent acceptance of mass unemployment, as an instrument for controlling inflation, was repellent'.[11]

However, despite the traumas that monetarism inflicted, these sentiments were very much in the minority after 1983. Conservative electoral triumph, despite high levels of unemployment, rather undermined the position of the economic dissenters. Moreover, most of the other planks of Thatcherism commanded wide support in the party. There were few Conservatives, of any persuasion, who were willing to criticise privatisation or tax cuts for the rich or the sale of council houses or the marginalisation of the unions. These policies were pursued with as much vigour by the Major government of 1990 to 1997 as the Thatcher administrations of 1979 to 1990. After all, 'the big bang was the dispute with the miners, which was carefully prepared for and conducted by Peter Walker. A man than whom there weren't any wetter.'[12]

1983–1987: Harmony?

The period of the second Thatcher government was, in many ways, both the high-water mark of Thatcherism and an era in which the UK's involvement with Europe became steadily deeper. A pro-European party put its anti-European opponents to the sword domestically and embraced developments in the EEC with apparent enthusiasm. How did this come about, and how does it sit with the broader picture of divergence between a neoliberal UK and a social democratic Europe? There were, in truth, two trends in this period. One saw the UK both promoting and embracing the development of the single market in Europe. However, alongside this there were the first glimmerings of tension between British advocacy of free markets within nation states and European ideas of social solidarity and European unity.

The second Thatcher term got off to a positive start at the Fontainebleau summit in 1984. The issue of the budget rebate, which had overshadowed British relations with the EEC in the first term, was finally resolved, and on terms broadly satisfactory to the UK. There was some sniping from right-wingers who had never warmed to Europe, such as *The Spectator*, but party sentiment was generally favourable.[13]

The broader thrust of British policy was to promote competition, free trade and deregulation. For example, the government submitted to the Fontainebleau summit a document entitled 'Europe – the future', which advocated freeing up European markets. This would see the 'internal barriers to business and trade come down [so that] the genuine common market in goods and services which is envisaged by the Treaty of Rome' could emerge. The next year, at Stresa, Howe (as Foreign Secretary) put forward a similar paper. He subsequently announced an 'action programme' for the forthcoming British presidency, intended to 'mobilize and energize the community to realize its full potential for generating jobs and prosperity'. This would occur through a freer internal market, the liberalisation of transport and more flexible labour markets.[14]

These efforts culminated in the Milan European Council of 1985, which agreed to take further steps towards the completion of the single market by 1992. This led to the adoption in 1986 of the SEA. The UK strongly supported and promoted the SEA. Indeed, the relevant Commissioner, Arthur Cockfield, 'the architect of the SEA', had previously been a Tory minister. The SEA set in motion steps towards the completion of the single market by 1992, but, in so doing, it required the Member States to accept a degree of common regulation and qualified majority voting on matters necessary to achieve that objective.[15]

There is no doubt that Thatcher and her government strongly supported the SEA. Chris Patten recalled that 'the views that are now associated with her on Europe are very different from what she was saying … when we were pioneers of the single market … when Norman Tebbit was being sent around the House of Commons to threaten and bully people into voting for more qualified majority voting'. Charles Moore, her sympathetic official biographer, does not doubt that Thatcher supported the SEA at the time, but thinks she was 'self-deceiving' about the loss of sovereignty and excessive regulation that the single market would involve. Indeed, according to Moore, Thatcher faithfully toed the Heath line on Europe until 1986, since 'it was only later that she worked out … what she thought'.[16]

With hindsight, Nick Crowson is surely right to see the SEA as 'the fracture point of the Thatcherite monetarist alliance'. Eurosceptics on the Right would come to see the SEA as a 'tool for further integration'. They claimed that, under the guise of perfecting the single market, the Commission would seek to take on powers to rival national governments and would use those powers to pursue a federalist agenda, in hot pursuit of Christian Democratic or even social democratic policies.[17]

However, it is not difficult to discern these tensions even in the relatively harmonious times when the SEA was under discussion. After all, in 1983 Thatcher had agreed (only days after her emphatic second election victory) to a 'Solemn Declaration on European Union' at Stuttgart. This did not seem entirely Thatcherite in tone:

> The Heads of State or Government of the Member States of the European Communities, meeting within the European Council, resolved to continue the work begun on the basis of the Treaties of Paris and Rome and to create a united Europe ... determined to work together to promote democracy on the basis of the fundamental rights recognized in the constitutions and laws of the Member States, in the European Convention for the Protection of Human Rights and the European Social Charter, notably freedom, equality and social justice, convinced that, in order to resolve the serious economic problems facing the Member States, the Community must strengthen its cohesion, regain its dynamism and intensify its action in areas hitherto insufficiently explored, resolved to accord a high priority to the Community's social progress and in particular to the problem of employment by the development of a European social policy ... have adopted the following: 1 Objectives 1.1 The Heads of State or Government, on the basis of an awareness of a common destiny and the wish to affirm the European identity, confirm their commitment to progress towards an ever closer union among the peoples and Member States of the European Community ... 1.3 In order to achieve ever increasing solidarity and joint action, the construction of Europe must be more clearly oriented towards its general political objectives, more efficient decision-making procedures, greater coherence and close coordination between the different branches of activity, and the search for common policies in all areas of common interest, both within the Community and in relation to third countries...[18]

One might dismiss this as grandiose rhetoric, but, when it came to practical politics, British Conservatives seemed more and more out of step with their supposed allies in Europe. For example, in June 1986, Kenneth Clarke (a junior minister within the Department of Employment, headed by the uber-Thatcherite Lord Young) blocked a proposal for statutory paternity leave for fathers at a meeting of the council of employment ministers. The British position on these issues was evident from a document tabled later the same year, 'Employment Growth in the 1990s: A Strategy for the Labour Market', which advocated flexible labour markets.[19]

Likewise, the December 1986 meeting of the European Council in London was only able to agree a communiqué on the basis that there was commitment to dialogue with 'the social partners'. Thatcher opposed this, but her ostensible European associates on the Right, such as Helmut Kohl, the West German Chancellor, insisted. *The Financial Times* commented that 'the debate emphasised the divide between the British Government's economic approach and that of most of the rest of the community'. At the beginning of 1987, the Commission put forward a package of proposed reforms to embody a 'social common market' approach. These included greatly increased support for regional aid and job training, with this to be paid for through a new system of funding based on relative GDPs. When these reforms were discussed at the June European Council in Brussels, Thatcher was intransigent and isolated in a 11 to 1 vote. Howe was said to have been 'shaking with anger' at her approach.[20]

Howe's fury illustrated the fact that, in the highest echelons of the Tory Party, there remained considerable enthusiasm for the EEC and for the Heathite approach to Europe. Thus, in 1984, one could find Jim Prior (a close associate of Heath who had been demoted by Thatcher and was soon to leave the government) deprecating a draft of the Conservative Manifesto for Europe on the basis that 'I don't believe that we need to go quite as far as this document presently does in giving quite such an overwhelming emphasis on fighting for British interests at the expense of the potential which the Community offers to all its members if we were able to widen the fields of co-operation'. Similarly, Howe was concerned about the isolation of British Conservative MEPs in the European Parliament, and keen that the party should 'establish a closer working relationship with the Christian Democrats, who are the mainstream centre-right parties throughout much of Europe'. This was all very well but, on practical issues where the 'social common market' reared its head, it was apparent that British Conservatives and European Christian Democrats by now had very different instincts, whatever they may have thought in the 1970s. This gulf would only widen with time.[21]

Indeed, this cosy prospectus of co-operation and Christian Democracy did not have universal appeal within the Tory Party. Here one needs to go back a little to understand the tensions that were beginning to emerge in the mid-1980s. There had always been some Conservatives who were strongly opposed to British membership of the EEC, primarily on nationalist and sovereignty grounds. However, they had been much marginalised by the Heath government, the result of the referendum and the defection of Powell, their most charismatic figure.

Nonetheless, by 1980, there were sufficient Tory MPs of this persuasion to form a 'Conservative European Reform Group'. The group had the initial support of 29 MPs (of a Tory contingent of 339). Its statement of aims was uncompromising and, on analysis, incompatible with continued membership:

> We believe in the urgent need for fundamental reform of the Common Market in the interest of securing genuine European co-operation based on the partnership of nation-states … we believe that there is an urgent need to adopt policies directed to: … the reassertion of the power of national Parliaments over the institutions of the Community.[22]

At this stage, senior ministers were dismissive of the group's concerns. Its 'objectives … are clearly beyond the possibility of being negotiable', according to the Party Chairman, Lord Thorneycroft. Or, as Ian Gilmour who, as Lord Privy Seal was in effect Deputy Foreign Secretary, more robustly put it, these objectives were 'incompatible with our continued membership of the Community. It is, therefore, a dud prospectus.'[23]

Dud or otherwise, Thatcher herself took the view that it was necessary to deal gently with the group. For example, she asked Gilmour to tone down the draft of a letter to the group on the basis that it was 'a little too confrontational' and she needed to 'keep the party together'. Thatcher perhaps had a point, since Gilmour's draft was provocative, telling them that 'any chance of success would be vitiated if the Government's commitment to the Community itself were in doubt. That is why I believe your approach is misconceived, and likely to impede rather than encourage reforms in the Community which will benefit Britain.'[24]

Ian Gow (Thatcher's PPS) observed in 1980 that 'this issue will not go away'. This prediction proved more accurate than many. Thatcher remained anxious to propitiate rather than confront the group, partly because she shared many of their instincts and partly owing to the need to 'keep the party together'. As to the latter consideration, there is at least some evidence that by the early 1980s Euroscepticism was on the march among the Tory grassroots. For example, at the 1981 party conference, Powell was 'given a hero's welcome by more than 400 representatives' as he shared a platform with eight Tory MPs and urged withdrawal from the EEC.[25]

Against that background, it is not surprising that the Conservative European Reform Group once more attracted attention in 1986, when the government was seeking parliamentary approval for the SEA. By then, it had the support of some 70 MPs (of a Conservative contingent now totalling 397), and 'an organization in the constituencies including some 24 Young Conservative groups'. Thatcher met the group's leaders in April 1986 and reassured them as to the government's intentions. Her message was that she had secured a good deal for the UK at Fontainebleau and that the SEA, and other developments within the EEC, did not give cause for alarm. The group was itself alarmist, stressing 'the dangers of the further undermining of our national sovereignty through the surrender of powers to the E.E.C.' and its concern that the SEA would ensure 'that this process will continue'. More broadly, they said, in words that foreshadowed the Bruges speech two years later, that 'their vision of the Community was of a free association of nation states, not a bureaucratic institution dedicated to imposing uniformity'.[26]

Thatcher may have felt it necessary to meet these Eurosceptic MPs as part of her role in keeping the party together, but other senior Conservatives took a more relaxed approach. In particular, Howe, Foreign Secretary from 1983 to 1989, was a striking case. Always a European enthusiast, Howe had steered the 1972 Act through the Commons and had also been central as Shadow Chancellor and then Chancellor from 1975 to 1983 in developing and implementing domestic Thatcherism. He saw no tension between these two lines of thought, and was dismissive of those on his own side who thought differently. In Howe's view it was necessary to co-operate in Europe in order to achieve the domestic policy objectives that the Conservatives advocated. As he told the Commons when commending the SEA:

> We are not talking about the declaration or proclamation of a United States of Europe or about vague political or legal goals. We are talking about practical steps towards the unity that is essential if Europe is to maintain and enhance its economic and political position in a harshly competitive world. These are steps to which all the member Governments are ready to agree. No doubt the House will hear a good deal from some of my hon. Friends and from some Opposition Members about the fearful constitutional fantasies that preoccupy them. Those are terrors for children; not for me. I hope that the House will put them aside. In a world where no European power can any longer stand on its own, our national goals can be achieved only in co-operation with our Community partners.[27]

This relatively complacent tone may have stemmed in part from the low profile that the European issue had with the wider public, who did not seem to share the 'constitutional fantasies that preoccupy' Eurosceptic MPs and did not appear to think in 1986 (as many would in 2016) that the UK was a 'power [which could] stand on its own'. At the 1987 general election, Europe was scarcely an issue. Labour was by now moving away from a policy of withdrawal. The SEA was not contentious. The Conservatives were re-elected, with a slightly reduced majority of

102. Few would then have predicted that, within three years, the three most senior members of the government (Thatcher, Howe and Lawson) would all have departed over matters related to Europe.[28]

1987–1990: Bruges and beyond

After this election victory, the position of the Conservatives generally, and Thatcher in particular, appeared unassailable. Labour had distanced itself from the Left and run an attractive campaign under a young new leader in Neil Kinnock. Nonetheless, the Conservatives had won overwhelmingly. In relation to Europe, they appeared to have a very strong hand. The principle of membership was now widely accepted in the UK, save for a few partisans of Left and Right still fighting the battles of the 1970s. Within the EEC, the UK's formula of co-operation to promote competition seemed to be encapsulated in the SEA. Yet within three years, Lawson had resigned as Chancellor over the ERM; Howe had been demoted from the Foreign Office for being too pro-European and then resigned from the government over European issues; and Thatcher herself had fallen, despite her electoral success, as her party feared popular rejection of her approach, not least over Europe.

How did all this come about, and what does it tell us about the wider relationship between British attitudes towards Europe and domestic social and economic policy? At first sight, the fall of Thatcher in 1990 might suggest that the Conservatives had begun to repent of their flirtation with Thatcherism and therefore decided to embrace something closer to Christian Democracy. In fact, this period encompassed at least two European narratives for the party. The first concerned the technical but important issue of membership of the ERM. The second was a much broader question as to the relationship between British and European social policy. On both matters, Thatcher found herself in a small minority in her own party at the time. However, if one took the slightly longer view, her position – that the UK should retain absolute independence for both its currency and its social policy – proved to be the prevailing Conservative view.

These two narratives, of course, were intertwined and were further complicated by differences over domestic issues, such as the poll tax, and by personal relationships. Nonetheless, it is right to say that by 1988 at the latest, Howe, Lawson, and a substantial number of other Conservatives, were strongly committed to the UK joining the ERM of the EMS. Howe, but not Lawson, wanted to go further and see the UK join the single currency. Some influential Conservatives shared this ambition, but many had reservations. Of course, as its opponents pointed out, a single currency necessarily involved considerable further integration. Thatcher, on the other hand, was opposed root and branch to the ERM, the single currency and further integration.[29]

The ERM issue had a lengthy gestation. By 1985, Lawson, Howe and other senior ministers had become convinced that the UK should join the ERM quite soon. A meeting of these senior figures in November 1985 arrived at a consensus to this effect, with the important exception of Thatcher, who said that she would resign if the UK joined the ERM. In the run-up to the 1987 election, Lawson once more prepared the ground and thought that Thatcher shared the commitment to join. After the election was won, he discovered that she remained strongly against: he was 'dismayed … she had simply been stringing me along in everything she said before the election, which obviously had not been uttered in good faith'. Relations between Thatcher and her Chancellor never recovered.[30]

While the British government was dithering, the EEC was moving forwards on the single currency. In 1988 the Hanover European Council agreed to set up the Delors Committee on the future of the EMS. The Committee reported in April 1989, recommending a three-stage process for monetary union (which the British government promptly rejected). At the June 1989 Madrid European Council, Thatcher appeared to adopt a more conciliatory line on the ERM, agreeing that the UK would join when certain conditions were met. However, any suggestion that the line was being softened was somewhat undermined by her refusal to set a date for entry. At the same time, the UK Treasury was developing plans for a 'hard ECU', a common currency that parties and countries would be free to use but which would not replace national currencies.[31]

At this stage, some little local difficulties arose. In July 1989, Thatcher demoted Howe from the Foreign Office, replacing him with John Major, who was thought more pliable, not least on European issues. In October 1989, Lawson resigned: the breaking point in his case was the malign influence of Thatcher's personal economic adviser, Alan Walters, who was vehemently opposed to the UK's membership of the ERM. There had, clearly, been a complete breakdown in relations between Lawson and Thatcher, and a fundamental disagreement over the ERM. It is important, at this point, to note that, personal matters aside, the policy difference was quite a slim one. Lawson's argument was for what Howe later dubbed 'Thatcherism on a European scale', but with the UK inside the ERM:

> Full United Kingdom membership of the EMS … would signally en-
> hance the credibility of our anti-inflationary resolve in general and the
> role of the exchange rate discipline in particular, and thus underpin the
> medium-term financial strategy … there is also a vital political dimen-
> sion.
>
> As my right hon. Friend the Prime Minister made clear in her Bruges
> speech, Britain's destiny lies in Europe as a member of the European
> Community – and let me be clear that I am speaking, as she speaks, of a
> Europe of nation states. Within that context, it is vital that we maximise
> Britain's influence in the Community so as to ensure that it becomes the
> liberal free-market Europe in which we on the Conservative Benches so
> firmly believe. I have little doubt that we will not be able to exert that
> influence effectively, and successfully provide the leadership, as long as
> we remain largely outside the EMS.[32]

Ironically, Thatcher's battle against the ERM proved in vain. Walters too resigned. Major replaced Lawson as Chancellor and himself began to agitate for the UK to join. In October 1990, the UK finally did join the system. By now, Thatcher's political position was much weakened both at home and abroad. At the Rome European Council in October 1990, she found herself outvoted 11 to 1 over proposals to move to the second stage of the Delors plan by January 1994. Her position over European issues was made weaker by the fact that the majority of the Cabinet no longer supported her on the single currency. In November 1990, Howe dramatically resigned, telling the Commons that 'the time has come for others to consider their own response to the tragic conflict of loyalties with which I have myself wrestled for perhaps too long'. His resignation speech precipitated a leadership contest, in which Major replaced Thatcher.[33]

Widespread Conservative support for the ERM, and the ruthless disposal of Thatcher, might suggest a more general Tory enthusiasm for European integration. As will be seen in discussing the second, social policy, strand this would be misleading. A number of factors led to Thatcher's demise, of which Europe was only one. Even in the context of debates over Europe, support for the ERM did not necessarily connote acquiescence in a Delors-style social project. As Lawson made clear in a speech at Chatham House in January 1989, one could argue for joining the ERM as an anti-inflationary mechanism and 'as an agreement between independent sovereign states', while also promoting 'the vision of a deregulated, free-market, open Europe'.[34]

What then of broader social policy? In this respect, 1988 proved to be a turning point. For Thatcher, 'the agenda in Europe began to take an increasingly unwelcome shape' during that year. In July, Delors told the European Parliament that 'we are not going to manage to take all the decisions needed between now and 1995 unless we see the beginnings of European government ... ten years hence, 80% of our economic legislation, and perhaps even our fiscal and social legislation as well, will be of Community origin'.[35]

Thatcher determined to respond to this challenge in a set-piece speech, the text of which became the subject of much debate within government. The Foreign Office pressed upon her a conventional draft, or what her confidant, Alan Clark, described as 'a really loathsome text, wallowing in rejection of our own national identity'. Thatcher, however, wished to 'press ahead with the Bruges notes [which she had drafted] virtually unchanged, in spite of FCO complaints'. These complaints were strongly expressed, Howe sending her detailed comments on the draft:

> The Secretary of State's overall comment is that there are some plain and fundamental errors in the draft and that it tends to view the world as though we had not adhered to any of the treaties. Nor does the speech accommodate the diversity of visions of Europe – even in one country ... a stronger Europe does not mean the creation of a new European superstate but does, has and will require the sacrifice of political independence and the rights of national parliaments. That is inherent in the treaties.[36]

Nothing daunted, Thatcher made her speech at Bruges on 20 September 1988. She rejected Howe's advice as to what was 'inherent in the treaties'. Whatever the treaties might say, for her Europe was about 'willing and active cooperation between independent sovereign states ... to try to suppress nationhood and concentrate power at the centre of a European conglomerate would be highly damaging and would jeopardise the objectives we seek to achieve'. The purpose of this limited cooperation was 'policies which encourage enterprise', for 'enterprise is the key. The basic framework is there: the Treaty of Rome itself was intended as a Charter for Economic Liberty. But that is not how it has always been read, still less applied.'[37]

The speech soon became almost a sacred text for a large section of the Tory Party. The *Daily Mail* praised 'the true British spirit' Thatcher had shown. A right-wing commentator in the *Daily Telegraph* thought that 'most younger Tories are happy to be Little Englanders, especially now that England does not seem so little'. The Bruges Group was established in February 1989 'to promote the idea of a less centralised European structure than that emerging in Brussels'. Later that year, Powell, addressing a meeting at the Conservative conference, observed that he found himself 'less on the fringe of [the] party than ... for 20 years'.[38]

From 1988 onwards, and despite the fall of Thatcher in 1990, the themes explored at Bruges became a central part of the anti-EEC narrative. Britain was an exceptional country, where (in the words of Lord Young, Secretary of State for Trade and Industry towards the end of the Thatcher era) 'we have shown ... that deregulation, openness and competition are central to economic success'. Europe should concentrate on promoting competition and free trade, and eschew the 'social dimension', since 'social gains are achieved not by legislation but by the operations of a healthy economy'. Above all, the EEC works best when 'following our lead ... [as] a deregulated, liberalised Europe'.[39]

There was, therefore, emerging by the late 1980s a sharp conflict, at least in many Tory minds, between European dirigisme and British economic liberalism. However, this struggle was not just about economics. Conservative Eurosceptics conjured up an alarming vision of the European superstate, bent on 'centralised interference ... [with] the unashamed desire to subvert the basis of the new Conservative creed of the predominance of market forces'. Thatcher herself, only days before her enforced departure, treated the Commons to a comprehensive denunciation of Delors and all his works:

> The Commission wants to increase its powers. Yes, it is a non-elected body and I do not want the Commission to increase its powers. ... The President of the Commission, Mr. Delors, said at a press conference the other day that he wanted the European Parliament to be the democratic body of the Community, he wanted the Commission to be the Executive and he wanted the Council of Ministers to be the Senate. No. No. No.[40]

Indeed, by the late 1980s many Conservatives had discovered that they were out of sympathy not only with the EEC as an institution but, more generally, with European economic and social policies, even as pursued by their ostensible Centre Right allies in Europe. The love affair of the 1970s with Christian Democracy and Ordoliberals had cooled. Affection for all things German had turned to something close to hostility. It turned out that, for Thatcherites, the German model was not what they had intended after all: it was a recipe for corporatism and regulation. Nicholas Ridley, a minister close to Thatcher, went so far as to say of proposals to confer increased powers on the Commission, 'you might just as well give [sovereignty] to Adolf Hitler, frankly'. EMU was 'all a German racket designed to take over the whole of Europe'. To emphasise the point, the Eurosceptic *Spectator*, in which this interview appeared, illustrated the article with two separate cartoons in which Helmut Kohl was depicted with a Führer-style moustache. The interviewer, Dominic Lawson, mischievously 'imagined ... that I could hear a woman's voice with the very faintest hint of Lincolnshire, saying "Yes, Nick, that's right, they are trying to take over everything."' Certainly, there was little love lost personally or philosophically between Thatcher and Kohl. Their understanding of Centre Right politics was fundamentally different. As a commentator observed:

> Kohl's Christian Democracy was close to the 'one nation' Toryism that Thatcher sought to destroy. Kohl believed that Thatcher was a Manchester liberal dedicated to the Ellbogengesellschaft – a society in which people elbow each other out of the way. His was the path of Mitbestimmung, in which workers and managers co-operate and in which a generous welfare state protects people from change. This was anathema to Thatcher, particularly when it manifested itself in European legislation.[41]

From this point onwards, the press, which, with the exception of *The Spectator*, had been generally supportive of British membership in the 1970s, also turned against Europe. The Murdoch titles led the charge. In November 1990, *The Sun* urged its readers 'to tell the French fool [Delors] where to stuff his ECU'. Where the tabloid press led, others followed. From the early 1990s onwards, the Tory press, including the *Telegraph*, poured forth a constant stream of hostile material. The EU was depicted as an out-of-control bureaucratic juggernaut, undemocratic and unBritish (or even anti-British).[42]

1990–1997: In Office but not in Power

When Major became Prime Minister in November 1990, he had three main tasks. The first was to find a way out of the Poll Tax, which was proving difficult and divisive. This was swiftly achieved with the new Council Tax. The second was to adopt a less confrontational and divisive tone, especially over Europe. This is discussed further below. Finally, the Conservatives sought to improve their electoral fortunes, and achieve a fourth successive election victory, a task that appeared hopeless to many of them under Thatcher. Major achieved this as well, although he may well have wished in due course that he had not done so.

What Major was not asked to do, and did not do, was to reverse or abandon Thatcherism. His government was, in nearly all respects, a continuation of what had occurred since 1979. Privatisation was extended to the railways, which, according to Patten, might have proved a bridge too far even for Thatcher. The battle against the trade unions continued, with the Trade Union Reform and Employment Rights Act 1993. Major and his Chancellors broadly continued the fiscal and monetary policies of the 1980s: indeed, Major was clear that 'the tax changes Nigel [Lawson] introduced [in 1988] were right. They ended the unjustifiably high taxation of income that had hampered investment.'[43]

In relation to Europe, Major initially pursued a 'strategy of conflict avoidance', through a policy of carefully crafted ambiguity. Thus, in March 1991 Major said, when visiting Germany, that he wished to be 'at the very heart of Europe', but, in October of the same year, told the Tory conference that 'being at the centre of Europe doesn't mean we've sold out, doesn't mean we've suddenly become Europhiles'. On the substance, however, many Conservatives were suspicious of what was developing within the EEC, in particular moves towards monetary union, and proposals for legislation on working hours and employee rights.[44]

These issues came together at the Maastricht summit in December 1991. This resulted in the Treaty on European Union, which, on the face of it, contained precisely the dangers of which British Eurosceptics were wont to complain. For example, the articles proclaimed:

> By this Treaty, the High Contracting Parties establish among themselves a European Union, hereinafter called 'the Union'. This Treaty marks a new stage in the process of creating an ever closer union among the peoples of Europe. … The Union shall set itself the following objectives: to promote economic and social progress which is balanced and sustainable, in particular through the creation of an area without internal frontiers, through the strengthening of economic and social cohesion and through the establishment of economic and monetary union, ultimately including a single currency in accordance with the provisions of this Treaty…[45]

However, Major was able to agree to the Treaty on the basis of two concessions by the other Member States. The first was that the 'Social Chapter', which put flesh on the bones of 'economic and social progress', was removed from the text and put in a separate protocol to which the other eleven states committed themselves. The second was that the UK secured an opt-out clause on monetary union. These essentially negative achievements by Major were sufficient to secure him 'ecstatic' press and party reaction on his return. However, his attempts to hold the party together, while successful in the short term, were, in the words of the veteran diplomat Sir Percy Cradock, 'at the expense of a greater impatience with British negativism among European governments and growing Euroscepticism at home'.[46]

In the short term, Maastricht was part of the run-in to the Tory victory at the 1992 election. The Conservative Manifesto for that election was soothingly vague, reassuring the voters that 'when or if other members of the EC move to a monetary union with a single currency, we will take our own unfettered decision on whether to join. That decision will be taken by the United Kingdom Parliament.' This stance came under little scrutiny. Europe attracted limited attention in the campaign. Neither of the main parties focused on European issues, and Labour was, by now, a thoroughly Europhile party.[47]

Major might have expected to bask in the adoration of a grateful party. He had dealt with the Poll Tax, secured a harmonious compromise in Europe and achieved, against all expectations, an overall majority of 21 at the April 1992 election. If so, he was to be disappointed. During the campaign, only Powell, by now in his late 70s and no longer an MP, saw fit to accuse Major of treachery at Maastricht. The complex psychodrama of the Tory Party would soon see others make similar allegations.

To understand these assertions, one needs to track back a little. In 1990, Thatcher and her closest allies did not, of course, want her to go. But they thought Major the most loyal of her potential successors. However, within a few months, and certainly by 1992, doubts were beginning to form. According to the Right, the post-war history of the Conservatives had, until the mid-1970s, been one of appeasement. Through what Joseph called the 'ratchet effect', the Right was constantly giving in to socialism, even when in power. After 1975, Thatcher stopped and then reversed this process, putting to flight at home socialists and trade unionists ('the enemy within') and Britain's enemies abroad. But, in this version of events, there remained within the party a large number of cowards, who had deserted Thatcher in her hour of need, and who would carry on the process of appeasement as soon as they could.

Quietly at first, but then more volubly, the Tory Right began to voice their suspicions that Major was not 'one of us'. Given that Major had not greatly deviated from the Thatcher line domestically, the chosen battleground was Europe; the fall of Thatcher in 1990 came to be characterised as 'a plot against the Lady' by pro-Europeans. By 1992, these forces were growing in strength. One hundred and thirty Tory backbenchers were associated with the 'Friends of Bruges Group'. New Eurosceptic organisations were coming into existence such as the Fresh Start Group and the European Foundation, the latter financed by the

wealthy businessman James Goldsmith. According to Major's close colleague Kenneth Clarke, by this stage, 'the former Conservative press
is now almost without exception edited by way-out Eurosceptics'. The
April 1992 Conservative intake was strongly Eurosceptic, providing 'the
Thatcherite army Mrs Thatcher had never had whilst in power'.[48]

The Lady herself poured fuel on these flames. In one of her last
Commons speeches, Thatcher called for a referendum on the single
currency. In a speech in May 1992, the now Lady Thatcher gave vent
to her feelings about Delors in terms scarcely less inflammatory than
those used by *The Sun*:

> M. Delors at least seems to be quite clear. Before the ink is even dry on
> the Maastricht Treaty, the President of the European Commission, who
> has always been admirably frank about his ambitions, is seeking more
> money and more powers for the Commission which would become the
> Executive of the Community, in other words a European Government.
> … So there is no doubt what the President of the Commission is aiming
> at – it is a tightly centralised European federal state. … This is not so
> much constructing a common European home – as a Common Euro-
> pean Prison.[49]

Major then had three pieces of bad luck. The first was that his
narrow majority provided a perfect platform for his internal enemies,
so that the government existed permanently on the edge of defeat. The
second was that, in June 1992, the Danes voted in a referendum to reject
Maastricht. At this point, according to Major's then Chancellor, 'the
pent-up frustrations over Maastricht now burst into the open' or, in
Major's own words, 'all hell broke loose'. Finally, on 16 September 1992,
Black Wednesday, the UK was driven out of the ERM despite desperate
efforts by the government, which included raising interest rates by 5%
in the course of the day. At this point, Major recalled, Black Wednesday 'turned a quarter of a century of unease into a flat rejection of any
wider involvement in Europe … emotional rivers burst their banks'. The
ERM disaster fatally undermined the credibility of the government, and

of Major personally: they had staked much of their authority on ERM membership, and the policy had failed spectacularly.[50]

Those who had opposed ERM membership from the start, most notably Thatcher, greeted this failure gleefully. Even before Black Wednesday, ministers close to Thatcher, like Michael Portillo and Peter Lilley, had been in near open revolt over Maastricht. But from September 1992 onwards, Thatcher, Tebbit and others were working 'openly to stoke the flames of rebellion'. As Major recalled, this was 'a unique occurrence in our party's history: a former prime minister openly encouraging backbenchers … to overturn the policy of her successor'. At the Conservative conference in October 1992, Tebbit received a standing ovation from the increasingly Eurosceptic activists as he denounced the ERM experiment and displayed 'a root-and-branch contempt for the European Community'.[51]

From the autumn of 1992 onwards, the Conservatives were essentially at war over Europe. The focus of Eurosceptic and Thatcherite ire was Major, whose PPS told him that 'the mood is very ugly. A lot of them have turned against you very badly. They'll get you out if they can. They thought you were phobic about Europe, and you're not.' Partly this was the result of the policy failure over the ERM and partly there remained bitterness over Thatcher's enforced departure. However, a key element in this sentiment was the suspicion, indeed paranoia, that the Europeans might somehow impose through the back door the socialism (as Thatcherites characterised it) that the British people had rejected. Within three days of Black Wednesday, Thatcher was calling for the government 'to make as complete a reversal of policy on Maastricht as has been done on the ERM. And of course, the connection is very close, economically and politically.' What was the connection? As she had previously told the Lords, Maastricht 'shackles and burdens our economies with the extra restrictions and intrusive regulations imposed by the Social Chapter'. Something different was required, she said in September 1992:

> We should aim at a multi-track Europe in which groups of different
> states forge varying levels of co-operation and integration on a case-
> by-case basis. Such a structure would lack graph paper neatness. But it
> would accommodate the variety of post-Communist Europe. Instead of
> a centralised bureaucracy laying down identical regulations, national
> governments should offer different mixes of taxes and regulations, com-
> peting with each other for foreign investments, top management and
> high earners.[52]

There could scarcely have been a less propitious environment in
which to seek the ratification of the Treaty. What ensued was months
of hard pounding, as the government struggled to pass the necessary
legislation in the face of repeated rebellions, encouraged from outside
the Commons by Thatcher, Tebbit and others. In November 1992, the
government scraped home by three votes amid 'extraordinary scenes'. In
March 1993, Major was 'humiliated' as the rebels inflicted a defeat, with
26 Tory MPs voting against the government and 18 abstaining. In May,
46 Tories defied the whip. Finally, in July the government lost a vote by
324 to 316 on an ostensibly technical issue concerning the composition
of the British delegation to the Committee of Regions. This was 'probably the most serious parliamentary defeat suffered by the Conservative
Party this century', and the government had to call a vote of confidence
the next day.[53]

What motivated these rebellions? Of course, there were personal and
political factors at work. However, the central argument was that the
government had simply underestimated the extent to which the Treaty
would undermine the UK's sovereignty, so that unwanted social protection would be imposed from Brussels. As Bernard Jenkin MP put it,

> Why should the social aspects be brought into the Community at all?
> The true intent of the Maastricht treaty is that it should lead to a federal
> Europe. Why should a truly separate economic pillar include matters such
> as social protection and social cohesion and solidarity, especially if our
> opt-out from the social chapter is to free us from those very activities?

Likewise, the notion of subsidiarity, which was enshrined in the Treaty (the principle whereby the EU does not take action, except in the areas that fall within its exclusive competence, unless it is more effective than action taken at national level), would 'instead make [parliament] ever more subsidiary to the institutions in Brussels'. And why was Labour so keen on the Social Chapter, asked Iain Duncan Smith, another rebel (and future Tory leader):

> [Labour's] real reason for wishing to incorporate the social chapter is the fact that it has lost all hope that a socialist party will ever be returned to power in this country. It needs all the assistance that it can find to ensure that someone else can do its dirty work for it.[54]

Events did not much assist the government. A key Eurosceptic argument was that Major's much-vaunted opt-outs would not in fact protect the UK from European social legislation. In June 1993, the Commission's proposals for the Working Time Directive passed into law, despite the opt-out, and a British challenge in the European Court subsequently failed. Likewise, British multinationals adopted measures such as the Works Council Directive, even though they were not strictly binding upon them. Developments such as these induced Thatcher to tell the Lords in June 1993 that she 'could never have signed this treaty':

> We have signed up to the objective of a high level of social protection. I wonder whether the social chapter will be brought in by the European Court to apply to Britain, because we have signed up to that high level of social protection. ... The voluntary alliance of 12 nations that we joined is being turned gradually into a new political entity – a European superstate. I doubt very much whether the people realise what is happening. Unification is supposed to be the natural direction of development. ... The Bill will pass considerable further powers irrevocably from Westminster to Brussels.[55]

For the Conservatives, therefore, the argument was not about the desirability of European-style social protection. They were, with few exceptions, opposed to that. The issue was whether Major's opt-out would ensure, as he claimed, that Tory supply-side reforms were not 'wrecked by the job-destroying legislation that coalition governments across the Community had inflicted'. It was on this basis that Major pleaded with the Commons to secure a vote of confidence in his government in July 1993:

> I support a Community which does not intrude into areas that are prop-
> erly the domain of the member states. That, I believe, is what the social
> chapter does. There is already concern across the House, not just on the
> Conservative Benches, at the Commission's attempts to use health and
> safety powers for social legislation. We will oppose any abuse of those
> powers. ... In the social protocol, through the opt-out that I negotiated
> with the consent of the House and a massive majority to do so, I have
> preserved the right of the House to decide. ... The one certain impact
> of the social chapter is that jobs will be lost and unemployment will be
> worse.[56]

Major eventually got his way on the Treaty, but the political costs for the government of the events of 1992/3 were extremely high, and its authority never recovered. One of the casualties was Norman Lamont, dismissed from the Chancellorship in June 1993, whose resignation speech warned that 'we give the impression of being in office but not in power'. Events seemed to bear this out, as Major cut an increasingly hapless figure. The next month, he inadvertently told a journalist that the Eurosceptic members of his Cabinet were 'bastards'. In November 1994, eight backbenchers abstained on a European vote and had the whip removed, thus reducing the government's majority to nil. In the same year, the European elections saw the Conservatives return their lowest national vote share in any twentieth-century poll. In 1995, Major was heckled when addressing the 'Fresh Start' group of MPs and stood down as leader of the party. In the subsequent election, Major defeated one of the 'bastards', Redwood, by 218 votes to 89, with 20 abstentions and spoilt ballots.[57]

In these challenging circumstances, the government sought to advance a nuanced approach to the EU, exemplified in the 1996 White Paper, 'A Partnership of Nations'. This advocated a 'union of nations cooperating together', but opposed 'extending Community competence over employment ... it is businesses which make jobs'. The Foreign Secretary, Malcolm Rifkind, commended this to the Commons on the footing that the UK wished 'to see a Europe ... that does only those things at the European level that need to be done at that level; and that is outward-looking, free-trading, democratic and flexible – a partnership of nations working together to advance their national interests'. The Conservative Manifesto for the 1997 general election was to similar effect, and also offered a referendum on the single currency.[58]

These pledges flowed from Major's belief that he had 'one foot planted on either side of the fault line that runs through the party on Europe. I have to keep the party together or we risk disaster.' On one side of the fault line, there remained a small number of Conservatives, like Clarke and Heseltine, who had been strong supporters of British membership since the 1960s. In the former's view, 'a Conservative Party isolated from the EU would become very right wing and nationalistic'. Major could not ignore these views, since Clarke was his Chancellor (succeeding Lamont in 1993) and Heseltine his deputy.[59]

Sentiment within the party was, however, flowing strongly in a Eurosceptic direction. In 1994, Lamont suggested that there should be a referendum on continued membership. Free-market economists began to argue that the costs of being in the EU, imposed by regulation and social protection, exceeded the benefits. At the 1995 party conference, another of the 'bastards', Portillo, the Defence Secretary, made an extraordinary speech in which he suggested that 'the European Court would probably want to stop our men fighting for more than 40 hours a week', and called, as others would in 2016, for children to be taught 'the history of this remarkable country ... the real history of heroes and bravery, of good versus evil ... of Nelson, Wellington and Churchill'.[60]

Major's efforts to keep his party united reaped few dividends. The Conservatives lost the 1997 election by a landslide to New Labour, securing only 165 seats. Their tally was the lowest since 1906, and the swing the largest since 1945. Tory divisions over Europe were a prominent feature of the campaign. In a survey of 385 Conservative candidates only three appeared pro-Europe (and one of these was Heath). The press gave these divisions considerable attention, in sharp contrast to 1992 where the European issue had scarcely appeared in the media. The Conservative position was also under pressure from the Right. Goldsmith had set up and funded the Referendum Party, 'for mobilisation against future betrayal'. The party fought 547 constituencies, with an average vote share of 3.1%, 'the strongest ever performance by a British minor party'. UKIP secured 1.2% of the vote in the 194 seats where they stood. Many Conservatives concluded from these figures that the government's feebleness over Europe was a substantial factor in their defeat, although the psephologists doubted this.[61]

What was not in doubt, however, was the view of the EU that had become common currency on the Right of the party and of which Thatcher remained the most charismatic exponent. She had, she proclaimed, been prophetic in her Bruges speech and in opposing the UK's membership of the ERM. She would be proved right over the dangers of the single currency and the Social Chapter. Above all, she said in 1996, the EU was now a vehicle to impose on the British people the socialism that they had repeatedly rejected:

> Almost fifty years ago, the Conservative journalist, Colm Brogan, wrote an incisive *critique* of the post-war Labour Government with its arrogant bossiness and intrusive cackhandedness. He called it *Our New Masters*. The title is equally appropriate to the 'new *European* masters'. And it is no surprise to me – as someone who always recognised the Socialist destination of this Euro-federalist dream – that now the Labour Party welcomes it all so warmly. What they can't achieve in an independent, free enterprise Britain, they can hope to secure in a Euro-

federalist Britain, whose people's instincts are ignored and whose parliamentary institutions are over-ridden.[62]

1997–2005: Banging on about Europe

Albert Einstein is credited, probably wrongly, with saying that 'the definition of insanity is doing the same thing, but expecting different results'. On that footing, the Conservatives were close to insane in the period from 1997 to 2005. They returned repeatedly to the issue of Europe, framed in a way that was tailored to the predilections of their backbenchers and activists, but which had little wider public appeal. They lost two elections and three leaders. Their conclusion always seemed to be that they needed to concentrate more on the European issue and seek to appeal more fervently to the Eurosceptics.

The 1997 defeat was devastating. Major resigned as party leader the next day. His successor, William Hague, received the imprimatur of Thatcher. His principal rival, Clarke, was one of the few remaining Europhiles in the upper echelons of the party. Hague was best placed to defeat him 'in a largely Eurosceptic, economically liberal, but socially conservative parliamentary party'. Indeed, 140 of the Tory contingent of 165 MPs were considered Eurosceptic. Hague reflected this in his senior appointments, with Lilley as Shadow Chancellor and Michael Howard Shadow Foreign Secretary (both 'bastards'). He condemned the ERM as 'a great mistake' at his first party conference, and held a referendum the next year among his activists on a pledge to rule out British membership of the Euro for two parliaments, for which he received overwhelming support.[63]

Policy remained largely unchanged in substance, albeit that the tone was a little more strident than in Major's time. The UK should be 'in Europe, but not run by Europe'. The EU should concentrate on market liberalisation, deregulation and the promotion of competition. The party therefore opposed the treaties of Amsterdam (1997) and Nice (2000) as overly integrationist. It was increasingly uncomfortable, therefore, to be a pro-European Tory. Europhiles were no longer welcome in the Shadow Cabinet. Former ministers criticised the party's policy on the Euro. By 1999, Heseltine was warning of the 'incalculable folly' of supporting withdrawal. He and Clarke shared a platform with Blair, at the launch of 'Britain in Europe'.[64]

Naturally enough, Hague concentrated heavily on Europe at the 2001 election. The party placed the Euro issue at the centre of its campaign, proclaiming in its manifesto that 'We will keep the pound. Labour's plan for early entry into the euro is the single biggest threat to our economic stability ... the guiding principle of Conservative policy towards the European Union is to be in Europe, but not run by Europe.' The voters decided that they did not wish to be run by a Conservative government, the party gaining only one seat and securing a vote share barely above 30%. In many ways, this was a worse defeat than 1997, since the party could not blame 18 years in power for wearying the electorate. Europe was, indeed, scarcely an issue in the campaign. The Referendum Party no longer existed, Goldsmith having died. UKIP 'failed to make the impact that the Referendum Party had done four years earlier', securing a 1.5% vote share and losing 422 deposits out of 428 candidates. Hostility to the Euro was greatest in constituencies with a large proportion of elderly or less well-educated voters (foreshadowing 2016 to some extent), but otherwise Hague's 'core vote strategy' was markedly unsuccessful.[65]

The response to this devastating defeat was to move further to the Right and to embrace Euroscepticism even more strongly. Hague resigned. The party chose Duncan Smith as his successor in preference to Clarke, in a contest for the first time decided by the membership rather than the MPs alone: a Maastricht rebel and social conservative, Duncan Smith was the perfect fit for a grassroots that regarded Europe as by far the most important political issue. Many Tory activists considered Clarke a 'traitor' for sharing a pro-European platform with Blair. Duncan Smith did not, in one sense, disappoint his supporters, pledging that the party would 'never' agree that the UK should join the single currency, which was by now a reality, the Euro having launched in 1999. Unfortunately, Duncan Smith was, by common consent, a disastrous leader, and his MPs removed him in October 2003: he was 'simply not up to it'.[66]

A core element in Duncan Smith's appeal in 2001 had been that he was a true Thatcherite. In case anyone had missed the point, Thatcher intervened in the election process, writing to *The Daily Telegraph* in support of Duncan Smith that she

> did not understand how Ken [Clarke] could lead today's Conservative Party to anything other than disaster. He is at odds with the majority of its members on too many issues ... he seems to view with blithe uncon-cern the erosion of Britain's sovereignty in Europe. And in the strategic choice of whether Britain aligns herself with an emerging European su-perstate or whether our relationship with America should remain para-mount, Ken would ... be on the side of Brussels.

This was an extraordinary intervention. It was hard to imagine, for example, Macmillan in 1975 telling his party that they should prefer Heath to Thatcher. Nonetheless, Thatcher was no doubt right in assert-ing that Clarke was 'at odds with the majority of its members', as the results duly proved.[67]

His replacement, Michael Howard, was also a Eurosceptic. Given the state of the Conservative Party at this stage, Howard's brief was essentially to secure a respectable rather than overwhelming defeat in the forthcoming general election. In these circumstances, he did not overly emphasise the European issue. For example, he did not pursue the idea, which some had suggested, that Tory MEPs should leave the main Centre-Right grouping in the European Parliament, the EPP–ED, on the grounds that it was overly federalist. Instead, Howard fought the 2005 election largely on the questions of immigration and asylum. He fulfilled his brief and then resigned after the election: although Blair secured a 'third historic victory', the Conservatives increased their vote share to 32% and their number of seats to 198.[68]

After three successive election failures, one might have thought that the Tories would conclude that a policy mix based on Euroscepticism and social conservatism would continue to spell defeat. As we shall see, this, to some extent, was the basis upon which Cameron became leader in 2005. However, despite this and despite the somewhat lower profile that Howard gave the issue, most Conservatives remained fixated upon antagonism towards the EU. Indeed, in private, Howard had considered offering a referendum on a fundamental renegotiation of the UK's membership of the EU, but had been talked out of it by his advisers, including David Cameron (then a new backbencher). Such thoughts gained some traction with the first glimmerings of the rise of UKIP. At the 2004 European elections, UKIP came third with 6% of the vote (more than doubling their share compared to 1999), and the Tory vote fell from 36% in 1999 to 27%, the lowest at a national election since 1832. UKIP also secured 3.2% of the vote in the 2005 general election, and both they and the British National Party (BNP) began to complain of the influx of immigrants from new members of the EU, an issue that would loom large in 2016. All this seemed to confirm to Eurosceptic Tories that their votes were draining away to the Right, and that the answer, in the words of the EU-obsessed backbencher Bill Cash, was 'to move to a fundamental renegotiation of the treaties'.[69]

Conclusions

Burke believed that society was a 'partnership not only between those who are living, but between those who are living, those who are dead, and those who are to be born'. Political parties are miniature societies, and their parliamentary contingents experience a rebirth every four years, as a general election brings in new MPs and flushes out the old. Political leaders therefore have to bring together their current followers (the living) and new potential supporters (those who are to be born). They have to pay some respect to the dead (the heroes of their party) and the living dead (MPs of an older generation, still imbued with the ideas of a previous era).

In the twenty years between 1983 and 2005, the Conservative Party saw itself transformed. The parliamentary party moved steadily to the Right and away from the pro-European, 'paternalistic progressivism' that had characterised the Macmillan and Heath leaderships. According to Tim Bale, a leading scholar of Conservatism, the make-up of the

Table 5.3 Rightward drift of the Conservative Parliamentary Party, 1992–2005[70]

Parliament	Free Marketeers	Eurosceptic	Socially Conservative
1992–7	56%	58%	N/A
1997–2001	68%	85%	N/A
2001–5	73%	90%	80%

parliamentary party had developed as indicated in Table 5.3.

What is striking about these figures is the direction of travel. Each new intake moved the party further to the Right. The party membership was even more strongly of these views, as was shown by its overwhelming support for Duncan Smith (part of the 1992 cohort) over Clarke (first elected in 1970 and a prime example of the living dead). There were pockets of resistance: for example, in 2002 one could find Douglas Hurd (Political Secretary to Heath, 1970–4; first elected MP 1974; Foreign Secretary, 1989–95) advocating a policy of constructive engagement with Europe and deprecating 'the relentless pressure to be hostile to the EU and nothing else'. But this was by now chatter at the margins: the Tory centre of gravity was elsewhere. Those who thought like this tended also to have serious reservations about the whole thrust of Conservative policy since 1979, and to be on their way out of the party. Thus in 1999, 10 former Tory MPs and MEPs lent their support to a fringe party, the 'Pro-Euro Conservative Party'. Some had their party membership terminated as a result. Their number included Ian Gilmour and Julian Critchley, who had been highly critical of Thatcherism from the start, and across the whole range of social and economic policy.[71]

Indeed, constructive engagement was not the hallmark of official Tory policy, which stressed the advantages of disengagement from Europe. Even in 2005, in an election where damage limitation was the order of the day, the manifesto message was unremittingly negative:

> we will co-operate with all those who wish to see the EU evolve in a more flexible, liberal and decentralised direction. We oppose the EU Constitution and would give the British people the chance to reject its provisions in a referendum within six months of the General Election. We also oppose giving up the valuable freedom which control of our own currency gives us. We will not join the Euro. … We will ensure that Britain once again leads the fight for a deregulated Europe by negotiating the restoration of our opt-out from the Social Chapter.[72]

What lay behind this? In part, there was, on the Eurosceptic Right, an underlying belief that the UK and Europe were fundamentally different and opposing entities. According to Menno Spiering, looking at the UK from outside, it was 'only in Britain that one can find the slogan "I am British, not European": there were "Europeans" and then there was the "proud and independent-minded island race". But it was not just nationalism that was at work. There was a growing gulf between British Conservatives, who admired free-market rigour of a Thatcherite or Reaganite variety, and the much more social democratic or Christian democratic approach in favour elsewhere in the EU.

In a sense, the Bruges speech explained everything one needed to know about the Conservative Party in this period, for all that it began the process that would lead to the fall of Thatcher. The Thatcher governments had by 1988 largely dismantled the structure of British social democracy, a structure within which many Conservatives had been content to exist until 1979. The post-1979 breed of Tories did not want to see social democracy return at home and they felt increasingly out of tune with the EU and, indeed, even with Christian Democrats in Europe, their one-time close allies.

The last word therefore belongs to Thatcher (speaking in 1998). Hers was overwhelmingly the dominant Conservative voice throughout these two decades, even though she had been forced from office in 1990:

> Among those who criticised my approach in the eighties were people who considered that … some half-way house between collectivism and the free market … preferable. There was, for example, an alternative European model on offer, sometimes described as 'the social market', which involved a large state sector and a fair amount of state planning but also a significant role for private enterprise. … Compromises of this sort are never very attractive … if … one reckons that prosperity and jobs really flow from the interaction of individual consumers and independent businesses, the role of government should be kept to the bare minimum. In any case, the jury is no longer out. We now know that it is the American model of free enterprise capitalism that works best to foster innovation and to create jobs. We know that the more statist economies of continental Europe are not so successful.[73]

6 Labour Changes Position, 1983–2005

Privatisation should have a role to play not out of dogmatism but out of pragmatism.

(Tony Blair, 1999, introducing White Paper on public service reform)[1]

I am a passionate pro-European. … I believe in Europe as a political project. I believe in Europe with a strong and caring social dimension. I would never accept a Europe that was simply an economic market.

(Tony Blair, speech to the European Parliament, 23 June 2005)[2]

Introduction

In 1983, Labour was a socialist party, mistrustful of capitalism and of the EEC, which most on the Left thought was an obstacle to building a socialist society in Britain. Labour was also a defeated party, looking to the future with apprehension. This was the appropriate emotion, since much defeat, both electoral and industrial, lay ahead. By 2005, Labour's policies and fortunes had been transformed. As the above quotations illustrate, Labour had embraced both the market and Europe (by now the EU) with enthusiasm. Electoral triumph had accompanied the new approach, and when Blair addressed the European Parliament, Labour had just won its third successive election victory: an unprecedented achievement for a party that had only twice before managed to achieve a comfortable majority in the House of Commons, in 1945 and 1966.

In this chapter, I will seek to explain how this transformation came about and to place it within the wider argument that British affection for Europe depended upon a reasonable degree of synergy between a 'Europe with a strong and caring social dimension' and a Britain that was essentially social democratic. On the face of it, Labour's conversion to Europeanism was a straightforward application of this principle: the party moved Right, abandoned socialism and embraced the EU. However, at a deeper level, this was a problematic conversion. It will be suggested that Labour not only forsook socialism, but also largely turned its back on its, alternative, social democratic traditions. In attempting a 'third way', the party found itself with a European policy that was shallow and half-hearted. Labour did not wish to seem anti-European, because this would undermine its credentials as a newly respectable party. On the other hand, it could not wholeheartedly accept 'Social Europe', for that was too social democratic for its tastes.

1983–1988: Yes to Delors

However, we should not get too far ahead of ourselves. It is 10 June 1983, and the sun is rising on a new Thatcherite dawn. The Conservatives have won an emphatic election victory. Labour is in disarray and the party's leader, Michael Foot, is about to resign. Tony Benn, standard-bearer of the Left, has lost his seat. The Left gather on the following Sunday for a 'post-mortem', and resolve to nominate a candidate for the impending leadership contest against Neil Kinnock, the front-runner. Kinnock had himself come from the Left, but the Left have no love for him now. According to Jeremy Corbyn, then a newly elected MP, 'Kinnock lost the deputy leadership for Tony in 1981' [by abstaining and urging others to do so]. In public, the Left remain defiant, with Benn claiming that 'for the first time since 1945, a political party with an openly socialist policy has received the support of over eight and a half million people'.[3]

The Left were right to be suspicious of Kinnock, who became party leader in October 1983, in a 'dream ticket' with Roy Hattersley (a pro-European from the party Right and formerly a Jenkinsite), easily beating a Left ticket composed of Eric Heffer and Michael Meacher. From then onwards, the Left, and their allies in the union movement, suffered defeat after defeat. When, five years later, Benn and Heffer stood against Kinnock and Hattersley, their result was an 'appalling' 11%. This was a stark contrast to 1981, when Benn had so nearly defeated Healey for the Deputy Leadership. What had gone wrong? The Left had suffered reverses on all fronts.[4]

The most conspicuous defeat was in the industrial sphere, and, above all, the miners' strike of 1984/5. The Thatcher government had appointed Ian MacGregor as Chairman of the National Coal Board (NCB) in 1983. In March 1984 the NCB announced that Cortonwood Colliery in Yorkshire was to close. Official area strikes started in Yorkshire and Scotland. The National Union of Mineworkers' (NUM) national executive called on other areas to back them. Many other coalfields stopped work. What was, in effect, a national strike continued for the next year. Following a massive and prolonged struggle, a majority of conference delegates voted in March 1985 to return to work, without a new agreement. The government mobilised all the powers at its disposal to defeat the NUM. During the strike over 11,000 people were arrested, of whom about 8,000 were charged. The Labour Movement was not united or effective at national level. Kinnock pleaded diary clashes when asked to share a platform with striking miners: this was thought 'absolutely pathetic'. He earned the nickname '"Kneel" Kinnock for his apparent subservience to the government'.[5]

Benn and the Left, and many in the union movement, had given unstinting support to the striking miners. However, the lesson of 1984/5 seemed to be that it was not possible to defeat the Thatcher government through industrial means. Moreover, Kinnock (himself a miner's son and with a mining constituency) and his allies drew the conclusion that their rupture with the Bennite Left must be total. In October 1985, Kinnock used a speech at the party's conference to attack Militant, a Trotskyite group in control of Liverpool City Council who had 'end[ed] up in the grotesque chaos of a Labour council, a Labour council, hiring taxis to scuttle round a city handing out redundancy notices to its own workers'. Heffer, a Liverpool MP, stormed from the platform in disgust.[6]

The leadership were also addressing policy, and by 1986, statements from Policy Review Groups were under consideration. These gave the first hint of what was, in due course, to be wholesale retreat from the 1983 manifesto. However, even then, Benn thought that Kinnock was 'advocating a Franklin D. Roosevelt approach ... individual freedom must come above equality, that production must come above redistribution, and that taxes would not be raised except on the very rich ... these statements ... put Kinnock and Hattersley squarely in the SDP camp'. This was a somewhat hyperbolic representation of Labour policy in 1986, but as a prediction of the New Labour future it was all too accurate, save that the Blair government would not unduly trouble 'the very rich'.[7]

Amid this drift to the Right, what then of the party's policy on Europe? One needs to begin, in this context, by recalling how deep-frozen was the party's anti-EEC sentiment in the early 1980s. When, in 1980, Callaghan resigned as party leader, three of the four candidates to replace him were opposed to the EEC, and the other, Healey, was 'only marginally less sceptical' – and this in a contest that the Bennite Left had boycotted. The young Tony Blair, when a candidate at the 1982 Beaconsfield by-election, advised his prospective voters that 'the E.E.C. takes away Britain's freedom to follow the economic policies we need'. Hugo Young is surely right to say that the move away from this Euro-sceptical consensus was at first grudging as 'under the curse of what seemed to be the interminable status of opposition, [Labour] evolved ... not because it saw the light but because it tired of the darkness'.[8]

The thaw was slow at first, but the signs were there to see even before Kinnock became leader. Even in 1971, he had told the party's special conference that he was 'against E.E.C. entry on these terms at this time', striking a less fundamentalist note than other speakers like Peter Shore. By September 1983, the about-to-be leader told the Socialist Group in the European Parliament that by 1988, when the next general election was due, withdrawal would be 'a last resort that is considered only if and when the best interests of the British people cannot be feasibly safeguarded by any other means'. Once elected leader, Kinnock told his front-bench spokespeople that the UK should not 'criticise ineffectively from the side-lines but… participate fully in the development of the EC'. Consistently with this, he developed close relations with European socialist leaders such as Brandt, Rocard and Gonzalez.[9]

However, in terms of concrete European policy, 1983–7 was a fairly thin period. In part, this was because the new leadership was seeking to obtain greater control over the party machine and to concentrate on recasting the party's economic policy. The party's 1984 manifesto for the European elections ruled out withdrawal, but only for the next five years. Conference did not even debate Europe in 1985 or 1986. Moreover, there remained significant elements within the party of fundamental opposition to the EEC, including (ironically) within the Labour Group in the European Parliament. Shore remained as Churchillian as ever, condemning the SEA on the basis that

> the European Communities (Amendment) Bill is not just another Bill relating to our domestic affairs … it gives legislative effect to a treaty concluded with other nations – the member states of the E.E.C. – and upon whose institutions it confers additional legislative powers. Once passed, this measure cannot be repealed by a subsequent Parliament.[10]

It is not surprising, therefore, that the party's official position on the SEA was equivocal, adopting the line that the single market would be acceptable but only if it were 'accompanied, as the President of the Commission said, by a considerable social obligation on the rest of the Community to ensure that that growth is accompanied by the protection of rights that have been won with such great difficulty'. This led Labour to vote against the European Communities (Amendment) Bill, which implemented the SEA, in what Hattersley was later to call 'the last throes of the old unthinking anti-Market position'.[11]

That position was withering by the time of the 1987 election. Labour fought a well-regarded campaign, using the media slickly. Kinnock was thought to have done well. Europe was scarcely an issue. The party's manifesto was suitably ambiguous, stating that 'Labour's aim is to work constructively with our E.E.C. partners to promote economic expansion and combat unemployment … [while] … stand[ing] up for British interests within the European Community and reject[ing] E.E.C interference with our policy for national recovery and renewal.' However, neither the slickness nor the ambiguity did much to slow down the Thatcher juggernaut, and the result represented only the most modest advance for Labour.

Party	Votes	Seats	Change	Vote share (%)
Conservative	13,760,583	376	−21	42.3
Labour	10,029,807	229	+20	30.8
Liberal/SDP	7,341,633	22	−1	22.5[12]

For Labour this was a disappointing result, although it could be regarded as progress compared with 1983. For the Liberal/SDP Alliance, the outcome was dispiriting. Roy Jenkins immediately resigned as SDP leader. David Owen succeeded him and conceived a new strategy for the party, taking it in search of Conservative votes. He therefore sought to abandon the party's 'Old Labour' inheritance (for example, public ownership), and advocate in its place 'social concern and market realism'. This 'sub-Thatcherite posture' was not to the taste of other members of the Gang of Four, who wanted the party to be 'unequivocally on the centre-left'. After 1987, the SDP disintegrated, and most of its members agreed to merge with the Liberals in 1988. An Owenite faction fought on, until 1990, at which point the party was wound up.[13]

These developments presented an opportunity for social democrats within Labour, since social democracy within the SDP had shrivelled and then died. After all, Labour's Deputy Leader, Hattersley, had been a Jenkinsite. Might Labour now become the natural home for the pro-European social democrat? Moreover, there was increasing warmth towards the EEC from some unlikely quarters. Frances Morrell, who had been a trusted adviser to Benn in government, and Hilary Wainwright, editor of *Red Pepper* magazine, both suggested in 1987 that Labour needed to take a more internationalist approach to the benefits of the EEC. Even Heffer, while maintaining that withdrawal was 'still essential', accepted the need to work with the European Left, since 'British socialism cannot build a wall around itself or solve its political and economic problems in isolation'.[14]

However, although these were encouraging straws in the wind for Labour pro-Europeans, the most powerful impetus for change came from the unions. The period from 1979 to 1987 had been one of uninterrupted misery for the Labour Movement as a whole, with three successive election defeats and victory for the Thatcher government in the greatest industrial dispute of the period. However, for the unions in particular, decline was both rapid and extensive. They had created Labour to be their voice in Parliament, and were beginning to wonder whether this now afforded them sufficient protection.

The only alternative source of such protection appeared to be the EEC. It was logical, therefore, that the unions began to apply pressure upon the party to reconsider its European policy and to see social and industrial problems in a European as well as a national context. Moreover, the EEC, with Delors at the helm, offered the prospect of applying restraint upon an otherwise uncontrolled British Tory government. And the union tradition of voluntarism was beginning to look a little less compelling in the face of declining union bargaining power. Rights were more likely to be conferred by legislation than by collective bargaining, and they were much more likely to come from Europe than from Thatcher.[15]

It was in these circumstances that David Lea (Assistant General Secretary of the TUC 1978–99) 'got Jacques Delors to speak to the TUC in 1988, that was against a background that we were moving in Brussels towards a social chapter whereby agreements could be made with the social partners and if they reached an agreement, be implemented by the Executive and the Council of Ministers, a remarkable arrangement'. The effect, as John Edmonds (a member of the TUC General Council 1986–2003) recalled, was electric:

> In August 1988, the TUC was against EC membership and calling for withdrawal, but by October, both the TUC and the Labour Party were in favour of membership … a veritable 'coup', and the TUC shift effectively determined Labour's, as the trade unions had the best part of 90% of votes at the Labour Party Conference … the more positive aim of this shift: reaping the benefits of the Social Dimension – new legal rights for working people … this represented a major shift for unions – collective bargaining had, hitherto, been the main focus – and a whole series of new opportunities opened up … unions did not simply fight in Britain for every change. Social partnership changed the question: would the UK implement the legal changes achieved in Brussels?[16]

Delors addressed the TUC at Bournemouth on 8 September 1988. Why did he produce such ecstasy in his audience, who serenaded him as 'Frère Jacques'? The essential argument advanced was that the unions, whose 'pioneering role' he praised, had nothing to fear and everything to gain from the single market when it came into effect in 1992. Under the heading of 'the social dimension', Delors told his listeners that it would be 'unacceptable for Europe to become a source of social regression', and that 'measures adopted to complete the large market should not diminish the level of social protection already achieved in the member states'. It was necessary to make concrete progress towards 'the establishment of a platform of guaranteed social rights, containing general principles, such as every worker's right to be covered by a collective agreement … the creation of a statute for European companies, which would include the participation of workers or their representatives'.[17]

To add to the unions' enthusiasm, Thatcher made her speech in Bruges between the TUC and Labour conferences: as Lea recalled, 'she

was so venomous about what Jacques Delors had to say at Bournemouth, not only the substance but the temerity of a foreign power'.
When Labour met at Blackpool in October, even anti-EEC veterans
such as Clive Jenkins (a prominent No campaigner in 1975) were in
Damascene mode: a new attitude to Europe was required and this was
'a hard process of learning from life itself'. Bill Jordan, President of
the Engineering Workers, moved a pro-EEC composite resolution and
argued that the party 'must seek to use or adapt community institutions
to promote democratic socialism'.[18]

On the face of it, therefore, Labour had reverted to social democratic
type and, in so doing, turned naturally to continental social democracy in the person of Delors for inspiration. There is some truth in this
analysis and, self-evidently, the rightward shift, and then implosion
of the SDP, gave social democrats within Labour space to maneouvre.
However, there are two very substantial qualifications to this picture.
One relates to the state of social democracy in the UK in 1988, and
the other concerns the nature of the conversion that had occurred at
Bournemouth.

Social democracy was not dead, but it was scarcely in rude health.
After all, the SDP had been created in 1981 for the sole purpose of promoting social democracy. After 1983, 'David Owen *was* the SDP and the
SDP *was* Owen'. A one-man operation did not look to have much of a
future ,and by 1990 the party was no more. Labour had not yet moved
as far and as fast to the right as Dr Owen, but was increasingly accepting
that it would have to regard large parts of the Thatcherite settlement as
irreversible, such as the (extensive) privatisation programme and the
sale of council houses. Labour remained in 1988 an egalitarian party,
but many of the pillars of its post-war legacy had been demolished, and
some in the party now doubted they could be rebuilt. Benn may have
been overstating things when he described the policy review process as
'the Thatcherism of the Labour Party', but the trend was clear enough:
the party would have to adapt itself to Thatcherism, rather than seeking
to replace this new orthodoxy.[19]

The conversion, too, was a fragile one. Thus, at the TUC in 1988, Ron Todd (General Secretary of the TGWU, historically sympathetic to the Left and hostile to the EEC) placed the union's weight behind the Delors agenda. Yet, at the Labour conference, where Kinnock announced a major modernisation of policy, Todd mocked the modernising philosophy, especially the party's abandonment of unilateral nuclear disarmament. And his support for Delors was expressed in strictly functional terms:

> In the short term we have not a cat in hell's chance in Westminster. The only card game in town at the moment is in a town called Brussels, and it is a game of poker where we have got to learn the rules and learn the rules fast. … We have to seize the initiative on this whole debate from the employers … social engineering is what 1992 is all about.[20]

This was hardly the zeal of the convert, let alone the vision of those enthusiasts for Europe in the 1960s and 1970s who had foreseen a wholehearted partnership between the UK and Europe. It was not even the more qualified assurance of Kinnock in 1983, who told his fellow socialists in the European Parliament that 'our future … lies with Europe … the inspiration of the E.E.C as an organisation to bind and stabilise the democracies of Western Europe was – and is – decent and desirable'.[21]

1988–1997: Labour moves to the Right and towards Europe

Between 1988 and 1997, Labour had three leaders: Kinnock until 1992, John Smith from 1992 until his sudden death in 1994, and Tony Blair from 1994 onwards. The party fought two general elections, losing narrowly and unexpectedly in 1992, and winning overwhelmingly in 1997. The general rightward drift in policy continued, and accelerated after 1994, with the rise of New Labour. New Labour was, according to Benn, 'the smallest political party that's ever existed in Britain': certainly, Blair, Gordon Brown, Peter Mandelson and a few others tightly controlled both the formation and the implementation of policy. In these years, the party's Europhilia also intensified: as Austin Mitchell, who had been an MP since 1977 and remained hostile to the EU, commented in 1995, 'in 1987 we were pro-Europe, by 1992 we were enthusiastic about Europe, and [we are now] positively bubbling with enthusiasm'.[22]

However, the move to the Right had rather more conceptual basis than did the new-found European enthusiasm. It will be suggested that there was little more to the latter than a desire on the part of successive Labour leaderships to demonstrate that they were not like the Tories (divided, nationalistic and backward-looking), and not like the Labour Party of the early 1980s either (also divided and looking to create an impossible 'socialism in one country'). In a sense, this was good opposition politics. As early as 1989, the Europhobic Tory MP Bill Cash had told Benn that 'the Tory Party was on the point of splitting over the federalisation of the Common Market, which would leave the British Parliament without power'. It was obviously tempting for Labour to sit back and enjoy the spectacle of Conservative dissension, a process that became more vicious after 1992. The only problem with this approach was that it left Labour with a vacuum at the heart of its European policy.[23]

There were, of course, a number of continuities in this period, most conspicuously the pragmatic zeal with which the unions embraced the single market, exemplified by the 1988 pamphlet 'Maximising the Benefits, Minimising the Costs'. A few years later, Chris Mullin (a Left-leaning MP) noted the TUC's 'growing team of lobbyists in Brussels', one of whom made the point to him that 'the TUC gets nowhere at Westminster, but achieves a lot of what it wants in Brussels'. Contrari-wise, the party still contained some vocal figures who were as fixated with, and hostile to, the EU, as Tory Eurosceptics such as Cash. Thus, MPs like Benn, Nigel Spearing and Denzil Davies criticised each new European development. For Davies, Maastricht had at its 'heart ... an economic ideology which would be anathema to everything Labour has stood for'. However, these views were becoming increasingly marginal, for, as Benn complained, Kinnock had managed to persuade all the key organs of the party of the wisdom of his pro-European views.[24]

The leadership pursued a line that largely ignored such Eurosceptic concerns and chimed with the unions' pragmatic zeal. Policy documents such as 'Britain in the World' and 'Meet the Challenge, Make the Change', published in 1989, recognised that 'some 60 per cent of Britain's trade is with our Community partners. We could not now withdraw without great damage to our economy.' Even those who had previously been supporters of the AES thought that 'the idea of national economies controlled by national Governments is dead', and that 'it's sad ... but it is the reality. We are in Europe. We are going to stay in Europe and what we have to do is to get the best out of Europe.'[25]

In terms of practical politics, the principal issues that arose before 1992 related to the intertwined questions of the ERM, EMU and the Social Chapter, questions that were causing such agonies for the Conservatives. Labour supported the UK's entry into the ERM in October 1990. The following month, the party's NEC issued a statement endorsing the principle of a single currency, albeit with no commitment as to date. When Major returned from Maastricht with his two opt-outs in December 1991, Kinnock chided him for his caution:

> the Government have returned from the Maastricht Council with a pair of opt-outs on the most vital matters of economic and monetary union and the social chapter. Their duty was to exert maximum influence on those fundamental issues. That required involvement; they have chosen isolation. ... The Government's duty was to resist the development of a two-speed Community. Instead, they have contrived to get a two-speed Community, and they have put Britain in the slow lane. A Prime Minister who said that he wanted Britain at the heart of Europe spent his whole time at the Council getting two escape clauses. That is not the action of a Prime Minister who wants to be at the heart of Europe but the action of a Prime Minister who wants Britain at the tail of Europe.[26]

There was, however, considerable imprecision at the core of Labour's position on Europe. In January 1991, John Smith, as Shadow Chancellor, distinguished between monetary union and 'the far from precise notion of economic union implying, as it might, the loss of fiscal and budgetary sovereignty'. However, was it really possible to be half-in and half-out of a process of economic and monetary union? Moreover, the turn towards Europe was happening at a time when Labour was busily ditching many of the policies that had been distinctive, but electorally unpopular, only a few years previously: nationalisation, unilateral nuclear disarmament, opposition to selling council houses. As Russell Holden has argued, Labour's new position on Europe 'lacked a coherent theoretical basis', so that 'the emerging social dimension [in Europe] filled the ideological vacuum'. Chris Smith MP (on the 'soft Left' and later a minister under Blair) observed: 'we were stuck with Thatcher's reactionary social policies: the EC began to appear as a haven of progressive ideas'.[27]

Labour approached the 1992 election in an optimistic frame of mind: surely, after thirteen years, the country would be tiring of Thatcherism? Its programme was now shorn of most of the socialist ideas of 1983; the party's support for the ERM was thought to give it anti-inflationary credibility; the Left had been sidelined. Pro-Europeanism gave the party yet further respectability, although, surprisingly in the light of later events, Maastricht was hardly an issue in the campaign. Labour, despite the winnowing of its programme, remained an egalitarian party. John Smith had devised a taxation scheme whereby the ceiling on national insurance contributions was abolished, and a new top rate income tax of 50 per cent was to apply to individuals with an income over £40,000. This duly featured in the manifesto. The Conservatives ruthlessly exploited 'Labour's Tax Bombshell', whereby 'a Labour Government would raise the top rate of tax from 40 to 59 per cent bringing in a new tax on talent'.[28]

These tactics proved effective, and Labour, although making progress, suffered another defeat, all the more devastating because of the high hopes which had marked the campaign.

This appeared to be an unequivocal triumph for Major, who had achieved a surprising victory and fulfilled the brief given him when he

Party	Votes	Seats	Change	Vote share (%)
Conservative	14,093,007	336	−40	41.9
Labour	11,560,484	271	+42	34.4
Liberal/SDP	5,999,606	20	−2	17.8

had succeeded Thatcher eighteen months previously. An overall majority of 21 offered an ostensibly secure future. As we have already seen, this victory proved pyrrhic indeed, and five miserable and fractious years lay ahead for the Conservatives. In the meantime, Labour needed a new leader, Kinnock having resigned following the defeat. In July 1992, John Smith succeeded him, overwhelmingly beating Bryan Gould. In a sense, this could not have been a starker indication of Labour's new attitude to Europe. Smith had been one of the Labour MPs who had defied a three-line whip in October 1971 to support Heath's application to join; Gould had long been anti-EEC.

Events then moved swiftly. On 16 September 1992, the UK was ejected from the ERM. Major's government never recovered from this blow to its credibility. In a sense, Labour and Smith ought to have suffered similar damage, since they had pressed a reluctant government to join the ERM from 1988 onwards. However, the party could now enjoy the luxury of opposition: losing the 1992 election proved a lucky escape. Indeed, the dramas suffered by the Major government over the ERM did not cause Labour to re-evaluate its ever more pro-EU position. At its 1992 conference, which fell just after Black Wednesday, the party resolved to support the Maastricht Treaty, which 'while not perfect, is the best that can currently be achieved'.[29]

Eurosceptics within the party were increasingly sidelined. In September 1992, Gould resigned from the Shadow Cabinet, saying that 'the gag and straitjacket' of collective responsibility prevented him from expressing his opposition to both Maastricht and the ERM. Gould, broadly on the Left and always anti-EEC, was probably the most substantial figure remaining in the upper echelons of the party who took this view. In 1994, he returned to his native New Zealand and left British politics. From afar, he disowned the 1997–2010 government, which he had 'watched … compromise its principles, embrace greed and take the UK into war and recession'.[30]

During the Maastricht debates of 1992/3, Labour broadly stuck to the line that they would support the treaty, but only if it also incorporated the Social Chapter. This led to a general policy of abstaining on the principal votes, which gave the government comfortable majorities. However, on a number of occasions, Labour combined with the Tory rebels to vote against the government, and Major's government hung on by its fingernails. This gave rise to the strange spectacle of a coalition of anti-Major forces composed of a Labour Party that supported the Treaty and the Social Chapter, and right-wing Conservatives who loathed both.

The furore over the Social Chapter was itself curious. Conservative hostility to the chapter played a large part in Major's troubles over Maastricht, despite the opt-out that he had negotiated. Listening to those debates, one might have thought that the chapter, if applied to the UK, would transform British society in an almost Soviet fashion. By the same token, Labour expressed lavish enthusiasm. Both parties appeared to agree that the chapter would deliver through the Brussels back door the socialist measures that would not pass through the Westminster front entrance.

In fact, the Social Chapter was a much more modest undertaking than British political rhetoric suggested. The Social Protocol to the Treaty on European Union, to give the correct title, did not impose any new social policies. Rather, it changed the procedure by which such policies might be introduced in future, bringing certain social topics within the scope of Qualified Majority Voting in the Council of Ministers. These related to a limited range of topics, such as health and safety, the consultation of workers and equality between men and women at work. A larger list of matters continued to require unanimity, such as social security and social protection of workers. Moreover, certain areas were specifically excluded, namely pay, the right of association, the right to strike and the right to impose lock-outs. Nor was the idea of EEC-wide social policy a new one. The Treaty of Rome contained as articles 117 to 122 what was, in effect, a Social Chapter, requiring

> close co-operation between Member States in the social field, particularly in matters relating to: employment; labour law and working conditions; basic and advanced vocational training; social security; prevention of occupational accident, and diseases; occupational hygiene; the right of association, and collective bargaining between employers and workers.[31]

The truth was that the divide between the parties over the Social Chapter was largely symbolic. As Lord Eatwell (an academic who had been chief economic adviser to Kinnock) pointed out in the Lords in 1993:

> the measures described in the social protocol are themselves innocuous. Nobody can seriously believe in the hyperbole which characterises the social protocol as a threat to British and European industry. ... The impact of the social protocol on workers' rights is minimal compared, for example, with the Government's own health and safety or wrongful dismissal legislation ... the social protocol, innocuous though it undoubtedly is, is a touchstone for profound differences in both the formation and implementation of economic policy. It defines the dividing line between those on the Government Benches who regard labour as a cost and those on these Benches who regard it as a resource.[32]

This analysis was illuminating, but if the Social Chapter was itself 'innocuous', then the EU might not be the 'haven of progressive ideas' that many within Labour had hoped it would be. And if there were 'profound differences in both the formation and implementation of economic policy' between the parties, as there clearly were, then these could only be resolved at Westminster, and Labour could only succeed in such debates if it could win a general election. These questions had scarcely been raised, let alone resolved, before Smith's death in May 1994. Smith had certainly established Labour's European credentials: indeed, shortly before his death, Major had characterised him as 'the man who likes to say yes in Europe – Monsieur Oui, the poodle of Brussels'. However, he had not had the time, or, perhaps, the inclination, to set out more fully to what he would be saying yes.[33]

In a party-political sense, a policy of fuzzy warmth towards Europe made sense, and was working electorally: in the 1994 European elections, Labour secured a vote share of 44% (the highest share in a national election since 1966), and the bitterly divided Tories, at 28%, obtained their lowest nationwide percentage poll of the twentieth century. However, the Labour approach in these years was vague, to say the least. Thus, in its manifesto for the previous European elections in 1989, the party had announced that 'we need a Europe which is created for the people … powerful enough to restrain the multinationals … but democratic enough to avoid the dangers of excessive centralisation'. But what exactly did this mean?[34]

As so often in the UK's engagement with Europe, Labour seemed reluctant to accept that membership of the EU might involve compromises between various inherently desirable objectives, and that there might therefore have to be an acceptance of some restriction on sovereignty, for example, in order to secure economic and social benefits. Thus, Benn told Cash in 1989 that Labour would support European social legislation, 'even though we share the constitutional argument' [of Eurosceptics like Cash]. But was it, more generally, necessary to accept some 'constitutional' diminution in order to secure social advance? There were some on the Left who thought that there was, indeed, scope for such a bargain. For example, Michael Barratt Brown, a leading figure in the development of the New Left in the 1950s and 1960s, was by 1991 arguing that 'full federation was preferable to a halfway house of an economic community of sovereign states … those who look to the European Community for the protection and the social provision that European nation states can no longer provide, will have to accept a common currency, but will need to insist on a common social budget'. Thus, rather than continuing to argue for 'socialism in one country', it might be better for the Left to seek a form of socialism in a European superstate, the very stuff of Thatcherite nightmares.[35]

That Labour was papering over the cracks, rather than developing a coherent policy, was, on occasions, apparent. It was all very well to point to the much wider fissures on the Tory side, and to use the Social Chapter to build a bridge between traditional Labour concerns and the need to embrace Europe, but there remained real disagreements within the party. For example, the party's official position was to abstain on the third reading of the Maastricht Bill, but, in the event, the party split three ways and 71 MPs (out of 271) voted against the party line: five actually supported the government. One of the five had, on an earlier occasion, explained his approach to ratification on the basis that

> there is no salvation for Labour as an anti-European or even a reluc-
> tantly European party. We must continue to develop our strategy and
> our policies within a European framework. Labour's future, like that of
> Britain as a whole, lies in the European Community.

Labour was no longer an anti-European party, although pockets of resistance remained. It was, however, 'a reluctantly European party', in the sense that the party was still unclear as to what elements of the European bargain it might accept in order to secure enhanced social protection in the UK.[36]

This was, roughly, the state of play when John Smith died suddenly on 12 May 1994. Within hours Blair had emerged as his likely successor. In July, he became leader, with 57% of the vote, easily beating much more experienced candidates in John Prescott and Margaret Beckett. Two important consequences flowed from these events. The first was that Blair's accession involved a deal with Gordon Brown (his chief competitor among the younger ranks of Labour MPs) whereby the latter stood down in his favour. The terms of this deal were to be hotly disputed over the next thirteen years, and the tempestuous relationship between the two rivals would dominate much of the Blair government. The second was that the party saw the rise of New Labour, of which Benn was scornfully to remark 'though almost certainly the smallest party in the history of British politics, is nevertheless a very powerful organisation, since most of its members are in the Cabinet'.[37]

'Old Labour', not then a phrase in common use, was mortally wounded in 1994, although not everyone then appreciated this. Until 1994, the party had sought to come to terms with electoral failure by reverting to its social democratic roots. Hattersley and Smith, for example, had both been ministers in the 1974–9 government, and they came from a position on the traditional Right of the party. Both had long been pro-European, and neither had been tempted to join the SDP, an attitude that was vindicated when the SDP collapsed. Although, inevitably, the 1983–94 leadership felt compelled to accept that some aspects of Thatcherism were irreversible, this remained recognisably a Labour Party. For example, links with the unions were still thought important, and redistribution was at the heart of policy: Hattersley had, earlier in his career, received the imprimatur of Crosland himself as 'an egalitarian'. New Labour, by contrast, represented a deliberate break with this approach. The 1992 defeat had convinced Blair, Brown and their small band of followers that nothing short of a rupture with Labour's egalitarian tradition would enable the party to return to power.[38]

The New Labour project took root in the remaining years of opposition. Although there was some continuity with the Kinnock Policy Review, Blair and Brown were very much at home with embracing the market and keeping the unions at arm's length. In 1995, the party adopted an amended version of clause IV of its constitution, which had, since 1918, committed the party (in theory at least) to 'the common ownership of the means of production, distribution, and exchange'. The new version referred to 'a dynamic economy, serving the public interest, in which the enterprise of the market and the rigour of competition are joined with the forces of partnership and co-operation to produce the wealth the nation needs'. Clause IV had caused considerable heartache for previous Labour leaders (Gaitskell in particular), but this change went through with little controversy.[39]

New Labour likewise embraced Europe as a symbol of the party's fresh modern, moderate and trustworthy nature. The UK should be 'at the centre of Europe' and 'set about building the alliances within Europe that enable our influence to grow'. The Tories, by contrast, were depicted as looking backwards and inwards: as the 1996 *Road to the Manifesto* put it, 'nothing is doing more to undermine Britain's ... influence than the doubt being created about our commitment to Europe'. Blair had numerous conversations in this period with the political commentator Hugo Young, and convinced him that he was 'a proper European ... not ... a Euro-sceptic ... prepared to align the island with its natural hinterland beyond'.[40]

However, even at this stage, one could doubt exactly what it was that the new leadership was committing itself to achieve. For one thing, New Labour was an intensely media-focused enterprise, and the press environment had turned increasingly hostile to all things European. Even by the mid-1990s this hostility verged on the hysterical. *The Daily Telegraph* reported complaints to the BBC about a children's programme that had 'contained positive statements about EU membership'. Following a sexual abuse scandal in Belgium, *The Daily Mail* concluded that the 'Europhile fantasy that Belgium was a successful precursor of a European superstate ... now lies in tatters'. Public opinion was also fickle, with the proportion of the public believing that the EU was 'a Good Thing' declining from 57% to 36% between 1991 and 1997. Blair, conscious of these considerations, and having made a 'Faustian bargain' with the Murdoch press, shared the following thoughts with the readers of *The Sun* during the 1997 election campaign:

> Tomorrow is St George's Day, the day when the English celebrate the pride we have in our nation. On the day we remember the legend that St George slayed a dragon to protect England, some will argue that there is another dragon to be slayed: Europe.[41]

Blair may, therefore, have convinced Young that he was 'a proper European', but he was not anxious to scare the horses by sharing this commitment more widely. Within Labour, there was no advantage to overdoing things, since the party was now generally pro-European. Most voters were not very interested one way or the other. In truth, Labour devoted little time to serious consideration of European issues. Policy was, in all respects, formulated in vague but attractive-sounding terms (for example, in 1996 Blair published a book entitle *New Britain – My Vision of a Young Country*). Above all, New Labour did not want to risk squandering its massive poll leads by detailed discussion of European issues that might offend some sections of the electorate: Blair was, said Roy Jenkins, 'like a man carrying a priceless Ming vase across a highly polished floor'.[42]

However, on the two principal European issues of the mid-1990s, the Social Chapter and the single currency, New Labour's instincts were cautious, if not hostile. The new leadership had little sympathy for Social Europe, being much more at home with the deregulatory approach now in vogue among President Clinton's Democrats. This, insofar as it meant anything at all, was the message to be gleaned from Blair's calls for 'institutional reform' and 'the third way, not old left or new right, a new centre and centre-left agenda'. In the context of the Social Chapter, 'the third way' was to support the chapter (unlike the Conservatives), but reassure sceptical business leaders that it meant very little (unlike Delors).[43]

The single currency was trickier. Could New Labour be both for it and, at the same time, against it? It seemed that it could. The party's official policy was to 'protect and advance', while, at the same time, offering a referendum before any decision was taken. There were, after all, some quite fundamental issues here for a party of the Left. Might it be the case, as the Labour Euro-Safeguards Campaign argued, that entry into the single currency would mean a permanent surrender to neoliberalism, so that 'we would not be able to function as a democratic socialist party'? Did New Labour, indeed, wish to 'function as a democratic socialist party'? Rather than confronting these difficulties it seemed much better to point to Tory disarray on the issue for, as Mullin noted, 'the trouble is that we are at least as divided. Most of us don't understand it and those who do are strongly opposed. The only reason it doesn't show is we are not the government.'[44]

When the much-anticipated election finally arrived in 1997, Blair kept the vase firmly in his clutches. Labour's operation was highly disciplined, and the party's commitments modest in the extreme. The campaign centred on five, fairly anodyne, pledges (for example, 'fast-track punishment for persistent young offenders by halving the time from arrest to sentencing'). One of the pledges committed a Labour government to 'no rise in income tax rates … inflation and interest rates as low as possible'. Fiscal and monetary credibility were all-important.

As we have seen in Chapter 5, Europe was an issue. However, rather than being a question that separated the main parties (as in 1983), the EU was, rather, a stick with which to beat the bitterly divided Tories: to a large extent, indeed, Conservatives eagerly beat each other. In this sense, Labour's stance was expansive, contrasting the party's 'fresh start in Europe', with the willingness of an 'increasing number of Conservatives [to support] withdrawal [which] would be disastrous for Britain … would relegate Britain from the premier division of nations'. Labour strategists clearly calculated that anti-EU voters were likely to peel off from the Tories towards the Eurosceptic fringe of the Referendum Party and UKIP, damaging the Conservatives and helping Labour's already strong position.

In terms of substance, however, the Labour position was vague and looked nervously towards the Eurosceptic press. The party's 'vision of Europe [was] of an alliance of independent nations … we oppose a European federal superstate'. In relation to the single currency, there were some warm words, but little enthusiasm:

> Any decision about Britain joining the single currency must be determined by a hard-headed assessment of Britain's economic interests …

there are formidable obstacles in the way of Britain being in the first wave of membership. … However, to exclude British membership of EMU forever would be to destroy any influence we have over a process which will affect us whether we are in or out. We must therefore play a full part in the debate to influence it in Britain's interests. In any event, there are three pre-conditions which would have to be satisfied before Britain could join during the next Parliament: first, the Cabinet would have to agree; then Parliament; and finally the people would have to say 'Yes' in a referendum.[45]

Likewise, in relation to Social Europe, the party's undertaking to sign the Social Chapter was hedged around with reassurance to business. The overall tone was consistent with the Thatcherite emphasis since the 1980s that social progress was best achieved through competition in free markets:

We will open up markets to competition; pursue tough action against unfair state aids; and ensure proper enforcement of single market rules. This will strengthen Europe's competitiveness and open up new opportunities for British firms. … The Social Chapter is a framework under which legislative measures can be agreed. Only two measures have been agreed. … The Social Chapter cannot be used to force the harmonisation of social security or tax legislation and it does not cost jobs. We will use our participation to promote employability and flexibility, not high social costs.

These oblique formulations proved highly successful in garnering votes. The 1997 result was more than a landslide, declared the political scientist Anthony King on election night, it was 'like an asteroid hitting the planet and destroying practically all life on earth'. Labour emerged with an overall majority of 179, 418 seats and 146 gains. It was clear that Labour had won, but much less apparent what this meant. Was this a victory for socialism? Very few people thought that. Some, like David Marquand, believed that New Labour had 'become an unequivocally social-democratic party in the mainstream of North European social democracy', able to resist 'rampant capitalism' with the 'benign, tamed capitalism of Keynes, Monnet, Beveridge and the rest'. Marquand, a political historian, was in a good position to judge, having been a Jenkinsite Labour MP from 1966 to 1977 before going to work for the European Commission during Jenkins's presidency. But some, like Lionel Jospin (a leading French Socialist) doubted the accuracy of the Marquand view. Blair himself did little to reassure those in 'the mainstream of North European social democracy', telling a European audience that the Third Way would see New Labour reject 'unbridled individualism and *laissez-faire*' but also 'the corporatism of 1960s social democracy'.[46]

1997–2005: New Labour in power

Labour came to power less than twenty years before the 2016 referendum, and left office thirteen years later. It is, therefore, too early to arrive at definitive judgements on this period in office, and most government papers remain withheld. However, one can already see two potential ways to frame the New Labour era. The first is to see the 1997–2010 period as a continuation and deepening of Thatcherism, softened at the edges with some presentational brio and social modernisation. Political practitioners have urged this view, Benn arguing that Blair 'transformed the Labour party from being a radical alternative to the Conservatives into a quasi-Thatcherite sect that made three electoral victories possible, with the backing of Rupert Murdoch and other proprietors'. Thatcher herself is said to have regarded Tony Blair and New Labour as her greatest achievement on the basis that 'we forced our opponents to change their minds'. Simon Jenkins, in his 2007 book, *Thatcher and Sons: A Revolution in Three Acts*, has sought to put factual flesh on these rhetorical bones, explaining in some detail the continuities between the Thatcher/Major and Blair/Brown projects.[47]

There is, of course, another view, which emphasises that New Labour sits within Labour's revisionist traditions. Steven Fielding, for example, has highlighted the connections between the policies of the Blair/Brown governments and those of previous, pragmatic Labour administrations. For obvious reasons, this is not a line with much appeal to New Labour or its opponents, but Fielding has sought to explain how this government, like its social democratic predecessors, sought to bring the party into line with 'contemporary developments in capitalism'.[48]

Whatever the merits of these debates, the 1997–2010 government was certainly not social democratic in the sense used in this book. There were strong continuities with Thatcherism and equally stark departures from what previous Labour (and some Tory) governments had attempted to achieve. A conspicuous example was privatisation. New Labour made no effort to reverse the extensive privatisations of the Thatcher/Major era and, indeed, sought to expand this programme. PFI, commenced somewhat hesitantly under Major, was greatly expanded. Outsourcing of government services was also extended. The Right to Buy scheme continued unabated, and very few council houses were built.

The state both rolled back, and rolled on, in a decidedly Thatcherite fashion. There was no attempt to restore tripartism. The unions were kept at arm's length. Union membership continued to decline. There was 'little sense of shared social purpose' between the industrial and political wings of the Labour Movement. Brown as Chancellor committed the government to keeping the income tax rates and public spending plans inherited from the Conservatives. To general surprise, he achieved this and public spending fell between 1997 and 2000 from 40.6% to 37% of GDP. Thereafter, public spending increased quite rapidly (at 4% pa from 2000 to 2006), but the areas favoured were those that had prospered under Thatcher: health, education and social security.

None of this is to deny that New Labour had solid achievements to its name, including achievements that had eluded previous Labour governments. From 1997 to 2007, at any rate, the economy grew strongly, and unemployment was low. The government took substantial steps to reduce child poverty. The National Minimum Wage was introduced, together with other measures to enhance employee rights. There was a new constitutional settlement in Scotland and Wales; the Good Friday Agreement in Northern Ireland; cultural modernisation, such as the enactment of civil partnerships. Indeed, one could argue, à la Fielding, that New Labour in fact achieved more in practice than previous Labour governments that had been elected with much more grandiose programmes. Nor should Blair's ability to appeal to Middle England be underestimated, a feat that had also eluded earlier generations of Labour politicians.[49]

What, however, the Blair government did not do was to reduce inequality. Mandelson had told a business audience in 1999 that New Labour was 'intensely relaxed about people getting filthy rich'. This part of the Blair agenda was certainly fulfilled, and the wealthy did very well for themselves. The share of the nation's wealth owned by the top 1% fell from 60% in the 1920s to 17% in 1991, but then rose to 24% in 2002: the rich were doing better under New Labour than they had under Thatcher. The poor fared less well. The IFS reported in 2005 that 'inequality remains slightly higher than in 1996/97'. The UK was the most unequal country in the OECD, apart from the USA and Eire.[50]

To some extent, this increasing inequality was the product of global changes over which any British government could have little influence. However, there was also a sense in which New Labour consciously sought a Third Way: not, perhaps, unqualified admiration for all aspects of capitalism, but certainly not the embrace of social democracy as it had been practised in the past in the UK and as still remained the norm in many parts of Europe. As Gordon Brown told the 2003 Labour Conference:

> the future will belong to those countries that by flexibly opening the doors of opportunity, nurture the full potential not just of a few – as in the industrial age – but of the many. And where America is enterprising but not today seen as fair, the rest of Europe more socially cohesive but not today seen as enterprising, I believe that we in Britain can – even amidst the pressures and insecurities of globalisation – become the first

country of this era to combine enterprise and economic strength with a strong public realm…[51]

What then was the attitude of New Labour to 'the rest of Europe' (the formulation itself suggesting a degree of distance)? There is no reason to doubt Blair's own account that he 'regarded anti-European feeling as hopelessly, absurdly out of date'. Other European leaders welcomed the new government, preferring to deal with a friendly and united Labour Party after the years of contending with the prickly and disunited Conservatives. In his early days, at least, Blair was 'the big act in Europe'.[52]

However, Blair also made clear from the outset that there would be much less change in substance than in tone. Nowhere was this more apparent than in relation to the Social Chapter. At his first European meeting as Prime Minister, he told his colleagues that there would be 'serious political difficulties in the United Kingdom if the British signature on the social chapter leads to further proposals for social regulation: we attach very high priority to the promotion of job creation, competitiveness and labour market flexibility'. These 'difficulties' included the 'furious' reaction of the CBI to this signature, 'having been told it would be soft-pedalled'. Blair 'reassured them that the Social Chapter was "only a set of principles", and that he had no intention of allowing the return of union power'.[53]

In practice, New Labour resisted every attempt to extend European competence in employment and social affairs. The IMF was impressed, commending Brown in 2007 for his refusal to implement 'hefty labour protection through regulation, as in France and Germany'. Brown was, after all, both an admirer of Adam Smith and an Americophile, approving 'the US productivity record, free of EU-type employment restrictions'. The unions were less enamoured than the IMF, noting that:

> the British government employed a number of key techniques to blunt the impact of Directives:

'the Blockage' – trying to stop 'unpleasant' Directives, (such as the Information and Consultation draft), from becoming law, in alliance with other hostile EU Member States (e.g., Ireland);

'Foot-dragging' on implementation – doing it slowly and minimally … when holiday rights rose from three weeks to four, the UK subsumed annual and public holidays into the entitlement…;

The inclusion of 'Opt out' clauses – the Working Time Directive gave member states the ability to 'opt out' … the UK allowed all individuals to do so.[54]

It was, in fact, New Labour's deregulatory enthusiasm that led to the fateful decision in 2004 not to impose transitional restrictions on immigration from the accession countries (ten in total, of which eight were from Eastern Europe). Ministers were advised that the net migration effect would be 'relatively small, at between 5,000 and 13,000 migrants per year up to 2010'. In fact, the peak annual figure was 250,000, and so this proved to be a massive miscalculation. However, the government had wished to be welcoming to the new members from the East since 'their free market and pro-NATO stances provided potential for us to strengthen a national alliance within the Union, against that led by France and Germany'.[55]

This immigration decision was not controversial within the government. The same could not be said for the debate over whether the UK should join the Euro. To set this debate in context, one needs to appreciate the importance which New Labour attached to cultivating good relations with the press, especially the Murdoch and Rothermere titles. In 1997, Murdoch 'was not theological about' the single currency, but by the following year, *The Sun* had, in this context, a front-page picture of a masked Blair with the headline 'Is this the most dangerous man in Britain?' Paul Dacre, editor of *The Daily Mail*, was convinced that 'we were going in by stealth'. The government had, therefore, to proceed with caution.[56]

Such caution was all the more necessary because the two leading figures in the government had irreconcilable views upon this central question. Blair, throughout, wanted the UK to join, for example seeking an assurance from Jack Straw, when appointed Foreign Secretary in 2001, that he would 'be onside' on the Euro. Brown, the all-powerful Chancellor, was never prepared to countenance British membership. In formulating the 'five tests' 'he'd not only set the exam paper but would be sitting it and marking it too, this was the one test in life he'd be determined to fail'.[57]

Brown first promulgated the five tests in a statement to the Commons in October 1997. Roy Jenkins told Blair that this was 'a grave mistake'. However, Blair was, in effect, held prisoner by the Treasury. It was a little difficult for any Prime Minister to insist on a policy which, he was advised, was against the nation's economic interests:

> if, in the end, the single currency is successful and the economic case is clear and unambiguous, the Government believe that Britain should be part of it…
>
> We conclude that the determining factor as to whether Britain joins a single currency is the national economic interest, and whether the economic case for doing so is clear and unambiguous. I turn now to the Treasury's detailed assessment of the five economic tests that define whether a clear and unambiguous case can be made. These tests are, first, whether there can be sustainable convergence between Britain and the economies of a single currency; secondly, whether there is sufficient flexibility to cope with economic change; thirdly, the effect on investment; fourthly, the impact on our financial services generally; and fifthly, whether it is good for employment…
>
> Applying those five economic tests leads the Government to the following clear conclusions. British membership of a single currency in 1999 could not meet the tests, and therefore is not in the country's economic interests. There is no proper convergence between the British economy and other European economies now…[58]

As the Euro became a reality in 1998/9, Blair was left 'as a man on a quayside waving others off on their great voyage': a typical British posture over the years of the UK's awkward engagement with Europe. In 1999, following further internal wrangling, Blair announced 'not a change of policy: it is a change of gear. If we wish to have the option of joining, we must prepare'. Technical preparations subsequently took place. Blair hinted that his own preference was to join, for, as he told the Labour Conference in 1999, 'our destiny is with Europe'. Brown, at about the same time, 'was clearly going cold on the euro'. Since, as he made clear in his 2000 Mansion House speech, the Treasury was 'guardian of the policy', there was little that other ministers could do.[59]

There matters stood as Labour entered the 2001 election against a Conservative party that had opted to make hostility to the Euro central to its campaign. Labour brushed the Conservatives aside, achieving a second successive landslide. Blair hinted that a re-elected Labour government might join the Euro: to rule this out would be 'isolationism … relegating Britain to the side-lines of Europe'. The fringe Eurosceptic Right did not seem much of a threat to Blair, his press secretary Alastair Campbell dismissing them in his diary as 'UKIP headbangers'.[60]

With the election won, Blair seemed in a strong position both within and outside the government. According to Brown, he then became 'a lot more bullish' about the Euro. Events, however, then intervened in the shape of the attack on the Twin Towers in New York on 11 September 2001. This was to prove the defining moment of Blair's premiership, as he embarked with Bush upon a 'joint plan to pursue regime change' in Iraq. The UK's subsequent closeness to the Republican Administration in the USA was to place considerable strains upon relations with the EU, not least because France and Germany did not support the invasion of Iraq in 2003.[61]

While the government was largely preoccupied with Iraq for much of its second term, its official position remained that the UK should join the Euro if and when the five tests were satisfied. The Treasury therefore embarked upon a detailed analysis of the evidence. According to Andrew Rawnsley, Brown was determined that this should be so 'authoritative and emphatically negative that no-one, especially not

[Blair] could argue with the conclusion'. Brown duly presented the report in April 2003. Two thousand pages of material led inexorably to the conclusion that the answer must remain No: four of the five tests had not been met. 'A furious shouting match' ensued, according to Brown. Or, as Rawnsley's sources have it, Blair told Brown that he did not accept the conclusions of the report; Brown retorted that he would have to accept it; Blair replied that Brown should 'consider your position', whereupon Brown stormed out, not sure whether he remained Chancellor.[62]

This confrontation was eerily reminiscent of the meeting of the leading figures in the Thatcher government in November 1985, at which Thatcher had declared that she would resign if the UK joined the ERM, as recommended by the Treasury. An equally isolated Blair, albeit from a different perspective, concluded that he could not enforce his will by removing Brown from the Chancellorship and installing a more biddable minister. In June 2003, the Cabinet agreed with Brown's advice, and he told the Commons that 'because we will never put stability at risk that the tests we set were, and indeed are, high ones: namely, to show a clear and unambiguous case for British membership … we have still to meet the two tests of sustainable convergence and flexibility'. Blair may have thought Brown was 'sabotaging his efforts to get into the Euro', but there was little he could do about it.[63]

On broader European issues, the government charted a hesitant course between the Europhile sentiments of at least some in the New Labour camp and the Europhobia of the press. In 1998, the government ratified the Amsterdam Treaty, but without accepting the Schengen acquis (to the security aspects of which the UK retained an 'opt-in', later exercised). The Foreign Secretary told the Commons, in an eerie foreshadowing of 2016, that 'because Britain is an island, it is sensible for us to retain controls at the point of entry … because of our long historical and cultural ties with other parts of the world, it is important to retain control of our own immigration policy'. In 2004 Blair and Straw agreed that there would be a referendum on the proposed treaty for a new

European Constitution. This followed a campaign in *The Sun*, personally authorised by Murdoch, which depicted Blair as the 'undertaker' of British sovereignty and demanded a referendum. In the event, the issue became academic after the French and Dutch voted to reject the Constitution.[64]

Labour secured a third term in 2005 with a reduced, but comfortable, overall majority of 66. The main beneficiaries of the traumas of the Iraq war were the Liberal Democrats, who won 62 seats and a vote share of 22%. The Conservatives made little progress, their vote increasing by only 0.7%. In this sense 2005 was a 'no change' election, but there were some hints of developments that would be important in 2016. Immigration had some weight as an issue, with both UKIP and the BNP demanding an end to the influx of migration from the new EU Member States. UKIP secured 3.2% of the vote and the BNP 0.7%. This confirmed a trend evident at the previous year's European elections, at which these Far-Right parties had obtained 16.1% (and third place with 12 seats) and 4.9% respectively.[65]

Conclusions

Labour's disastrous defeat in 1983 led, in fairly short order, to the party abandoning the socialist policies that it had advocated at that election. These included nationalisation and economic planning, and the necessary concomitant of the AES, withdrawal from the EEC/EU. In that sense, Labour became, for a period, both a social democratic party and a pro-European one. Certainly, in 1992, Labour faced the electorate with a programme that remained egalitarian and a Shadow Chancellor with a substantial record of supporting the UK's engagement with Europe. Defeat in that election, and the death of John Smith in 1994, ushered in the New Labour era.

The Blair/Brown regime, while disavowing withdrawal, in the end pursued policies that left the UK once more on the periphery of a Europe with whose social democratic instincts they felt little sympathy.

The Euro was the key symbol of this tangled relationship, and it was not a merely technical issue as Brown sought to suggest. As Hugo Young observed in 1999, it seemed that New Labour was

> determined to relegate the question of the Euro to the technical realm, as if its only political significance lay in its capacity to destabilise his government rather than its central import to a political leader claiming as strenuously as he does to be a British European.[66]

This relegation was not for want of powerful voices pointing out the political significance of this question. For example, in 1998 some senior pro-European politicians of the *ancien régime* (including Clarke, Heath and Heseltine) wrote to the newspapers to say that 'Conservatives committed to Britain at the heart of Europe will support [Blair] in making the right decision on the difficult challenges that lie ahead … nowhere will … the need for support [be] greater than on economic and monetary union'. In February 1999, Blair saw Heseltine privately at the time of the 'change of gear' announcement and assured him that it remained the government's intention to join. Later that year, Blair and Brown launched the cross-party 'Britain in Europe', together with Clarke, Heseltine and Charles Kennedy, the leader of the Liberal Democrats.[67]

There were, of course, legitimate economic and political arguments against joining the Euro. Indeed, some have argued that the five tests represented an intelligent way to depoliticise the issue in the face of a hostile press and sceptical public. However, it is hard to avoid the conclusion that New Labour's hesitancy over the Euro was part of a wider anxiety about European integration. Blair might be happy to address the French National Assembly in French and contrast New Labour's modernising fervour with the Tories' outdated nationalism. But did he not also believe that the attitudes of France and Germany to social protection equally outdated? As Blair told the Lisbon summit in 2000, 'there is now a new direction for Europe, away from the social regulation agenda of the 80s and instead a direction of enterprise, innovation competition and employment'. Or, as Labour's 2005 manifesto promised, 'During

Britain's EU presidency this year, we will work to promote economic reform, bear down on regulation.'[68]

In truth, New Labour was pursuing a line on Europe which, while overtly friendly to the EU, contained the seeds of much of the destruction that was to come. On the one hand, Blair and Brown were not willing to commit the UK either to economic and monetary union or to Social Europe. Coupled with the UK's isolation over the Iraq war, this, once more, left a British government 'on a quayside waving others off on their great voyage'. On the other hand, the priorities of New Labour favoured openness to the importation of cheap labour from the East and an indulgence of the interests of the City, both of which would prove costly once boom turned to bust. By 2003, the IMF was warning that the UK's economic growth was based on 'domestic demand … sustained by high and increasing levels of household debt, fuelled by house price inflation and low interest rates'. Moreover, the 'Sultans of Spin' were always inclined to give a power of veto to the Eurosceptic press. It was only dissidents like Robin Cook who dared to challenge this veto. Cook had been a pro-European Foreign Secretary from 1997 to 2001, before being demoted after the 2001 election and then resigning over the Iraq war in 2003. In his view, 'the patriotic agenda that the *Sun* advocates is an American one, not a British one'.[69]

7 Crisis, Renegotiation and Referendum, 2005–2016

> Instead of talking about the things that most people care about, we talked about what we cared about most. While parents worried about childcare, getting the kids to school, balancing work and family life – we were banging on about Europe.
>
> (David Cameron, Conservative conference, 2006)[1]

> The British people have voted to leave the European Union and their will must be respected … have made a very clear decision to take a different path and as such I think the country requires fresh leadership to take it in this direction.
>
> (David Cameron, 24 June 2016)[2]

Introduction

Tony Blair led the Labour Party between 1994 and 2007. Throughout this period, New Labour controlled the Party and Labour, likewise, dominated the political scene. The UK remained an 'awkward partner' for the Europeans, but, notwithstanding press sentiment and the views of an increasing number of Conservatives, it seemed very unlikely that the UK would depart the EU.

Brown replaced Blair as Prime Minister in June 2007. Thereafter, the world was turned upside down. The financial crisis of 2007–9 sent the British economy into its worst recession since the 1930s, following two decades of solid growth. This had a substantial negative effect on the public finances: debt and deficit became central political preoccupations. The Conservatives, now under fresh leadership in the shape of Cameron and Osborne, capitalised on alleged Labour profligacy. However, they were unable to win the 2010 general election outright and were obliged to enter into a coalition with the Liberal Democrats.

The coalition government of 2010–15 saw the coming together of like-minded politicians in these two parties, notably Cameron, Osborne, and the Liberal Democrats under Nick Clegg, who had become the party's leader in 2007. On both sides, there was enthusiasm for economic and social liberalism. The government embarked on a deficit reduction strategy ('austerity'), which involved large public spending cuts. Except for the very rich, living standards fell. Public services were reduced. Economic growth slowed.

The financial crisis, and the austerity policies that followed, contributed to the rise of the Far Right (UKIP and the BNP). Immigration became a central political concern. At the same time, Conservative Eurosceptics continued to press for fundamental change in the UK's relationship with the EU. In deference to these developments, Cameron announced in 2013 that a future Conservative government would offer an 'In/Out Referendum'. Austerity proved challenging for Labour as well. Ed Miliband replaced Brown as leader in 2010, having been a New Labour adviser and then minister prior to 2010. However, the party found it difficult to shake off the Tory charge that it was responsible for the size of the deficit. Nor could Labour decide what its position was on austerity.

The Conservatives narrowly won the 2015 election. The Liberal Democrats were crushed. Labour performed disappointingly, especially in Scotland, and Miliband resigned. In the ensuing leadership contest, Jeremy Corbyn defeated a number of New Labour candidates. Corbyn was on the hard Left, a Eurosceptic of long standing, and *plus Benniste que le Benn*. Labour therefore appeared to have changed overnight from being a hesitantly social democratic party to an outright socialist one.

This, very roughly, was the stage upon which the 2016 In/Out Referendum took place. The forces in this battle were disposed very differently from those who had contested the 1975 referendum. The Out, or Leave, campaign principally consisted of the Far Right and the Tory Right (including some dissenting ministers), with the vocal support of much of the media. The In, or Remain, camp was dominated by Conservatives loyal to Cameron and Osborne. Labour provided some, but largely invisible, support. The shattered Liberal Democrats were of marginal importance. Following a bitter campaign, Leave won by 52% to 48%. Cameron resigned immediately. Corbyn barely survived. On the early morning of 2 May 1997, following Labour's landslide, Blair had told his cheering supporters that 'a new dawn has broken'. He could scarcely have foreseen that 19 years later, another Prime Minister would face another dawn in which the UK was about to 'go it alone' outside the EU.

This chapter will seek to make sense of this dizzying sequence of events. In this short period, a large number of received wisdoms were shown to be false. It had been said that the Left was dead, that the press was of no political importance in a digital age, that the electorate was indifferent to political issues, that the UK was now a comfortably multi-cultural society. As it turned out, none of this was true. Most relevantly for present purposes, it also turned out that the UK's future did not lie with Europe, as many had thought in the 1960s and 1970s.

I will examine, therefore, successively the decline of New Labour from 2005 to 2010, the austerity policies of the Coalition from 2010 to 2015 and the upsurge of the Far Right, and the ever-rising tide of Conservative Euroscepticism from 2005 to 2016, before finally considering the denouement of 2015/16. The central argument of this chapter is that the financial crisis, and the measures to deal with it, exposed the hollowed-out nature of what was left of British social democracy, a fragility that had been concealed before boom turned to bust. There were no social democrats left in the Conservative Party, and precious few among the Liberal Democrats. Labour struggled to decide whether it was a social democratic party or not, before concluding that it was, after all, a socialist party. Without the stoutly social democratic framework that had brought the UK into Europe in 1973, and kept it there in 1975, the pro-European case simply lacked sufficient robustness to fight off the nationalist forces ranged against it.

New Labour in decline: 2005–2010

Blair's final day as Prime Minister was 27 June 2007. He departed to a standing ovation in the Commons. The scene affected even the caustic Mullin: he noted that 'several people … were wiping tears from their eyes'. Blair earned at least some of the plaudits that he received. There had been forty successive quarters of economic growth, 'the longest on post-war record for any G7 economy'. In 2007, 61% of those polled thought that the preceding decade had been prosperous for them and their families. They were right to do so. GDP per head in the UK doubled in the New Labour years before the crash, from US\$ 26,000 in 1997 to US\$ 50,000 in 2007. Median real wages grew consistently by around 2% per year.[3]

Moreover, the New Labour economic record won praise beyond the partisan confines of the Commons. The IMF strongly approved the government's policies, which favoured the City, liberalised markets and the bracing forces of globalisation. Mindful of the fate of previous Labour governments, Brown as Chancellor identified, and then kept to, the 'golden rule', whereby he would not permit borrowing to finance current spending over the economic cycle. Between 1997/8 and 2007/8, indeed, although public spending increased, tax receipts increased more quickly and net public debt fell. All in all, Brown felt that he could afford to be a little triumphalist when delivering his last budget in March 2007:

> the British economy is today growing faster than all the other G7 economies. Growth is stronger this year than in the euro area, stronger than in Japan, and stronger even than in America. After 10 years of sustained growth, Britain's growth will continue into its 59th quarter – the forecast end of the cycle – and then into its 60th, 61st and 62nd quarter

and beyond. Before 1997 we were bottom in the G7 for national income per head. We were seventh out of seven, behind Germany, Italy, France, Canada and Japan. Now we are second only to America and ahead of all those other countries. … We will not return to the old boom and bust.[4]

Brown's European inheritance from Blair was also comparatively serene. In May 2005, the French and Dutch had rejected the proposed EU constitution. This allowed the government to dispense with its offer of a referendum, to 'huge relief'. Membership of the Euro had receded as a possibility. Some tabloid sniping apart, the New Labour position of warm verbal engagement with the EU, tempered by a cool detachment from most proposals for Social Europe, was broadly successful in finessing many of the difficulties that had overwhelmed the Major government. However, as Rawnsley observes,

> Blair was better at selling Britain and its pro-reform agenda to Europe than he was at selling Europe and the European ideal to Britain … what he did not succeed in doing was draining Europhobia from the body politic.

As to the former, the UK had been able to promote market liberalisation and enlargement, and resist further moves towards a federal Europe. However, as to the latter, Blair himself acknowledged that:

> The dilemma of a British Prime Minister over Europe is acute to the point of the ridiculous. Basically you have a choice: co-operate in Europe and you betray Britain; be unreasonable in Europe, be praised back home, and be utterly without influence in Europe. It's sort of: isolation or treason…
>
> There is no other way for Britain. Britain won't leave Europe. No Government would propose it. And despite what we are often told, the majority of the British people, in the end, would not vote for withdrawal.[5]

There were, however, clouds on the horizon for New Labour when Brown took over in 2007. Self-evidently, the government's standing depended very largely upon its reputation for economic competence. The balancing act in relation to Europe was a delicate one. And 'the smallest party in the history of British politics' had a very limited talent pool. When Wilson resigned as Labour leader in 1976, there were six candidates to replace him (Benn, Callaghan, Crosland, Foot, Healey and Jenkins). Each was a giant in Labour politics, and the field represented the full spectrum of views within the party from Left to Right. By contrast, in 2007, Brown 'stood head, shoulders and torso above everyone else in the government'. He was the only candidate to succeed Blair.[6]

Brown's last budget speech had shown signs of hubris, but nemesis lay in wait. In his first few weeks as Prime Minister, Labour's private polling showed the party well ahead, and there was talk of a snap election. In the event, Brown was outmanoeuvred by the new Tory leadership and decided not to go the country. This turned out to be a fateful decision. In mid-September 2007, depositors began queuing to withdraw funds from the Northern Rock building society. This developed into a fully fledged failure, the first run on a bank since 1866; the government had to nationalise the society.[7]

The relief was only temporary. In the autumn of 2008, there was a massive international financial crisis, triggered by the collapse of Lehman Brothers in New York. Panic ensued. By mid-September 'the world financial system [was] on the brink of meltdown … our television screens are showing erstwhile Masters of the Universe emerging ashen-faced from Lehman Brothers' gleaming tower in Canary Wharf'. Two big British banks (RBS and Lloyds) collapsed and the government had to nationalise them as well. Such was the international scale and depth of the crisis that an emergency meeting of G7 finance ministers convened in Washington DC over the weekend of 10 to 13 October 2008 in order to avert the collapse of the entire international banking system.[8]

The crisis had a number of important consequences. The real economy suffered a deep recession. The public finances plunged into deficit as a result. New Labour's boast that it had abolished 'boom and bust' was exposed. However, and paradoxically, the government embarked on what looked very much like 'Old Labour' policies to deal with the effects of the recession. As Alastair Darling (Brown's successor as Chancellor) wryly remarked during the crisis, 'All my political career people have been telling me to stop being so left wing, to give up on socialism … now they want me to nationalise the bloody banks!'[9]

The British economy suffered its deepest recession since the 1930s. Output fell by 7.1% from its pre-recession peak at the end of 2007 to the trough in the second quarter of 2009. The effect on government finances was dramatic and immediate. Borrowing reached £152bn (9.9% of GDP) in 2009/10. The recession both pushed up government spending and reduced government revenue. Spending rose from 39% of GDP in 2007/8 to 45% in 2009/10. Revenue fell from 36% to 35% of GDP.[10]

Of course, the crisis was not confined to the UK. Almost all Western economies were badly affected, but the more fragile suffered particularly badly. In Europe, Greece experienced a severe debt crisis: its public debt amounted to 113% of GDP, nearly double the Eurozone limit of 60%. This in turn gave rise to a bitter conflict between successive Greek governments and the EU authorities. The former, especially the left-wing, anti-austerity, Syriza party, sought renegotiation of the bailout terms which the EU and the country's creditors had imposed, debt cancellation and increased public sector spending. The latter, whose will eventually prevailed, imposed stringent austerity terms as a condition of financial assistance, and appeared to many to place the sanctity of the Euro and the maintenance of the Eurozone above the interests of the Greek people. The EU emerged from the crisis as a force for neoliberalism and financial orthodoxy. Notions of social solidarity took a poor second place. The Euro became less a symbol of European unity than of prolonged austerity.[11]

At the same time, social democracy was facing a wider predicament throughout Western Europe. In Greece itself, PASOK, which had been in and out of government for decades, struggled to provide answers to the crisis and found itself usurped on the Left by Syriza. In Germany's 2009 parliamentary elections, the SPD experienced a massive fall in support, winning just 23% of the national vote, and failed to improve its position substantially thereafter. Even in Sweden, where the Social Democrats had dominated politics since the 1930s, the party lost office. Social democrats throughout Europe found it hard to provide a convincing response to the financial crisis and its aftermath or an electorally attractive alternative to neoliberalism.[12]

These developments, both domestic and international, created a major political problem for New Labour, which the Conservatives were swift to exploit. Brown's economic policies had been predicated upon 'light-touch' financial regulation, an all-powerful Treasury and the encouragement of a City plutocracy. This was intended to deliver prudence in the public finances. All this looked more than a little suspect as the 'meltdown' in the City caused the government to plunge into the red. Labour's reputation for economic competence was fatally damaged. One could argue that the Conservatives would have spent as much, taxed as little and tolerated the City very much the same. But the political world does not comprehend such subtleties. Labour had been in charge when the crisis hit, and would be punished for it, just as the Conservatives had been in 1992.[13]

However, nothing became Brown in his political life like the leaving of it. From October 2008 onwards, the government both embarked on aggressive domestic policies to soften the impact of the crash and sought to lead international policymakers along similar lines. The Bank of England massively loosened monetary policy. Interest rates were cut to 0.5%. A substantial quantitative easing programme was undertaken. However, the government also sought to assist recovery through fiscal policy. In November 2008, Darling announced a stimulus of £20bn. The crisis also offered the opportunity for more redistributive policies, with the top rate of income tax being increased to 45% and then 50%. In 2009, Brown hosted a G7 summit in which the leaders agreed to inject £681bn into the world economy.[14]

The financial crisis, and the measures to deal with it, overshadowed the Brown government. European policy took a back seat. However, there was substantial continuity: Brown had been as much the architect of New Labour's approach to Europe as Blair. Moreover, he appointed as Foreign Secretary David Miliband, who had formerly run Blair's policy unit. Miliband, in his first major speech in that role, struck an appropriately Blairite note:

> we are members of the EU. That membership is an asset in economic terms – guaranteeing open markets and setting common standards where needed … it needs to be a greater asset in foreign policy – not substituting for nation states but giving better expression to the common commitments of nation states. That is why we support the proposal to amend the EU Treaties so that we have at our disposal a single Representative to take forward our Common Foreign and Security Policy where all 27 Member States wish to act together and give authority to do so.[15]

Such remained the authentic voice of New Labour. There was no trace of the Conservative hostility to Europe, but the relationship remained a fundamentally cautious one. In one respect, Brown's administration was more confined in its approach. Within weeks of his elevation, it became apparent that 'the Murdoch press would be my adversary'. The *casus belli* was the Lisbon Treaty, which was the somewhat more anodyne replacement for the Constitutional Treaty, which had foundered in 2005. For example, no additional exclusive competences were transferred to the EU, and, unlike the Constitutional Treaty, Lisbon contained no article formally enshrining the supremacy of EU law over national legislation. Nonetheless, Eurosceptics viewed Lisbon with suspicion, and the tabloid press was 'vitriolic' in its demands for a referendum.[16]

Brown's response to this pressure was 'not to take on the argument, but to hope it would go away if he kept his head down for long enough'. For example, in December 2007 he signed the treaty, 'alone and behind closed doors after he skipped the televised signing ceremony with the 26 other EU heads of state'. This neither endeared him to his European colleagues nor satisfied the Eurosceptic press. Such dithering was curious, in that the finer points of European constitutional law did not appear to have much traction with the public, however much the press fulminated. The same was not true of immigration, which, as will be seen, was gaining increasing salience even before the financial crisis: in March 2008, the government introduced a 'points-based' system for non-EU migrants.[17]

Despite the vigorous counter-measures adopted, Labour's credibility did not recover after the crisis and the party lost the 2010 election. Its share of the vote was lower than at any time since the 1983 catastrophe. However, the Conservatives failed to win an overall majority, and the result left the Commons exquisitely balanced. The precise disposition of forces was to prove important in what came next.

Party		Seats	Net votes	%	±%
Con	306	+96	10,703,744	36.1	+3.7
Lab	258	−90	8,606,518	29.0	−6.2
LD	57	−5	6,836,198	23.0	+1.0
DUP	8	−1	168,216	0.6	−0.3
SNP	6	0	491,386	1.7	+0.2
SF 5	0	171,942		0.6	
PC 3	+1	165,394		0.6	
SDLP 3	0	110,970		0.4	−0.1
Green 1	1	284,823		1.0	+1
All	1	+1	42,762	0.1	
Ind	1	0	229,021	0.8	+0.4
Spkr	1		22,860	0.1	N/A
(326 seats being required for an overall majority)					

Coalition Government, 2010–2015: all in it together?

The deficit had increased rapidly once the crash occurred. In 2008/9 it was £101.5bn or 6.6% of GDP, and this figure rose to £158.3bn in 2009/10 (10.3%). How to deal with the deficit was a central issue in the general election, albeit that, as a Tory insider recalled, 'there was a sort of mutual pact between the parties about not being too upfront about future pain; everyone wanted to avoid debate about what was to come'. Nonetheless, it was clear to those who looked carefully at the Conservative Manifesto that the Tories would seek 'to eliminate the bulk of the structural deficit over a Parliament', and would do this primarily through cutting spending. Given that the election had produced a hung parliament, but with the ostensibly 'progressive' forces (Labour, Lib Dems and others) outnumbering the Conservatives by 328 seats to 306, how did it come about that the Conservatives took office?[18]

The Liberal Democrats held talks after the election with both main parties, but it is evident from Andrew Adonis's account that they were never serious about forming a pact with Labour (Adonis had been a minister in the Brown government and was involved in these negotiations). The leadership of the Liberal Democrats, in particular Clegg, Laws and Alexander, were much more temperamentally sympathetic to the Cameron/Osborne Conservatives than to Labour. Partly this seemed to be personal and social, Clegg and Cameron coming from similarly privileged public school backgrounds.[19]

However, this was more than the old school tie at work. The Liberal Democrats had undertaken an ideological journey to the Right since the formation of the Alliance in 1983 as the 'defender of the Butskellite consensus'. The party's broad stance in the 1980s and 1990s had been Keynesian, interventionist and redistributive. Under the leadership of Paddy Ashdown (1988–99) and Charles Kennedy (1999–2006), the Liberal Democrats had aimed to be 'the most socially progressive party in British politics'. Kennedy had come into politics via the SDP, and his approach remained social democratic. He resigned as leader in

2006 and was replaced by Menzies Campbell, who gave way to Clegg in 2007.[20]

Clegg came from a quite different tradition. He was 'a liberal by temperament, by instinct and by upbringing'. In particular, he was party to the 'Orange Book', co-edited by Laws, a 2004 publication that sought to reclaim the supposed Liberal tradition of economic liberalism. Laws argued that over a long period from the 1930s to the 1980s the party's commitment to 'free market principles, and to economic liberalism, was slowly watered down'. This process had reached its apogee in the merger with the SDP of the mid-1980s, 'which saw many individuals who had believed in state solutions to economic problems participate in' the new party. The Liberal Democrats should now embrace competition and the private sector, 'reducing the state's role in the economy, including investigating the case for privatising the Royal Mail'. While still leader, Kennedy was suspicious of this new agenda, not least since he was one of the 'many individuals' who had joined the merged party in the 1980s. However, the new leadership had little truck with his talk of a 'war against poverty', being more concerned with the need to court better-off voters.[21]

On this footing, the Liberal Democrats were now, in a real sense, neoliberals. Much of what they proposed was a perfect fit with the new direction of the Conservatives: Thatcherite economics tempered by a more 'modern' approach to social issues such as gay marriage. Indeed, Laws quoted approvingly Jo Grimond, a former Liberal leader, who had observed in the 1980s that 'much of what Mrs Thatcher and Sir Keith Joseph say and do is in the mainstream of liberal philosophy'. Social democracy seemed to be dead within the Liberal Democrats. The SDP heritage had evaporated. Of course, some within the party retained social democratic sympathies. For example, the Treasury spokesperson, Vince Cable, had served as a special adviser to the Secretary of State for Trade and Industry, John Smith, in the Callaghan government and later joined the SDP. However, Cable was ruthlessly marginalised in the Coalition negotiations. His pro-Keynesian sympathies were not those of the party leadership: according to Adonis, 'on this central strategic issue, they were at one' with the Tories. The 'issue' was the need for 'swifter action to tackle the deficit, willingness to hold an Emergency Budget'.[22]

The involvement of the Liberal Democrats was not, therefore, as some may have thought, an unhappy marriage of convenience brought about by the quirks of the electoral system. Rather, as the cultural theorist Stuart Hall argued, this was an ideological choice by those in the party who favoured neoliberalism. And this new project was not really new and not merely the product of the financial crisis. It formed part of successive waves of neoliberalism since the mid-1970s, in which 'the state [was] cast as tyrannical and oppressive'. The apparent harmony of Clegg and Cameron as they '"kissed hands" in the No. 10 rose garden' was a victory for 'neoliberal-inclined Orange Book supporters, who favoured an alliance with the Conservatives, against the "progressives", including former social democrats, who leaned towards Labour'. Or, as Adonis (not a Marxist like Hall, but a New Labour technocrat and former SDP member) has put it, 'Laws and the neoliberals believe in the "failure of the social-democratic experiment" as an article of faith. They emphatically reject the label "social democrat"'.[23]

Bringing these ideas up to date, the parties in 2010 stood shoulder to shoulder on the need for austerity. The Coalition Agreement entered into on 20 May 2010 was explicit on the point:

> We recognise that deficit reduction, and continuing to ensure economic recovery, is the most urgent issue facing Britain. We will significantly accelerate the reduction of the structural deficit over the course of a Parliament, with the main burden of deficit reduction borne by reduced spending rather than increased taxes. … We will set out a plan for deficit reduction in an emergency budget.[24]

Osborne duly announced the emergency budget on 22 June 2010. In it he set out the principles that were to underlie the 2010–15 government. The state had grown too large under Labour, and it was this extravagance that had led to an unsustainable deficit. It was necessary to take strong measures to avoid the fate of economies like Greece, which were struggling to borrow sufficient monies to keep their state services from entire collapse. These measures would principally involve cutting spending rather than increasing taxes, for 'the coalition believes that the bulk of the reduction must come from lower spending rather than higher taxes. The country has overspent; it has not been under-taxed … that is the origin of our 80:20 rule of thumb – roughly, 80% through lower spending and 20% through higher taxes.'[25]

Thereafter, the government embarked upon a policy that came to be known as 'expansionary fiscal contraction'. The Brown government's monetary policies – low interest rates and quantitative easing – remained in place. But instead of a fiscal stimulus, there ensued a significant fiscal squeeze. This, it was said, would promote growth, since it was necessary to move, in Osborne's words, to 'an economy where the state does not take almost half of all our national income, crowding out private endeavour'. The reduction in the size of the state was substantial. Local government in particular suffered a 52% real-terms cut in central government support between 2010/11 and 2015/16. However, the picture generally was bleak for government spending. As the IFS reported:

> Between 2010–11 and 2014–15, total public spending has been cut by 3.0% in real terms, resulting in a dramatic fall in public spending as a share of national income. Different areas of spending have fared very differently over this period of austerity. Between 2010–11 and 2014–15, departmental spending was cut by 9.1%, compared with a 2.4% increase in non-departmental spending. Within departmental spending, health, schools and official development assistance have been protected, while other areas have been cut dramatically.[26]

Although there was some softening of austerity in 2012/13, and although the government eventually recognised that it could not eliminate the deficit within a single parliament, the direction of travel was relentless. Following the 2011 Autumn Statement, the Treasury Chief Secretary (the Liberal Democrat, Danny Alexander) told the BBC that at the next election he would be 'promising further billions of cuts in spending'. In 2013, Osborne proclaimed a new, long-term, economic plan with the aim of reducing public spending to 'its lowest level in 80 years' as a proportion of GDP. This was to be achieved as to 98% by cuts and 2% by tax increases. As in the 1980s, there was, it appeared, no alternative, since 'even if the improving economic news eventually leads to an improvement in the fiscal outlook, the job will not be done. More tough choices will be required after the next election to find many billions of further savings and anyone who thinks those decisions can be ducked is not fit for government.'[27]

Of course, the austerity programme was not without its critics. There were two broad points made. The first was that the reason that the deficit had increased so much in 2008/9 was that the economy had contracted so sharply, pushing up social spending and reducing tax revenues. To reduce the deficit, it was necessary to promote economic growth, which would reduce social spending and increase tax revenues, thus narrowing the deficit. Since the government was, in the short to medium term, able to finance the deficit by borrowing at reasonable rates, this was the way back from the crisis. In his memoirs, Brown argued this very point: the post-crash fiscal stimulus 'drove the economic recovery … leading to even faster growth in mid-2010 than in 2007. But this was then killed off by austerity.' The figures appeared to bear this out. The policy of expansionary fiscal contraction proved more successful at the latter than the former. The plans of June 2010 had been premised upon achieving nearly 9% growth by June 2013. The actual figure was only 3.2%. Indeed, one could see, as Brown suggested, a promising recovery being snuffed out by the austerity programme (see Table 7.1).

The austerity programme was also criticised by those who disputed that, as Osborne claimed in 2010, 'we are all in this together'. Certainly, the coalition was at pains to ensure that the wealthy did not suffer undue hardship. For example, in the 'millionaire's budget' of 2012, the highest rate of income tax was cut from 50% (the rate to which Darling had increased it post-crash) to 45%. The poor, especially those dependent on benefits, took the brunt of the pain. The 'bedroom tax' (a cut in housing benefit for those living in social housing classed as having a spare bedroom) was a particular source of grievance. Indeed, most ordinary wage earners fared poorly. The ONS reported in 2011 that 'in 2010 … real disposable income actually fell – by 0.8 per cent … the first annual fall since 1981 and the largest since 1977. The squeeze continued in the first quarter of 2011 when real households' disposable income fell by 2.7% compared with the same period of 2010.' These were very significant reductions: there was considerable truth in the charge that the burden of the financial crisis fell not upon those who had caused it, and had benefited from the previous boom, but upon those who had played no part in the crisis.[29]

The coalition government proved a difficult period for Labour. The Conservatives, aided and abetted by their coalition partners, kept to an insistent theme. Labour had brought the country to its knees by spending and borrowing too much. Without stern measures to cut the deficit, the UK would be reduced to bankruptcy, like Greece. Labour found itself impaled upon the horns of a dilemma. If it agreed with this analysis, the party had to explain how this unhappy state of affairs had come about and why, if this was so, there was any point in voting Labour. If it did not agree, the party had to identify some alternative course.[30]

Unfortunately for the party, Labour after 2010 never seemed clear in its own mind what answer it proposed to this dilemma. Following Brown's resignation, Ed Miliband became leader, defeating his brother David, Ed Balls, Andy Burnham and Diane Abbott. With the exception of Abbott, all the candidates had been advisers and then ministers under New Labour. The only real distinction between them was that Balls and Ed Miliband were 'Brownites' and Burnham and David Miliband 'Blairites'. However, all were tarnished with the Tory charge that irresponsible public spending by the government in which they had served had created the deficit crisis. The inability to mount an effective challenge to this allegation left Labour unable to regain the mantle of economic credibility and forced it to espouse a confused message on the central

question of public spending. At one moment, the leader would address
The People's Assembly Against Austerity. At another Balls, as Shadow
Chancellor, would pledge Labour to accept Osborne's spending plans.
As *Private Eye* had it, Ed Miliband was prepared 'to join your protest
against some of the cuts, though obviously not all of them because let's
face it if we'd been elected we would have to have made some too'.[31]

The muddled narrative over austerity was symptomatic of a wider
confusion within the party. The new leadership sought to draw upon
multiple sources of ideas, in contrast to the strict message discipline of
the Blair years. However, as Peter Mandelson (the arch disciplinarian
of that period) remarked, the new message 'did not cohere or become
a compelling narrative'. Ideas ('Responsible capitalism', 'One Nation
Labour', 'Blue Labour') came and went without ever forming a cogent
counter-narrative to the coalition account of a nation laid low by Labour
profligacy. The party gave the impression of writing out a shopping list
of 'micro-policies' on matters such as energy bills or the bedroom tax,
without any overarching philosophy to hold these disparate themes
together.[32]

During the 2010–15 Parliament, Labour, in addition to its other
woes, suffered a massive haemorrhage on its Scottish flank. Support
for the SNP had been building steadily since 2010. In 2014, a referendum was held on independence. The campaign went much better than
the Nationalists may have feared. In early September, a YouGov poll
showed that 51% of respondents supported independence. Panic ensued
among the unionist forces: Cameron and Miliband missed PMQs to fly
to Scotland and promise more extensive devolution. In the event, the
nationalists lost the referendum by 45% to 55%. However, for Labour
the victory was pyrrhic indeed. The party's close identification with the
Conservatives during the referendum campaign proved toxic. At the
2015 election, Labour lost all but one of its 41 Scottish MPs, with the
SNP securing 56 of 59 seats north of the border. The SNP was 'widely
seen as to the left of Labour' albeit that there was some policy overlap.
However, the anti-austerity and anti-Tory rhetoric of the nationalists

Table 7.1 GDP growth 2008–2013

2008 Q1	0.3
2008 Q2	−0.7
2008 Q3	−1.6
2008 Q4	−2.2
2009 Q1	−1.6
2009 Q2	−0.2
2009 Q3	0.2
2009 Q4	0.3
2010 Q1	0.5
2010 Q2	0.9
2010 Q3	0.5
2010 Q4	0.1
2011 Q1	0.6
2011 Q2	0.1
2011 Q3	0.4
2011 Q4	0.2
2012 Q1	0.6
2012 Q2	−0.1
2012 Q3	1.2
2012 Q4	−0.1
2013 Q1	0.6
2013 Q2	0.5[28]

played well in Scotland. Labour's equivocal stance on austerity and apparent closeness to English Conservatism did not.[33]

All in all, social democracy in the UK (or, at least, in England) was in a somewhat sickly state during this period. As has been rightly said, the 'dominance of neoliberalism has ensured that it has come to define the terms of discussion', not only in the UK but elsewhere. Certainly, the neoliberal desire to reduce the size and role of the state was central to the coalition's austerity programme. However, even within Labour, there was a fundamental division between 'those who did not question New Labour's economic model and those who argued for a more social democratic agenda', with the leadership poised uncomfortably atop this divide. Some, like Roy Hattersley, who was Old Labour to his fingertips, and who had served in the Wilson and Callaghan governments, continued to argue for traditional social democratic values. However, at least some of those advising the new leadership shuddered at such 'statist philosophy'.[34]

Revolt of the 'left behind': the rise of UKIP

The British economy was on something of a rollercoaster ride after 2005. Boom turned to bust. A promising recovery gave way to austerity. GDP per head in the UK fell from US$ 50,000 in 2007 to US$40,000 by 2016. Earnings fell sharply from 2008 onwards. Between 2008 and 2017, real weekly wages for the median worker decreased by about 5%, almost a 20% drop relative to the trend in real wage growth from 1980 to the early 2000s.[35]

However, we were not 'all in this together'. The rich were different, and they did very well out of the crash and its aftermath. Quantitative easing, low interest rates and international economic conditions resulted in considerable asset price inflation. Anyone fortunate enough to own property in Kensington and Chelsea in September 2008 would have seen the investment increase in value by about 50% by the time of the 2016 referendum. In the former mining district of Mansfield, house prices did not rise at all over the same period. The retail price index had risen by about 25%, so asset-holders in Kensington enjoyed a real-terms increase and those who owned property in Mansfield saw it shrinking in value. The difference between these local authority areas (and there were numerous other similar comparisons that could be made) was stark when the referendum votes were counted: the Remain vote in the former was 69% and the latter 29%. Moreover, those who had presided over the banking collapse emerged unscathed. The smirking Fred Goodwin, Chief Executive of RBS, suffered the minor inconvenience of losing his knighthood, but could console himself with a pension for life of £603,000 per annum and a tax-free lump sum of £2.7m.[36]

Life was very different for those who lived in areas where UKIP was to prosper. To set UKIP's dramatic rise in context, it is worth going back a little in time. The party's origins lay in the Anti-Federalist League, which had been set up by Alan Sked (an academic at the LSE) in 1991 to campaign against Maastricht. UKIP itself was formed in 1993, and was initially overshadowed by Goldsmith's Referendum Party. From then onwards, UKIP made steady but unspectacular progress. In 1997 it had fielded 194 candidates, who secured 1% of the vote in the seats they contested. By 2010, the figures were 558 and 3.5%. It was, curiously enough, in European elections that the party made most impact before 2010. By 2004, it had 12 MEPs and was in third place overall. In 2009, a 'potent mix of Eurosceptic, populist and anti-immigration messages' secured 16.5% of the poll. At the same election, the BNP received 6.2% of the vote and its first two MEPs were elected. Labour suffered its worst postwar election result and was beaten into third place. Labour's share of the vote was 15.3%, so that the two Far Right parties easily outpolled it.[37]

Nonetheless, and bearing in mind that the European elections attracted a turn-out of only 34%, UKIP's standing at the 2010 elections presented an equivocal picture. On the one hand, this was still a very amateurish operation. The party's leader, Lord Pearson, presented an eccentric face to the world. Its most charismatic figure, Farage, very nearly died during the campaign in an election stunt that went wrong. The party's policies were incoherent. As Farage himself was later to remark, the 2010 manifesto 'was 486 pages of drivel ... It was a nonsense.' On the other hand, this was the 'largest minor party challenge ever to be mounted, and generated the largest share of the vote ever won by a minor party'. Furthermore, the BNP fielded 338 candidates and secured 1.9% of the votes, 'easily the highest vote ever cast for a far-right party in a UK general election'. UKIP's manifesto, even if it was 'drivel', anticipated many of the themes that would surface at the 2016 referendum:

> UKIP will … regain control of UK borders. This can only be done by leaving the European Union … maintain a trade-based relationship with our European neighbours using a Swiss-style free trade agreement as the EU's largest single trading partner. … European companies sell us more than we sell them; we are their largest client. So our trade and jobs would continue if we left the EU, and we would benefit by escaping from its crippling overregulation … Regain Britain's dormant seat at the World Trade Organisation. From here, a UKIP government will be free to pursue Britain's national interests. The current situation leaves Britain unable directly to negotiate its own trade deals because vital national interests are subsumed in a common EU position that frequently reflects the interests of France and Germany.[38]

The evidence from 2010 was uncertain as to the impact of the issues that were to dominate the Brexit referendum six years later. Labour focus groups found that immigration was a major concern, and Brown had a disastrous confrontation with an elector whom he described as 'this sort of bigoted woman', even though she was a handpicked Labour voter. The Conservatives proposed an annual cap on immigration: even so, it appeared that there was a negative effect on their vote where UKIP polled strongly. However, polling suggested that most voters thought economic issues far more important than immigration or asylum. A theme of the election was Cleggmania – a cartoon in the *Telegraph* showed a man on crutches outside a Clegg rally saying 'I don't want to ask him about the NHS, I want him to heal me' – and yet the Liberal Democrats were the most relaxed of the major parties on immigration. Most strikingly of all, there was little discussion of Europe. As the official history of the election observed, 'an outsider might have been struck by the parochialism of Britain in 2010'.[39]

Between 2004 and 2010, support for UKIP had hovered between 3% and 6% in the polls. After 2010, with Farage restored to the leadership (a role he had previously held from 2006 to 2009), the party's fortunes took off, with a poll rating of about 14%. Farage noted 'a rebirth of identity politics' among those disenchanted with 'the political class'. This took the form, after 2010, of a huge surge in support in areas with 'a financially disadvantaged and working-class electorate', a trend first observable at the Oldham by-election in January 2011. In similar seats, such as Rotherham and South Shields, the party increased its vote share by between 16% and 24%; it also achieved a similar showing in the more prosperous, southern, seat of Eastleigh. In some, short-term, senses the period after the 2010 general election was tailor-made for a protest party of the Right. A Centre Right party was in government, but without a majority. The traditional party of by-election dissent was now in office. The BNP had disintegrated. Labour was ineffectual, and unable to articulate a clear line on anything, let alone speak to the concerns of its erstwhile supporters on immigration. 'The political class' seemed to be doing everything possible to invite the derision of the voters. The by-elections at Rotherham, South Shields and Eastleigh arose from respectively: the imprisonment of the former MP for fiddling his expenses, the departure of David Miliband to a lucrative job in New York and the jailing of the departing MP for perjury.[40]

UKIP's rise continued in dramatic fashion in the 2014 European elections. Farage welcomed the result as putting pressure on the other parties: it was 'an earthquake … never before in the history of British politics has a party seen to be an insurgent party ever topped the polls in a national election'. He also predicted that this result would overshadow Cameron's negotiating stance in Europe. It was, indeed, the first time in a century that neither main party had won first place in a national election. More impartial commentators agreed that the results were 'remarkable'; this was 'the first new movement for almost a century to win a nationwide election'.

Party	Vote share	Change	Seats	Change
UKIP	27.49	(+10.99)	24	+11
Labour	25.40	(+9.67)	20	+7
Cons	23.93	(−3.80)	19	−7
Green	7.87	(−0.75)	3	+1
Lib Dem	6.87	(−6.87)	1	−10[41]

Although UKIP had been doing particularly well in areas that usually voted Labour, the contagion began to spread to Conservative seats as well. In the autumn of 2014, two right-wing Tory MPs (Carswell and Reckless) defected to UKIP. They had both been urging a more Eurosceptic stance upon the government. Both held their seats for UKIP at the subsequent by-elections at Clacton and Rochester. There was panic among at least some Conservatives as to how they might win back voters lost to UKIP. The offer of an In/Out Referendum did not seem to have worked.[42]

What explained this upsurge in support for a party that put forward 'drivel' by way of policy? The rise of UKIP prompted considerable scholarly work on the nature of that support. It 'had a distinctive geographical pattern. It was anchored in left-behind communities that … had few good reasons to feel optimistic about the future.' Clacton was a case in point. Although in the generally prosperous South-East, one town within the constituency, Jaywick, had been categorised as the most deprived place in England. Of course, this 'pattern' had deep and longstanding roots. Deprivation had not happened overnight. As was observed, these communities had been lagging over a long period during which 'a deep divide has opened up between struggling, working-class voters who have been left behind by the economic and social transformation of Britain, and the university educated middle class, who have prospered and risen to numerical and political dominance.'[43]

This long-term explanation is all very well, but one needs to understand how and why UKIP went so quickly from being 'cranks and political gadflies' (in the words of Michael Howard in 2004) to being a formidable political force. And how, by 2014, had they become 'the most working-class-dominated party since Michael Foot's Labour in 1983' (when, of course, Labour had been defeated on a leftist platform)?[44]

The former question is perhaps easier to answer. The impact of the crash, and subsequent austerity, affected those 'left behind' particularly severely. Between 2008 and 2013, UKIP saw its support rise fastest among working-class voters, pensioners and those who had left school at 16. The proportion of UKIP voters who thought, in 2014, that the financial situation of their household would get worse over the next year was far higher than among more prosperous Tory or Liberal Democrat voters and similar to that for Labour voters.[45]

The latter question – the inroads of UKIP into traditional Labour territory – requires a more complex response. Clearly immigration played a large part in the defection of Labour voters. Some working-class former Labour voters had lost faith with the party's apparently liberal stance on migration. This disaffection became more pronounced after the crash, as economic conditions worsened. However, the disillusionment of these voters was not just over migration. They thought that Labour wanted to help the rich as much as the poor. They did not believe that the party now spoke to their economic insecurity. It was striking that on an assessment of Left/Right values, 72% of UKIP supporters thought that 'ordinary working people do not get their fair share' and 68% that 'privatisation has gone too far'. These were not the views of the Maastricht rebels or, indeed, the neoliberals in charge of the coalition. Certainly, UKIP voters were overwhelmingly in favour of leaving the EU, but it was not obvious that they shared the concern of the Tory Right over issues such as the Customs Union, the jurisdiction of the European Court or the danger of regulatory overload.[46]

However, although UKIP's policies might have been 'a nonsense' and although the new party certainly lacked the message discipline of the larger parties, it had a clear ideology. This was not confined to immigration. Indeed, the remarkable feature of UKIP's programme in the 2010–15 period was how closely the party anticipated the themes that the Vote Leave campaign would articulate in 2016: the threat from new Member States, such as Turkey; the burden of the UK's financial contributions; the need to 'leave the EU and make our own laws'; the possibility of 'build[ing] trade links with emerging and growing, not declining economies'. Above all, UKIP expressed the dominant refrain of 2016, the need to take back control. As its 2015 General Election manifesto – in which the word 'control' or its variants occurred 42 times – put it:

> until we leave the EU. We will never control our borders or manage immigration. ... A British exit from the EU, 'Brexit,' is the only choice open to us, if we are to make our own laws and control our own destiny. Unless we leave, our democracy, our law-making powers and our sovereignty will continue to be salami sliced away by the EU.[47]

In the 2015 general election, UKIP stood in all 573 seats in England and Wales for the first time. The surge continued, with the party securing 12.6% of the overall vote, and improving its share by 10.7% in the seats where it had stood in 2010. It did particularly well in those areas where unemployment had risen sharply over the previous decade and where a high proportion of the electorate was 'White British'. However, this was a curious campaign for a country that was about to vote to 'take back control'. The EU was hardly mentioned. UKIP took ownership of immigration as a concern but, said the official historians, 'overall the issue did not register on the election agenda as it had done in previous campaigns'.[48]

UKIP had, therefore, come a long way since its formation in 1993. Most of its new supporters were probably little acquainted with the minutiae of the Maastricht Treaty, the Major government's acceptance of which had prompted the formation of the new party. Equally, the central concerns of those voters from 2010 onwards – immigration and austerity – scarcely registered in the 1990s. However, UKIP were also able to speak very successfully to the anxieties of the 'left behind' on matters that went well beyond the narrow question of the UK's relationship with the EU. The party skilfully exploited a wider disillusionment with the 'political class' over such issues as the expenses scandal of 2009, in which many MPs were revealed to have been falsifying, or, at least, over-claiming their expenses. The party's poster message at the 2010 election, 'Sod the Lot' (over pictures of Brown, Cameron and Clegg), captured this anti-political mood. The politicians did not help themselves. At the same election, Brown and other leading Labour figures engaged only with carefully selected small groups of reliable voters: as a wag remarked, it was as if they were moving 'from safe house to safe house'. By contrast, Farage could command attendances of 1,000 or more at public meetings in working-class strongholds like Gateshead. His message, albeit with an anti-European flavour, spoke directly to those who were dissatisfied with modern Britain, who believed (wrongly but angrily) that 'schools … can't hold nativity plays or harvest festivals … you can't wear an England shirt on the bus … you can't even smack your child':

> We have been lied to. … I do not want the European Union passport! I do not want that flag. … I do not want 75 per cent of my laws made somewhere else! I do not want to pay £55 million a day! And I do not want a total open border to 485 million people…[49]

The Conservatives and Europe, 2005–2016: the Eurosceptics march on

Until some point after 2005, the Conservatives had no real prospect of office. Their debates on Europe, and, indeed, everything else, therefore enjoyed a somewhat unreal quality for a party that had been extraordinarily successful electorally throughout the twentieth century and whose guiding principle was the pursuit and retention of political power. As New Labour began to falter, and the possibility of office became real once again, those debates of necessity took on a different quality. At this stage it is, therefore, helpful to distinguish a little more precisely the shades of opinion within the party between Europhiles, Eurosceptics and Europhobes.

Europhile Conservatives believed wholeheartedly in the European ideal. They were relaxed about the sharing of sovereignty that the EU entailed, and broadly favourable in principle to the grant of additional powers to Brussels: one could, therefore, imagine them supporting the UK's adoption of the Euro, and many of them did so. Above all, the Europhiles regarded Europe as a political as well as an economic project. As Geoffrey Rippon (who had led the negotiations for the UK's accession in 1973) put it in 1974:

> The fundamental political argument for British membership of the European Community has always been that our national circumstances are so similar to those of our fellow member states and our national objectives so much the same as theirs that it must be right for this country to work with them in the creation of an evolving Community whose joint strength and influence is so much greater than our own. ... As a full member of the Community, we are pooling our sovereignty in the specific areas covered by the Treaties, so that we may have a share in the much more effective sovereignty of the Community as a whole.[50]

At the other end of the spectrum were the Europhobes. They generally protested that they had nothing against Europe and, indeed, were more than happy for the UK to stay in the EU. However, on analysis, this continued membership was to be on a radically different basis from the footing on which the Accession and subsequent Treaties had been agreed. The UK would trade freely with other Member States but would require a renegotiation that did away with the supremacy of EU law, the jurisdiction of the European Court and the indissolubility of the four freedoms. In other words, this was such a fundamental change in the terms of British engagement that it, in reality, necessitated departure.

Between these two extremes, there were many Conservatives who were Eurosceptic in a real sense. Their essential mantra was 'so far and no further'. The UK should remain within the EU and needed to do so for primarily economic reasons. But it should oppose all developments that smacked of federalism or Social Europe and should seek as many opt-outs as possible to accommodate British interests. Eurosceptics viewed the EU with suspicion, and certainly did not think that the UK's 'national objectives [were] so much the same as theirs' or that 'this country [should] work with them in the creation of an evolving Community'. The UK's relationship should be guarded and transactional, with primary emphasis upon the British national interest.

Of course, there were degrees of Euroscepticism, with some close to the views of the Europhobes. However, as at 2005, it was these two strands that dominated Conservative opinion. Most of the Europhiles were either, like Rippon and Heath, dead, or had retired from front-line politics: Heseltine, Howe, Hurd and Patten. The party's three most recent leaders had been, at least, Eurosceptics, and its most recent Prime Minister had, after much agonising, arrived at a position that was essentially Eurosceptic. Moreover, for many Conservatives Europe was not one issue among many: it was *the* all-important question that dominated all their political discourse. Eurosceptic think tanks and lobby groups proliferated. Ambitious new MPs were anxious to demonstrate their Eurosceptic credentials. The leadership could always hear, ever more loudly, 'Britain's Tea Party ... baying for a final reckoning with the European Union'. The party's mainstream was located on the border between Euroscepticism and Europhobia. Thus, in 2011, a new group, Fresh Start, had the support of over 100 Tory MPs for the following prospectus:

> The Fresh Start Project's sole objective is to build a better relationship for Britain within the EU. It is not focused on leaving the EU, nor is it focused on reforming the EU, it is only concerned with reforming Britain's role within the EU. The Fresh Start Project is in the process of comprehensively researching the different options for renegotiating and reforming – ie taking back – the areas of competency Britain currently cedes to the EU.[51]

Since the 1990s, the party had, therefore, been Eurosceptic, with an increasing number of Europhobes. It had also identified a loyal core vote of about 30% of the electorate, who were broadly Eurosceptic, socially conservative, anxious about immigration and committed to the free market. The difficulty for the party was that this had, in the three most recent general elections, produced no more than 198 seats, far behind Labour and well short of the necessary winning margin. The party had, therefore, to persuade some voters who supported other parties to come over to the Conservative camp. Where were those voters to come from? The most obvious pool of potential converts was the Liberal Democrats, with 22% of the total in 2005, nearly ten times the share secured by UKIP. The question for the Conservatives was, therefore, how they could win over such voters. The Liberal Democrats were probably the most Europhile of all the political parties. How was a Eurosceptic party to appeal to them?

This was the setting, and these were the challenges, when the party once more considered the leadership in 2005, having lost the general election and, with it, Michael Howard. Four candidates emerged: Clarke; David Davis; Liam Fox; and Cameron. Clarke was no longer a credible candidate: in Tim Bale's words, 'a Europhile in a party whose MPs, activists, ordinary members, and financial and media backers were overwhelmingly Eurosceptic'. Davis and Fox were Europhobes. Cameron's position on Europe, and everything else, was elusive. He had 'little ideological baggage', and won easily. His broad pitch was a Tory form of Blairism: youthful, modernising and undogmatic, leading 'a sensible centre-right party to sort things out in a sensible way … [in] the ground on which this Party's success has always been built. The centre ground of British politics.'[52]

This all made sense if the Conservatives were to win over some of those Liberal Democrat voters. And, on that basis, Cameron could afford to dismiss UKIP as 'fruitcakes, loonies and closet racists'. His difficulty, apparent even during the leadership election, was that many Tories shared the preoccupations of the 'loonies'. When Fox pledged that, were he leader, Conservative MEPs would leave the main EPP–ED group in the European Parliament, Cameron gave the same undertaking. A 2006 poll of grassroots Tories found that this had been Cameron's most popular promise in the campaign. In 2009, the MEPs duly left the EPP–ED group, and helped to create the 'European Conservatives and Reformists group'. Of the 55 members, 26 were Tory MEPs, with 24 of the others from the Czech Republic and Poland. The Conservatives were no longer in the centre ground of European politics, but Cameron was compelled to this course for reasons of party management. In the 1980s and 1990s, the party had had tense relations with European Christian Democrats, but by 2009 the rupture was nearly total.[53]

The new leadership struck a consistently Eurosceptic tone, although on occasions giving the impression that this was more an attempt to appease the Europhobes on the backbenches and in the press than a matter of genuine conviction. Thus in 2007, Cameron offered in *The Sun* 'this cast-iron guarantee: if I become PM a Conservative government will hold a referendum on any EU treaty that emerges from these negotiations' (i.e. those leading to the Lisbon Treaty). His choice of newspaper was significant: the Murdoch empire was increasingly Europhobic and anti-Labour. However, two years later, Cameron told *The Guardian* that 'our campaign for a referendum on the Lisbon treaty is … over … because it is no longer a treaty: it is being incorporated into the law of the European Union'. Not 'cast-iron', after all, and the Europhobes promptly denounced him for 'treachery' and 'contempt'.[54]

Likewise, on the issue of human rights, which much of the press sought to conflate with 'Europe', Cameron came under pressure to repeal the Human Rights Act. Labour had introduced this in 1998 to incorporate the provisions of the European Convention of Human Rights into domestic law. To many Europhobes this was an affront, albeit not, in fact, an EU matter at all. Cameron promised to replace the Act with a 'British Bill of Rights'. This was an unworkable proposal, which never saw the light of day, but which gave the necessary impression of resisting foreign incursions into 'our laws'. Clarke denounced the idea as 'xenophobic and legal nonsense'.[55]

At the 2010 general election, the Conservatives struck a note on Europe that was Eurosceptic, with a hint of Europhobia. The Cameron/Osborne leadership was not willing to make a positive case for the UK's engagement with the EU. Indeed, Steve Hilton, Cameron's policy adviser, was already urging that they plan for the UK's departure. The manifesto did not promise this, but it did offer plenty of material to keep Eurosceptics happy:

> We will ensure that by law no future government can hand over areas of power to the EU or join the Euro without a referendum of the British people. We will work to bring back key powers over legal rights, criminal justice and social and employment legislation to the UK. We believe Britain's interests are best served by membership of a European Union that is an association of its Member States. We will never allow Britain to slide into a federal Europe. Labour's ratification of the Lisbon Treaty without the consent of the British people has been a betrayal of this country's democratic traditions. In government, we will put in place a number of measures to make sure this shameful episode can never happen again. In future, the British people must have their say on any transfer of powers to the European Union. … The steady and unaccountable intrusion of the European Union into almost every aspect of our lives has gone too far.[56]

The 2010 election provided an ambiguous verdict on the approach of the new leadership, both on Europe and generally. On the one hand, the Conservatives were back in power, and the modernising 'Cameroons' readily found like-minded partners in the Liberal Democrats. On the other hand, Cameron had failed to secure a majority of his own, even against a Labour Party gravely damaged by the financial crisis. In internal, party, terms, he also faced a considerable challenge over Europe. For many in his party, this issue dwarfed all others, and they demanded either the sort of fundamental renegotiation at which the manifesto hinted, or withdrawal. Yet, this issue had scarcely featured at the election, as was reflected in the fact that these manifesto commitments were buried at pages 113 and 114 of a 119-page document. Moreover, in a sense the real winners of the election were the Liberal Democrats, with whom the new Tory leadership agreed on virtually everything, except Europe. Their 23% of the poll was, surely, the only pool of votes from which the Conservatives might plausibly seek to construct a majority of their own. Seeking to win over these voters looked a more promising strategy for the future than courting the 3% of irreconcilable Europhobes who had supported UKIP.

The EU was a trickier issue than most in the May 2010 coalition talks. The party leaders therefore agreed that European policy should be put 'in the deep freeze'. The UK should move neither towards, nor away from, the EU. Consistently with this, the government passed the European Union Act 2011, which provided for a referendum on any proposed EU treaty or Treaty change that would transfer powers from the UK to the EU. In the words of the Conservative Foreign Secretary, William Hague, this 'put into the British people's hands a referendum lock'. The following year, the government launched a review of the 'balance of competences' between the UK and the EU: a massive undertaking, but not one likely to get many pulses racing. On occasions, even within the higher echelons of the government, the 'iceberg of European Union politics … broke the surface of British politics'. In December 2011, Cameron vetoed a proposed 'fiscal compact' to deal with the crisis in the Eurozone, and did so without consulting his coalition partners. The next year, the UK secured a police and criminal justice opt-out, only to opt back into many of the same provisions.[57]

In reality, however, this was not so much an issue for the government as for the Conservatives internally. The EU was 'a totemic issue for [Cameron's] tribe' in a party divided 'only between different kinds of Eurosceptic'. Between 2010 and 2014, 101 different Tory MPs rebelled on European issues. In October 2011, 81 MPs defied a three-line whip to support a referendum on membership. In June 2012, Cameron told

Clegg that he would be writing a newspaper article hinting that this could become party policy, telling him 'I have to do this. It is a party management issue. I am under a lot of pressure on this.' The pressure did not lessen; by the autumn of that year, senior ministers were stating semi-publicly that the government should say to the EU 'give us back our sovereignty or we will walk out'.[58]

It was at this stage that Cameron appears to have decided that he could hold out no longer, and would have to offer his party a commitment to renegotiate with the EU and then hold a referendum. UKIP were doing well in the polls. In November 2012, Labour gained Corby in a by-election, with UKIP securing 14% of the poll. Cameron explained his approach to Clegg on the basis that 'what else can I do? My backbenchers are unbelievably Eurosceptic and UKIP are breathing down my neck.' To underline the former point, 100 Tory MPs wrote to Cameron to demand 'a commitment on the statute book to hold such a referendum [which] would address the very real lack of trust when people hear politicians making promises', a thinly veiled reference to Cameron's backsliding over Lisbon.[59]

In January 2013, Cameron made his fateful Bloomberg speech, in which he announced that, since 'democratic consent for the EU in Britain is now wafer thin', he was 'in favour of a referendum' but only after 'a negotiation with our European partners'. As Clegg and others pointed out, this was an obvious attempt to paper over the cracks: there surely could not be a renegotiation that could both satisfy his party and press critics, and also be acceptable to the EU. Nonetheless, senior Tories had by 2013 concluded that, if they did not offer a referendum, they would 'be destroyed by UKIP'.[60]

Despite Bloomberg, Cameron struggled to keep his party in order or UKIP at bay. In 2013, he took the unprecedented step of allowing a free vote on the Queen's Speech on an amendment regretting the absence of a bill for a referendum. In 2014, Carswell and Reckless defected and won their respective by-elections. Tories were worried that the trend towards UKIP was hurting them more than the other parties, with 42%

of UKIP voters polled recalling having voted Conservative in 2010. Yet, despite all this, Cameron's heart did not really seem in the anti-European crusade. Privately he told Clegg that he did not want to 'be spelling out for some time what I am going to negotiate on', and that his 'hunch' was that the next election would produce another hung parliament (thus avoiding the need to call the referendum). Publicly, even in the Bloomberg speech, Cameron found it difficult to sound like a proper Eurosceptic, let alone a Europhobe, declaring that:

> We will have to weigh carefully where our true national interest lies. ... Continued access to the Single Market is vital for British businesses and British jobs. ... There are some who suggest we could turn ourselves into Norway or Switzerland – with access to the single market but outside the EU. But would that really be in our best interests?... The fact is that if you join an organisation like the European Union, there are rules. You will not always get what you want. But that does not mean we should leave – not if the benefits of staying and working together are greater.[61]

The truth was that there was some justice in the claim made by Bernard Jenkin, the veteran Europhobe, that Cameron was trying to lead the Conservatives in a direction in which they did not wish to be led. Many influential Tories had become convinced that it made no sense for the UK to remain shackled to a slow-moving continental bureaucracy in a fast-paced digital age. The country needed to look outwards towards the competitive, rapidly modernising economies of the Far East (Singapore was a particular favourite), rather than to the declining social democracies of Europe. As the authors of *Britannia Unchained*, a pamphlet published in 2012 by five recently elected Tory MPs, argued, 'Britain must learn the rules of the 21st century, or face a slide into mediocrity ... [emulating] the nations that are triumphing in this new age.' At times, Cameron felt it necessary to speak in a similar vein, telling his party conference in 2012:

the old powers are on the slide. What do the countries on the rise have in common? They are lean, fit, obsessed with enterprise, spending money on the future – on education, incredible infrastructure and technology. And what do the countries on the slide have in common? They're fat, sclerotic, over-regulated, spending money on unaffordable welfare systems, huge pension bills, unreformed public services. I sit in those European Council meetings where we talk endlessly about Greece, while on the other side of the world, China is moving so fast it's creating a new economy the size of Greece every three months.[62]

It was on this somewhat conflicted basis that the Tories fought the 2015 election, offering 'a new settlement for Britain in Europe, and then ask[ing] the British people whether they want to stay in the EU on this reformed basis or leave … we will hold that in–out referendum before the end of 2017 and respect the outcome'. The party was scarcely less conflicted on immigration, divided between those who wanted to reduce it massively (and who were often Europhobes as well) and those who favoured an open economy. The manifesto commitment in this regard also tended to the former position, promising 'annual net migration in the tens of thousands, not the hundreds of thousands, control[ling] migration from the European Union', although it was far from clear how any of this was to be achieved.[63]

The election produced a result that surprised many commentators. UKIP increased their vote share but won only one seat. Labour was wiped out in Scotland, and made modest progress elsewhere. The SNP won 56 out of 59 seats in Scotland. The Liberal Democrats, having sat contentedly atop the Tory tiger for the previous five years, found themselves devoured whole. The upshot was a small overall Tory majority of 12. Cameron's 'hunch' that there would be another hung Parliament turned out to be wrong. He would have to deliver on his referendum pledge. He was more in hock than ever to his 'unbelievably Eurosceptic' backbenchers.

Renegotiation and Referendum, 2015–2016

On the face of it, Cameron had so designed matters that he would be able to reproduce the scheme that Wilson had successfully pursued in 1975: a commitment to a general renegotiation, followed by a referendum, and with the clear hint that the government's ultimate position would be to stay in. This should, in principle, have been a mirror image of 1975, with a government composed of a party divided over Europe, and an opposition party broadly united in support of continued membership. The only difference was that the governing party was now Conservative and the opposition Labour. In fact, 2016 turned out to be very different from 1975, and Cameron's gamble, unlike Wilson's, went disastrously wrong.

The government, as in 1975, passed the necessary legislation and conducted negotiations with the EU. However, even at this stage, Cameron found himself outmanoeuvred in a way that Wilson had not been. Under pressure from his backbenchers, the European Union Referendum Act 2015 provided that 'the alternative answers to that question that are to appear on the ballot papers are – "Remain a member of the European Union … Leave the European Union."' This was a much more neutral formula than in 1975, when the ballot referred in terms to the renegotiations and asked whether the UK should stay in the Common Market. The government also conceded that 'purdah' should apply to the campaign, the month-long period before a poll when government announcements and spending are restricted. Once the renegotiations started at the end of 2015, Cameron 'appeared to have little idea what he wanted to achieve'. In 1974/5, Wilson and Callaghan had concentrated on 'practical improvements that targeted specific grievances'; the latter irritated his European colleagues by relentlessly returning to the issues that were raised in the Labour manifesto. Cameron, by contrast, sought only more and more opt-outs: but, if opting out was such a good idea, why not opt out entirely? In 1975, the polls shifted in the government's favour in March 1975, once the renegotiations were complete: no such change was to happen in 2016.[64]

Once the campaign got under way, there were some echoes of 1975. Dissenting ministers were, once more, given an agreement to differ. The senior figures in the government, notably Cameron and Osborne, supported continued membership. The CBI, and most of the business community, took the same view. The Bank of England, the Treasury and the BBC were widely thought to favour staying in. The government received 'third-party endorsements from the great and the good', most notably President Obama, who declared in April 2016 that 'the UK is going to be in the back of the queue' for trade deals if it left the EU. The problem with all this was that the voters no longer 'listened to the people they were used to following', as Roy Jenkins had somewhat smugly noted in 1975. On the contrary, Obama's intervention was 'seen by voters as patronising', and they did not 'care what the CBI thinks'.[65]

In formal terms, the conduct of the campaign was similar to 1975. The government recommended staying in, and produced official literature to explain this recommendation. There was an umbrella group, separate from government, which supported the Remain position, Britain Stronger in Europe. BSIE, as in 1975, brought together the 'pluralist, liberal, centrist, force in British politics'. The Leave campaign had its own umbrella organisation, Vote Leave, in which the leading figures were two senior Tories (Michael Gove and Boris Johnson) and a Labour MP, Gisela Stuart. Leave.Eu, a distinct organisation closely associated with UKIP, ran its own campaign. Unlike 1975, when essentially the Left had sought to organise the anti-EEC forces on a shoestring, the Leavers were well-financed; Arron Banks, an associate of Farage, spent £11m on social media between 2015 and polling day.[66]

The differences from 1975 were much more marked than any superficial similarities. For one thing, relations within the governing party were rancorous in the extreme. In 1975, the Left had made exit their cause, but they had done so in a dignified fashion. There was little dignified about 2016. As Cameron set off on his negotiations in November 2015, a Europhobic backbencher, Jacob Rees-Mogg, warned him that his starting position was 'pretty thin gruel … its whole aim is to make Harold

Wilson's renegotiation look respectable'. On his return, Rees-Mogg told him that 'the thin gruel has been further watered down'. Another Europhobe announced that 'this in-at-all-costs deal looks and smells funny … he has been reduced to polishing poo'. During the campaign itself, there were incessant 'blue on blue' attacks, with, for example, the Home Secretary asserting during a television debate that 'the only number Boris [Johnson] is interested in is Number 10'.[67]

The truth was that, although the party had just fought and won a general election on the basis of potentially wide-ranging discussions with the EEC, there were many Conservatives who were satisfied that this could only ever be a 'patsy renegotiation', and were determined, before those discussions had started, to 'prepare for an "out" campaign'. Euroscepticism was not, for such people, one issue among many. It was almost the only matter that really counted. The Left, in 1975, had sought a No vote as a means towards the end, namely the implementation of the AES. For the Right in 2016, a vote to leave had become almost an end in itself. As Liam Fox, a senior Europhobe, remarked, 'Dave and George are furious at the lack of deference from the 2010 or, even more, the 2015 intake. They were unprepared for the level of ideology. For them Euroscepticism has always been a tool to use, not a position they actually believe in. They thought everyone behaved like that. They miscalculated'.[68]

Press coverage in 2016 was very different from 1975, and, despite the rise of the digital media, and the relative impartiality of the broadcasters, the print titles were influential in shaping the debate. The most obvious change was that most of the Conservative-supporting newspapers had changed sides: the *Mail*, *Express*, *Telegraph* and *Sun* titles were now strongly pro-leave. Their coverage of the campaign was vitriolic: for example, Remain claims about the economic effects of Brexit were routinely dismissed as 'scaremongering'. Cameron's deal with the EU was condemned by *The Sun* as a 'steaming pile of manure'. In sharp contrast to 1975, pro-European advice from leading politicians and others received short shrift. The Leave-supporting press derided such guidance as 'Project Fear'. This merged into a broader theme that the Remain campaign represented the 'Establishment' or elites, whose interests were opposed to those of 'the people'.[69]

However, the most marked difference in the media coverage concerned immigration. It was the central issue by far, and the Leave-supporting press was none too fastidious in its approach: for example, there was little attempt to distinguish between the effects of EU and non-EU migration. An exhaustive study of the subject concluded that 'coverage of the effects of immigration was overwhelmingly negative. Migrants were blamed for many of Britain's economic and social problems – most notably for putting unsustainable pressure on public services. Specific nationalities were singled out for particularly negative coverage – especially Turks and Albanians, but also Romanians and Poles'. (Neither Turkey nor Albania were members of the EU, but the Leave campaign were 'relentlessly highlighting' the prospect that 88 million citizens of these and other countries could 'soon' have 'the right to live and work here'.[70])

In contrast to an aggressive and effective campaign on the Leave side, the Remain voice in the media stuttered. There were, of course, supportive voices: *The Guardian* and the *Financial Times* had not greatly shifted their positions since 1975. However, the BBC, the subject of the unrelenting hostility of many in the Leave camp (not all of it for reasons related to Europe), was hesitant in its coverage. Moreover, the voices featured in the debate were overwhelmingly on the Right. Labour struggled to make itself heard: 'Jeremy Corbyn attracted very little attention, being quoted in just 3–4% of articles in the *Guardian* and *Mirror*, about a third as many times as David Cameron or Boris Johnson'. *The Guardian* and *Mirror* were broadly pro-Remain and pro-Labour: elsewhere the position was worse. This was symptomatic of a wider issue in the reporting. Views obtained much more attention if they were pro-Leave. For example, an analysis concluded that Professor Patrick Minford, a pro-Brexit, monetarist, economist who had advised Thatcher, alone accounted for a fifth of all quotes from academics during the campaign.[71]

All of this presented a considerable structural problem for the Remain camp. Cameron and Osborne were accustomed to strong press support, and to the press turning most of its fire on Labour. However, in 2016, the press were 'acrimonious and divisive', but much of the acrimony was directed at the Conservative leaders of the Remain campaign. Again, this was very different from 1975, when the Tory press had held its nose and backed Wilson against the Left. Another contrast to 1975 was that then the 'Yes' operation had been a harmonious one embracing the Labour Right, the Liberals and most mainstream Conservatives. It was difficult to achieve the same level of harmony when the Labour part of Remain achieved such limited prominence; and, of course, the Tory press loathed Corbyn even more than they despised Cameron and the EU. As one of Cameron's advisers reflected on the press coverage, 'We're discovering what it's like to be Ed Miliband.'[72]

Miliband had, in fact, resigned as Labour leader immediately after the 2015 defeat. The candidates to replace him were two New Labour former ministers (Burnham and Cooper), a Blairite MP (Kendall) – and Corbyn. Corbyn had been a backbench MP since 1983, and was, at all times, 'unapologetically on the hard left … a mini-opposition within his own party'. He was also a longstanding Eurosceptic, having voted No in 1975 and opposed the Maastricht Treaty. For most of his career, the Left had been marginalised in the party. In the Blair years, they had very nearly disappeared. Corbyn struggled to obtain the necessary nominations from MPs, and was reluctant to stand at all. And yet, when the votes of party members were counted, Corbyn won overwhelmingly, with nearly 60% of the vote.[73]

The rise of Corbyn was both a symptom of a wider change and the cause of a major problem for the Remain Campaign. The change was that New Labour seemed to have run out of ideas. Its prospectus had been exposed by the financial crisis, and it had struggled to respond to austerity. Immediately after the 2015 defeat, 10 new Labour MPs had demanded a new leader who would 'set out an alternative to austerity', and the majority of those 600,000 party members who took part in the leadership election agreed. The problem was that, unlike in 1975, the main opposition party in the referendum campaign was decidedly lukewarm in its approach. Corbyn described the EU as 'an exclusive club' and Treasury forecasts as to the effect of Brexit as 'histrionic'. He refused to share a platform with Blair or Cameron, and kept Labour Remain campaigners at arm's length. It was scarcely surprising that many Labour voters did not know what their own party's attitude to the EU was. Labour had gone, it appeared, overnight from neoliberalism to socialism, without passing social democracy.[74]

As the press coverage made clear, another massive difference from 1975 was the centrality of immigration to the debate. Some Loyalists had then been troubled by the prospect of 'foreign labour' in Northern Ireland, but, otherwise, the issue scarcely featured. In 2016, the Leave campaign focused relentlessly on immigration. On 26 May 2016, an ONS report revealed a net immigration figure of 333,000, the second highest ever recorded. The Leave campaign made much of this: it showed that 'Brussels has taken away our control of immigration'. The polls shifted immediately, with a small majority for Leave, which persisted until polling day: there had been a 10% margin the other way a week earlier. The Leave campaign pressed home its advantage by offering an 'Australian style points system'. This, a Vote Leave strategist told a journalist, 'was all about sending out a signal to white voters. Australia … is probably the nation most commonly perceived by Britons to be overwhelmingly "white"'. Likewise, the Leavers warned of the dangers of Turkey joining the EU, with a flood of migrants 'since the birth rate in Turkey is so high' and the government powerless 'to exclude Turkish criminals from entering the UK'.[75]

The government, and the Remain campaign, seemed bemused by the focus on immigration and, certainly, unable to counter it effectively. For supporters of EU membership, it seemed obvious that departure would have severe economic consequences. After all, 90% of economists had confirmed that this was so. And was not the Leave campaign's pledge to leave the Single Market an act of wilful economic self-harm? Yet for the Leavers, such concerns could simply be brushed aside: after all, as Gove observed, 'people in this country have had enough of experts'; the public should 'trust themselves' and 'take back control'. In any event, such 'expert' concerns over the economics were simply overshadowed by the 'nasty and brutal' propaganda on immigration.[76]

Indeed, in marked contrast to 1975, the debate was unremittingly negative. Then, Winston Churchill MP (grandson of the wartime PM) had proclaimed proudly that 'we have not gone into Europe in order to lose sovereignty but to regain and embrace it'. Such sentiments were rare forty years later. The government concentrated on what the Leavers called 'Project Fear': exit would lead to a recession, a £4,300 cut in family income and the need for an emergency budget. In short, 'leaving is a leap in the dark and would mean years of uncertainty'. Official propaganda emphasised that the UK would 'have new powers to block or remove unwanted European laws' and that there would be 'tough new restrictions on access to our welfare system for new EU migrants'. It was as if the UK needed to be protected from Europe and Europeans: there was little prospect of 'embracing' anything. Only at the margins of the Remain campaign could one see much spirit of idealism on issues such as climate change, workers' rights and the need to 'have a bigger say in the world'.[77]

The Leave campaign, although ostensibly two distinct organisations, had a single message, peddled 'with metronomic relentlessness'. In the words of a UKIP leaflet, 'we will take back control of our borders … we will make all our laws in Westminster, not Brussels … we will save £55m every day in membership fees, money better spent on the NHS'. Vote Leave's literature contrasted 'out of control' immigration (with a photograph of swarthy migrants burrowing under a barbed wire fence and a graphic showing Turks bound for the UK) with a golden future in which £350m a week would be available for the NHS. BSIE was left flailing at 'Leave myths', but the damage was done.[78]

One of the noticeable features of 2016, again by contrast with 1975, was the very different nature of the campaign and outcome in Scotland.

Support for the EEC/EU actually rose in Scotland between 1975 and 2016 (from 58% to 62%), whereas England was the bedrock of the Leave vote and those who identified as 'English' the most hostile to Europe. The explanation for this lay in the very different nature of politics north of the border. Scotland had never taken to Thatcherism and by 1997 was a 'Tory-free zone', with no remaining Conservative MPs. The Blair government, keen to protect its Caledonian flank against the SNP, then implemented devolution. However, rather than sating the demand for nationalism, this paradoxically strengthened the position of the SNP. The nationalists, once romantically Right of Centre, had developed into an unashamedly social democratic party, aspiring to emulate the Scandinavian social model. Their electoral position gradually improved, culminating in victory in the elections for the Scottish Parliament in 2011. Thereafter, the Scottish government contrasted its anti-austerity policies with those pursued at Westminster by the coalition. The party was also enthusiastically pro-Europe, believing that 'the best way to build a more prosperous and equal Scotland is to be a full independent member of the EU'. In Scotland, therefore, support for the EU went hand in hand with this social democratic perspective.[79]

For all the sound and fury, what was most deafening in the campaign was the sound of the politicians avoiding the real issue. Almost everyone could agree that, in principle, the UK should have full sovereignty over all aspects of policy, and that (to quote Benn in 1975) 'the Parliamentary democracy we have developed and established in Britain is based, not upon the sovereignty of Parliament, but upon the sovereignty of the People, who, by exercising their vote lend their sovereign powers to Members of Parliament, to use on their behalf, for the duration of a single Parliament only'. Likewise, most agreed that, in principle, the UK would benefit economically from unrestricted access to the Single Market. The real question was the extent to which it was necessary or desirable to trade off one of these desirable objectives against the other.[80]

So far as the Remain camp was concerned, there is some truth in the allegation that, since 1975, British supporters of EEC/EU membership had been coy about conceding that this involved some degree of shared sovereignty. The truth, perhaps, was that absolute sovereignty was an illusion in a globalised world and that, moreover, the sharing of sovereignty that the EEC/EU involved was a price worth paying for the benefits that accrued thereby, just as membership of NATO brought advantages in security in exchange for restrictions on 'sovereignty'. However, this was a truth that politicians, faced with the unremitting hostility of the Eurosceptic press, were reluctant to admit.

The Leavers were no more candid. Boris Johnson often joked that his 'policy on cake is pro having it and pro eating it': in other words, the UK could so renegotiate its arrangements with the EU that it would continue to enjoy the benefits of the Single Market, without incurring any of the burdens that that entailed for other Member States. Or, as he put it in his *démarche* in *The Daily Telegraph* in February 2016, 'there is only one way to get the change we need – and that is to vote to go; because all EU history shows that they only really listen to a population when it says No'.[81]

However, what all this left hanging in the air was the degree of compromise of 'sovereignty' that might be acceptable to secure those benefits, and the nature of the relationship with the EU that this might involve, if the EU required the UK to choose between having its cake and eating it. Was the UK to be like Norway or Switzerland or Canada? This was a debate that would only really begin after the votes were counted. Even then, the victorious Leave campaigners were reassuring that the UK could have the best of both worlds. According to Johnson, 'British people will still be able to go and work in the EU; to live; to travel; to study; to buy homes and to settle down.' Or as David Davis, the Secretary of State for Exiting the European Union, assured the Commons in 2017, 'what we have come up with … is the idea of a comprehensive free trade agreement and a comprehensive customs agreement that will deliver the exact same benefits as we have, but also enable my right hon. Friend the Secretary of State for International Trade to go and form trade deals with the rest of the world'. But what if the EU would not agree, for example, to allowing British citizens to continue to enjoy the right of free movement within the EU, while that right was denied to EU citizens within the UK? And if the EU would not agree to a 'best of all possible worlds' renegotiation, what, if any, compromise would be acceptable? After all, the notion of compromise had not loomed large in the referendum campaign.[82]

Indeed, the abiding impression of 2016 was how 'nasty and brutal' the campaign had proved to be. Tony Benn, without whom the referenda of 1975 and 2016 might never have happened, described elections as a 'healing process'. This was not true of 2016. A single day encapsulated the darkness of the campaign: on 16 June 2016, a week before the vote, Farage unveiled a poster with the message 'Breaking Point', which appeared to show dusky migrants surging into the UK. In fact, these were Syrian refugees, and the image had been doctored to remove any white faces. It was, therefore, nothing to do with the debate over free movement within the EU. Osborne, and others, compared it to Nazi propaganda. Later the same day, a Labour MP, Jo Cox, was murdered by a man who shouted 'Britain First' as he stabbed her. The reaction was calculated and cynical: Priti Patel, a Tory minister in Vote Leave, emailed Leave.Eu on the need 'to avoid any activities that could be viewed as insensitive … this is now a balancing act'.[83]

This may have been the worst single day of the campaign, but the 'Breaking Point' poster was the tip of a very unsavoury iceberg. Race, identity and nativism were constant features of the Brexit debate. Johnson attacked Obama in *The Sun* for allegedly removing a bust of Churchill from the Oval Office and asked whether this was 'a symbol of the part-Kenyan President's ancestral dislike of the British Empire'. He also claimed, disingenuously, that the Leave proposal on immigration was merely that control should rest with Westminster rather than Brussels, whereas, as he must have known, in 'post-war estates in working-class areas … "control" had been interpreted as "closing the door"'.[84]

Some material was darker still. Vote Leave put out an extraordinary video advertisement attacking Mark Carney, who was not only 'a close family friend of George Osborne', but also formerly a senior director of Goldman Sachs. The video, to the sound of ominous music, showed Carney chortling at black tie events while Greece was in flames and contained the line 'some say Goldman Sachs is still pulling the strings today'. The conclusion was that the voters should not 'let Goldman Sachs profit from our EU membership: this is your last chance'. The video did not say in terms that there was a conspiracy of Jewish bankers against the people, but the implication was clear. Similarly, Daniel Korski, an adviser to Cameron, was attacked by the Leave-supporting press for his alleged role in the dismissal of John Longworth, the pro-Brexit director-general of the British Chambers of Commerce. Korski believed that 'the way he was depicted by the media as the puppeteer of "dark forces" against Brexiteers was anti-Semitic'.[85]

Conclusions

Events unfolded at terrifying speed between 2005 and 2016. An apparently buoyant economy moved almost overnight from boom to bust. A settled political situation, in which New Labour dominated, became very unsettled indeed. The UK's engagement with the EU, which seemed to be enduring if, at times, reluctant, came to a sudden halt. The Conservatives revived, and regained power, but remained bitterly divided. The Liberal Democrats joined forces with the Tories and then disintegrated. The Left, who had seemed fatally wounded in 1975, somehow came back to life in time for the 2016 referendum.

1975 had been noteworthy for the uniform response of the British people across ages, classes and regions. Virtually everywhere, about two-thirds of the electorate were willing to trust the judgement of those politicians who had overseen the post-war social democratic model, such as Heath and Jenkins. 2016 revealed a very much more divided nation. The old voted to leave (66%/34%), the young to stay (25%/75%). The better-off were Remainers (A/B: 35%/65%) and the working-class Leavers (C2: 63%/37%; D/E: 64%/36%). The regional variations were stark. It is estimated that only about 20% of parliamentary constituencies voted to leave in London and Scotland, whereas in the Midlands and the North the proportions were 88% and 77%.[86]

What had caused these very substantial changes over these four decades? Of course, no single account will unravel this complex story. For example, a wider disillusionment partially explains the voting patterns: 80% of the most socially conservative voters supported Leave, whereas 90% of the most socially liberal were for Remain. Yet, the EU had little to do with the issues that agitated these voters, such as same-sex marriage, and, in any event, there were, no doubt, at least equal numbers of social conservatives among the electorate in 1975.[87]

In the short term, it seems clear that the financial crisis and the subsequent austerity programme made the Remain campaign's task very much harder. After 2010, voters became increasingly pessimistic both about the national economy and their own finances. This coincided with the rise of UKIP from marginal force to major players, at least in the opinion polls and European elections. The proportion of those polled who 'approved' EU membership fell from 48% in 2009 to 35% in 2011. At the same time, concern over immigration both increased and became strongly associated with hostility towards the EU. However, the crisis on its own will not suffice to explain the result of the 2016 referendum. After all, in 1975 the UK was feeling the full effects of the oil price increase of 1973/4. Inflation was 25%, the economy was in recession and the government was about to introduce a pay and prices policy.[88]

The difference between the two periods was more political than economic. In 1975, the broad Centre of British politics was social democratic, and prepared to implement policies that ensured that we were, indeed, all in it together. The same could not be said forty years later. Labour, the obvious candidate to be the party of social democracy, had sold its soul to the neoliberal devil. Once this experiment had run its course, the social democrats within Labour were too enfeebled to resist the rise of the Corbynistas. The Liberal Democrats had become embarrassed by their social democratic heritage, and embraced economic liberalism. The Conservatives remained unashamed Thatcherites, and it was to them that the Liberal Democrats naturally turned for alliance, not Labour. It was, perhaps, no coincidence that George Osborne was the public face of Tory mourning at Thatcher's funeral in 2013, of austerity from 2010 to 2016, and of the ill-fated Remain campaign in 2016. Only in Scotland was there a party of government that was happy in its social democratic skin, and able to deliver a clear majority for Remain.[89]

Conclusion

What matters is what works.

(Tony Blair, 1998)[1]

I didn't come into politics to make cuts. Neither did Nick Clegg. ... We're tackling the deficit because we have to – not out of some ideological zeal. This is a government led by people with a practical desire to sort out this country's problems, not by ideology.

(David Cameron, 2010)[2]

This book has sought to argue that Britain operated a social democratic system between 1945 and 1979. This system came under strain in the mid-1970s, as the post-war economic Golden Age drew to a close. It was steadily dismantled after 1979, and has not been reinstated since. The highwater mark of British social democracy coincided with the UK's most enthusiastic engagement with Europe, from the late 1950s to the early 1980s. British social democratic leaders were the keenest to take Britain 'into Europe'. Thereafter, but especially from 1988 onwards, the Right has wholly abandoned social democracy and turned strongly against the EEC/EU. The mainstream Left's grasp on social democracy has been tenuous, and its engagement with Europe superficial. These circumstances created the perfect conditions for the UK to vote to leave the EU, as it did in 2016. What then has the evidence shown about this argument?

It is, I would suggest, clear that Britain operated as a social democratic system in the post-war period, and did so with reasonable stability. The mixed economy, strong trade unions, and activist social policies in areas such as education and housing, were constant features of this landscape. The consequence was that, by the mid-1970s, the UK was more equal than it had ever been. Of course, this was no paradise, and there were plenty of critics of Left and Right. The Left were impatient with social democracy's accommodation with capitalism. The Right thought there was too little capitalism and too much quasi-socialism.

Of course, as we have seen, the system came under strain during the 1970s, as the simultaneous increase in inflation, unemployment and industrial militancy evidenced the end of the Golden Age. For the critics of social democracy, this was a crisis not to be wasted. To the Left, the economic downturn showed that social democrats had been foolish to seek to save capitalism from itself. The time had come to replace capitalism. To the Right, it was apparent that this diluted form of capitalism could not succeed: the free market should be set free. There were, however, still plenty of defenders of the post-war system, and they were well represented in both main parties.

As has been discussed in previous chapters, British social democracy did not function within any very exact ideological structure. However, that is not to say that there was a shortage of ideas, only that those ideas were relatively fluid. After all, the distinguished scholar E.H.H. Green could devote thirty lucid pages to 'the Political Economy of Harold Macmillan', and acknowledge that 'the range of his intellectual engagement was wide' – and Green, in the words of his obituarist, was a 'historian drawn to investigating the Conservative party though never tempted to vote for it'. On any view, Crosland made a major intellectual contribution to the development of British social democracy, and interest in his work remains considerable, forty years after his death. It has been said recently that his arguments have 'stood the test of time rather than crumbling to dust'. If future scholars are to work on the Political Economy of Blair or Cameron, they will have thin pickings indeed (a point to be returned to below).[3]

It also seems obvious that there occurred, in about 1979, what Avner Offer has dubbed 'the market turn': 'social democracy strove to provide employment, education, healthcare, social insurance, housing, and physical infrastructure. Market liberalism held out property ownership as an alternative source of economic security.' Privatisation, the rundown of social housing, the marginalisation of the trade unions: all these proceeded unabated. New Labour did not reverse these changes, and seemed unconcerned at increasing disparities of income and wealth. If Arthur Lewis was right to say that 'a passion for equality is the one thing that links all socialists' then New Labour were not socialists of any kind – and outside the realms of Conservative propaganda in the early Blair years, few suggested that they were.[4]

Offer's analysis is not universally accepted. Andrew Hindmoor, for example, has protested against the 'remorselessly bleak and miserabilist view of our recent political history' prevalent on the Centre Left. He argues that the increased state spending of the New Labour years (especially on the NHS and education), and the wave of social reform in this period (gay marriage, progress towards racial and gender equality), show that social democracy is in better fettle than often thought. However, to my mind, this presents altogether too cheerful a picture of the society that voted for Brexit, in which deep and bitter divisions between young and old, rich and poor, big cities and smaller towns, were all too apparent.[5]

Whatever view one takes of Hindmoor's argument, the approach of the British Centre Left to Europe has followed very closely the fortunes of social democracy within the Labour Movement. From the late 1950s to the late 1970s, it was the Jenkinsites who were the most fervent in support of joining, and then staying in, Europe. Although there were exceptions, the Labour Right was broadly in favour of EEC membership. There was an obvious and satisfactory fit between the EEC and British social democracy. Indeed, as Roy Jenkins argued in 1978, it was perhaps a necessary condition of preserving the health of the latter that the former should progress and prosper. Social democracy had succeeded in Europe. Quite apart from the economic advantages of membership, where else might British social democrats look to for support than the continent?[6]

In this period, the social democratic Right was broadly in control of Labour. The Left did not want to settle for the compromises of the mixed economy at home, and was, generally, hostile to the capitalist European club. It was not surprising, therefore, that the party, at least when in government, showed reasonable enthusiasm for the EEC and that the Left raged furiously, but largely impotently, against such engagement. When the Right lost control, after 1979, and socialists from the Left held greater sway, the party swung sharply away from the EEC. 'Socialism in one country' had no need for European structures, indeed saw them as a major obstruction to domestic policy development. As the social democratic Right regained control from the mid-1980s onwards, so the party moved back towards engagement with Europe. And, of course, the short-lived SDP had bottomless enthusiasm for the EEC and for social democracy. The engagement of the Labour Movement became, of course, more intense after 1988, as Social Europe became both the great hope of the British Left and a key dividing line in the UK between Left and Right.

There are, of course, anomalies in some of the positions that Labour politicians adopted. There were a few voices on the Left supportive of membership, but not very many. For most of this period, the Left's mind was closed on Europe. On the Right, one must acknowledge that Gaitskell opposed Macmillan's application, but, as he did so, 'all the wrong people [were] cheering' and the Gaitskellites were aghast. What Gaitskell might have done if he had been Prime Minister after 1964 is a matter of speculation but, certainly, most of his supporters were strongly pro-EEC. Likewise, one can point to Crosland's somewhat lukewarm attitude to Europe in the 1970–4 period as evidence of a lack of engagement. However, I would suggest that his behaviour, and that of others on the Labour Right, was indicative of the need to keep the party together in difficult times, rather than a lack of European fervour.

Crosland was 'an instinctive pro-European', and he, and his colleagues on the Right of the party, gave strong support to Labour governments that sought to get the UK to join, and then stay in, the EEC.[7]

These incongruities apart, one has, therefore, a good degree of correlation between the health of British social democracy within Labour, and the UK's engagement with Europe. Thus, the easy victory of the Yes campaign in 1975 was at a time when social democracy still appeared strong both in the party and in Britain generally. In one sense, New Labour can easily be accommodated within this framework. Insofar as New Labour fits into Labour's traditions at all, it was social democratic rather than socialist and, in the Blair/Brown years, Britain's relationship with the EEC was comparatively untroubled. Certainly, it is hard to imagine a New Labour government leading the UK out of the EEC. What is more debatable is the depth of the dedication of New Labour either to social democracy or to the EU. The shallowness of those commitments was not a problem when times were good, but this began to matter very much once the financial crisis had occurred in 2008.

What then of the Right? The Conservative story is, in one sense, less tangled and complex than Labour's. The Tories were, in the main, very keen on the EEC from the early 1960s until the late 1980s. Opinion then turned sharply against Europe. The party was divided between those who, in reality, wanted the UK to leave and those who wished the country to remain, but in a semi-detached position.

The second half of this story – from 1988 onwards – is perhaps easier to explain. There had always been irreconcilables in the party, who took a Powellite view of the EEC. However, during the course of 1988, it seems to have occurred to Thatcher for the first time that Europe, rather than being an external force supportive of free-market policies at home, might actually prevent a British Tory government from implementing such a programme. It was also evident to all concerned that Thatcherite Conservatives no longer needed the EEC as an insurance against socialism at home. The unions had been defeated; Labour, even under new and more engaging leadership, had just lost its third successive election;

the Republicans were about to win a third presidential term, even without the charismatic Reagan. People were beginning to say that the Tories (and Republicans) were bound to keep winning almost regardless, as demographic change came to their aid. And the TUC's warmth towards Delors was scarcely a commendation.

Thatcher's acolyte Alan Clark advised her, as the drafts of the Bruges speech went to and fro:

> I have … seen the second draft – which I was glad to see resisted many of the changes suggested by FCO but is already at, or very close to, the dilution threshold. For example, the excellent passages (pp 29–32) of the original draft of which the essence was the para on page 30 –
>
> > Let me say bluntly on behalf of Britain: we have not embarked on the business of throwing back the frontiers of the state at home, only to see a European superstate getting ready to exercise a new dominance from Brussels.
>
> – have been very greatly curtailed.
>
> Furthermore, it is my opinion that Delors, by coming over here and addressing what to all intents and purposes is an Opposition Conference, offering them the 'deal' of a return to their old non-elective privileges if they support him – has put himself outside any immunity that might attach to his position as President. This speech is of crucial importance. It will signal our attitudes to developments in the Community both micro and macro over the next decade.[8]

Not everyone took Clark seriously, but his was not a lone voice within government. Just after Bruges, another of Thatcher's close advisers, Charles Powell, presented her with a detailed memorandum, which officials had prepared about future developments within the EEC. Powell's advice, was blunt:

> we need to remain alert to the Commission's activities … be prepared to 'terrorise' the Commission politically on the lines of the Bruges speech,

and confront them directly when they try to move into really sensitive areas such as tax harmonisation, frontier control and above all any attempted invasion of the heartland of economic policy-making. I think it would be useful for the note to have a wider circulation in Whitehall, with your endorsement of the need to respond firmly to the Commission's expansionary tendencies. Agree?[9]

Thatcher wrote on this document 'Yes – very much so'. From 1988 onwards, it became increasingly the case that Conservatives would, in effect, say 'We are all Powellites now' on Europe (whether of the Enoch or Charles variety), notwithstanding the removal of Thatcher in 1990. It was said, in the McCarthyite era, that, once one became convinced someone was a communist, everything they did reinforced that belief, even such unrevolutionary activities as joining a country club or working on Wall Street. Likewise, every event after 1988 served to convince Conservative Eurosceptics of the wisdom of Thatcher's approach: the UK's ignominious exit from the ERM, Maastricht, subsequent treaties and so on. Conservative leaders (such as Major from 1992 to 1997 and Cameron from 2005 onwards) could seek to stem the tide of Europhobia in their party, but, in the end, they were always overwhelmed by it. The party was much more at ease when under strictly Eurosceptic leadership, as it was between 1997 and 2005.

In this context, the period from 1975 to 1988 should be seen as a sort of interregnum. For the first part of this period, with new leadership and many internal battles to fight, Thatcher and her allies had neither the strength nor the inclination to add Europe to the list of foes to be vanquished. The SEA seemed, at first blush, to confirm the view that they affected to have that the EEC was an arrangement whereby the UK could enjoy the advantages of free trade within a much larger market, but with no commensurate disadvantages or restrictions on domestic policy. Once Thatcher had demolished Galtieri, Scargill, the Left and the wets in her own party, attention shifted to the EEC. It turned out that this was not merely a free-trade association. Howe might seek to tell her that this was all 'inherent in the treaties' by which the UK had joined the EEC, but this inconvenient message was ignored.

If one then goes back a stage further, to the period when the Conservatives were most at ease with Europe, one can see that there were excellent domestic and foreign policy reasons for that approach. Of course, many Tories were not social democrats, even in the loosest sense. Even in the 1950s and 1960s, there were many Conservatives who would attest to the bracing effects of competition and inequality, and this was a decidedly different emphasis from (say) the Jenkinsites within Labour. But most Conservatives acknowledged that they had to live within the social democratic system of the times. That meant that accommodation with Europe was both logical and comforting, providing, if nothing else, protection against something worse than social democracy: full-blooded socialism.

In some, important, cases, the Tory affinity with both social democracy and Europe went beyond mere accommodation. To a modern Conservative, like Nick Timothy (Theresa May's Downing Street Chief of Staff), the pre-Thatcher policy mix was simply unthinkable. Writing in 2018, he would wonder 'How can the same philosophical tradition spawn the near-socialism of Harold Macmillan as well as the free market beliefs of Margaret Thatcher?' Conservatives of the Macmillan/Heath era did not accept all of what some have called the post-war settlement, but they certainly did place emphasis on the maintenance of full employment. For Macmillan, unemployment was the overriding issue: he was 'determined, as far as it lies within human power, never to allow this shadow to fall again upon our country'. Heath thought much the same, and saw the connection between domestic and European policy as critical. He was 'sometimes accused of being oversensitive about unemployment [but did] not believe that that is possible, certainly not for anyone who lived through the 1930s and saw the political consequences of high unemployment throughout Western Europe and what happened in 1939'.[10]

And so, to recapitulate, in the period between the early 1960s and the financial crisis of 2008, the European case was most strongly supported by British social democrats and was at its strongest when Britain was operating within a securely social democratic system. The Bennite Left and the Powellite Right never had any time for the EEC, but their influence was quite limited prior to the mid-1970s. For the next decade or so, this issue saw the Left struggling to advance a case for withdrawal in the face of the hostility of the press, the Labour Right and most of the Conservative Party. It was after 1988 that the Powellite Right, now ascendant in the Tory Party and the press, began to take up the anti-European case with fervour, as the Left receded and a pro-EU consensus settled upon Labour. This, roughly, was the state of play between 1988 and 2008.

Before coming to the crisis and its aftermath, one should deal with the suggestion made in some quarters that the UK did not leave the EU: rather the EU left the UK. On this basis, the EEC of the 1970s was a loose free-trade association: a Common Market and no more. That was what Britain agreed to join. Since then, it has been claimed, the 'European Project' has run out of control, seeking to regulate every aspect of our lives. The project has spawned a number of schemes, which were both overblown in conception and disastrous in execution: the Social Chapter, the Euro, open borders for asylum seekers. It is no wonder, some say, that the British people voted to accept a Common Market in 1975 but decided in 2016 to leave this superstate.

The difficulty with this argument (slightly, but only slightly, caricatured above) is that, as we have seen, the turn against the EEC had occurred well before any of these developments. Moreover, the fact that there was a European blueprint, which went well beyond free trade between otherwise wholly independent nation states, was obvious from the outset. After all, quite apart from what was 'inherent in the treaties', the wider ambitions at work had been evident from 1955, when the six Member States of the European Coal and Steel Community met at Messina and pledged that:

further progress must be [made] towards the setting up of a united Europe by the development of common institutions, the gradual merging of national economies, the creation of a common market, and the gradual harmonization of their social policies … as far as the social field is concerned, the six Governments consider it imperative to study the progressive harmonization of the regulations now in force in the various countries, especially those relating to working hours … length of statutory holidays and holiday-pay.[11]

How, then, did it come about that, 40 years later, Norman Lamont (Chancellor under Major, and every inch a Thatcherite) would seek to quell the fears of his Eurosceptic backbenchers by telling them that 'I do not believe that social policy should be decided in Brussels. I believe that it should be decided in this country and in this House'? There was certainly deception in play here. To be charitable, one might accept a degree of self-deception; the less forgiving might see this as very selective amnesia indeed. Certainly, it seems that it was only after 1988 that most Conservatives began to see a substantial conflict between their domestic and European objectives.[12]

There is, however, one final puzzle to be resolved. Between 2008, when the crisis struck, and 2016, when the UK voted to leave the EU, Britain remained in the care of politicians who were strongly pro-Remain. New Labour, and the coalition, were led by Remainers, and they all worked hard during the referendum to secure a vote to stay. Why could not the British Centre achieve in 2016 the outcome that had been secured in 1975 by the then generation of Centrists?

Of course, the circumstances in 2016 were very different. By 2016, the UK had endured six years of austerity. The recession had been the deepest since the war. Those who had done well out of the preceding boom did, if anything, better during the ensuing bust. Austerity and inequality were a toxic combination. The situation was ideal for populists of Left and Right to emerge, and they duly did so. Corbyn, Rees-Mogg and the 'pound shop Enoch Powell', Farage, had no love for the EU and little affection for the new consensus that had emerged since 1979. For Corbyn, the 2008 crash showed that he had been right all along to oppose any compromise with capitalism. For the Right, the problem of public debt had created a watershed moment, in which it would be possible to move towards the smaller state to which they aspired. To both Left and Right, the EU was at best an irrelevance and at worst an obstruction. These were strange bedfellows, admittedly, and many of the arguments that they deployed were curious. After all, as Major pointed out of the self-styled saviours of the NHS:

> The concept that the people running the Brexit campaign would care for the National Health Service is a rather odd one. I seem to remember Michael Gove wanted to privatise it, Boris wanted to charge people for using it and Iain Duncan Smith wanted a social insurance system. The NHS is about as safe with them as a pet hamster would be with a hungry python.[13]

This all serves to explain why the Left and Right were, by 2016, hopeful that a sustained attack on the established order might succeed. But why was that established order so enfeebled? I would suggest that the answer lies in the system over which New Labour had presided since 1997, which did not have the robustness of the post-war order, and which placed little emphasis on equality.

When the financial crisis occurred in 2008, the cupboard was relatively bare in terms of ideas. Most British political leaders had invested heavily in neoliberalism. They could not readily admit that this choice had been ill-advised, nor easily find another ideological model within which to shelter. Thus, in June 2006, one could find Brown heaping lavish praise on his City hosts for making London 'the capital marketplace of the world'. This had been achieved through (his) policy framework of 'light touch regulation, a competitive tax environment and flexibility'. The very next day Cameron told another audience of financiers that 'the lessons from the City are clear. Low tax. Low regulation ... these are the keys to success.'[14]

But were these really the only lessons from the City? Was it wise for British leaders to be so close to the bankers, and so reliant upon a single industry? After all, a previous generation of politicians had taken a very different view, but had nonetheless presided over unprecedented economic growth. Macmillan, for example, 'entertained a profound suspicion of the banking sector' and was concerned that the failure of the banks to co-operate with the authorities would take the country 'very near the crash'. Wilson denounced the 'casino mentality' of the City and the 'spivs' paradise' of the Stock Exchange. Of course, some of this was crowd-pleasing rhetoric, but caution about the financiers was coupled with a depth of thinking that went well beyond passive acquiescence in the desires of the very wealthy. Macmillan saw 'engagement with ideas … [as] an essential part of the policy-making process', and, like Keynes, believed 'positive action by the State [was] essential'. It was hard to imagine Brown or Cameron engaging on equal terms with a Keynes, as had Macmillan, even assuming that such an economist had been available.[15]

Robert Skidelsky, Keynes's biographer, is surely right in his explanation of the reasons why policymakers, after a brief flurry of renewed interest in Keynesianism immediately after the crash, soon reverted to type: quoting Marx, he suggests that 'The ideas of the ruling class are in every epoch the ruling ideas.' The more thoughtful of the neoliberal ruling class did have some ideas. But they were not social democratic ideas, and they were not likely to do much to restore the sense of social solidarity that had been lost since 1975, or to reduce the levels of inequality that had developed. After all, it was apparent that the keenest brain in the coalition, Osborne, had a long-term vision for the country that would emerge from the crisis. High levels of public debt were the opportunity not merely for short-term adjustments, but to cut the state down to size in the long term. Osborne thought that Thatcher was 'a great prime minister – probably the greatest in our peacetime history – and we are fortunate to live in a country she did so much to transform'. That transformation was not over, for, as he told an American audience (although he would not have been so brutally candid at home):

Some say that if there are people lacking work, the government should create jobs itself through more spending. If we want a more equal society, they say the answer is a bigger welfare budget. But it is simply not sustainable to attempt to swim against the tide with ever more government spending. We have seen how that approach sows the seeds of its own destruction – not only because the spending becomes unaffordable but also because it creates dependency and ends up harming the very people it is designed to help. Instead we need to equip our citizens to succeed in the world as we find it. … We need to ensure that work always pays by cutting income taxes and reforming welfare. We need to reduce the business taxes and regulatory barriers that hold back the creation of new good jobs.[16]

But was it possible to remain a member of the EU while pursuing these policies to shrink the state and deregulate business? Could the UK embrace such a Reaganite approach and still be a full member of a European Union? Was it likely that the UK could accept the 'the gradual harmonization of their social policies' upon which the Europeans had embarked in 1955? The answer to all these questions from the referendum was, it appeared, no. This was no coincidence. As Thomas Piketty has shown, the abandonment of domestic policies to promote greater equality makes the case for external engagement much more difficult: 'without a strong egalitarian-internationalist platform, it is difficult to unite low-education, low-income voters from all origins within the same coalition and to deliver a reduction in inequality'. The British social democrats who campaigned for membership in the 1960s and 1970s were both egalitarian and internationalist. Without such a programme, it did not prove possible to sustain the necessary breadth of support for Britain in Europe.[17]

Notes to the Text

Abbreviations used in the notes

CAB	Records of the Cabinet Office, The National Archives
CBI MSS	Confederation of British Industry Collection, The Modern Records Centre, Warwick University
CCA	printed items and pamphlets connected with the 2016 Referendum on the United Kingdom's Membership of the European Union, Cambridge University Library
CCO/CRD	Conservative Central Office Papers / Conservative Party Archive, Bodleian Library, Oxford
HC Deb	House of Commons Debates
HL Deb	House of Lords Debates
HLSM	Papers of Lord Hailsham, Churchill Archives Centre, Cambridge
HMSO	Her/His Majesty's Stationery Office
KJ	Papers of Keith Joseph, Conservative Party Archive, Bodleian Library, Oxford
ODNB	Oxford Dictionary of National Biography
POLL	Papers of Enoch Powell, Churchill Archives Centre, Cambridge
PREM	Records of the Prime Minister's Office, The National Archives
SELO	Papers of Selwyn Lloyd, Churchill Archives Centre, Cambridge
THCR	Papers of Margaret Thatcher, Churchill Archives Centre, Cambridge
TNA	The National Archives
TUC MSS	Trades Union Congress Collection, The Modern Records Centre, Warwick University

Notes to Introduction, pages 1–20

[1] www.cvce.eu/obj/address_given_by_edward_heath_brussels_29_january_1963-en-d6b554fe-bb82-4499-85fa-02b2407adc65.html, accessed 4 September 2018.

[2] www.telegraph.co.uk/news/2016/06/24/david-cameron-announces-his-resignation---full-statement/, accessed 4 September 2018.

3   www.independent.co.uk/news/uk/politics/eu-referendum-nigel-farage-4am-victory-speech-the-text-in-full-a7099156.html, accessed 5 September 2018.

4   www.bbc.co.uk/news/business-36611512, accessed 5 September 2018.

5   www.theguardian.com/business/2016/jun/24/bank-of-england-mark-carney-says-brexit-contingency-plans-under-way; www.independent.co.uk/news/uk/politics/anna-soubry-finally-reveals-where-george-osborne-disappeared-to-after-the-referendum-result-a7104646.html, both accessed 5 September 2018.

6   www.theguardian.com/politics/2016/jun/26/labour-crisis-how-coup-plot-jeremy-corbyn-gathered-pace; www.bbc.co.uk/news/uk-politics-36647458, both accessed 5 September 2018.

7   Statement by Edward Heath (Paris, 10 October 1961), www.cvce.eu/en/obj/statement_by_edward_heath_paris_10_october_1961-en-d990219a-8ad0-4758-946f-cb2ddd05b3c0.html; blogs.lse.ac.uk/brexit/2016/09/06/i-want-my-country-back-the-resurgence-of-english-nationalism/, both accessed 5 September 2018.

8   Of course, more broadly based explanations are beginning to emerge: see, for example, the argument that the UK has long been in thrall to the idea of the 'Anglosphere': Michael Kenny and Nick Pearce, *Shadows of Empire: The Anglosphere in British Politics* (London: Penguin, 2018).

9   Martin Daunton, *Just Taxes: The Politics of Taxation in Britain, 1914–1979* (Cambridge: Cambridge University Press, 2002), pp. 302, 322, 328.

10 HC Deb, 28 October 1971, vol. 823, cc. 2205–12.

Notes to Chapter 1, pages 21–58

1   Leader's speech, Scarborough 1948, www.britishpoliticalspeech.org/speech-archive.htm?speech=158, accessed 20 August 2018.

2   Interview for *Woman's Own*, www.margaretthatcher.org/document/106689, accessed 20 August 2018.

3   www.kings.cam.ac.uk/files/services/sermon-20140601-bennett.pdf, accessed 13 August 2018.

4   Where appropriate, the post-1979 domestic policy landscape is addressed in more detail in the relevant chapter below; Inaugural Address, 20 January 1981, at www.presidency.ucsb.edu/ws/index.php?pid=43130, accessed 28 August 2018.

5   See e.g. Arthur Marwick, 'Middle Opinion in the Thirties: Planning, Progress and Political "Agreement"', *English Historical Review*, vol. 79, no. 311 (April 1964), pp. 285–98; Vernon Bogdanor and Robert Skidelsky, *The Age of Affluence, 1951–64* (London: Macmillan, 1970); Paul Addison, *The Road to 1945: British Politics and the Second World War* (rev. edn, London: Pimlico, 1994), p. 290.

6   www.theguardian.com/commentisfree/2007/may/31/thewitandwisdomoftonybenn, accessed 17 August 2018.

7   Sean Glynn and Alan Booth (eds), *The Road to Full Employment* (London:

Allen & Unwin, 1986), pp. 6, 18; HC Deb, 15 April 1929, vol. 227, c. 54.

8   *Employment Policy* (London: HMSO, 1944), Cmnd. 6527; W. John Morgan
    (ed.), *The Rise and Fall of Full Employment 1944–1994* (Nottingham: University
    of Nottingham, 1994), pp. 17, 31–2.

9   Stanley Crooks, *Peter Thorneycroft* (Winchester: George Mann, 2007),
    pp. 88–92; Hailsham 'Note on Economic Policy', May 1962, HLSM 2/5/18;
    Reginald Maudling, *Memoirs* (London: Sidgwick & Jackson, 1978), pp. 102–4.

10 Memorandum, Trend to Heath, 18 January 1972, PREM 15/1079; Budget
    statement, 21 March 1972, HC Deb, vol. 833, cols 1346–7; www.guardian.co.uk/
    news/datablog/2009/nov/25/gdp-uk-1948-growth-economy#chart, accessed 17
    August 2018.

11 Richard Toye, *The Labour Party and the Planned Economy, 1931–1951*
    (Woodbridge: RHS, 2003); Daniel Ritschel, *The Politics of Planning* (Oxford:
    Clarendon Press, 1997), pp. 144–279; Harold Macmillan, *The Middle Way*
    (London: Macmillan, 1938), pp. 238–9, 260–2 and 289–300.

12 Daniel Chester, *The Nationalisation of British Industry, 1945–51* (London:
    HMSO, 1975), pp. 1–2; Martin Chick, *Industrial Policy in Britain, 1945–1951:
    Economic Planning, Nationalisation and the Labour Governments* (Cambridge:
    Cambridge University Press, 1998), p. xi; Samuel Brittan, *Steering the Economy*
    (rev. edn, Harmondsworth: Pelican, 1971), at pp. 238–45, 290; Selwyn Lloyd,
    press release, 19 July 1962, SELO 5/83.

13 Labour Party, *Labour Party Election Manifesto* (London: Labour Party, 1964);
    The National Plan (London: HMSO, 1965), Cmnd. 2764, p. (v); Jim Tomlinson,
    The Labour Governments 1964–1970, Volume 3: Economic Policy (Manchester:
    Manchester University Press, 2003), pp. 94–123; Jim Tomlinson, *Government
    and the Enterprise since 1900: The Changing Problem of Efficiency* (Oxford:
    Oxford University Press, 1994) at pp. 263–74; Joan Mitchell, *Groundwork to
    Economic Planning* (London: Secker, 1966).

14 Robert Taylor, 'The Heath Government, Industrial Policy and the "New
    Capitalism"', in A. Seldon and S. Ball (eds), *The Heath Government, 1970–1974:
    A Reappraisal* (London: Routledge, 1996), at pp. 139–59; *An Approach to
    Industrial Strategy* (London: HMSO, 1975), Cmnd. 6315, at p. 7; Wyn Grant,
    The Political Economy of Industrial Policy (London: Butterworth, 1982),
    pp. 49/50; J.D. McCallum, 'The Development of British Regional Policy',
    pp. 3–41, in D. MacLennan and J. Parr, *Regional Policy: Past Experience and
    New Directions* (Oxford: Robertson, 1979), at pp. 24–8.

15 1944 White Paper, quoted in Morgan (ed.), *Rise and Fall of Full Employment*,
    p. 33.

16 Macmillan in 1962, quoted in Robert Taylor, 'The Need for an Incomes Policy',
    pp. 149–67, in R. Charter et al., *Incomes Policy* (Oxford: Clarendon Press,
    1981), at p. 149; *Incomes Policy: The Next Step* (London: HMSO, 1962), Cmnd.
    1626, at paras 3 and 5; Mark Wickham-Jones, 'The Debate about Wages: The
    New Left, the Labour Party and Incomes Policy', *Journal of Political Ideologies*,
    vol. 18, no. 1 (2013), pp. 83–105.

17 HL Deb, 16 December 1964, vol. 262, cc. 461–2; *Prices and Incomes Policy* (London: HMSO, 1965), Cmnd. 2639, paras 3 and 11; NBPI, *Machinery of Prices and Incomes Policy* (London: HMSO, 1965), Cmnd. 2577, para 18; HC Deb, 16 December 1964, vol. 704, c. 382.

18 Campbell Balfour, *Incomes Policy and the Public Sector* (London: Routledge, 1972), at pp. 236–7, and e.g. *Prices and Incomes Standstill* (London: HMSO, 1966), Cmnd. 3073; *Prices and Incomes Standstill: Period of Severe Restraint* (London: HMSO, 1966), Cmnd. 3150.

19 Notes for the Record of meetings with the CBI and Vic Feather of the TUC, 7 June 1971, PREM 15/315; Trend, Memo, 26 September 1972, 'Prices and Incomes Policy: Discussions with the CBI and TUC', CAB 129/164/18; Note of meeting at Chequers, 28 October 1972, pp. 9/10, PREM 15/820.

20 Labour Party, *Election Manifesto February 1974* (London: Labour Party, 1974); for the 'voluntary' pay policy, see e.g. Trades Union Congress, *The Development of The Social Contract* (London: TUC, 1975), at pp. 13–14 and *The Attack on Inflation* (London: HMSO, 1975), Cmnd. 6151, paras 6–10.

21 'Economic Policy: The British Experiment', 18 June 1984, Thatcher Foundation, www.margaretthatcher.org/document/109504, accessed 18 August 2018. Excerpt from 'Economic policy: The British Experiment', Lord Nigel Lawson 1984 Mais Lecture. Published by The City University Business School and reprinted by permission of Lord Lawson.

22 Mandelson speech to 2009 Labour Conference, www.theguardian.com/politics/2009/sep/28/lord-mandelson-speech-in-full, accessed 18 August 2018; John Grieve Smith, *Full Employment: A Pledge Betrayed* (Basingstoke: Macmillan, 1997), p. 100.

23 Chris Wrigley, *British Trade Unions since 1933* (Cambridge: Cambridge University Press, 2002), at pp. 18/19; women: see Robert Taylor, *The Fifth Estate: Britain's Unions in the Seventies* (London: Routledge, 1978), pp. 12–13; insurance etc.: Hugh Clegg, *The Changing System of Industrial Relations in Great Britain* (Oxford: Blackwell, 1979), Table 8, p. 179; wages: Andrew Glyn and Bob Sutcliffe, *British Capitalism, Workers and the Profits Squeeze* (Harmondsworth: Penguin, 1972), at pp. 58–9.

24 Quoted in Ruth Dukes, 'Otto Kahn-Freund and Collective Laissez-Faire: An Edifice without a Keystone?', *The Modern Law Review*, vol. 72, no. 2 (March 2009), pp. 220–46, at p. 221; see generally, Peter Dorey, *British Conservatism and Trade Unionism, 1945–1964* (Aldershot: Routledge, 2009), esp. at pp. 129, 173–7; Harriet Jones, '"New Conservatism"? The Industrial Charter, Modernity and the Reconstruction of British Conservatism after the War', in B. Conekin et al., *Moments of Modernity: Reconstructing Britain, 1945–1964* (London: Rivers Oram Press, 1999), at pp. 180–1: the word 'Conservative' had been obscured; ODNB entry for Monckton.

25 Meeting, 21 March 1977, p. 125, TUC MSS.292D/40.2LPMR/1; from 1968 to 1979, statutes dealt with such topics as racial discrimination, unfair dismissal and the promotion of collective bargaining: Paul Davies and Mark Freedland,

Labour Legislation and Public Policy: A Contemporary History (Oxford: Clarendon Press, 1993), pp. 186–237, 376–7, 422–3.

[26] See Bob Hepple and Sandra Fredman, *Labour Law and Industrial Relations in Great Britain* (Deventer: Kluwer, 1986), at pp. 49–51. For details of the legislation in the Thatcher era, see Davies and Freedland, *Labour Legislation and Public Policy*, chapters 9 and 10; Robert Taylor, *The Trade Union Question in British Politics* (Oxford: Blackwell, 1993), at p. 273, Table 8.2; www.statista.com/statistics/287232/trade-union-density-united-kingdom-uk-y-on-y/, accessed 18 August 2018; Alastair Reid, *United We Stand: A History of British Trade Unions* (London: Allen Lane, 2004), pp. 388–9.

[27] HC Deb, 17 October 1945, vol. 414, cc. 1222–3.

[28] John Boughton, *Municipal Dreams: The Rise and Fall of Council Housing* (London: Verso, 2018), chapters 3–5, p. 165; Philip Bentley, 'The Becontree Estate before 1945: "Like Heaven with the Gate Open"' (2006, held at Barking and Dagenham, Archives and Local Studies Centre), p. 11; Robert Home, *The Largest Council Housing Estate in the World: The Planning History of Becontree/Dagenham* (1995, held at Barking and Dagenham, Archives and Local Studies Centre), p. 29; the deputy librarian of Barking in 1961, quoted in Roy Greenslade, *Goodbye to the Working Class* (London: Marion Boyars, 1976), at p. 14.

[29] Harlow Development Commission, 27th Annual Report, 1974, p. 161; File C3, Surveys, 1976 Household Survey, report 8, 'Household Characteristics and Dwelling Sizes', p. 4, Harlow Archive, papers held at the Museum of Harlow; 'Harlow 30 years after: how the dream stands up to reality', *The Times*, 16 December 1977; *Harlow Gazette and Citizen*, 23 April 1976, p. 5.

[30] Alice Coleman, *Utopia on Trial: Vision and Reality in Planned Housing* (2nd edn, London: Shipman, 1990), pp. 3, 6, 185.

[31] Boughton, *Municipal Dreams*, pp. 167–9.

[32] C.A.R. Crosland, *The Future of Socialism* (London: Cape, 1956; 1980 reissue), p. 188; Hunter Davies, *The Co-Op's Got Bananas: A Memoir of Growing Up in the Post-War North* (London: Simon & Schuster, 2016), ch. 7.

[33] David Rubinstein and Brian Simon, *The Evolution of the Comprehensive School, 1926–1972* (2nd edn, London: Routledge, 1973), pp. 85–6; Susan Crosland, *Tony Crosland* (London: Cape, 1982), p. 148.

[34] Rubinstein and Simon, *Evolution of the Comprehensive School*, pp. 108, 117; Clyde Chitty, *Education Policy in Britain* (3rd edn, Basingstoke: Palgrave, 2014), p. 29; Charles Moore, *Margaret Thatcher: The Authorized Biography, Volume One: Not For Turning* (London: Penguin, 2013), p. 217.

[35] Rubinstein and Simon, *Evolution of the Comprehensive School*, p. 104; John Rae, *The Public Schools Revolution: Britain's Independent Schools 1964–1979* (London: Faber & Faber, 1981), p. 13.

[36] *The Daily Telegraph*, 'Blair: comprehensives have failed', 13 February 2001; Chitty, *Education Policy in Britain*, pp. 29–31, 103. For the overlap between the approaches of Boyle and Crosland, which was substantial: Maurice Kogan,

The Politics of Education: Edward Boyle and Anthony Crosland in Conversation with Maurice Kogan (Harmondsworth: Penguin, 1974), pp. 16–25.

37 Chitty, *Education Policy in Britain*, pp. 111–16.

38 Chitty, *Education Policy in Britain*, p. 259; 'Rose garden was like the "Dave and Nick Show"', news.bbc.co.uk/1/hi/uk_politics/8678370.stm, 12 May 2010; Michael Gove, 'I refuse to surrender to the Marxist teachers hell-bent on destroying our schools', *The Daily Mail*, 23 March 2013.

39 Alec Cairncross, *The British Economy since 1945: Economic Policy and Performance, 1945–1995* (2nd edn, Oxford: Blackwell, 1995), p. 192; Douglas Wass, *Decline to Fall* (Oxford: Oxford University Press, 2008), pp. 99, 121–5.

40 www.ifs.org.uk/tools_and_resources/fiscal_facts/public_spending_survey/ total_public_spending, figure 1a, accessed 17 November 2016; data.oecd.org/ gga/general-government-spending.htm, accessed 21 August 2018.

41 Michael Moran, *The British Regulatory State: High Modernism and Hyper-innovation* (Oxford: Oxford University Press, 2003); Michael Power, *Audit Society: Rituals of Verification* (Oxford: Oxford University Press, 1999); www.independent.co.uk/news/people/obituary-lord-jay-5625483.html, accessed 21 August 2018.

42 Martin Daunton, *Just Taxes: The Politics of Taxation in Britain, 1914–1979* (Cambridge: Cambridge University Press, 2002), pp. 195, 277–8; www.ifs.org. uk/ff/vat.xls, accessed 17 November 2016; www.ifs.org.uk/bns/bn09.pdf, Table 1, p. 5, accessed 21 August 2018.

43 Daunton, *Just Taxes*, pp. 229, 236, 278; Heather Richardson, *To Make Men Free: A History of the Republican Party* (New York: Basic Books, 2014), pp. 236–7.

44 Anthony Barber, *Taking the Tide: A Memoir* (Norwich: Russell, 1996), pp. 103–5; Elizabeth Knowles and Angela Partington (eds), *The Oxford Dictionary of Quotations* (5th edn, Oxford: Oxford University Press, 1999), p.366.

45 For the rates of tax after 1979, see: www.ifs.org.uk/uploads/publications/ff/ income.xls, accessed 1 December 2016; budget statement and suspension: HC Deb, 15 March 1988, vol. 129, cc. 1006–13.

46 Daunton, *Just Taxes*, pp. 195, 213, 278; John Campbell, *Roy Jenkins: A Well-Rounded Life* (London: Cape, 2014), pp. 126–7.

47 For the Wealth Tax, Daunton, *Just Taxes*, pp. 316–18 (Conservatives) and pp. 328–33 (Labour); Notes of third session of Selsdon Conference, p. 11, and fourth session, p. 4: both 31 January 1970, CRD 3/7/7/7; Healey: HC Deb, 26 March 1974, vol. 871, cc. 312–14; Cedric Sandford, 'The Diamond Commission and the Redistribution of Wealth', *British Journal of Law and Society*, vol. 7, no. 2 (Winter 1980), pp. 286–96.

48 www.ifs.org.uk/bns/bn09.pdf, Table 1, p. 5, accessed 21 August 2018.

49 Glyn and Sutcliffe, *British Capitalism, Workers and the Profits Squeeze*, pp. 180–1; Anthony Atkinson, *Top Incomes in the United Kingdom over the Twentieth Century* (Oxford: Oxford University Press, 2002), Table 4, p. 28,

p. 38; Danny Dorling, *Peak Inequality: Britain's Ticking Time Bomb* (London: Policy Press, 2018), Figure 2.2.1, p. 30.

50 Facundo Alvaredo et al., *Top Wealth Shares in the UK over More than a Century* (London: Centre for Economic Policy Research, 2017), Figure 1, p. 3; www.ons.gov.uk/peoplepopulationandcommunity/birthsdeathsandmarriages/lifeexpectancies/bulletins/englishlifetablesno17/2015-09-01, accessed 23 August 2018; Dorling, *Peak Inequality*, pp. 182–4 and Table 4.5.1, p. 185.

51 Atkinson, *Top Incomes in the United Kingdom*, Table 4, p. 28, p. 38; Dorling, *Peak Inequality*, p. 28; Alverado et al., *Top Wealth Shares in the UK*, p. 50. Reprinted with permission from Trades Union Congress. www.tuc.org.uk.

52 Howard Reed and Jacob Mohun Himmelweit, *Where Have All The Wages Gone?* (London: TUC, 2012), p. 8 and Table 1, p. 12. Reprinted with permission from Trades Union Congress. www.tuc.org.uk.

53 www.gov.uk/government/publications/health-profile-for-england/chapter-1-life-expectancy-and-healthy-life-expectancy, accessed 23 August 2018; Dorling, *Peak Inequality*, pp. 69–70.

54 Dorling, *Peak Inequality*, pp. 73–5 and Table 3.11.1, p. 143.

55 The term 'Great Divergence' has been coined to refer to the much more rapid growth of the economies of Europe than that of China during the Era of Mercantilism and Industrialisation; for the differences in income inequality between Continental Europe and the English-speaking countries: A.B. Atkinson and Thomas Piketty (eds), *Top Incomes over the Twentieth Century: A Contrast between European and English-speaking Countries* (Oxford: Oxford University Press, 2007), pp. 539–44; for the U-shaped trend, www.newyorker.com/news/john-cassidy/pikettys-inequality-story-in-six-charts, accessed 3 January 2019; David Davis in 2016, quoted in Michael Kenny and Nick Pearce, *Shadows of Empire: The Anglosphere in British Politics* (London: Penguin, 2018), p. 154.

56 Jeffrey Weeks, *Sex, Politics and Society: The Regulation of Sexuality since 1800* (3rd edn, Harlow: Pearson, 2012), pp. 339–40.

57 *In Place of Strife: A Policy for Industrial Relations* (London: HMSO, 1969), Cmnd 3888, paras 10–17, 86–92 and 93–8; Michael Moran, *The Politics of Industrial Relations: The Origins, Life, and Death of the 1971 Industrial Relations Act* (London: Palgrave, 1977).

58 Wass, *Decline to Fall*, pp. 114–16; Joe Haines, *The Politics of Power* (London: Cape, 1977), pp. 44–59, at p. 58; John Shepherd, *Crisis? What Crisis?: The Callaghan Government and the British 'Winter of Discontent'* (Manchester: Manchester University Press, 2013).

59 A.W. Phillips, 'The Relation Between Unemployment and the Rate of Change of Money Wage Rates in the United Kingdom, 1861–1957', *Economica*, vol. 25, no. 100 (1958), pp. 283–99, at p. 299; Jim Tomlinson, *The Politics of Decline: Understanding Post-War Britain* (Harlow: Routledge, 2000), Table 6.1, p. 91; for unemployment figures in more detail: www.ons.gov.uk/ons/rel/.../unemployment--trends-since-the-1970s.pdf, accessed 24 August 2018.

[60] Leader's speech, Blackpool, 28 September 1976, www.britishpoliticalspeech. org/speech-archive.htm?speech=174, accessed 24 August 2018; Denis Healey, *The Time of My Life* (London: Joseph, 1989), pp. 378–9.

[61] *The Independent*, 'UK unemployment rate hits lowest since 1975 but wage growth still weak', 16 August 2017; Healey, *The Time of My Life*, p. 443 (a reference to Peter Jay, then married to Callaghan's daughter, and a monetarist economist).

[62] *Public Expenditure to 1979–80* (London: HMSO, February 1976), Cmnd. 6393, para 2; quoted in Edmund Dell, *A Hard Pounding: Politics and Economic Crisis, 1974–1976* (Oxford: Oxford University Press, 1991), p. 273.

[63] Crosland, *Tony Crosland*, pp. 374–83; IEA, *The Rebirth of Britain* (London: IEA, 1964); *Swinton Journal*, Editorial, vol. 14, no. 3 (1968), pp. 2–4, at p. 4.

[64] www.margaretthatcher.org/speeches/displaydocument.asp?docid=110607 (Preston speech, 5 September 1974); Keith Joseph, 'Inflation: The Climate of Opinion is Changing', in *Stranded on the Middle Ground?: Reflections on Circumstances and Policies* (London: CPS, 1976); speech at Oxford, 14 March 1975, KJ 30/2; Keith Joseph and Jonathan Sumption, *Equality* (London: Murray, 1979).

[65] W. Arthur Lewis, *The Principles of Economic Planning* (London: Routledge, 2003 edn; originally published 1949), p. 10.

[66] Macmillan, *The Middle Way*; for Eisenhower and the Middle Way: Richardson, *To Make Men Free*, pp. 234–5; Crosland, *The Future of Socialism*, p. 148.

[67] Crosland, *Tony Crosland*, pp. 66–7, 92–4; Tony Benn (ed. Ruth Winstone), *Years of Hope: Diaries, Letters and Papers, 1940–1962* (London: Hutchinson, 1994), pp. 317–21. Crosland was, by 1960, fearful that Labour was doomed to steady decline unless it could 'acquire a broader appeal and a relatively classless image': Anthony Crosland, *Can Labour Win?* (London: Fabian Society, 1960), pp. 23, 24.

[68] Susan Howson, *British Monetary Policy 1945–51* (Oxford: Clarendon Press, 1993), pp. 63–8; for the progressive 1930s Tories: Robert Rhodes James, *Bob Boothby: A Portrait* (Sevenoaks: Hodder, 1991), pp. 72–4, 87–8.

[69] Ben Jackson, *Equality and the British Left: A Study in Progressive Political Thought, 1900–64* (Manchester: Manchester University Press, 2007), pp. 29–30, 168; Lawrence Goldman, *The Life of R.H. Tawney: Socialism and History* (London: Bloomsbury, 2014), pp. 173, 192–3, 267.

[70] Jackson, *Equality and the British Left*, pp. 117–19; Goldman, *Life of R.H. Tawney*, pp. 179, 193; Kenneth O. Morgan, *Ages of Reform: Dawns and Downfalls of the British Left* (London: Tauris, 2011), p. 143.

[71] Jackson, *Equality and the British Left*, pp. 108–19; Evan Durbin (ed. David A. Reisman), *The Politics of Democratic Socialism* (London: William Pickering, 1994; originally published 1940), pp. xi, 305–6, 321, 326, 332.

[72] Jackson, *Equality and the British Left*, pp. 137, 205.

[73] Morgan, *Ages of Reform*, p. 145; Kevin Jefferys, *Anthony Crosland: A New*

Biography (London: Politico's, 2000), p. 63.

74 Jefferys, *Anthony Crosland*, pp. 59–60, 63.

75 Crosland, *The Future of Socialism*, pp. 35–42, 148, 169, 246, 288, 340.

76 Crosland, *The Future of Socialism*, pp. 355, 357; Roy Jenkins, *Europe: Why Social Democrats Should Support a New Advance* (London: Rita Hinden Memorial Fund, 1978), p. iii.

77 Crosland, *The Future of Socialism*, p. 355.

78 David Lipsey and Dick Leonard (eds), *The Socialist Agenda: Crosland's Legacy* (London: Cape, 1981), p. 22.

79 Morgan, *Ages of Reform*, p. 143.

80 Jenkins, quoted in Tudor Jones, *The Revival of British Liberalism: From Grimond to Clegg* (Basingstoke: Palgrave, 2011), p. 90; for a view sympathetic to Thatcherism, see e.g. Nicholas Crafts, *British Economic Growth Before and After 1979: A Review of the Evidence* (London: Centre for Economic Policy Research, 1988).

Notes to Chapter 2, pages 59–92

1 HL Deb, 13 November 1984, vol. 457, c. 240.

2 Julian Critchley, *Westminster Blues* (London: Futura, 1986), pp. 40–1.

3 EFDD Group, *The EU Referendum Deal*, 2016, www.efddgroup.eu/images/publications/Referendum_book.pdf, accessed 20 July 2018.

4 *Bulmer* v *Bollinger* [1974] Ch. 401, 411; Robert Saunders, *Yes to Europe! The 1975 Referendum and Seventies Britain* (Cambridge: Cambridge University Press, 2018), pp. 231–3, 380.

5 See Lynton Robins, *The Reluctant Party: Labour and the EEC, 1961–1975* (Ormskirk: Hesketh, 1979); Crosland, *Tony Crosland*, pp. 219–30.

6 Coincidentally, or otherwise, all three attended Balliol College, Oxford: Macmillan (1912–14), Heath (1935–9) and Jenkins (1938–41).

7 The Monday Club was formed in 1963 'as a Right-wing counterblast to the Bow Group': *The Times*, 7 October 1963. See generally: Mark Pitchford, *The Conservative Party and the Extreme Right, 1945–75* (Manchester: Manchester University Press, 2011), pp. 75, 81, 172; *Monday World* (Summer 1971), Editorial, p. 2.

8 For the Treaty: ec.europa.eu/romania/sites/romania/files/tratatul_de_la_roma.pdf, accessed 27 July 2018; *Flaminio Costa* v *ENEL (Procedure)*: ECJ, 15 July 1964, C-6/64 (1964) CMLR 425.

9 Martin Dedman, *The Origins and Development of the European Union, 1945–95: A History of European Integration* (London: Routledge, 1996), pp. 105, 107 and 111–15.

10 Alan Milward, *The Rise and Fall of a National Strategy, 1945–1963* (London: Whitehall History, 2002), pp. 357, 416.

11 For considerations of sovereignty: Milward, *Rise and Fall of a National Strategy*, pp. 344–5, 444–9; for the accusations of lying, Referendum Party

Advertisement, *The Times*, 10 January 1997; HL Deb, 2 August 1961, vol. 234, cc. 1119–20.

12   For a full account of this application: Stephen Wall, *The Official History of Britain and the European Community, Volume II: From Rejection to Referendum, 1963–1975* (London: Routledge, 2013), pp. 137–265.

13   Cabinet Minutes, 13 April 1967, CAB 128/42/20; Wilson and White Paper, quoted in Wall, *From Rejection to Referendum*, pp. 166–7, 440.

14   For the 1970–1 negotiations: Wall, *From Rejection to Referendum*, pp. 360–412; for Howe's views: Hugo Young, *This Blessed Plot: Britain and Europe from Churchill to Blair* (London: Macmillan, 1998), p. 250; Wall, *From Rejection to Referendum*, pp. 440–1; Geoffrey Howe, *Conflict of Loyalty* (London: Pan, 1995), p. 67.

15   Alistair Horne, *Macmillan, 1894–1956, Volume 1 of the Official Biography* (London: Macmillan, 1988).

16   Harold Macmillan, *The Middle Way: A Study of the Problem of Economic and Social Progress in a Free and Democratic Society* (London: Macmillan, 1938), pp. 192, 217, 301–11; Horne, *Macmillan, 1894–1956*, p. 109.

17   For the debate about Macmillan's own beliefs: Horne, *Macmillan, 1894–1956*, pp. 313–15, 350–1, and Jacqueline Tratt, *The Macmillan Government and Europe: A Study in the Process of Policy Development* (Basingstoke: Macmillan, 1996), pp. 12–15.

18   Horne, *Macmillan, 1894–1956*, pp. 362–4; Alastair Horne, *Harold Macmillan, 1957–1986, Volume II of the Official Biography* (London: Macmillan, 1989), pp. 30–1; Dedman, *Origins and Development*, p. 107; Wendy Brusse, *Tariffs, Trade, and European Integration, 1947–1957: From Study Group to Common Market* (Basingstoke: Palgrave, 1997), pp. 169/170; Simon Bulmer, 'Britain and European Integration: Of Sovereignty, Slow Adaptation and Semi-detachment', pp. 1–29, in Stephen George (ed.), *Britain and the European Community: The Politics of Semi-detachment* (Oxford: Oxford University Press, 1992), p. 7.

19   Dedman, *Origins and Development*, p. 111. D.R. Thorpe, *Supermac: The Life of Harold Macmillan* (London: Chatto, 2010), pp. 452–3; Tratt, *The Macmillan Government and Europe*, pp. 95–101, 126–7.

20   Harold Macmillan, *At the End of the Day, 1961–1963* (London: Macmillan, 1973), pp. 5–16; Cabinet Minutes, 27 July 1961, TNA, CAB/128/35; Philip Ziegler, *Edward Heath: The Authorised Biography* (London: Harper, 2010), p. 117; Milward, *Rise and Fall of a National Strategy*, pp. 341–51.

21   HC Deb, 2 August 1961, vol. 645, cc 1490–1.

22   Note to Cabinet by Heath, 16 October 1961, CAB/129/107.

23   Peter Catterall (ed.), *The Macmillan Diaries, Volume 2: Prime Minister and After, 1957–66* (London: Macmillan, 2011), entries for 29 January and 22 July 1961, pp. 358, 399; Macmillan, *At the End of the Day*, pp. 14, 31, 33.

24   Macmillan, *At the End of the Day*, p. 140; Harold Macmillan, *Britain, the Commonwealth and Europe* (London: Conservative Political Centre, 1962).

25 www.britishpoliticalspeech.org/speech-archive.htm?speech=111, accessed 27
    July 2018.
26 Catterall (ed.), *The Macmillan Diaries, Volume 2*, entry for 11 October 1962,
    p. 505; Horne, *Harold Macmillan: 1957–1986,* pp. 222, 444–51; Young, *This
    Blessed Plot,* p. 144.
27 Catterall (ed.), *The Macmillan Diaries, Volume 2*, entry for 5 August 1961,
    p. 404; Macmillan, *At the End of the Day,* p. 16.
28 Macmillan, *At the End of the Day,* p. 16; Tratt, *The Macmillan Government and
    Europe,* p. 86.
29 Catterall (ed.), *The Macmillan Diaries, Volume 2*, entries for 5 August, 21
    September and 4 October 1961, pp. 401–4, 498 and 503.
30 Macmillan, *At the End of the Day,* pp. 15, 25–6.
31 John Bew, *Citizen Clem: A Biography of Attlee* (London: Quercus, 2017),
    pp. 487–8.
32 For biographical details: John Campbell, *Roy Jenkins* (London: Vintage Books,
    2015) and Roy Jenkins, *A Life at the Centre* (London: Papermac, 1994).
33 Campbell, *Roy Jenkins,* pp. 189, 214–16; Jenkins, *A Life at the Centre,* pp. 27–58,
    144; HC Deb, 28 June 1961, vol. 643, c. 541.
34 Douglas Jay and Roy Jenkins, *The Common Market Debate* (London: Fabian
    International Bureau, 1962), p. 15; Campbell, *Roy Jenkins,* pp. 221–4; George
    Brown, *In My Way: The Political Memoirs of Lord George-Brown* (London:
    Gollancz, 1971), pp. 203, 212–13; Peter Paterson, *Tired and Emotional: The Life
    of Lord George-Brown* (London: Chatto, 1993), p. 234.
35 Campbell, *Roy Jenkins,* p. 224; LCE, *Europe Left,* no. 1 (1963), pp. 2, 6–7 and
    11–13; no. 4 (1964), pp. 7–9, 20.
36 LCE, *Europe Left,* no. 5 (1964), p. 2; Roger Broad, *Labour's European
    Dilemmas: From Bevin to Blair* (Basingstoke: Palgrave, 2001), p. 57.
37 Richard Crossman, *The Diaries of a Cabinet Minister, Volume One* (London:
    Cape, 1975), entries for 3 April and 31 July 1966, pp. 492 and 594; Campbell,
    Roy Jenkins, pp. 284–5; Jenkins features only marginally in the official history
    of this application: Wall, *From Rejection to Referendum,* pp. 194–5.
38 Cabinet Minutes, 30 April 1967, CAB 128/42/26.
39 Eric Heffer, *Never a Yes Man: The Life and Politics of an Adopted Liverpudlian*
    (London, New York: Verso, 1991), p. 129; Barbara Castle, *The Castle Diaries,
    1964–70* (London: Weidenfeld & Nicolson, 1984), entry for 5 October 1967,
    p. 305; Paterson, *Tired and Emotional,* pp. 233–4.
40 Campbell, *Roy Jenkins,* p. 375; Jenkins, *A Life at the Centre,* pp. 317, 323; HC
    Deb, 21 January 1971, vol. 809, cc. 1316–17.
41 Campbell, *Roy Jenkins,* p. 380; Jenkins, *A Life at the Centre,* pp. 330, 338.
42 Jenkins, *A Life at the Centre,* pp. 330–4; Crosland, *Tony Crosland,* pp. 224–6,
    229, 242; Roy Jenkins, *European Diary, 1977–1981* (London: Collins, 1989), p. 4.
43 Letter to *The Times,* 20 November 1971.
44 Brown, foreword, in Joan Mitchell, *Groundwork to Economic Planning*
    (London: Secker, 1966), pp. 5–6; for Brown's role in the National Plan:

Paterson, *Tired and Emotional*, pp. 165–91; HC Deb, 17 October 1972, vol. 843, cc. 71–2.

45 Jenkins, *Europe: Why Social Democrats Should Support a New Advance*, pp. iii–iv.

46 Jack Jones, *Union Man: The Autobiography of Jack Jones* (London: HarperCollins, 1986), p. 215. For biographical details: Ziegler, *Edward Heath* and John Campbell, *Edward Heath: A Biography* (London: Jonathan Cape, 1993).

47 HC Deb, 26 June 1950, vol. 476, cc. 1960–4; the position of the Attlee government on the Schuman Plan was unenthusiastic: see Bew, *Citizen Clem*, pp. 489–90.

48 Ziegler, *Edward Heath*, pp. 112–15, 130; Campbell, *Edward Heath*, pp. 112–13.

49 Campbell, *Edward Heath*, pp. 117, 119, 127; HC Deb, 17 May 1961, vol. 640, c. 1390.

50 Campbell, *Edward Heath*, pp. 121, 131.

51 Campbell, *Edward Heath*, p. 247; Nigel Lawson, 'The Need for a National Policy', pp. 47–63, in *Conservatism Today: Four Personal Points of View* (London: CPC, 1966), p. 60; *The Spectator*, 14 July 1990; Nicholas Ridley, *Towards a Federal Europe* (London: CPC, 1969).

52 www.britishpoliticalspeech.org/speech-archive.htm?speech=113, accessed 27 July 2018.

53 Edward Heath, *Old World, New Horizons: Britain, Europe, and the Atlantic Alliance* (Cambridge, MA: Harvard University Press, 1970), pp. 19, 20, 30 and 57–8.

54 Andrew Roth, *Heath and the Heathmen* (London: Routledge, 1972), pp. 203–6; Ziegler, *Edward Heath*, pp. 192–5. For the negotiations: Ziegler, *Edward Heath*, pp. 271–83 and Campbell, *Edward Heath*, pp. 299–300 and 352–63. For the Cabinet decision: Cabinet Minutes, 1 July 1971, CAB 128/49/36.

55 Richard Kelly, 'The Party Conferences', pp. 221–60, in A. Seldon and S. Ball (eds), *Conservative Century: The Conservative Party since 1900* (Oxford: Oxford University Press, 1994), p. 250. As to the May 1970 speech: 'Heath warns Six: Never again if entry talks fail', *The Guardian*, 6 May 1970, and 'Heath warns Six to negotiate in right spirit', *The Times* (London), 6 May 1970; as to haunting: Wall, *From Rejection to Referendum, 1963–1975*, p. 360, and e.g. Simon Heffer, 'How for 40 years, the British Public has been lied to', *Daily Mail*, 15 May 2003. For public opinion: Campbell, *Edward Heath*, p. 397; and for discussion of a referendum: Ziegler, *Edward Heath*, p. 286.

56 Campbell, *Edward Heath*, pp. 402–5, 439.

57 White Paper, quoted in Campbell, *Edward Heath*, p. 397; HC Deb, 28 October 1971, vol. 823, cc. 2205–12.

58 'Mr Heath foresees a Europe wielding real influence', *The Times*, 25 January 1972; Campbell, *Edward Heath*, pp. 441–2; Ziegler, *Edward Heath*, p. 291.

59 Jim Prior, *A Balance of Power* (London: Hamilton, 1986), p. 85; Catherine Hynes, *The Year that Never Was: Heath, the Nixon Administration and the Year*

of Europe (Dublin: University College Dublin Press, 2009), p. ix.

60 Bank of England papers, quoted in David Marsh, *The Euro: The Politics of the New Global Currency* (New Haven, CT: Yale University Press, 2009), p. 55.

61 Anon., 'Public Opinion and the EEC', *Journal of Common Market Studies*, vol. 6, no. 3 (September 1967), pp. 231–49; Young, *This Blessed Plot*, pp. 129–30, 223, 287.

62 Wall, *From Rejection to Referendum*, p. 137.

Notes to Chapter 3, pages 93–124

1 www.cvce.eu/content/publication/1999/1/1/a3d116ff-3ebe-44ee-99b8-e2b038253def/publishable_en.pdf, accessed 6 September 2018.

2 www.theguardian.com/world/2016/jun/09/eu-enoch-powell-common-market-conservative-party, accessed 6 September 2018.

3 Richard Crossman, *The Diaries of a Cabinet Minister, Volume Three* (London: Cape, 1977), entry for 29 April 1969, p. 464.

4 The stated aim of LCE, of which Jenkins was Chairman: LCE, *Europe Left*, no. 1 (London, 1963); Heath, 10 October 1961, quoted in Edward Heath, *Our Community* (London: CPC, 1977), p. 3.

5 Crossman, *The Diaries of a Cabinet Minister, Volume Three*, entry for 20 April 1970, p. 894.

6 Patrick Bell, *The Labour Party in Opposition, 1970–1974* (London: Routledge, 2004), pp. 192–209.

7 Simon Heffer, *Like the Roman: The Life of Enoch Powell* (London: Weidenfeld & Nicolson, 1998), pp. 247–8, 952; Kenneth Morgan, *Michael Foot: A Life* (London: Harper, 2007), pp. 248–9.

8 Tony Benn, *Office without Power: Diaries, 1968–1972* (London: Arrow, 1989), entry for 16 April 1969, p. 161; HC Deb, 27 October 1971, vol. 823, c. 1762; Benn, *Office without Power*, entry for 28 October 1971, p. 382.

9 Richard Crossman, *The Backbench Diaries of Richard Crossman* (London: Cape, 1981), entry for June 1961, p. 951; 1970 pamphlet, quoted in Broad, *Labour's European Dilemmas*, p. 81; LCE, *Europe Left*, no. 1 (London, 1963), Editorial, p. 2.

10 For a full account of the speech, the background and aftermath: Philip Williams, *Hugh Gaitskell: A Political Biography* (London: Cape, 1979), pp. 702–49.

11 Castle, *The Castle Diaries, 1964–70*, entry for 9 May 1966, pp. 123–4; Tony Benn, *Out of the Wilderness: Diaries, 1963–1967* (London: Arrow, 1988), entry for 14 January 1965, p. 204; Crossman, *The Diaries of a Cabinet Minister, Volume One*, entries for 19 February 1966, p. 461 and 3 April 1966, p. 492.

12 Labour Party, *Election Manifesto* (London: Labour Party, 1966).

13 Crossman, *The Diaries of a Cabinet Minister, Volume One*, entry for 25 May 1966, pp. 527–8; Benn, *Out of the Wilderness*, entry for 22 October 1966, p. 480.

14 Cabinet Minutes, 21 March 1967, CAB/128/42; Cabinet Minutes, 30 April 1967, CAB/128/42; Benn, *Out of the Wilderness*, entry for 30 April 1967, p. 496.

15 HC Deb, 8 May 1967, vol. 746, cc. 1096–7.

16 Benn, *Out of the Wilderness*, entry for 7 March 1966, pp. 396–7; Castle, *The Castle Diaries, 1964–70*, entry for 30 April 1967, pp. 248–50; Crossman, *The Diaries of a Cabinet Minister, Volume One*, entry for 30 April 1967, p. 335.

17 HC Deb, 8 May 1967, vol. 746, cc. 1117–18.

18 See Chapter 2.

19 Labour Party, *Election Manifesto* (London: Labour Party, 1970).

20 Castle, *The Castle Diaries, 1964–70*, entry for 5 October 1967, p. 305; Heffer, *Never a Yes Man*, p. 129.

21 See e.g. Michael Hodges, *Multinational Corporations and National Government: A Case Study of the United Kingdom's Experience, 1964–1970* (Farnborough: Saxon, 1974); Benn, *Office without Power*, entry for 6 April 1970, p. 258.

22 Benn, *Office without Power*, entries for 22 July 1969 and 28 September 1969, pp. 192 and 203, and also notes p. 313; David Butler and Uwe Kitzinger, *The 1975 Referendum* (London: Macmillan, 1976), Table 1, p. 247.

23 Bell, *The Labour Party in Opposition*, pp. 13–19, 163–71, 174–5 and 177–80; the arguments presented by Holland between 1971 and 1974 are summarised in Stuart Holland, *The Socialist Challenge* (London: Quartet Books, 1975), chapters 7 and 8.

24 Bell, *The Labour Party in Opposition*, p. 17; Broad, *Labour's European Dilemmas*, pp. 74–5; Benn, *Office without Power*, entries for 11 November 1970, 18 January 1971 and 3 March 1971, pp. 315, 325–6 and 337.

25 Morgan, *Michael Foot*, pp. 273/4; Bell, *The Labour Party in Opposition*, pp. 80/81; Robins, *The Reluctant Party*, pp. 81, 83/4.

26 Bell, *The Labour Party in Opposition*, pp. 79, 84–5; Broad, *Labour's European Dilemmas*, pp. 79–85.

27 Bell, *The Labour Party in Opposition*, p. 85; Benn, *Office without Power*, entries for 19 and 28 October 1971, pp. 379–82; HC Deb, 27 October 1971, vol. 823, c. 1906.

28 Crosland, *Tony Crosland*, pp. 225–7; Benn, *Office without Power*, entries for 13 January and 30 May 1971, pp. 324–5, 345–6.

29 Broad, *Labour's European Dilemmas*, pp. 94–5; Heffer, *Never a Yes Man*, p. 142; Benn, *Office without Power*, entry for 21 September 1973, pp. 454--5.

30 Broad, *Labour's European Dilemmas*, pp. 92–3; Benn, *Office without Power*, entries for 18 April 1972 and 11 June 1972, pp. 427 and 431, and text of speech at pp. 522–7.

31 Labour Party, *Election Manifesto February 1974* (London: Labour Party, 1974).

32 Tony Benn, *Against the Tide: Diaries, 1973–1976* (London: Hutchinson, 1990), entry for 11 April 1974, p. 138; Note of meeting, CBI with Wilson and Healey, 10 January 1975, CBI MSS.200/C/3/DG2/11.

33 Benn, *Against the Tide*, entries for 21 November 1974 and 9 April 1975,

pp. 269–70 and 364–5; Heffer, *Never a Yes Man*, pp. 146–7.

34 Barbara Castle, *The Castle Diaries, 1974–76* (London: Weidenfeld & Nicolson, 1982), entries for 14 March 1974 and 22 May 1975, p. 400, 441; HC Deb, 21 July 1975, vol. 896, c. 71.

35 For the AES, see e.g. John Eaton, *An Alternative Economic Strategy for the Labour Movement* (Nottingham, 1975); Benn, *Against the Tide*, entry for 25 February 1975 and Appendix IV, pp. 324–5 and 725–7.

36 Broad, *Labour's European Dilemmas*, pp. 100–5; Cabinet Minutes, 5 December 1974 and 17 March 1975, CAB/128/55/25 and /56/13.

37 Broad, *Labour's European Dilemmas*, p. 102; Benn, *Against the Tide*, entries for 26 to 28 December 1974 and 18 March 1975, pp. 288–91 and 342–9; Morgan, *Michael Foot*, pp. 326–7; Cabinet Minutes, 21 January 1975, CAB/128/56/4.

38 Castle, *The Castle Diaries, 1974–76*, entries for 26 March and 26 April 1975, pp. 354–7, 379 and text of motion p. 750; Broad, *Labour's European Dilemmas*, pp. 106–9.

39 Broad, *Labour's European Dilemmas*, pp. 108–9; *The Castle Diaries, 1974–76*, entry for 16 September 1974, pp. 182–3.

40 *New Left Review*, no. 69 (September 1971), pp. 2–28; Tom Nairn, *The Left against Europe?* (Harmondsworth: Penguin, 1973); Stuart Holland et al., *Sovereignty and Multinational Companies* (London: Fabian Society, 1971), p. 27; Holland, *The Socialist Challenge*, pp. 319–23; Stuart Holland, *Beyond Capitalist Planning* (Oxford: Blackwell, 1978).

41 Stuart Holland, *Uncommon Market: Capital, Class and Power in the European Community* (London: Macmillan, 1980), p. xiii; Delors contributed to *Beyond Capitalist Planning*.

42 Broad, *Labour's European Dilemmas*, Table 7.2, p. 118; Castle, *The Castle Diaries, 1974–76*, entry for 22 April 1975, pp. 373–4.

43 Conservative Research Department, *Campaign Guide for Europe 1979* (London, 1979), p. 216; Memo Howell to Howe, 13 October 1977, THCR 2/6/1/13.

44 Margaret Thatcher, *The Path to Power* (London: HarperCollins, 1995), p. 343.

45 Anti Common Market League and Keep Britain Out literature quoted in Uwe Kitzinger, *Diplomacy and Persuasion: How Britain joined the Common Market* (London: Thames & Hudson, 1973), pp. 233, 247; Pitchford, *The Conservative Party and the Extreme Right*, p. 75.

46 Quoted in T.E. Utley, *Enoch Powell: The Man and His Thinking* (London: Kimber, 1968), p. 114.

47 Speech to Mont Pelerin Society, September 1968, POLL 4/1/3; speech in Leicestershire, August 1968, ibid.; *The Times*, 29 January 1964; Enoch Powell, edited by John Wood, *Freedom and Reality* (London: Elliot, 1969), pp. 53–4, 84, 92, 147.

48 Heffer, *Like the Roman*, pp. 449–59.

49 One Nation Group of MPs, *One Europe* (London: CPC, 1965), p. 8; Heffer, *Like the Roman*, p. 304; Anthony Forster, *Euroscepticism in Contemporary British*

Politics: Opposition to Europe in the British Conservative and Labour Parties since 1945 (London: Routledge, 2002), p. 21.

50   Heffer, *Like the Roman*, pp. 517–18, 528–30; Andrew Roth, *Enoch Powell: Tory Tribune* (London: Macdonald & Co., 1970), pp. 375–8; John Turner, *The Tories and Europe* (Manchester: Manchester University Press, 2000).

51   Conservative Party, *Conservative Manifesto* (London: Conservative Party, 1970); Heffer, *Like the Roman*, p. 554; HC Deb, 25 February 1970, vol. 796, cc. 1265–6.

52   Heffer, *Like the Roman*, pp. 592, 602–4; Enoch Powell, *The Common Market: The Case Against* (Kingswood: Elliot, 1971), pp. 9, 15, 111; Kelly, 'The Party Conferences', pp. 221–60, p. 250.

53   Heffer, *Like the Roman*, pp. 606–7, 618–19; HC Deb, 28 October 1971, vol. 823, c. 2186.

54   Heffer, *Like the Roman*, pp. 705–8, 723.

55   Barry Hedges and Roger Jowell, *Britain and the E.E.C.: Report on a Survey of Attitudes towards the European Economic Community* (London: SCPR, 1971), pp. 27–34, 35, 45–6, 51–2; Douglas Schoen, *Enoch Powell and the Powellites* (London: Macmillan, 1977), pp. 79, 128–33 and 276–7.

56   *The Spectator*, 3 July 1971, p. 3; *The Spectator*, 10 July 1971, pp. 44–5, 83.

57   Turner, *The Tories and Europe*, pp. 64/65; *One Europe*, p. 9; speeches at Preston, 23 September and Croydon, 27 September 1971, Enoch Powell, *Still to Decide* (London: Batsford, 1972), pp. 224–9.

58   *The Daily Telegraph*, 12 July 2017; Heffer, *Like the Roman*, pp. 562–3.

59   Powell, *The Common Market: The Case Against*, p. 119.

Notes to Chapter 4, pages 125–62

1   Thatcher, *The Path to Power*, p. 334; Lomas, quoted in Broad, *Labour's European Dilemmas*, p. 118.

2   For full analysis of the results: Butler and Kitzinger, *The 1975 Referendum*, pp. 263–78.

3   Mark Baimbridge (ed.), *1975 Referendum on Europe, Volume 1: Reflections of the Participants* (Exeter: Imprint, 2007), pp. 75, 77, 78, 83–4.

4   Wilson statement: HC Deb, 7 April 1975, vol. 889, c. 350-1W.

5   Butler and Kitzinger, *The 1975 Referendum*, pp. 94, 95, 229; Baimbridge (ed.), *1975 Referendum on Europe*, memoir by Bernard Donoughue, p. 131.

6   Baimbridge (ed.), *1975 Referendum on Europe*, memoir by Bernard Donoughue, p. 131; Referendum Act 1975, schedule 1.

7   *Britain's New Deal In Europe* (London: HMSO, 1975).

8   Butler and Kitzinger, *The 1975 Referendum*, pp. 73, 82; Body quoted (speaking in 1995), Broad, *Labour's European Dilemmas*, p. 118; Campbell, *Roy Jenkins*, p. 444; for adverts, e.g. *The Daily Mirror*, 31 May 1975, p. 27; *The Sun*, 19 May 1975, p. 19, 3 June 1975, p. 19.

9   Philip Goodhart, *Full-hearted Consent: The Story of the Referendum Campaign*

and the Campaign for the Referendum (London: Davis-Poynter, 1976), pp. 161–2; CBI, *British Industry and Europe* (London: CBI, 1975); Memo from Chairman of GKN, 30 May 1975, POLL 3/2/1/22.

10 Butler and Kitzinger, *The 1975 Referendum*, pp. 166, 182, 184; Campbell, *Roy Jenkins*, p. 448.

11 Campbell, *Edward Heath*, pp. 614–19; Butler and Kitzinger, *The 1975 Referendum*, p. 161.

12 Campbell, *Roy Jenkins*, pp. 444–5; Campbell, *Edward Heath*, p. 684; Michael Bloch, *Jeremy Thorpe* (London: Little, Brown, 2014), pp. 416–17.

13 Campbell, *Roy Jenkins*, pp. 460–3; www.oxforddnb.com/view/10.1093/ref:odnb/9780198614128.001.0001/odnb-9780198614128-e-95228#odnb-9780198614128-e-95228-div1-d1105804e3066, accessed 21 February 2018; John Preston, *A Very English Scandal: Sex, Lies and a Murder Plot at the Heart of the Establishment* (London: Penguin, 2017).

14 Britain in Europe, *Referendum on the European Community (Common Market): Why You Should Vote Yes* (London: HMSO, 1975); Goodhart, *Full-hearted Consent*, pp. 153–5, 165.

15 *Bulmer* v *Bollinger* [1974] Ch. 401, 411; Campbell, *Roy Jenkins*, p. 446; *The Times*, 2 June 1975.

16 Baimbridge (ed.), *1975 Referendum on Europe*, pp. 86–7.

17 Goodhart, *Full-hearted Consent*, pp. 124, 125; Whitelaw's views: Hailsham, note of Shadow Cabinet meeting, 11 April 1975, HLSM 1/1/10 Part 1.

18 269 MPs out of a total of 330; 65% of European Movement speakers were also members of the CGE: CGE Report, 12 July 1973, CCO 507/2/3; Conservative Research Department, *Britain in Europe* (London: Conservative Party, 1975); leaflet at CCO 508/19.

19 Goodhart, *Full-hearted Consent*, pp. 170–1; Butler and Kitzinger, *The 1975 Referendum*, pp. 184, 185; Colin Kidd, 'Upside Down, Inside Out', *London Review of Books*, vol. 40, no. 20 (25 October 2018), pp. 29–30.

20 Thatcher, *The Path to Power*, pp. 283, 335; Benn, *Against the Tide*, entries for 18 and 23 February 1975, pp. 319, 322, 323; *The Sun*, 2 June 1975, p. 2; *The New Statesman*, vol. 84, no. 2307 (6 June 1975), p. 751.

21 Speech, 16 April 1975: www.margaretthatcher.org/document/10267; *The Daily Mail*, 4 June 1975, p. 9.

22 Benn, *Against the Tide*, entry for 14 May 1975, p. 377; Butler and Kitzinger, *The 1975 Referendum*, p. 211.

23 Butler and Kitzinger, *The 1975 Referendum*, pp. 226–7, Table 2.

24 *The Daily Mirror*, 29 May 1975, p. 1, 2 June 1975, pp. 1–2, and 4 June 1975, p. 2; *The Sun*, 4 June 1975, p. 14.

25 *The Daily Express*, 27 May 1975, p. 8, 5 June 1975, p. 10; *The Daily Mail*, 27 May 1975, p. 6, 4 June 1975, p .6.

26 *The Daily Telegraph*, 26 May 1975, p. 8, 29 May 1975, p. 16, 5 June 1975, p. 16.

27 *The Daily Express*, 29 May 1975, p. 10, 2 June 1975, p. 8, 4 June 1975, p. 8; for criticism of Du Cann, *The Daily Express*, 4 June 1975, p. 8; for turmoil: *The*

Daily Telegraph, same day, p. 1; for the jobs claim, e.g. *The Daily Mirror*, 2 June 1975, pp. 1–2; *The Sun*, 28 May 1975, pp. 1–2; *The Daily Mail*, 27 May 1975, p. 6.

28 For 27 May 1975: *The Daily Mirror*, 27 May 1975, p. 1; *The Daily Mail*, pp. 1–3; *The Daily Express*, pp. 1–2; *The Sun*, 3 June 1975, p. 1, 5 June 1975, p. 5; *The Daily Mail*, 31 May 1975, p. 1; *The Daily Telegraph*, 24 May 1975, p. 1.

29 Inflation: *The Sun*, 19 May 1975, p. 1, *The Daily Express*, 19 May 1975, p. 2; strikes, e.g. *The Daily Telegraph*, 31 May 1975, p. 1.

30 Goodhart, *Full-hearted Consent*, pp. 122–4, 130–1; Butler and Kitzinger, *The 1975 Referendum*, pp. 97–110; Castle, *The Castle Diaries, 1974–76*, entries for 1 June and 3 June 1975, pp. 403–6.

31 Butler and Kitzinger, *The 1975 Referendum*, pp. 109, 136–9; *The Sunday Express*, 27 April 1975, p. 16 (Heath), 25 May 1975, p. 14 (Hailsham); Benn, *Against the Tide*, entries for 20 March and 4 May 1975, pp. 350–5, 372; withdrawal plan: *The Times*, 21 April 1975, p. 4.

32 For public meetings, e.g. Benn, *Against the Tide*, entry for 3 June 1975, p. 384; for the role of the Left: Andrew Mullen, *The British Left's 'Great Debate' on Europe* (London: Continuum, 2007), pp. 109–19.

33 Benn, *Against the Tide*, entry for 26 April 1975, p. 369; Morgan, *Michael Foot*, p. 327; Heffer, *Like the Roman*, pp. 754–5; NRC, *Referendum on the European Community (Common Market): Why You Should Vote No* (London: HMSO, 1975).

34 Butler and Kitzinger, *The 1975 Referendum*, pp. 273–4.

35 Benn, *Against the Tide*, entry for 18 March 1975, p. 346.

36 Butler and Kitzinger, *The 1975 Referendum*, p. 168; David Dimbleby chaired a debate on *Panorama* on 2 June 1975: www.youtube.com/watch?v=_zBFh6bpcMo, accessed 21 February 2018.

37 *The Daily Express*, 15 May 1975; quoted in Butler and Kitzinger, *The 1975 Referendum*, p. 229.

38 Letter from Ken Tynan, quoting Jenkins, *The New Statesman*, 13 June 1975, p. 779; Patrick Cosgrave, a polemical journalist close to Thatcher, so argued in *The Spectator*, no. 7668, 14 June 1975, p. 709.

39 Telegram from Christian Democrats, 6 June 1975, THCR 2/6/1/111; Butler and Kitzinger, *The 1975 Referendum*, pp. 252, 271; Colin Braham and Jim Burton, *The Referendum Reconsidered* (London: Fabian Society, 1975); Roger Jowell and James Spence, *The Grudging Europeans: A Study of British Attitudes towards the EEC* (London: SCPR, 1975), pp. 14, 34, 35.

40 Benn, *Against the Tide*, entry for 6 June 1975, p. 387; Forster, *Euroscepticism in Contemporary British Politics*, p. 55.

41 Minutes of Shadow Cabinet, 19 April 1978, LCC/78/200, THCR 2/6/1/162 and *Frankfurter Allgemeine Zeitung*, 25 April 1978, no. 3, p. 3; Minutes of Second Meeting of Policy Group on Direct Elections, 18 November 1975, THCR 2/6/1/75; Report 'Direct Elections to the European Parliament', 1 July 1977, THCR 2/6/1/48; Powell speech on direct elections, May 1978, POLL 3/2/1/21; Nick Crowson, *The Conservative Party and European Integration since 1945: At*

the Heart of Europe (Abingdon: Routledge, 2007).

⁴² Patten interview; Letter. Joseph to Chairman of Unilever, 18 April 1974, KJ 10/8; Memo, Adam Butler to Thatcher, 'What's in a Name?', 8 February 1977, THCR 2/6/1/23.

⁴³ Stephen George, *An Awkward Partner: Britain in the European Community* (3rd edn, Oxford: Oxford University Press, 1998), p. 148; Turner, *The Tories and Europe*, pp. 100–1; Moore, *Margaret Thatcher, Volume One*, pp. 489–94; Ian Gilmour, *Dancing with Dogma: Britain under Thatcherism* (London: Simon & Schuster, 1992), p. 240; Cabinet Minutes, 6 December 1979, CAB/128/66/24, p. 6.

⁴⁴ Moore, *Margaret Thatcher, Volume One*, pp. 485, 487; Thatcher Press Conference after Dublin European Council, 30 November 1979, www. margaretthatcher.org/document/104180, accessed 2 March 2018.

⁴⁵ Memo, Reece to Ryder, 28 November 1979, THCR 2/6/2/134; Note, Gomersall to Alexander, 12 December 1980, PREM 19/1754 f 91; George, *An Awkward Partner*, pp. 150–1.

⁴⁶ Address by Roy Jenkins on creation of EMU, 27 October 1977, www.cvce. eu/content/publication/2010/11/15/98bef841-9d8a-4f84-b3a8-719abb63fd62/ publishable_en.pdf, accessed 7 September 2018.

⁴⁷ Conclusions of European Council, 6 and 7 July 1978 in Bremen, quoted in Peter Ludlow, *The Making of the European Monetary System: A Case Study of the Politics of the European Community* (London: Butterworth, 1982), p. 301.

⁴⁸ Memo from Howe, 31 October 1978, THCR 2/1/1/32.

⁴⁹ HC Deb, 29 November 1978, vol. 959, c. 480; Briefing Note for *Weekend World* Interview, January 1979, THCR 5/1/2/235; statement by Howe and Pym, 6 December 1978, THCR 2/6/2/65.

⁵⁰ Conservative Party, *Conservative Manifesto for Europe* (London, 1979); Howe, *Conflict of Loyalty*, pp. 273–6.

⁵¹ Biffen to Thatcher, 11 July 1978, THCR 2/1/2/2; Note of 27 October 1978, THCR 2/1/2/2; Speech at Uxbridge, 9 August 1978, POLL 4/2/4; *The Times* and *Financial Times*, 4 October 1978.

⁵² Benn, *Against the Tide*, entry for 20 March 1975, p. 355.

⁵³ Bell, *The Labour Party in Opposition, 1970–1974*, at pp. 171–7 and 236–9.

⁵⁴ *Public Expenditure to 1979–80*, para 2.

⁵⁵ Benn, *Against the Tide*, entries for 20 April and 9 June 1975, pp. 365, 389; Scott Newton and Dilwyn Porter, *Modernization Frustrated: The Politics of Industrial Decline in Britain since 1900* (London: Unwin, 1988), p. 175; for the IMF crisis: Kathleen Burk and Alec Cairncross, *'Goodbye, Great Britain': The 1976 IMF Crisis* (New Haven, CT: Yale University Press, 1992).

⁵⁶ Broad, *Labour's European Dilemmas*, pp. 120–38.

⁵⁷ Tony Benn, *Conflicts of Interest: Diaries 1977–1980* (London: Hutchinson, 1990), entries for 25 October 1977 and 28 November 1978, pp. 234, 400; Stuart Holland, *The Regional Problem* (London: Palgrave, 1976), pp. 83–6, 152–3.

⁵⁸ Broad, *Labour's European Dilemmas*, pp. 125, 128, 130–1; Mullen, *The British*

Left's 'Great Debate' on Europe, pp. 121–4.

59   Healey, *The Time of My Life*, pp. 438/9; Benn, paper for Cabinet, 13 July 1978, PREM 16/1635; Mullen, *The British Left's 'Great Debate' on Europe*, p. 124; Memo by Bryan Gould and other Labour MPs, October 1978, TUC MSS.292D/409/565/1.

60   Broad, *Labour's European Dilemmas*, p. 134; Mullen, *The British Left's 'Great Debate' on Europe*, pp. 124–8.

61   Benn, *Conflicts of Interest*, entries for 26 May and 29 July 1977, pp. 153, 205.

62   Labour Party, *1979 Labour Party Election Manifesto* (London, 1979); Broad, *Labour's European Dilemmas*, pp. 135–8; David Butler and Dennis Kavanagh, *The British General Election of 1979* (London: Macmillan, 1980), p. 173; Mullen, *The British Left's 'Great Debate' on Europe*, p. 125.

63   Mullen, *The British Left's 'Great Debate' on Europe*, p. 124; LCMSC, *The Common Market: Labour and the General Election* (Glasgow: LCMSC, 1978), p. 24.

64   Colin Hay, 'The Winter of Discontent after Thirty Years', *Political Quarterly*, vol. 80, no. 4 (2009), pp. 545–61; Shepherd, *Crisis? What Crisis?*

65   Ken Coates (ed.), *What Went Wrong* (Nottingham: Spokesman Books, 2008; first published 1979), pp. 1, 20.

66   Richard Hill, *The Labour Party's Economic Strategy, 1979–1997: The Long Road Back* (Basingstoke: Palgrave, 2001), pp. 21–3, 25–8, 92–5, 125–35.

67   John Callaghan, *The Labour Party and Foreign Policy* (Abingdon: Routledge, 2007), pp. 280–3.

68   Forster, *Euroscepticism in Contemporary British Politics*, p. 68.

69   Broad, *Labour's European Dilemmas*, pp. 140–2, 145–6; Benn, *Conflicts of Interest*, entry for 3 December 1979, p. 561; Tony Benn, *The End of an Era: Diaries 1980–90* (London: Hutchinson, 1992), entry for 1 October 1980, p. 31.

70   Broad, *Labour's European Dilemmas*, pp. 148–54; Morgan, *Michael Foot*, p. 388; Mullen, *The British Left's 'Great Debate' on Europe*, pp. 133–49.

71   Broad, *Labour's European Dilemmas*, pp. 147–8.

72   Labour Party, *1983 Labour Party Election Manifesto* (London, 1983); David Butler and Dennis Kavanagh, *The British General Election of 1983* (London: Macmillan, 1999 edn), pp. 199, 256.

73   For the early history of the SDP: Anthony King and Ivor Crewe, *SDP: The Birth, Life, and Death of the Social Democratic Party* (Oxford: Oxford University Press, 1995), pp. 43–7, 57–8, 74–5, 92–4, 98, 144, 155 and 177.

74   E.H.H. Green, *Ideologies Of Conservatism: Conservative Political Ideas in the Twentieth Century* (Oxford: Oxford University Press, 2004), p. 239.

75   For the policy approaches of the SDP and Liberals: King and Crewe, *SDP*, pp. 44, 57, 60, 107 and 119; for Hayek, Letter to *The Times*, 24 March 1977, www.margaretthatcher.org/document/114626. For the development of SDP European policy: Mullen, *The British Left's 'Great Debate' on Europe*, pp. 145–7.

76   *The Spectator*, vol. 241, no. 7849 (9 December 1978), p. 3 (from a longstanding anti-EEC position).

Notes to Chapter 5, pages 163–200

1   Margaret Thatcher, Speech to the College of Europe ('The Bruges Speech'), 20 September 1988, www.margaretthatcher.org/document/107332.

2   Quoted in Tim Bale, *The Conservative Party from Thatcher to Cameron* (Cambridge: Polity, 2010; 2011 edn), p. 212.

3   Burk and Cairncross, '*Goodbye, Great Britain*', p. xi; Press Release of 31 January 1977, THCR 2/6/1/153.

4   Unemployment rates: www.ons.gov.uk/ons/rel/lms/labour.../unemployment-since-1881.pdf.Table 1 and statswales.wales.gov.uk/Catalogue/Business-Economy-and-Labour-Market/People-and-Work/Unemployment/ILO-Unemployment/CHART-ILOUnemploymentRates-by-UKCountry-Quarter, both accessed 9 July 2013.

5   Peter King, *Housing Policy Transformed* (Bristol: Policy Press, 2010), pp. 60–9.

6   Source: www.ifs.org.uk/uploads/publications/ff/income.xls, accessed 1 December 2016; IIS was Investment Income Surcharge, an additional charge on 'unearned' income.

7   Robert Taylor, *The Trade Union Question in British Politics* (Oxford: Oxford University Press, 1993), p. 273, Table 8.2; also pp. 264, 269.

8   www.ifs.org.uk/tools_and_resources/fiscal_facts/public_spending_survey/total_public_spending, figure 1a, accessed 17 November 2016.

9   Nigel Lawson, *The View from No. 11: Memoirs of a Tory Radical* (London: Bantam Press, 1992), p. 339.

10 Monks interview.

11 Prior, *A Balance of Power*, p. 71; Edward Heath, *The Course of My Life: My Autobiography* (London: Hodder, 1998), pp. 301–2.

12 Patten interview; Walker, a Conservative politician who was close to Heath, was Energy Secretary during the 1984/5 dispute.

13 Charles Moore, *Margaret Thatcher: The Authorized Biography, Volume Two: Everything She Wants* (London: Allen Lane, 2015), pp. 377–82.

14 George, *An Awkward Partner*, pp. 174–85; Moore, *Margaret Thatcher, Volume Two*, p. 394.

15 Crowson, *The Conservative Party and European Integration*, p. 51; for the details of the SEA: A. Campbell, 'The Single European Act and the Implications', *International & Comparative Law Quarterly*, vol. 35, no. 4 (October 1986), pp. 932–9.

16 Patten interview; Moore, *Margaret Thatcher, Volume Two*, pp. 394 and 408.

17 Crowson, *The Conservative Party and European Integration since 1945*, pp. 101–2.

18 aei.pitt.edu/1788/1/stuttgart_declaration_1983.pdf, accessed 9 May 2018.

19 George, *An Awkward Partner*, pp. 186–7.

20 George, *An Awkward Partner*, pp. 188–9.

21 Letter, Prior to Howe, 26 April 1984; note. Howe to Thatcher, 22 June 1984, THCR 2/7/4/13/f3.

22 Statement of Aims: 1 November 1980, THCR 2/11/7/1; list of members: 17 November 1980, www.margaretthatcher.org/document/119519.

23 Memo, Thorneycroft to Gow, 5 December 1980, and reply from Gow, 8 December 1980, THCR 2/11/7/1; HC Deb, 3 December 1980, vol. 995, c. 260.

24 No. 10 letter to Ian Gilmour, 15 December 1980, PREM19/1754 f89.

25 Gow's prediction: memo of 8 December 1980, THCR 2/11/7/1; Heffer, *Like the Roman*, p. 847.

26 Letter, Teddy Taylor to PM's office, 26 March 1986; letter, Budd to Powell, 7 April 1986; note of meeting 8 April 1986, PREM/1754/ f62,f17 and f9.

27 European Communities (Amendment) Bill, HC Deb, 23 April 1986, vol. 96, cc 325–6.

28 Butler and Kavanagh, *The British General Election of 1987*, pp. 14, 72, 221, 226.

29 Howe, *Conflict of Loyalty*, p. 534.

30 Lawson, *The View from No. 11*, pp. 488–9, 497–500, 663–4, 772.

31 George, *An Awkward Partner*, pp. 190–2, 216–17, 227.

32 Howe, *Conflict of Loyalty*, pp. 456, 576–80, 586–7; Lawson, *The View from No. 11*, pp. 960–8; HC Deb, 31 October 1989, vol. 159, cc. 208–9.

33 Nicholas Ridley, *My Style of Government: The Thatcher Years* (London: Hutchinson, 1991), pp. 226, 230; Crowson, *The Conservative Party and European Integration since 1945*, p. 54; George, *An Awkward Partner*, p. 228; HC Deb, 13 November 1990, vol. 180, c. 465.

34 Lawson, *The View from No. 11*, pp. 899, 910.

35 Margaret Thatcher, *The Downing Street Years* (London: Harper, 1993; 2011 edn), p. 737; Delors speech, 6 July 1988, www.margaretthatcher.org/document/113689, accessed 12 September 2018.

36 Alan Clark, *Diaries* (London: Phoenix, 1994), entries for 14 and 16 September 1988, pp. 225–6; Wall memo, 1 September 1988, www.margaretthatcher.org/document/111785, accessed 12 September 2018.

37 Bruges speech.

38 Benjamin Grob-Fitzgibbon, *Continental Drift: Britain and Europe from the End of Empire to the Rise of Euroscepticism* (Cambridge: Cambridge University Press, 2016), pp. 442–3; www.brugesgroup.com/about/the-bruges-group, accessed 12 September 2018; Heffer, *Like the Roman*, p. 927.

39 Lord Young, HL Deb, 3 May 1989, vol. 507, c. 158; David Young, 'Speech to Bruges Group', in Nicholas Ridley et al., *Shared Thoughts, Shared Values: A First Collection of Public Speeches to the Bruges Group* (London: Bruges Group, 1990), pp. 33–44.

40 Conrad Black, 'Conservatism and the Paradox of Europe', in Patrick Robertson, with foreword by Margaret Thatcher, *Reshaping Europe in the Twenty-first Century* (Basingstoke: Macmillan in association with the Bruges Group, 1992), p. 66 (speech at 1990 Conservative conference); HC Deb, 30 October 1990, vol. 178, c. 873.

41 Patrick Minford, 'Mrs Thatcher's Economic Reform Programme', pp. 93–106, in Robert Skidelsky (ed.), *Thatcherism* (London: Chatto, 1988), p. 94; Keith

Joseph, *The Social Market: Containing Some Lessons from Germany* (London: CPS, 1992), pp. 20–1; The *Spectator*, 14 July 1990, p. 8; Alan Watson, 'Europe's Odd Couple', *Prospect Magazine*, no. 10, July 1996.

42 For changing press attitudes: George Wilkes and Dominic Wring, 'The British Press and European Integration 1948 to 1996', in David Baker and David Seawright (eds), *Britain For and Against Europe: British Politics and the Question of European Integration* (Oxford: Clarendon Press, 1998).

43 Patten Interview; John Major, *The Autobiography* (London: HarperCollins, 1999), p. 106.

44 George, *An Awkward Partner*, pp. 239–40; Turner, *The Tories and Europe*, p. 143.

45 europa.eu/europeanunion/sites/europaeu/.../treaty_on_european_union_en.pdf, Treaty on European Union, accessed 14 May 2018.

46 George, *An Awkward Partner*, p. 243; Grob-Fitzgibbon, *Continental Drift*, p. 460; Alasdair Blair, *Dealing with Europe: Britain and the Negotiation of the Maastricht Treaty*, pp. 215, 220.

47 David Butler and Dennis Kavanagh, *The British General Election of 1992* (London: Macmillan, 1999 edn), pp. 107, 110, 120, 165.

48 Forster, *Euroscepticism in Contemporary British Politics*, pp. 85–93.

49 HC Deb, 20 November 1991, vol. 199, c. 297; 15 May 1992 speech in The Hague, www.margaretthatcher.org/document/108296.

50 Major, *The Autobiography*, pp. 347, 352; Norman Lamont, *In Office* (London: Little, Brown, 1999), pp. 198/199.

51 Turner, *The Tories and Europe*, pp. 162–3; Lamont, *In Office*, p. 200; Major, *The Autobiography*, p. 361; George, *An Awkward Partner*, p. 249.

52 Major, *The Autobiography*, p. 364; HL Deb, 2 July 1992, vol. 538, c. 900; 19 September 1992 speech to CNN World Economic Development Conference, www.margaretthatcher.org/document/108304.

53 *The Times*, 5 November 1992, 9 March 1993, 21 May 1993; *The Independent*, 22 July 1993; George, *An Awkward Partner*, p. 254. For further details of Maastricht rebellions: Hugh Berrington and Rod Hague, 'Europe, Thatcherism and Traditionalism: Opinion, Rebellion and the Maastricht Treaty in the Backbench Conservative Party, 1992–1994', *West European Politics*, vol. 21, no. 1 (1998), pp. 44–71; Christopher Gill, *Whips' Nightmare* (Spennymoor: Memoir, 2003).

54 Forster, *Euroscepticism in Contemporary British Politics*, pp. 93–5; HC Deb, 20 January 1993, vol. 217, c. 410 (Duncan Smith), c. 419 (Jenkin); HC Deb, 8 March 1993, vol. 220, c. 748 (Jenkin); Iain Duncan Smith et al., *Maastricht; Game, Set and Match?* (London: Conservative Way Forward, 1993).

55 Jim Buller, *National Statecraft and European Integration: The Conservative Government and the European Union, 1979–1997* (London: Pinter, 2000), pp. 142–59; HL Deb, 7 June 1993, vol. 546, c. 565.

56 Major, *The Autobiography*, p. 273; HC Deb, 22 July 1993, vol. 229, c. 527.

57 HC Deb, 9 June 1993, vol. 226, c. 285; *The Independent*, 24 July 1993 and 29

November 1994; Turner, *The Tories and Europe*, pp. 169–70; George, *An Awkward Partner*, pp. 237–8.

58 White Paper, quoted in David Gowland and Arthur Turner, *Britain and European Integration, 1945–1998: A Documentary History* (London: Routledge, 2000), pp. 195–9; HC Deb, 12 March 1996, vol. 273, c. 785.

59 David Heathcoat-Amory, *Confessions of a Eurosceptic* (Barnsley: Pen & Sword, 2012), pp. 66, 72.

60 Forster, *Euroscepticism in Contemporary British Politics*, pp. 110, 114; Patrick Minford, 'The Price of Monetary Unification', pp. 149–66, in Martin Holmes (ed.), *The Eurosceptical Reader* (Basingstoke: Macmillan, 1996); Brian Hindley and Martin Howe, *Better Off Out? The Benefits or Costs of EU Membership* (rev. edn, London, IEA, 2007; originally published 1996); Portillo speech, quoted in Gowland and Turner, *Britain and European Integration, 1945–1998*, pp. 202–3.

61 David Butler and Dennis Kavanagh, *The British General Election of 1997* (Basingstoke: Macmillan, 1997), pp. 103, 107, 166, 175, 244, 255, 305–8.

62 11 January 1996, Keith Joseph Memorial Lecture, www.margaretthatcher.org/document/108353.

63 Bale, *The Conservative Party from Thatcher to Cameron*, pp. 67, 71, 79–80.

64 Bale, *The Conservative Party from Thatcher to Cameron*, p. 105; Philip Lynch, 'The Conservatives and Europe, 1997–2001', pp. 146–63, in Mark Garnett and Philip Lynch, *The Conservatives in Crisis* (Manchester: Manchester University Press, 2003).

65 David Butler and Dennis Kavanagh, *The British General Election of 2001* (Basingstoke: Palgrave, 2002), pp. 103, 244, 252, 260, 324–7.

66 Bale, *The Conservative Party from Thatcher to Cameron*, pp. 138–46.

67 Letter to *The Daily Telegraph*, 21 August 2001.

68 Bale, *The Conservative Party from Thatcher to Cameron*, p. 208; Dennis Kavanagh and David Butler, *The British General Election of 2005* (Basingstoke: Palgrave Macmillan, 2006), pp. 59, 91, 196, 204.

69 Bale, *The Conservative Party from Thatcher to Cameron*, pp. 216–17; Kavanagh and Butler, *The British General Election of 2005*, pp. 77, 204, 246.

70 Robert Blake, *The Conservative Party from Peel to Major* (London: Heinemann, 1997), pp. 300–1; Bale, *The Conservative Party from Thatcher to Cameron*, pp. 136, 141.

71 Nick Watts, with foreword by Douglas Hurd, *Working Together: A New Approach to European Policy Making for Conservatives* (London: Action Centre for Europe Ltd, 2002), p. 1; Lynch, 'The Conservatives and Europe, 1997–2001', p. 156. For criticism of Thatcher and Thatcherism: Critchley, *Westminster Blues* (London: Futura, 1986), pp. 1–14; Ian Gilmour, *Dancing with Dogma: Britain under Thatcherism* (London: Simon & Schuster, 1992).

72 Conservative Party, *Conservative Manifesto* (London: Conservative Party, 2005).

73 Menno Spiering, *A Cultural History of British Euroscepticism* (Basingstoke:

Palgrave Macmillan, 2015), pp. 29, 45, 75; 25 June 1998, speech to the American Enterprise Institute, www.margaretthatcher.org/document/108377.

Notes to Chapter 6, pages 201–34

1   Quoted in Simon Jenkins, *Thatcher and Sons: A Revolution in Three Acts* (London: Penguin, 2007), p. 259.
2   www.theguardian.com/politics/2005/jun/23/speeches.eu, accessed 1 June 2018.
3   Tony Benn, *The Benn Diaries 1940–1990* (London: Arrow, 1994), entries for 12 and 22 June, pp. 550/1, 552; Benn, quoted in labourlist.org/2014/03/praise-benn-but-never-forget-the-damage-he-did-to-labour/, accessed 5 June 2018.
4   Benn, *The Benn Diaries 1940–1990*, entry for 2 October 1988, p. 614.
5   See e.g. Geoffrey Goodman, *The Miners' Strike* (London: Pluto, 1985); Lodge Secretary, quoted in Andrew Richards, *Miners on Strike: Class Solidarity and Division in Britain* (Oxford: Berg, 1996). p. 143; Beverley Trounce, *From a Rock to a Hard Place: Memories of the 1984/85 Miners' Strike* (Stroud: The History Press, 2015), p. 92.
6   www.ukpol.co.uk/neil-kinnock-1985-labour-party-conference-speech/: accessed 29 May 2018.
7   Benn, *The Benn Diaries 1940–1990*, entry for 9 February 1986, p. 581.
8   Forster, *Euroscepticism in Contemporary British Politics*, p. 68; Young, *This Blessed Plot*, pp. 473, 480–3.
9   Grob-Fitzgibbon, *Continental Drift*, p. 431; Broad, *Labour's European Dilemmas*, pp. 80, 158; Young, *This Blessed Plot*, p. 478.
10 Russell Holden, *The Making of New Labour's European Policy* (Basingstoke: Palgrave, 2002), pp. 34, 46–9; Broad, *Labour's European Dilemmas*, p. 158; HC Deb, 1 July 1986, vol. 100, c. 937.
11 George Robertson MP, HC Deb, 26 June 1986, vol. 100, c. 546; Broad, *Labour's European Dilemmas*, p. 167.
12 David Butler and Dennis Kavanagh, *The British General Election of 1987* (London: Macmillan, 1999 edn), esp. pp. 14, 72, 221, and Table 10.3, p. 226.
13 King and Crewe, *SDP*, pp. 303, 331–5, 364–410, 439–40.
14 Broad, *Labour's European Dilemmas*, p. 169; Eric Heffer, *Labour's Future* (London: Verso, 1986), pp. 123–4.
15 Holden, *The Making of New Labour's European Policy*, pp. 50–9; Broad, *Labour's European Dilemmas*, pp. 162–3.
16 Lea Interview; History & Policy Trade Union Forum, 27 November 2010, www.historyandpolicy.org/trade-union-forum/meeting/how-the-tuc-learned-to-love-the-european-union-and-how-the-affair-turned-ou, accessed 5 June 2018.
17 europa.eu/rapid/press-release_SPEECH-88-66_en.htm, accessed 5 June 2018.
18 Lea Interview; Broad, *Labour's European Dilemmas*, pp. 172–3.
19 King and Crewe, *SDP*, p. 303; Benn, *The Benn Diaries 1940–1990*, entry for 25 May 1986, pp. 611–12.

20 Obituary of Todd: www.theguardian.com/news/2005/may/02/ guardianobituaries.politics, accessed 5 June 2018; quoted in Broad, *Labour's European Dilemmas*, p. 171.

21 Quoted in Grob-Fitzgibbon, *Continental Drift*, pp. 431–2.

22 Benn, quoted in *The Independent*, 28 June 1999; Mitchell, quoted in Broad, *Labour's European Dilemmas*, p. 192.

23 Benn, *The End of an Era*, entry for 9 March 1989, pp. 560–1; Forster, *Euroscepticism in Contemporary British Politics*, p. 95; Tony Benn, *Free At Last: Diaries 1991–2001* (London: Arrow, 2003), entry for 17 November 1991, p. 56.

24 Chris Mullin, *A Walk-on Part: Diaries 1994–1999* (London: Profile, 2011), entry for 27 September 1994, p. 24.

25 Grob-Fitzgibbon, *Continental Drift*, p. 447; Brian Sedgemore MP and Doug Hoyle MP, respectively, quoted in Broad, *Labour's European Dilemmas*, p. 183.

26 Broad, *Labour's European Dilemmas*, pp. 178–9; HC Deb, 18 December 1991, vol. 201, cc. 286–7.

27 Broad, *Labour's European Dilemmas*, p. 179; Holden, *The Making of New Labour's European Policy*, pp. 71, 75, 87.

28 Conservative Party Press Release, 17/92, 7 January 1992.

29 Broad, *Labour's European Dilemmas*, pp. 186–7.

30 *The Times*, 28 September 1992, p. 6; 'I disown this government', www. theguardian.com/commentisfree/2009/feb/20/labour-foreign-policy, accessed 31 May 2018.

31 For further details: researchbriefings.files.parliament.uk/documents/RP97-102/RP97-102.pdf; Treaty of Rome, article 118, ec.europa.eu/romania/sites/ romania/files/tratatul_de_la_roma.pdf, both accessed 31 May 2018.

32 HL Deb, 22 July 1993, vol. 548, c. 841.

33 George, *An Awkward Partner*, p. 257.

34 George, *An Awkward Partner*, p. 259; *Meeting the Challenge in Europe*, quoted in Gowland and Turner, *Britain and European Integration*, p. 179; Labour Party, *European Election Manifesto* (London, 1984).

35 Benn, *The End of an Era*, entry for 9 March 1989, pp. 560–1; Barratt Brown, quoted in Broad, *Labour's European Dilemmas*, p. 184.

36 *The Times*, 21 May 1993; Giles Radice MP, HC Deb, 21 May 1992, vol. 208, c. 545.

37 James Naughtie, *The Rivals: The Intimate Story of a Political Marriage* (London: Fourth Estate, 2001), pp. 53–75; Benn, *Free At Last*, p. xi.

38 Crosland, *Tony Crosland*, p. 236.

39 Steven Fielding, *The Labour Party: Continuity and Change in the Making of New Labour* (Basingstoke: Palgrave Macmillan, 2003), pp. 74–8; Williams, *Hugh Gaitskell*, pp. 537–73.

40 Young, *This Blessed Plot*, pp. 484–5, 515; Holden, *The Making of New Labour's European Policy*, pp. 127, 138.

41 Young, *This Blessed Plot*, pp. 499–500, 506–7; quoted in Andrew Rawnsley, *Servants of the People* (London: Penguin, 2003), p. 73.

42 Holden, *The Making of New Labour's European Policy*, pp. 133, 136, 140; Simon Jenkins, quoted in labourlist.org/2015/03/milibands-carefully-calibrated-balancing-act/, accessed 17 June 2018.

43 Holden, *The Making of New Labour's European Policy*, pp. 134–5; Young, *This Blessed Plot*, pp. 490–1.

44 Young, *This Blessed Plot*, pp. 487–8; Broad, *Labour's European Dilemmas*, p. 191; Mullin, *A Walk-on Part*, entry for 1 March 1995, p. 69.

45 Labour Party, *Labour Party Election Manifesto* (London, 1997).

46 Quoted in David Marquand, *Britain since 1918: The Strange Career of British Democracy* (London; Orion, 2008), prologue; Marquand, writing in *The New Statesman*, 6 October 1995, p. 18; Broad, *Labour's European Dilemmas*, pp. 202–3.

47 www.theguardian.com/politics/2010/sep/05/tony-blair-journey-tony-benn; conservativehome.blogs.com/centreright/2008/04/making-history.html, both accessed 18 June 2018.

48 Fielding, *The Labour Party*, pp. 70–4, 175, 209.

49 For these paragraphs: Matt Beech and Simon Lee, *Ten Years of New Labour* (Basingstoke: Palgrave Macmillan, 2008), pp. 44–9, 58–9, 68–88, 120–35; Jenkins, *Thatcher and Sons*, pp. 230, 256–60, 264.

50 Quoted in Rawnsley, *Servants of the People*, p. 213; www.geog.ox.ac.uk/research/transformations/gis/papers/dannydorling_publication_id3089.pdf, and www.ifs.org.uk/comms/comm99.pdf, both accessed 6 June 2018; Beech and Lee, *Ten Years of New Labour*, p. 38.

51 www.theguardian.com/politics/2003/sep/29/labourconference.labour1, accessed 18 June 2018.

52 Tony Blair, *A Journey* (London: Hutchinson, 2010), p. 533; Sir John Kerr of the Foreign Office, quoted in Chris Mullin, *A View from the Foothills: The Diaries of Chris Mullin* (London: Profile, 2009), pp. 22–3, entry for 16 September 1999.

53 *The Independent*, 24 May 1997; Edmonds, History & Policy Trade Union Forum, 27 November 2010.

54 IMF, quoted in Jenkins, *Thatcher and Sons*, p. 273; Edmonds, History & Policy Trade Union Forum.

55 Jack Straw, *Last Man Standing: Memoirs of a Political Survivor* (London: Macmillan, 2012), pp. 422–3; Straw was Foreign Secretary from 2001 to 2006.

56 Alastair Campbell, *The Alastair Campbell Diaries, Volume Two: Power and the People, 1997–1999* (London: Hutchinson, 2010), entries for 5 October and 27 October 1997 and 23 February 1999, pp. 165, 193, 665.

57 Straw, *Last Man Standing*, pp. 326–7.

58 Jenkins, quoted in Rawnsley, *Servants of the People*, p. 87; HC Deb, 27 October 1997, vol. 299, c. 584.

59 Rawnsley, *Servants of the People*, pp. 88, 321, 387–8; Brown, HC Deb, 23 February 1999, vol. 326, c. 180.

60 Rawnsley, *Servants of the People*, p. 497; Alastair Campbell, *The Alastair Campbell Diaries, Volume Three: Power and Responsibility, 1999–2001* (London:

Hutchinson, 2011), entry for 5 June 2001, p. 629.

61 Gordon Brown, *My Life, Our Times* (London: Bodley, 2017), p. 181; Tom Bower, *Broken Vows: Tony Blair The Tragedy of Power* (London: Faber Paperback, 2016), p. 277; Chris Gifford, *The Making of Eurosceptic Britain* (2nd edn, Farnham: Ashgate, 2014), pp. 140–3.

62 For accounts of the April 2003 showdown: Andrew Rawnsley, *The End of the Party* (London: Penguin, 2010), pp. 194–5; Brown, *My Life, Our Times*, pp. 173–4, 182–3.

63 HC Deb, 9 June 2003, vol. 406, c. 407; Brown, *My Life, Our Times*, pp. 182–4.

64 Rawnsley, *The End of the Party*, p. 258; Straw, *Last Man Standing*, pp. 420–1; for Schengen, which has created the Schengen Area of 22 EU Member States and four non-EU Member States, in which there are no internal border checks between countries: researchbriefings.parliament.uk/ResearchBriefing/Summary/LLN-2016-0013#fullreport, accessed 13 September 2018.

65 Butler and Kavanagh, *The British General Election of 2005*, pp. 77, 91, 204, 246.

66 Quoted in Holden, *The Making of New Labour's European Policy*, pp. 178–9.

67 Letter to *The Independent*, 5 January 1998, quoted in Gowland and Turner, *Britain and European Integration*, pp. 221–2; Campbell, *The Alastair Campbell Diaries, Volume Two*, entry for 23 February 1999, p. 665; Brown, *My Life, Our Times*, p. 181.

68 For the depoliticisation argument: Jim Buller, 'New Labour and the European Union', in Beech and Lee, *Ten Years of New Labour*, pp. 136–50; Gifford, *The Making of Eurosceptic Britain*, pp. 132–3, 138–9.

69 IMF and Cook, quoted in Gifford, *The Making of Eurosceptic Britain*, pp. 137, 146; Nicholas Jones, *Sultans of Spin: The Media and the New Labour Government* (London: Gollancz, 2000).

Notes to Chapter 7, pages 235–82

1 Leader's speech, Bournemouth Conference 2006, www.britishpoliticalspeech.org/speech-archive.htm?speech=314, accessed 21 June 2018.

2 David Cameron's resignation speech, 24 June 2016, edition.cnn.com/2016/06/24/europe/david-cameron-full-resignation-speech/index.html, accessed 7 July 2018.

3 Chris Mullin, *Decline and Fall: Diaries 2005–2010* (London: Profile, 2010), entry for 27 June 2007, pp. 185–6; Simon Lee, 'The British Model of Political Economy', pp. 17–34, in Beech and Lee, *Ten Years of New Labour*, at p. 17; Nicholas Allen, 'Labour's Third Term: A Tale of Two Prime Ministers', pp. 1–36, in Nicholas Allen and John Bartle (eds), *Britain at the Polls 2010* (London: Sage, 2011), p. 12; data.worldbank.org/indicator/NY.GDP.PCAP.CD?locations=GB; Rui Costa and Stephen Machin, *Real Wages and Living Standards in the UK*, cep.lse.ac.uk/pubs/download/ea036.pdf, both accessed 20 June 2018.

4 Lee, 'The British Model of Political Economy', pp. 17–29; publications.

parliament.uk/pa/cm200607/cmhansrd/cm070321/debtext/70321-0004.htm, cc.815-816, accessed 21 June 2018.

5   Mullin, *Decline and Fall*, entry for 7 June 2005, p. 13; Rawnsley, *The End of the Party*, p. 446; Blair, speech on the future of Europe, 2 February 2006, webarchive.nationalarchives.gov.uk/20080909044415/http://www.number10. gov.uk/Page9003, accessed 22 June 2018.

6   Allen, 'Labour's Third Term', pp. 7–8.

7   Rawnsley, *The End of the Party*, pp. 496–514; Michael Moran, Sukhdev Johal and Karel Williams, 'The Financial Crisis and its Consequences', pp. 89–119, in Allen and Bartle, *Britain at the Polls 2010*, p. 89.

8   Mullin, *Decline and Fall*, entry for 16 September 2008, pp. 264–5; Moran et al., 'The Financial Crisis and its Consequences', p. 109.

9   Rawnsley, *The End of the Party*, p. 584.

10 www.bankofengland.co.uk/-/media/boe/files/quarterly-bulletin/2010/the-uk-recession-in-context-what-do-three-centuries-of-data-tell-us.pdf, and researchbriefings.files.parliament.uk/documents/SN06167/SN06167.pdf, both accessed 30 June 2018; *Financial Times*, 5 October 2011, 'UK recession deeper than first thought'.

11 For the debt crisis, see e.g. www.cfr.org/timeline/greeces-debt-crisis-timeline, accessed 4 January 2019; Yanis Varoufakis, *Adults In the Room: My Battle with Europe's Deep Establishment* (London: Bodley Head, 2018).

12 See generally Michael Keating and David McCrone, *The Crisis of Social Democracy in Europe* (Edinburgh: Edinburgh University Press, 2015).

13 For a review of New Labour's economic approach: Moran et al., 'The Financial Crisis and its Consequences', pp. 96–100.

14 Allen, 'Labour's Third Term', p. 14; Moran et al., 'The Financial Crisis and its Consequences', p. 109.

15 For policy continuity: Oliver Daddow, *New Labour and the European Union: Blair and Brown's Logic of History* (Manchester: Manchester University Press, 2011), pp. 243–53; David Miliband speech, 'New Diplomacy: Challenges For Foreign Policy', 19 July 2007, davidmilibandarchive.blogspot.com/2013/09/new-diplomacy-challenges-for-foreign.html, accessed 1 July 2018.

16 Brown, *My Life, Our Times*, p. 220; for Lisbon: www.europarl.europa.eu/atyourservice/en/displayFtu.html?ftuId=FTU_1.1.5.html, accessed 21 June 2018; for the vitriol: Rawnsley, *The End of the Party*, p. 525.

17 Rawnsley, *The End of the Party*, p. 525; *The Guardian*, 13 December 2017, 'Brown flies to Lisbon for belated EU treaty signing'; Allen, 'Labour's Third Term', pp. 19–20.

18 For deficit figures: www.ons.gov.uk/economy/governmentpublicsectorandtaxes/publicspending/bulletins/ukgovernme ntdebtanddeficitforeurostatmaast/aprtojune2016#summary-of-general-government-deficit-and-gross-debt, accessed 2 July 2018; Dennis Kavanagh and Philip Cowley, *The British General Election of 2010* (Basingstoke: Palgrave, 2010), p. 347.

19   Andrew Adonis, *5 days in May: The Coalition and Beyond* (London: Biteback Publishing, 2013).

20   Kevin Hickson (ed.), *The Political Thought of the Liberals and Liberal Democrats since 1945* (Manchester: Manchester University Press, 2009), pp. 41–2, 111 and 114.

21   David Laws, 'Reclaiming Liberalism: A Liberal Agenda for the Liberal Democrats', pp. 18–42, in Paul Marshall and David Laws (eds), *The Orange Book: Reclaiming Liberalism* (London: Profile, 2004), pp. 28, 33, 41; Hickson (ed.), *The Political Thought of the Liberals and Liberal Democrats since 1945*, pp. 43–5.

22   Laws, 'Reclaiming Liberalism', p. 28; Adonis, *5 days in May*, pp. 70, 85, 114–15.

23   'The march of the neoliberals', *The Guardian*, 12 September 2011; for the longer view: Stuart Hall, 'The Neo-liberal Revolution', *Cultural Studies*, vol. 25, no. 6 (2011), pp. 705–28; Andrew Adonis on the May 2010 behind-the-scenes coalition negotiations: www.newstatesman.com/books/2010/11/lib-dem-coalition-laws-labour, accessed 3 January 2019.

24   H.M. Government, *The Coalition: Our Programme for Government* (London: Cabinet Office, 20 May 2010).

25   Budget statement, 22 June 2010, HC Deb, vol. 512, cc. 168–9.

26   HC Deb, vol. 512, c. 167; Matt Beech and Simon Lee (eds), *The Conservative–Liberal Coalition: Examining the Cameron–Clegg Government* (Basingstoke: Palgrave, 2015), pp. 154/5; www.ifs.org.uk/tools_and_resources/fiscal_facts/public_spending_survey/cuts_to_public_spending, accessed 23 June 2018.

27   Matthew D'Ancona, *In It Together: The Inside Story of the Coalition Government* (London: Viking, 2013), p. 223; Beech and Lee (eds), *The Conservative–Liberal Coalition*, pp. 23–6; Osborne speech, September 2013, www.gov.uk/government/speeches/chancellor-speech-on-the-economy, accessed 26 June 2018.

28   For the anti-austerity case: William Keegan, *Mr Osborne's Economic Experiment* (London: Searching Finance, 2014); Brown, *My Life, Our Times*, pp. 346–8. For growth: Beech and Lee (eds), *The Conservative–Liberal Coalition*, p. 22; www.ons.gov.uk/economy/grossdomesticproductgdp/timeseries/ihyq/pgdp, accessed 26 June 2018.

29   www.ons.gov.uk/...impact-of-the-recession-on-household-income--expenditure, accessed 30 June 2018.

30   'Osborne compares UK to Greece', 28 April 2010, uk.reuters.com/article/britain-election-osborne-idUKLNE63R06Y20100428, accessed 27 June 2018.

31   Philip Cowley and Dennis Kavanagh, *The British General Election of 2015* (Basingstoke: Palgrave, 2016), pp. 69, 81; Eunice Goes, *The Labour Party under Ed Miliband: Trying but Failing to Renew Social Democracy* (Manchester: Manchester University Press, 2016), pp. 178–9; Private Eye, *Private Eye Annual 2011* (London: Private Eye, 2011), p. 49.

32   Cowley and Kavanagh, *The British General Election of 2015*, p. 78; Goes, *The Labour Party under Ed Miliband*, pp. 178–9.

33 Cowley and Kavanagh, *The British General Election of 2015*, pp. 89, 126–39, 189, 436.

34 Goes, *The Labour Party under Ed Miliband*, p. 180; Roy Hattersley and Kevin Hickson, 'In Praise of Social Democracy', *Political Quarterly*, vol. 83, no. 1 (2012), pp. 5–12, and response by Marc Stears p. 15.

35 data.worldbank.org/indicator/NY.GDP.PCAP.CD?locations=GB; Costa and Machin, *Real Wages and Living Standards in the UK*, both accessed 20 June 2018.

36 landregistry.data.gov.uk/;www.ons.gov.uk/economy/inflationandpriceindices/ timeseries/chaw/mm23; www.theguardian.com/business/2009/mar/17/fred-goodwin-pension-lord-myners, all accessed 24 June 2018.

37 Robert Ford and Matthew Goodwin, *Revolt on the Right: Explaining Support for the Radical Right in Britain* (London: Routledge, 2013), pp. 21–2, 76, 87.

38 Ford and Goodwin, *Revolt on the Right*, pp. 78–83; www.bbc.co.uk/news/ uk-politics-25879302, accessed 22 June 2018; Kavanagh and Cowley, *The British General Election of 2010*, pp. 116–20, 404–5; UKIP, *General Election Manifesto* (London, 2010).

39 Kavanagh and Cowley, *The British General Election of 2010*, pp. 163, 166, 174, 257, 346 and 407.

40 Ford and Goodwin, *Revolt on the Right*, pp. 90–5; Matthew Goodwin and Caitlin Milazzo, *UKIP: Inside the Campaign to Redraw the Map of British Politics* (Oxford: Oxford University Press, 2015), pp. 108–9.

41 *The Guardian*, 26 May 2014; www.bbc.co.uk/news/events/vote2014/eu-uk-results, accessed 26 June 2018. For analysis: Goodwin and Milazzo, *UKIP*, p. 53.

42 Goodwin and Milazzo, *UKIP*, pp. 151–2.

43 For Jaywick: www.bbc.co.uk/news/av/magazine-32396977/election-2015-politics-in-a-poor-seaside-town, accessed 4 July 2018; Ford and Goodwin, *Revolt on the Right*, pp. 107–38; Goodwin and Milazzo, *UKIP*, pp. 76–7.

44 *The Daily Telegraph*, 'Howard rages at UKIP "gadflies"', 31 May 2004; *The Guardian*, 'White face, blue collar, grey hair: the "left behind" voters only UKIP understands', Matthew Goodwin and Robert Ford, 5 March 2014.

45 Ford and Goodwin, *Revolt on the Right*, p. 172, Table 4.6; Goodwin and Milazzo, *UKIP*, p. 97.

46 Ford and Goodwin, *Revolt on the Right*, pp. 85, 91 (Table 5.2), 93, 95 (Table 5.3); Goodwin and Milazzo, *UKIP*, pp. 133 (Figure 3.7) and 279 (Figure 7.2); Harold D. Clarke, Matthew Goodwin and Paul Whiteley, *Brexit: Why Britain Voted to Leave the European Union* (Cambridge: Cambridge University Press, 2017), p. 120 (Figure 6.2).

47 Suzanne Evans, *Why Vote UKIP 2015* (London: Biteback Publishing, 2014), pp. 8, 14–15, 24–40; UKIP, *General Election Manifesto* (London, 2015).

48 Cowley and Kavanagh, *The British General Election of 2015*, pp. 112–13, 330, 402–4.

49 For the expenses scandal and 'Sod the Lot': www.telegraph.co.uk/news/

newstopics/mps-expenses/6499657/MPs-expenses-scandal-a-timeline.html, accessed 4 July 2018, and Kavanagh and Cowley, *The British General Election of 2010*, p. 118; for the 'safe house' campaign: Kavanagh and Cowley, *The British General Election of 2010*, pp. 172–3; for the attitudes of UKIP voters: Cowley and Kavanagh, *The British General Election of 2015*, p. 110; for Farage's Gateshead rally and its relationship to wider disillusionment: Goodwin and Milazzo, *UKIP*, pp. 1–10 and Figures 2.5 and 2.6, pp. 25–6.

[50] Geoffrey Rippon, *Our Future in Europe: The Case for Staying in the European Community* (London: Conservative Political Centre, 1974).

[51] Gifford, *The Making of Eurosceptic Britain*, pp. 158–60; Commentary, 'Britain's Tea Party', *Political Quarterly*, vol. 83, no. 1 (2012), pp. 1–3; www. conservativehome.com/thetorydiary/2012/05/what-is-the-fresh-start-project-mbarrettch-profiles-the-tory-mps-trying-to-forge-a-new-uk-eu-relatio.html, accessed 25 June 2018.

[52] Bale, *The Conservative Party from Thatcher to Cameron*, pp. 269–70, 282; Leader's speech, Bournemouth Conference 2006, www.britishpoliticalspeech. org/speech-archive.htm?speech=314, accessed 21 June 2018.

[53] news.bbc.co.uk/1/hi/uk_politics/4875502.stm, 4 April 2006; Bale, *The Conservative Party from Thatcher to Cameron*, pp. 271, 294; *The Guardian*, 22 June 2009, 'Tories unveil group of controversial new allies in European parliament'.

[54] *The Sun*, 26 September 2007; *The Guardian*, 4 November 2009; Barry Legg (ex-Tory MP), 'Cameron's EU treaty treachery', *The Guardian*, 4 November 2009.

[55] Bale, *The Conservative Party from Thatcher to Cameron*, pp. 306–7.

[56] For Hilton's views: D'Ancona, *In It Together*, pp. 196–7; Conservative Party, *Conservative Manifesto* (London: Conservative Party, 2010).

[57] David Laws, *Coalition: The Inside Story of the Conservative–Liberal Democrat Coalition Government* (London: Biteback, 2016), pp. 16, 238; D'Ancona, *In It Together*, pp. 237–8, 242, 246; Philip Lynch, 'The Coalition and the European Union', pp. 243–58, in Cowley and Kavanagh, *The British General Election of 2015*, p. 248.

[58] Laws, *Coalition*, pp. 240–1; D'Ancona, *In It Together*, pp. 239, 248; Lynch, 'The Coalition and the European Union', p. 253.

[59] Laws, *Coalition*, p. 237; D'Ancona, *In It Together*, pp. 251–3, 257.

[60] Cameron, Bloomberg speech, 23 January 2013, www.gov.uk/government/ speeches/eu-speech-at-bloomberg, accessed 21 June 2018; Laws, *Coalition*, pp. 242, 246.

[61] Laws, *Coalition*, p. 246; Lynch, 'The Coalition and the European Union', pp. 253–4.

[62] Douglas Carswell, *The End of Politics and the Birth of iDemocracy* (London: Biteback, 2012); Kwasi Kwarteng et al., *Britannia Unchained: Global Lessons for Growth and Prosperity* (Basingstoke: Palgrave, 2012); www.telegraph.co.uk/news/politics/conservative/9598534/

David-Camerons-Conservative-Party-Conference-speech-in-full.html, accessed 23 June 2018.

63 Conservative Party, *Conservative Manifesto* (London: Conservative Party, 2015).

64 For the 1975 question: Referendum Act 1975, c. 33, schedule 1; for backbench pressure: Tim Shipman, *All Out War: The Full Story of Brexit* (updated edn, London: Collins, 2017), pp. 81–7; for purdah: www.theguardian.com/politics/2015/sep/07/eu-referendum-david-cameron-suffers-defeat-in-parliament-over-purdah-rules, accessed 27 June 2018; for the contrast between 1975 and 2016 renegotiations: Saunders, *Yes to Europe!*, pp. 86–94, 377–8.

65 Shipman, *All Out War*, pp. 90–1, 192, 231.

66 Geoffrey Evans and Anand Menon, *Brexit and British Politics* (Cambridge: Polity, 2017), pp. 66–8; Shipman, *All Out War*, p. 412.

67 Rees-Mogg, HC Deb, vol. 602, c .235, 10 November 2015 and vol. 605, c. 946, 3 February 2016; Baker, HC Deb, vol. 605, c. 783, 2 February 2016; Shipman, *All Out War*, pp. 207, 26–78, 336.

68 Owen Bennett, *The Brexit Club: The Inside Story of the Leave Campaign's Shock Victory* (London: Biteback Publishing, 2016), pp. 35–6, 40; Fox, quoted in Shipman, *All Out War*, p. 188.

69 Shipman, *All Out War*, pp. 130–1.

70 Martin Moore and Gordon Ramsay, *UK Media Coverage of the 2016 EU Referendum Campaign* (London: Centre for the Study of Media, 2017), p. 9; Shipman, *All Out War*, p. 299.

71 For the BBC: Shipman, *All Out War*, pp. 310–21; for Corbyn and Minford: David Levy et al., *UK Press Coverage of the EU Referendum*, p. 5, reutersinstitute.politics.ox.ac.uk/sites/default/files/2017-06/UK%20Press%20Coverage%20of%20the%20EU%20Referendum_0.pdf, accessed 28 June 2018.

72 For 'acrimonious and divisive': Moore and Ramsay, *UK Media Coverage of the 2016 EU Referendum Campaign*, p. 10; for the Miliband reference: Craig Oliver, *Unleashing Demons: The Inside Story of Brexit* (London: Hodder, 2017), p. 74.

73 Rosa Prince, *Comrade Corbyn: A Very Unlikely Coup: How Jeremy Corbyn Stormed to the Labour Leadership* (London: Biteback Publishing, 2016), pp. 49, 90–2, 100, 237, 258–9, 317, 344.

74 Shipman, *All Out War*, pp. 73, 78, 339–65; Oliver, *Unleashing Demons*, pp. 256–7, 305; Evans and Menon, *Brexit and British Politics*, pp. 66–8.

75 Saunders, *Yes to Europe!*, p. 309; Jason Farrell and Paul Goldsmith, *How to Lose a Referendum: The Definitive Story of Why the UK Voted for Brexit* (London: Biteback Publishing, 2017), pp. 450–5; Gary Gibbon, *Breaking Point: The UK Referendum on the EU and its Aftermath* (London: Haus, 2016), p. 21.

76 Oliver, *Unleashing Demons*, p. 260; Farrell and Goldsmith, *How to Lose a Referendum*, pp. 425–6; Shipman, *All Out War*, pp. 245–6.

77 Saunders, *Yes to Europe!*, p. 230; Shipman, *All Out War*, pp. 230, 247, 376; H.M. Government, *The Best of Both Worlds: The United Kingdom's Special Status in a Reformed European Union* (London: HMSO, February 2016), p.11;

Leaflet, 'Why the Government believes that voting to remain in the European Union is the best decision for the UK'; Conservative Remain, Scottish Liberal Democrat and Green Party leaflets, CCA.6.9.22 and 24.

78 UKIP leaflet, 'The People's Army needs you now', CCA.6.9.24; www. voteleavetakecontrol.org/why_vote_leave.html, accessed 11 July 2018; BSIE leaflet, 'Leave Myths Busted'.

79 Saunders, *Yes to Europe!*, p. 376; for SNP policy on Europe: www.snp.org/ pb_what_is_the_snp_s_position_on_the_eu , accessed 7 July 2018.

80 Benn, letter to constituents in 1975, reproduced at blogs.spectator. co.uk/2016/05/a-lesson-from-the-1975-referendum/, accessed 1 July 2018.

81 Boris Johnson, 'There is only one way to get the change we want – Vote Go', *The Daily Telegraph*, 22 February 2016.

82 Boris Johnson, 'I cannot stress too much that Britain is part of Europe', *The Daily Telegraph*, 26 June 2016; HC Deb, 24 January 2017, vol. 620, c. 169.

83 Oliver, *Unleashing Demons*, p. 331; Arron Banks, *The Bad Boys of Brexit: Tales of Mischief, Mayhem & Guerrilla Warfare in the EU Referendum Campaign* (London: Biteback, 2017), pp. 290–2.

84 Bennett, *The Brexit Club*, p. 253; Gibbon, *Breaking Point*, p. 22.

85 'Mark Carney and Goldman Sachs – The Truth', www.youtube.com/ watch?v=iOWx_OhtCiA, accessed 18 May 2019; Shipman, *All Out War*, pp. 192–3.

86 Clarke et al., Brexit, pp. 151–2, 155.

87 Evans and Menon, Brexit and British politics, p. 74, figure 4.1.

88 Clarke at al., Brexit, figure 4.1 p. 65 and figure 6.2, p. 120; Brexit and British politics p. 19, figure 1.1.

89 There was also a majority for Remain in Northern Ireland, but that was a special case.

Notes to Conclusion, pages 283–96

1 Tony Blair, *The Third Way: New Politics for the New Century* (London: Fabian Society, 1998).

2 David Cameron, New Year message, 31 December 2010, webarchive. nationalarchives.gov.uk/20130102233042/http://www.number10.gov.uk/news/ new-year-podcast/, accessed 11 September 2018.

3 Obituary, 29 September 2006, www.theguardian.com/news/2006/sep/29/ guardianobituaries.obituaries, accessed 12 September 2018; Green, *Ideologies of Conservatism*, pp. 157–91; on Crosland, e.g. Patrick Diamond, *The Crosland Legacy: The Future of British Social Democracy* (Bristol: Policy Press, 2016), esp. p. 320; Peter Hain, *Back to the Future of Socialism* (Bristol: Policy Press, 2015).

4 Avner Offer, 'The Market Turn: From Social Democracy to Market Liberalism', *Economic History Review*, vol. 70, no. 4 (2017), pp. 1051–71.

5 Andrew Hindmoor, *What's Left Now?: The History and Future of Social*

Democracy (Oxford: Oxford University Press, 2018).

6   Jenkins, *Europe: Why Social Democrats Should Support a New Advance.*

7   For Crosland's approach to Europe: Diamond, *The Crosland Legacy*, pp. 153–9.

8   Alan Clark minute, 14 September 1988, THCR 5/1/5/569 f251.

9   Charles Powell minute, 5 October 1988, THCR 1/8/14 f38.

10 Nick Timothy, 'The Crisis of Conservatism', *The New Statesman*, 20 June 2018; Green, *Ideologies of Conservatism*, p. 158; HC Deb, 30 January 1978, vol. 000, c. 71.

11 www.cvce.eu/obj/resolution_adopted_by_the_foreign_ministers_of_the_ecsc_member_states_messina_1_to_3_june_1955-en-d1086bae-0c13-4a00-8608-73c75ce54fad.html, accessed 17 September 18.

12 HC Deb, 20 May 1993, vol. 225, c. 467.

13 www.huffingtonpost.co.uk/entry/sir-john-major-launches-emotional-attack-on-deceitful-brexit-campaign_uk_5753fc19e4b0b23a261a4cbf, 5 June 2016, accessed 17 September 2018.

14 Speech at the Mansion House, 21 June 2006, webarchive.nationalarchives.gov.uk/20100407173744/http://www.hm-treasury.gov.uk/speech_chex_210606.htm; speech to Euromoney Conference by David Cameron, 22 June 2006, conservative-speeches.sayit.mysociety.org/speech/600032, both accessed 6 September 2018.

15 Green, *Ideologies of Conservatism*, pp. 168, 178; Ben Pimlott, *Harold Wilson* (London: Harper, 1992), p. 222.

16 George Eaton, 'Keynes's Biographer Robert Skidelsky: "I've become more and more persuaded by Marx"', *The New Statesman*, 19 September 2018; *The Daily Mail*, 18 April 2013; Chancellor's speech to the American Enterprise Institute in Washington, 11 April 2014, www.gov.uk/government/speeches/chancellors-speech-to-the-american-enterprise-institute, accessed 17 September 2018.

17 Thomas Piketty, *Brahmin Left vs Merchant Right: Rising Inequality & the Changing Structure of Political Conflict (Evidence from France, Britain and the US, 1948–2017)*, http://piketty.pse.ens.fr/files/Piketty2018.pdf, accessed 18 September 2018.

Bibliography and Other Sources

Primary Sources

Manuscripts

Cambridge, Churchill Archives Centre, the Papers of Lord Hailsham (HLSM)
Cambridge, Churchill Archives Centre, the Papers of Selwyn Lloyd (SELO)
Cambridge, Churchill Archives Centre, the Papers of Enoch Powell (POLL)
Cambridge, Churchill Archives Centre, the Papers of Margaret Thatcher (THCR)
Cambridge University Library, printed items and pamphlets connected with the
    2016 Referendum on the United Kingdom's Membership of the European
    Union (CCA)
The National Archives, Records of the Cabinet Office (CAB)
The National Archives, Records of the Prime Minister's Office (PREM)
Oxford, Conservative Party Archive, Bodleian Library, Conservative Central
    Office Papers, Conservative Central Office Papers (CCO/CRD)
Oxford, Conservative Party Archive, Bodleian Library, Papers of Keith Joseph
    (KJ)
Warwick University, The Modern Records Centre, Confederation of British
    Industry Collection (CBI MSS)
Warwick University, The Modern Records Centre, Trades Union Congress
    Collection (TUC MSS)

Official documents

Employment Policy (London: HMSO, 1944), Cmnd. 6527.
Incomes Policy: The Next Step (London: HMSO, 1962), Cmnd. 1626.
The National Board for Prices and Incomes: *Machinery of Prices and Incomes
    Policy* (London: HMSO, 1965), Cmnd. 2577.
Prices and Incomes Policy (London: HMSO, 1965), Cmnd. 2639.
Joint Statement of Intent on Productivity, Prices and Incomes: The National Plan
    (London: HMSO, 1965), Cmnd. 2764.
Prices and Incomes Standstill (London: HMSO, 1966), Cmnd. 3073.
Prices and Incomes Standstill: Period of Severe Restraint (London: HMSO, 1966),
    Cmnd. 3150.
In Place of Strife: A Policy for Industrial Relations (London: HMSO, 1969), Cmnd
    3888.
Harlow Development Commission, 27th Annual Report, 1974.

Britain's New Deal in Europe (London: HMSO, 1975).

The Attack on Inflation (London: HMSO, 1975), Cmnd. 6151.

An Approach to Industrial Strategy (London: HMSO, 1975), Cmnd. 6315.

Public Expenditure to 1979–80 (London: HMSO, February 1976), Cmnd. 6393.

H.M. Government, *The Coalition: Our Programme for Government* (London: Cabinet Office, 20 May 2010).

H.M. Government, *The Best of Both Worlds: the United Kingdom's Special Status in a Reformed European Union / Presented to Parliament Pursuant to Section 6 of the European Referendum Act 2015* (London: HMSO, February 2016).

H.M. Government, *Rights and Obligations of European Union Membership / Presented to Parliament Pursuant to Section 7 of the European Union Referendum Act 2015* (London: HMSO, April 2016).

Hansard

Newspapers and periodicals (hard copy and online)

BBC News website

CNN

The Daily Express

The Daily Mail

The Daily Mirror

The Daily Telegraph

Financial Times

Frankfurter Allgemeine Zeitung

The Guardian

Harlow Gazette and Citizen

Huffington Post

The Independent

Monday World

New Left Review

The New Statesman

Reuters

The Spectator

The Sun

Swinton Journal

The Times

Books, articles and chapters

Adonis, Andrew, *5 Days in May: The Coalition and Beyond* (London: Biteback, 2013).

Anon., 'Public Opinion and the EEC', *Journal of Common Market Studies*, vol. 6, no. 3 (September 1967), pp. 231–49.

Balfour, Campbell, *Incomes Policy and the Public Sector* (London: Routledge, 1972).

Banks, Arron, *The Bad Boys of Brexit: Tales of Mischief, Mayhem & Guerrilla*

Warfare in the EU Referendum Campaign (London: Biteback, 2017).

Barber, Anthony, *Taking the Tide: A Memoir* (Norwich: Russell, 1996).

Benn, Tony, *Out of the Wilderness: Diaries, 1963–1967* (London: Arrow, 1988).

——, *Office without Power: Diaries, 1968–1972* (London: Arrow, 1989).

——, *Against the Tide: Diaries, 1973–1976* (London: Hutchinson, 1990).

——, *Conflicts of Interest: Diaries, 1977–1980* (London: Hutchinson, 1990).

——, *The End of an Era: Diaries, 1980–90* (London: Arrow, 1994).

——, *Free At Last: Diaries, 1991–2001* (London: Arrow, 2003).

——, *The Benn Diaries 1940–1990* (London: Arrow, 1994).

——, ed. Ruth Winstone, *Years of Hope: Diaries, Letters and Papers, 1940–1962* (London: Hutchinson, 1994).

Bennett, Owen, *The Brexit Club: The Inside Story of the Leave Campaign's Shock Victory* (London: Biteback, 2016).

Bentley, Philip, 'The Becontree Estate before 1945: "Like Heaven with the Gate Open"' (2006, held at Barking and Dagenham, Archives and Local Studies Centre).

Black, Conrad, 'Conservatism and the Paradox of Europe', pp. 54–71, in Patrick Robertson (ed.), with foreword by Margaret Thatcher, *Reshaping Europe in the Twenty-first Century* (Basingstoke: Macmillan in association with the Bruges Group, 1992).

Blair, Tony, *The Third Way: New Politics for the New Century* (London: Fabian Society, 1998).

——, *A Journey* (London: Hutchinson, 2010).

Braham, Colin and Jim Burton, *The Referendum Reconsidered* (London: Fabian Society, 1975).

Britain in Europe, *Referendum on the European Community (Common Market): Why You Should Vote Yes* (London: HMSO, 1975).

Brittan, Samuel, *Steering the Economy* (rev. edn, Harmondsworth: Pelican, 1971).

Brown, George, *In My Way: The Political Memoirs of Lord George-Brown* (Harmondsworth: Pelican, 1972).

Brown, Gordon, *My Life, Our Times* (London: Bodley Head, 2017).

Campbell, Alastair, *The Alastair Campbell Diaries, Volume Two: Power and the People, 1997–1999* (London: Hutchinson, 2010).

——, *The Alastair Campbell Diaries, Volume Three: Power and Responsibility, 1999–2001* (London: Hutchinson, 2011).

Carswell, Douglas, *The End of Politics and the Birth of iDemocracy* (London: Biteback, 2012).

Castle, Barbara, *The Castle Diaries, 1964–70* (London: Weidenfeld & Nicolson, 1984).

——, *The Castle Diaries, 1974–76* (London: Weidenfeld & Nicolson, 1982).

Catterall, Peter (ed.), *The Macmillan Diaries, Volume 2: Prime Minister and After, 1957–66* (London: Macmillan, 2011).

CBI, *British Industry and Europe* (London: CBI, 1975).

Clark, Alan, *Diaries* (London: Phoenix, 1994).

Coates, Ken (ed.), *What Went Wrong* (Nottingham: Spokesman Books, 2008; first published 1979).

Coleman, Alice, *Utopia on Trial: Vision and Reality in Planned Housing* (2nd edn, London: Shipman, 1990).

Commentary, 'Britain's Tea party', *Political Quarterly*, vol. 83, no. 1 (2012), pp. 1–3.

Conservative Party, *Conservative Manifesto* (London: Conservative Party, 1970).

Conservative Party, *Conservative Manifesto for Europe* (London: Conservative Party, 1979).

Conservative Party, *Conservative Manifesto* (London: Conservative Party, 2005).

Conservative Party, *Conservative Manifesto* (London: Conservative Party, 2010).

Conservative Party, *Conservative Manifesto* (London: Conservative Party, 2015).

Conservative Party Press Release, 17/92, 7 January 1992.

Conservative Research Department, *Britain in Europe* (London: Conservative Party, 1975).

Conservative Research Department, *Campaign Guide for Europe 1979* (London: Conservative Party, 1979).

Critchley, Julian, *Westminster Blues* (London: Futura, 1986).

Crosland, C.A.R., *The Future of Socialism* (London: Cape, 1956; 1980 reissue).

Crosland, Anthony, *Can Labour Win?* (London: Fabian Society, 1960).

Crosland, Susan, *Tony Crosland* (London, Cape, 1982).

Crossman, Richard, *The Diaries of a Cabinet Minister, Volume One* (London: Cape, 1975).

——, *The Diaries of a Cabinet Minister, Volume Three* (London: Cape, 1977).

——, *The Backbench Diaries of Richard Crossman* (London: Hamilton, Cape, 1981).

Davies, Hunter, *The Co-Op's Got Bananas: A Memoir of Growing Up in the Post-War North* (London: Simon & Schuster, 2016).

Duncan-Smith, Iain et al., *Maastricht; Game, Set and Match?* (London: Conservative Way Forward, 1993).

Eaton, John, *An Alternative Economic Strategy for the Labour Movement* (Nottingham, 1975).

EFDD Group, *The EU Referendum Deal, 2016*, www.efddgroup.eu/images/publications/Referendum_book.pdf, accessed 20 July 2018.

Evans, Suzanne, *Why Vote UKIP 2015: The Essential Guide* (London: Biteback, 2014).

Farrell, Jason and Paul Goldsmith, *How to Lose a Referendum: The Definitive Story of Why the UK Voted for Brexit* (London: Biteback, 2017).

File C3, Surveys, 1976 Household Survey, report 8, 'Household Characteristics and Dwelling Sizes', p. 4 (Harlow Archive, papers held at the Museum of Harlow).

Gill, Christopher, *Whips' Nightmare* (Spennymoor: The Memoir Club, 2003).

Glyn, Andrew and Bob Sutcliffe, *British Capitalism, Workers and the Profits Squeeze* (Harmondsworth: Penguin, 1972).

Goodhart, Philip, *Full-hearted Consent: The Story of the Referendum Campaign* and the Campaign for the Referendum (London: Davis-Poynter, 1976).

Greenslade, Roy, Goodbye to the Working Class (London: Marion Boyars, 1976).

Haines, Joe, The Politics of Power (London: Cape, 1977).

Healey, Denis, The Time of My Life (London: Joseph, 1989).

Heath, Edward, Old World, New Horizons: Britain, Europe, and the Atlantic Alliance (Cambridge, MA: Harvard University Press, 1970).

——, Our Community (London: CPC, 1977).

Heathcoat-Amory, David, Confessions of a Eurosceptic (Barnsley: Pen & Sword Politics, 2012).

Hedges, Barry and Roger Jowell, Britain and the E.E.C.: Report on a Survey of Attitudes Towards the European Economic Community (London: Social and Community Planning Research, 1971).

Heffer, Eric, Labour's Future: Socialist or SDP Mark 2? (London: Verso, 1986).

——, Never a Yes Man: The Life and Politics of an Adopted Liverpudlian (London and New York: Verso, 1991).

Hindley, Brian and Martin Howe, Better Off Out? The Benefits or Costs of EU Membership (rev. edn, London, IEA, 2007; originally published 1996).

Hodges, Michael, Multinational Corporations and National Government: A Case Study of the United Kingdom's Experience, 1964–1970 (Farnborough: Saxon House, 1974).

Holland, Stuart, The Price of Europe: A Reassessment (London: SGS Associates (Education) Ltd, 1971).

——, The Socialist Challenge (London: Quartet Books, 1975).

——, The Regional Problem (London: Palgrave, 1976).

——, Beyond Capitalist Planning (Oxford: Blackwell, 1978).

Holland, Stuart et al., Sovereignty & Multinational Companies (London: Fabian Society, 1971).

Home, Robert, The Largest Council Housing Estate in the World: The Planning History of Becontree/Dagenham (1995, held at Barking and Dagenham, Archives and Local Studies Centre).

Howe, Geoffrey, Conflict of Loyalty (London: Pan, 1995).

IEA, The Rebirth of Britain (London: IEA, 1964).

Jay, Douglas and Roy Jenkins, The Common Market Debate (London: Fabian International Bureau, 1962).

Jenkins, Roy, Europe: Why Social Democrats Should Support a New Advance (London: Rita Hinden Memorial Fund, 1978).

——, European Diary, 1977–1981 (London: Collins, 1989).

——, A Life at the Centre (London: Papermac, 1994).

Jones, Jack, Union Man: The Autobiography of Jack Jones (London: HarperCollins, 1986).

Joseph, Keith, 'Inflation: The Climate of Opinion is Changing', in Stranded on the Middle Ground?: Reflections on Circumstances and Policies (London: CPS, 1976).

——, The Social Market: Containing Some Lessons from Germany (London: CPS,

1992).

—— and Jonathan Sumption, *Equality* (London: Murray, 1979).

Jowell, Roger and James Spence, *The Grudging Europeans: A Study of British Attitudes Towards the EEC* (London: SCPR, 1975).

Keegan, William, *Mr Osborne's Economic Experiment: Austerity 1945–51 and 2010–* (paperback, London: Searching Finance, 2014).

Kenny, Michael and Nick Pearce, *Shadows of Empire: The Anglosphere in British Politics* (London: Penguin, 2018).

Kitzinger, Uwe, *Diplomacy and Persuasion: How Britain Joined the Common Market* (London: Thames & Hudson, 1973).

Kogan, Maurice, *The Politics of Education: Edward Boyle and Anthony Crosland in Conversation with Maurice Kogan* (Harmondsworth: Penguin, 1974).

Kwarteng, Kwasi et al., *Britannia Unchained: Global Lessons for Growth and Prosperity* (Basingstoke: Palgrave Macmillan, 2012).

Labour Committee for Europe, *Europe Left* (n.d.).

Labour Common Market Safeguards Campaign, *The Common Market: Labour and the General Election* (Glasgow: LCMSC, 1978).

Labour Party, *1964 Labour Party Election Manifesto* (London: Labour Party, 1964).

——, *Election Manifesto* (London: Labour Party, 1966).

——, *Election Manifesto* (London: Labour Party, 1970).

——, *Election Manifesto February 1974* (London: Labour Party, 1974).

——, *1979 Labour Party Election Manifesto* (London: Labour Party, 1979).

——, *1983 Labour Party Election Manifesto* (London: Labour Party, 1983).

——, *European Election Manifesto* (London: Labour Party, 1984).

——, *Labour Party Election Manifesto* (London: Labour Party, 1997).

Lamont, Norman, *In Office* (London: Little, Brown, 1999).

Laws, David, 'Reclaiming Liberalism: A Liberal Agenda for the Liberal Democrats', pp. 18–42, in Paul Marshall and David Laws (eds), *The Orange Book: Reclaiming Liberalism* (London: Profile, 2004).

——, *Coalition: The Inside Story of the Conservative–Liberal Democrat Coalition Government* (London: Biteback, 2016).

Lawson, Nigel, 'The Need for a National Policy', pp. 47–63, in *Conservatism Today: Four Personal Points of View* (London: CPC, 1966).

——, *The View from No. 11: Memoirs of a Tory Radical* (London: Bantam Press, 1992).

Lewis, W. Arthur, *The Principles of Economic Planning* (London: Routledge, 2003; originally published 1949).

Lipsey, David and Dick Leonard (eds), *The Socialist Agenda: Crosland's Legacy* (London: Cape, 1981).

Macmillan, Harold, *The Middle Way* (London: Macmillan, 1938).

——, *At the End of the Day, 1961–1963* (London: Macmillan, 1973).

——, *Britain, the Commonwealth and Europe* (London: Britain in Europe, 2001; first published 1962).

Major, John, *The Autobiography* (London: HarperCollins, 1999).

Maudling, Reginald, *Memoirs* (London: Sidgwick & Jackson, 1978).

Minford, Patrick, 'Mrs Thatcher's Economic Reform Programme', pp. 93–106, in Robert Skidelsky (ed.), *Thatcherism* (London: Chatto, 1988).

——, 'The Price of Monetary Unification', pp. 149–66, in Martin Holmes (ed.), *The Eurosceptical Reader* (Basingstoke: Macmillan, 1996).

Mitchell, Joan, *Groundwork to Economic Planning* (London: Secker, 1966).

Mullin, Chris, *A View From The Foothills: The Diaries of Chris Mullin* (London: Profile, 2009).

——, *Decline and Fall: Diaries 2005–2010* (London: Profile, 2010).

——, *A Walk-on Part: Diaries 1994–1999* (London: Profile, 2011).

Nairn, Tom, *The Left against Europe?* (Harmondsworth: Penguin, 1973).

NRC, *Referendum on the European Community (Common Market): Why You Should Vote No* (London: HMSO, 1975).

Oliver, Craig, *Unleashing Demons: The Inside Story of Brexit* (London: Hodder & Stoughton, 2017).

One Nation Group of MPs, *One Europe* (London: CPC, 1965).

Phillips, A.W., 'The Relation Between Unemployment and the Rate of Change of Money Wage Rates in the United Kingdom, 1861–1957', *Economica*, vol. 25, no. 100 (1958), pp. 283–99.

Powell, Enoch, ed. John Wood, *Freedom and Reality* (London: Elliot, 1969).

——, *The Common Market: The Case Against* (Kingswood: Elliot, 1971).

——, *Still to Decide* (London: Batsford, 1972).

Prince, Rosa, *Comrade Corbyn: A Very Unlikely Coup: How Jeremy Corbyn Stormed to the Labour Leadership* (London: Biteback, 2016).

Prior, Jim, *A Balance of Power* (London: Hamilton, 1986).

Private Eye, *Private Eye Annual 2011* (London: Private Eye, 2011).

Ridley, Nicholas, *Towards a Federal Europe* (London: CPC, 1969).

——, *My Style of Government: The Thatcher years* (London: Hutchinson, 1991).

Rippon, Geoffrey, *Our Future in Europe: The Case for Staying in the European Community* (London: Conservative Political Centre, 1974).

Roth, Andrew, *Enoch Powell: Tory Tribune* (London, Macdonald & Co., 1970).

——, *Heath and the Heathmen* (London: Routledge, 1972).

Rubinstein, David and Brian Simon, *The Evolution of the Comprehensive School, 1926–1972* (2nd edn, London: Routledge, 1973).

Sandford, Cedric, 'The Diamond Commission and the Redistribution of Wealth', *British Journal of Law and Society*, vol. 7, no. 2 (Winter 1980), pp. 286–96.

Schoen, Douglas, *Enoch Powell and the Powellites* (London: Macmillan, 1977).

Shipman, Tim, *All Out War: The Full Story of Brexit* (rev. and updated edn, London: William Collins, 2017).

Straw, Jack, *Last Man Standing: Memoirs of a Political Survivor* (London: Macmillan, 2012).

Thatcher, Margaret, *The Path to Power* (London: HarperCollins, 1995).

——, *The Downing Street Years* (London: Harper, 1993; 2011 edn).

Trades Union Congress, *The Development of the Social Contract* (London: TUC, 1975).

Trounce, Beverley, *From a Rock to a Hard Place: Memories of the 1984/85 Miners' Strike* (Stroud: The History Press, 2015).

UKIP, *General Election Manifesto* (London, 2010).

UKIP, *General Election Manifesto* (London, 2015).

Utley, T.E., *Enoch Powell: The Man and His Thinking* (London: Kimber, 1968).

Varoufakis, Yanis, *Adults in the Room: My Battle with Europe's Deep Establishment* (London: Bodley Head, 2018).

Watson, Alan, 'Europe's Odd Couple', *Prospect*, no. 10 (July 1996).

Watts, Nick, *Working Together: A New Approach to European Policy Making for Conservatives* (London: Action Centre for Europe Ltd, 2002).

Young, David, 'Speech to Bruges Group', pp. 33–44, in Nicholas Ridley et al., *Shared Thoughts, Shared Values: A First Collection of Public Speeches to the Bruges Group* (London: Bruges Group, 1990).

Interviews

Lord (David) Lea	7 November 2012.
Lord (John) Monks	15 October 2012.
Lord (Chris) Patten	14 January 2013.

Online sources

aei.pitt.edu/1788/1/stuttgart_declaration_1983.pdf, accessed 9 May 2018.

blogs.lse.ac.uk/brexit/2016/09/06/i-want-my-country-back-the-resurgence-of-english-nationalism/, accessed 5 September 2018.

British Political Speech Archive (various).

www.brugesgroup.com/about/the-bruges-group, accessed 12 September 2018.

www.cfr.org/timeline/greeces-debt-crisis-timeline, accessed 4 January 2019.

conservativehome.blogs.com/centreright/2008/04/making-history.html, accessed 18 June 2018.

www.conservativehome.com/thetorydiary/2012/05/what-is-the-fresh-start-project-mbarrettch-profiles-the-tory-mps-trying-to-forge-a-new-uk-eu-relatio.html, accessed 25 June 2018.

conservative-speeches.sayit.mysociety.org/speech/600032 accessed 6 September 2018.

Costa, Rui and Stephen Machin, *Real Wages and Living Standards in the UK*, cep.lse.ac.uk/pubs/download/ea036.pdf, accessed 20 June 2018.

www.cvce.eu/content/publication/1999/1/1/a3d116ff-3ebe-44ee-99b8-e2b038253def/publishable_en.pdf, accessed 6 September 2018.

www.cvce.eu/obj/address_given_by_edward_heath_brussels_29_january_1963-en-d6b554fe-bb82-4499-85fa-02b2407adc65.html, accessed 4 September 2018.

www.cvce.eu/en/obj/statement_by_edward_heath_paris_10_october_1961-en-d990219a-8ad0-4758-946f-cb2ddd05b3c0.html, accessed 5 September 2018.

www.cvce.eu/obj/resolution_adopted_by_the_foreign_ministers_of_the_ecsc_

member_states_messina_1_to_3_june_1955-en-d1086bae-0c13-4a00-8608-73c75ce54fad.html, accessed 17 September 2018.

www.cvce.eu/content/publication/2010/11/15/98bef841-9d8a-4f84-b3a8-719abb63fd62/publishable_en.pdf, accessed 7 September 2018.

data.oecd.org/gga/general-government-spending.htm, accessed 21 August 2018.

data.worldbank.org/indicator/NY.GDP.PCAP.CD?locations=GB, accessed 20 June 2018.

davidmilibandarchive.blogspot.com/2013/09/new-diplomacy-challenges-for-foreign.html, accessed 1 July 2018.

europa.eu/romania/sites/romania/files/tratatul_de_la_roma.pdf, accessed 27 July 2018.

europa.eu/europeanunion/sites/europaeu/.../treaty_on_european_union_en.pdf Treaty on European Union, accessed 14 May 2018.

europa.eu/rapid/press-release_SPEECH-88-66_en.htm, accessed 5 June 2018.

www.europarl.europa.eu/atyourservice/en/displayFtu.html?ftuId=FTU_1.1.5.html, accessed 21 June 2018.

www.geog.ox.ac.uk/research/transformations/gis/papers/dannydorling_publication_id3089.pdf accessed 6 June 2018.

www.gov.uk/government/publications/health-profile-for-england/chapter-1-life-expectancy-and-healthy-life-expectancy, accessed 23 August 2018.

www.gov.uk/government/speeches/chancellors-speech-to-the-american-enterprise-institute, accessed 17 September 2018.

www.gov.uk/government/speeches/eu-speech-at-bloomberg, accessed 21 June 2018.

History & Policy Trade Union Forum, 27 November 2010, www.historyandpolicy.org/trade-union-forum/meeting/how-the-tuc-learned-to-love-the-european-union-and-how-the-affair-turned-ou, accessed 5 June 2018.

www.ifs.org.uk/tools_and_resources/fiscal_facts/public_spending_survey/total_public_spending, figure 1a, accessed 17 November 2016.

www.ifs.org.uk/ff/vat.xls, accessed 17 November 2016.

www.ifs.org.uk/tools_and_resources/fiscal_facts/public_spending_survey/cuts_to_public_spending, accessed 23 June 2018.

www.ifs.org.uk/bns/bn09.pdf, accessed 21 August 2018.

www.ifs.org.uk/uploads/publications/ff/income.xls, accessed 1 December 2016.

www.ifs.org.uk/comms/comm99.pdf, accessed 6 June 2018.

www.kings.cam.ac.uk/files/services/sermon-20140601-bennett.pdf, accessed 13 August 2018.

labourlist.org/2014/03/praise-benn-but-never-forget-the-damage-he-did-to-labour/, accessed 5 June 2018.

labourlist.org/2015/03/milibands-carefully-calibrated-balancing-act/, accessed 17 June 2018.

landregistry.data.gov.uk, accessed 24 June 2018.

www.margaretthatcher.org. (various).

Andrew Adonis on the May 2010 behind-the-scenes coalition negotiations, www.

newstatesman.com/books/2010/11/lib-dem-coalition-laws-labour, accessed 3 January 2019.

www.newyorker.com/news/john-cassidy/pikettys-inequality-story-in-six-charts, accessed 3 January 2019.

www.ons.gov.uk/economy/inflationandpriceindices/timeseries/chaw/mm23, accessed 24 June 2018.

www.ons.gov.uk/...impact-of-the-recession-on-household-income--expenditure, accessed 30 June 2018.

www.ons.gov.uk/peoplepopulationandcommunity/birthsdeathsandmarriages/lifeexpectancies/bulletins/englishlifetablesno17/2015-09-01.

www.ons.gov.uk/economy/governmentpublicsectorandtaxes/publicspending/bulletins/ukgovernmentdebtanddeficitforeurostatmaast/aprtojune2016#summary-of-general-government-deficit-and-gross-debt, accessed 2 July 2018.

www.ons.gov.uk/economy/grossdomesticproductgdp/timeseries/ihyq/pgdp, accessed 26 June 2018.

www.presidency.ucsb.edu/ws/index.php?pid=43130, accessed 28 August 2018.

publications.parliament.uk/pa/cm200607/cmhansrd/cm070321/debtext/70321-0004.htm, cc.815-816, accessed 21 June 2018.

researchbriefings.files.parliament.uk/documents/RP97-102/RP97-102.pdf accessed 31 May 2018.

researchbriefings.parliament.uk/ResearchBriefing/Summary/LLN-2016-0013#fullreport, accessed 13 September 2018.

www.snp.org/pb_what_is_the_snp_s_position_on_the_eu, accessed 7 July 2018.

www.ukpol.co.uk/neil-kinnock-1985-labour-party-conference-speech/, accessed 29 May 2018.

www.voteleavetakecontrol.org/why_vote_leave.html, accessed 11 July 2018.

webarchive.nationalarchives.gov.uk/20130102233042/http://www.number10.gov.uk/news/new-year-podcast/, accessed 11 September 2018.

webarchive.nationalarchives.gov.uk/20100407173744/http://www.hm-treasury.gov.uk/speech_chex_210606.htm.

webarchive.nationalarchives.gov.uk/20080909044415/http://www.number10.gov.uk/Page9003, accessed 22 June 2018.

www.youtube.com/watch?v=_zBFh6bpcMo, accessed 21 February 2018.

www.youtube.com/watch?v=iOWx_OhtCiA, accessed 11 July 2018.

Secondary sources

Books, articles and chapters

Addison, Paul, *The Road to 1945: British Politics and the Second World War* (rev. edn, London: Pimlico, 1994), p. 290.

Allen, Nicholas, 'Labour's Third Term: A Tale of Two Prime Ministers', pp. 1–36, in Nicholas Allen and John Bartle (eds), Britain *at the Polls 2010* (London:

Sage, 2011.

Alvaredo, Facundo et al., *Top Wealth Shares in the UK over more than a Century* (London: Centre for Economic Policy Research, 2017).

Atkinson, Anthony, *Top Incomes in the United Kingdom over the Twentieth Century* (Oxford: Oxford University Press, 2002).

—— and Thomas Piketty (eds), *Top Incomes over the Twentieth Century: A Contrast between European and English-speaking Countries* (Oxford: Oxford University Press, 2007).

Baimbridge, Mark (ed.), *1975 Referendum on Europe, Volume 1: Reflections of the Participants* (Exeter: Imprint, 2007).

Bale, Tim, *The Conservative Party from Thatcher to Cameron* (Cambridge: Polity, 2010; 2011 edn).

Beech, Matt and Simon Lee, *Ten Years of New Labour* (Basingstoke: Palgrave Macmillan, 2008).

—— (eds), *The Conservative–Liberal Coalition: Examining the Cameron–Clegg Government* (Basingstoke: Palgrave Macmillan, 2015).

Bell, Patrick, *The Labour Party in Opposition, 1970–1974* (London: Routledge, 2004).

Berrington, Hugh and Rod Hague, 'Europe, Thatcherism and Traditionalism: Opinion, Rebellion and the Maastricht Treaty in the Backbench Conservative Party, 1992–1994', *West European Politics*, vol. 21, no. 1 (1988), pp. 44–71.Blair, Alasdair, *Dealing with Europe: Britain and the Negotiation of the Maastricht Treaty* (Aldershot: Ashgate, 1999).

Bew, John, *Citizen Clem: A Biography of Attlee* (London: Quercus, 2017).

Blake, Robert, *The Conservative Party from Peel to Major* (London: Heinemann, 1997).

Bloch, Michael, *Jeremy Thorpe* (London: Little, Brown, 2014).

Bogdanor, Vernon and Robert Skidelsky, *The Age of Affluence, 1951–64* (London: Macmillan, 1970).

Boughton, John, *Municipal Dreams: The Rise and Fall of Council Housing* (London: Verso, 2018).

Bower, Tom, *Broken Vows: Tony Blair, The Tragedy of Power* (London: Faber Paperback, 2016).

Broad, Roger, *Labour's European Dilemmas: From Bevin to Blair* (Basingstoke: Palgrave, 2001).

Brusse, Wendy, *Tariffs, Trade, and European Integration, 1947–1957: From Study Group to Common Market* (Basingstoke: Palgrave, 1997).

Buller, Jim, *National Statecraft and European Integration: The Conservative Government and the European Union, 1979–1997* (London: Pinter, 2000).

——, 'New Labour and the European Union', pp. 136–50, in Matt Beech and Simon Lee (eds),

Ten Years of New Labour (Basingstoke: Palgrave Macmillan, 2008).

Bulmer, Simon, 'Britain and European Integration: Of Sovereignty, Slow Adaptation and Semi-detachment', pp. 1–29, in Stephen George (ed.), *Britain and the European Community: The Politics of Semi-detachment* (Oxford: Oxford University Press, 1992).

Burk, Kathlee and Alec Cairncross, *'Goodbye, Great Britain': The 1976 IMF Crisis* (New Haven, CT: Yale University Press, 1992).

Butler, David and Uwe Kitzinger, *The 1975 Referendum* (London: Macmillan, 1976).

Butler, David and Dennis Kavanagh, *The British General Election of 1979* (London: Macmillan, 1980).

——, *The British General Election of 1983* (London: Macmillan, 1999 edn).

——, *The British General Election of 1987* (London: Macmillan, 1999 edn).

——, *The British General Election of 1992* (London: Macmillan, 1999 edn).

——, *The British General Election of 1997* (Basingstoke: Macmillan, 1997).

——, *The British General Election of 2001* (Basingstoke: Palgrave, 2002).

——, *The British General Election of 2005* (Basingstoke: Palgrave, 2005).

Cairncross, Alec, *The British Economy since 1945: Economic Policy and Performance, 1945–1995* (2nd edn, Oxford: Blackwell, 1995).

Callaghan, John, *The Labour Party and Foreign Policy* (Abingdon: Routledge, 2007).

Campbell, A., 'The Single European Act and the Implications', *International & Comparative Law Quarterly*, vol. 35, no. 4 (October 1986), pp. 932–9.

Campbell, John, *Edward Heath: A Biography* (London: Jonathan Cape, 1993).

——, *Roy Jenkins: A Well-Rounded Life* (London: Cape, 2014).

Chester, Daniel, *The Nationalisation of British Industry, 1945–51* (London: HMSO, 1975).

Chick, Martin, *Industrial Policy in Britain, 1945–1951: Economic Planning, Nationalisation and the Labour Governments* (Cambridge: Cambridge University Press, 1998).

Chitty, Clyde, *Education Policy in Britain* (3rd edn, Basingstoke: Palgrave, 2014).

Clarke, Harold D., Matthew Goodwin and Paul Whiteley, *Brexit: Why Britain Voted to Leave the European Union* (Cambridge: Cambridge University Press, 2017).

Clegg, Hugh, *The Changing System of Industrial Relations in Great Britain* (Oxford: Blackwell, 1979).

Cowley, Philip and Dennis Kavanagh, *The British General Election of 2015* (Basingstoke: Palgrave Macmillan, 2016).

Crafts, Nicholas, *British Economic Growth Before and After 1979: A Review of the Evidence* (London: Centre for Economic Policy Research, 1988).

Crooks, Stanley, *Peter Thorneycroft* (Winchester: George Mann, 2007).

Crowson, N.J., *The Conservative Party and European Integration since 1945: At the Heart of Europe?* (Abingdon: Routledge, 2007).

D'Ancona, Matthew, *In It Together: The Inside Story of the Coalition Government* (London: Viking, 2013).

Daddow, Oliver, *New Labour and the European Union: Blair and Brown's Logic of History* (Manchester: Manchester University Press, 2011).

Daunton, Martin, *Just Taxes: The Politics of Taxation in Britain, 1914–1979* (Cambridge; Cambridge University Press, 2002).

Davies, Paul and Mark Freedland, *Labour Legislation and Public Policy: A Contemporary History* (Oxford: Clarendon Press, 1993).

Dedman, Martin, *The Origins and Development of the European Union, 1945–95: A History of European Integration* (London: Routledge, 1996).

Dell, Edmund, *A Hard Pounding: Politics and Economic Crisis, 1974–1976* (Oxford: Oxford University Press, 1991).

Diamond, Patrick, *The Crosland Legacy: The Future of British Social Democracy* (Bristol: Policy Press, 2016).

Dorey, Peter, *British Conservatism and Trade Unionism, 1945–1964* (Abingdon: Routledge, 2009).

Dorling, Danny, *Peak Inequality: Britain's Ticking Time Bomb* (London: Policy Press, 2018).

Dukes, Ruth, 'Otto Kahn-Freund and Collective Laissez-Faire: An Edifice without a Keystone?', *The Modern Law Review*, vol. 72, no. 2 (March 2009), pp. 220–46.

Evans, Geoffrey and Anand Menon, *Brexit and British Politics* (Cambridge: Polity, 2017).

Fielding, Steve, *'Labourism' and Locating the British Labour Party within the European Left* (Salford: European Studies Research Institute, 1996).

——, *The Labour Party: Continuity and Change in the Making of New Labour* (Basingstoke: Palgrave Macmillan, 2003).

Ford, Robert and Matthew Goodwin, *Revolt on the Right: Explaining Support for the Radical Right in Britain* (London: Routledge, 2013).

Forster, Anthony, *Euroscepticism in Contemporary British Politics: Opposition to Europe in the British Conservative and Labour Parties since 1945* (London: Routledge, 2002).

George, Stephen, *An Awkward Partner: Britain in the European Community* (3rd edn, Oxford: Oxford University Press, 1998).

Gibbon, Gary, *Breaking Point: The UK Referendum on the EU and its Aftermath* (London: Haus, 2016).

Gifford, Chris, *The Making of Eurosceptic Britain* (2nd edn, Farnham: Ashgate, 2014).

Gilmour, Ian, *Dancing with Dogma: Britain under Thatcherism* (London: Simon & Schuster, 1992).

Glynn, Sean and Alan Booth (eds), *The Road to Full Employment* (London: Allen & Unwin, 1986).

Goes, Eunice, *The Labour Party under Ed Miliband: Trying but Failing to Renew Social Democracy* (Manchester: Manchester University Press, 2016).

Goldman, Lawrence, *The Life of R.H. Tawney: Socialism and History* (London: Bloomsbury, 2014).

Goodman, Geoffrey, *The Miners' Strike* (London: Pluto Press, 1985).

Goodwin, Matthew and Caitlin Milazzo, *UKIP: Inside the Campaign to Redraw the Map of British Politics* (Oxford: Oxford University Press, 2015).

Gowland, David and Arthur Turner, *Britain and European Integration, 1945–1998: A Documentary History* (London: Routledge, 2000).

Grant, Wyn, *The Political Economy of Industrial Policy* (London: Butterworth, 1982).

Green, E.H.H., *Ideologies of Conservatism: Conservative Political Ideas in the Twentieth Century* (Oxford: Oxford University Press, 2004).

Grieve Smith, John, *Full Employment: A Pledge Betrayed* (Basingstoke: Macmillan, 1997).

Grob-Fitzgibbon, Benjamin, *Continental Drift: Britain and Europe from the End of Empire to the Rise of Euroscepticism* (Cambridge: Cambridge University Press, 2016).

Hain, Peter, *Back to the Future of Socialism* (Bristol: Policy Press, 2015).

Hall, Stuart, 'The Neo-liberal Revolution', *Cultural Studies*, vol. 25, no. 6 (2011), pp. 705–28.

Hattersley, Roy and Kevin Hickson, 'In Praise of Social Democracy', *Political Quarterly*, vol. 83, no 1 (2012), pp. 5–12.

Hay, Colin, 'The Winter of Discontent after Thirty Years', *Political Quarterly*, vol. 80, no. 4 (2009), pp. 545–61.

Heffer, Simon, *Like the Roman: The Life of Enoch Powell* (London: Weidenfeld & Nicolson, 1998).

Hepple, Bob and Sandra Fredman, *Labour Law and Industrial Relations in Great Britain* (Deventer: Kluwer, 1986).

Hickson, Kevin (ed.), *The Political Thought of the Liberals and Liberal Democrats since 1945* (Manchester: Manchester University Press, 2009).

Hill, Richard, *The Labour Party's Economic Strategy, 1979–1997: The Long Road Back* (Basingstoke: Palgrave, 2001).

Hindmoor, Andrew, *What's Left Now?: The History and Future of Social Democracy* (Oxford: Oxford University Press, 2018).

Holden, Russell, *The Making of New Labour's European Policy* (Basingstoke: Palgrave, 2002).

Horne, Alistair, *Macmillan, 1894–1956, Volume 1 of the Official Biography* (London: Macmillan, 1988).

——, *Harold Macmillan: 1957–1986, Volume II of the Official Biography* (London: Macmillan, 1989).

Howson, Susan, *British Monetary Policy 1945–51* (Oxford: Clarendon Press, 1993).

Hynes, Catherine, *The Year that Never Was: Heath, the Nixon administration and the Year of Europe* (Dublin: University College Dublin Press, 2009).

Jackson, Ben, *Equality and the British Left: A Study in Progressive Political Thought, 1900–64* (Manchester: Manchester University Press, 2007).

Jefferys, Kevin, *Anthony Crosland: A New Biography* (London: Politico's, 2000).

Jenkins, Simon, *Thatcher and Sons: A Revolution in Three Acts* (London: Penguin, 2007).

Jones, Harriet, '"New Conservatism"? The Industrial Charter, Modernity and the Reconstruction of British Conservatism after the War', pp. 171–88, in B. Conekin et al., *Moments of Modernity: Reconstructing Britain, 1945–1964* (London: Rivers Oram Press, 1999).

Jones, Nicholas, *Sultans of Spin: The Media and the New Labour Government* (London: Gollancz, 2000).

Jones, Tudor, *The Revival of British Liberalism: From Grimond to Clegg* (Basingstoke: Palgrave, 2011).

Kavanagh, Dennis and Philip Cowley, *The British General Election of 2010* (Basingstoke: Palgrave Macmillan, 2010).

Keating, Michael and David McCrone, *The Crisis of Social Democracy in Europe* (Edinburgh: Edinburgh University Press, 2015).

Kelly, Richard, 'The Party Conferences', pp. 221–60, in A. Seldon and S. Ball (eds), *Conservative Century: The Conservative Party since 1900* (Oxford: Oxford University Press, 1994).

King, Anthony and Ivor Crewe, *SDP: The Birth, Life, and Death of the Social Democratic Party* (Oxford: Oxford University Press, 1995).

King, Peter, *Housing Policy Transformed* (Bristol: Policy Press, 2010).

Knowles, Elizabeth and Angela Partington (eds), *The Oxford Dictionary of Quotations* (5th edn, Oxford: Oxford University Press, 1999).

Lee, Simon, 'The British Model of Political Economy', pp. 17–34, in Matt Beech and Simon Lee (eds), *Ten Years of New Labour* (Basingstoke: Palgrave Macmillan, 2008).

Ludlow, Peter, *The Making of the European Monetary System: A Case Study of the Politics of the European Community* (London: Butterworth; 1982).

Lynch, Philip, 'The Conservatives and Europe, 1997–2001', pp. 146–63, in Mark Garnett and Philip Lynch, *The Conservatives in Crisis* (Manchester: Manchester University Press, 2003).

——, 'The Coalition and the European Union', pp. 243–58, in Philip Cowley and Dennis Kavanagh, *The British General Election of 2015* (Basingstoke: Palgrave Macmillan, 2016).

Marquand, David, *Britain since 1918: The Strange Career of British Democracy* (London; Orion, 2008).

Marsh, David, *The Euro: The Politics of the New Global Currency* (New Haven, CT: Yale University Press, 2009).

Marwick, Arthur, 'Middle Opinion in the Thirties: Planning, Progress and Political "Agreement"', *The English Historical Review*, vol. 79, no. 311 (April 1964), pp. 285–98.

McCallum, J.D., 'The Development of British Regional Policy', pp. 3–42, in D. MacLennan and J. Parr, *Regional Policy: Past Experience and New Directions* (Oxford; Robertson, 1979).

Milward, Alan, *The Rise and Fall of a National Strategy, 1945–1963* (London: Whitehall History, 2002).

Moore, Charles, *Margaret Thatcher: The Authorized Biography, Volume One: Not For Turning* (London: Penguin, 2013).

——, *Margaret Thatcher: The Authorized Biography, Volume Two: Everything She Wants* (London: Allen Lane, 2015).

Moore, Martin and Gordon Ramsay, *UK Media Coverage of the 2016 EU Referendum Campaign* (London: Centre for the Study of Media, Communication and Power, 2017).

Moran, Michael, *The Politics of Industrial Relations: The Origins, Life, and Death of the 1971 Industrial Relations Act* (London: Palgrave, 1977).

——, *The British Regulatory State: High Modernism and Hyper-innovation* (Oxford: Oxford University Press, 2003).

Moran, Michael, Sukhdev Johal and Karel Williams, 'The Financial Crisis and its Consequences', pp. 89–119, in Nicholas Allen and John Bartle (eds), *Britain at the Polls 2010* (London: Sage, 2011).

Morgan, Kenneth, *Michael Foot: A Life* (London: HarperCollins, 2007).

——, *Ages of Reform: Dawns and Downfalls of the British Left* (London: Tauris, 2011).

Morgan, W. John (ed.), *The Rise and Fall of Full Employment 1944–1994* (Nottingham: University of Nottingham, 1994).

Mullen, Andrew, *The British Left's 'Great Debate' on Europe* (London: Continuum, 2007).

Naughtie, James, *The Rivals: The Intimate Story of a Political Marriage* (London: Fourth Estate, 2001).

Newton, Scott and Dilwyn Porter, *Modernization Frustrated: The Politics of Industrial Decline in Britain since 1900* (London: Unwin, 1988).

Offer, Avner, 'The Market Turn: From Social Democracy to Market Liberalism', *Economic History Review*, vol. 70, no. 4 (2017), pp. 1051–71.

Paterson, Peter, *Tired and Emotional: The Life of Lord George-Brown* (London: Chatto & Windus, 1993).

Pimlott, Ben, *Harold Wilson* (London: HarperCollins, 1992).

Pitchford, Mark, *The Conservative Party and the Extreme Right, 1945–75* (Manchester: Manchester University Press, 2011).

Power, Michael, *Audit Society: Rituals of Verification* (Oxford: Oxford University Press, 1999).

Preston, John, *A Very English Scandal: Sex, Lies and a Murder Plot at the Heart of the Establishment* (London: Penguin, 2017).

Rae, John, *The Public Schools Revolution: Britain's Independent Schools 1964–1979* (London: Faber & Faber, 1981).

Rawnsley, Andrew, *Servants of the People* (London: Penguin, 2003).

——, *The End of the Party* (London: Penguin, 2010).

Reed, Howard and Jacob Mohun Himmelweit, *Where Have All The Wages Gone?* (London: TUC, 2012).

Reid, Alastair, *United We Stand: A History of British Trade Unions* (London: Allen Lane, 2004).

Rhodes James, Robert, *Bob Boothby: A Portrait* (Sevenoaks: Hodder, 1991).

Richards, Andrew, *Miners on Strike: Class Solidarity and Division in Britain*

(Oxford: Berg, 1996).

Richardson, Heather, *To Make Men Free: A History of the Republican Party* (New York: Basic Books, 2014).

Ritschel, Daniel, *The Politics of Planning* (Oxford: Clarendon Press, 1997).

Robins, Lynton, *The Reluctant Party: Labour and the EEC, 1961–1975* (Ormskirk: Hesketh, 1979).

Saunders, Robert, *Yes to Europe! The 1975 Referendum and Seventies Britain* (Cambridge: Cambridge University Press, 2018).

Shepherd, John, *Crisis? What Crisis?: The Callaghan Government and the British 'Winter of Discontent'* (Manchester: Manchester University Press, 2013).

Spiering, Menno, *A Cultural History of British Euroscepticism* (Basingstoke: Palgrave Macmillan, 2015).

Taylor, Robert, *The Fifth Estate: Britain's Unions in the Seventies* (London: Routledge, 1978).

——, 'The Need for an Incomes Policy', pp. 149–67, in R. Charter et al., *Incomes Policy* (Oxford: Clarendon Press, 1981).

——, *The Trade Union Question in British Politics* (Oxford: Blackwell, 1993).

——, 'The Heath Government, Industrial Policy and the "New Capitalism"', pp. 139–59, in A. Seldon and S. Ball (eds), *The Heath Government, 1970–1974: A Reappraisal* (London: Routledge, 1996).

Thorpe, D.R., *Supermac: The life of Harold Macmillan* (London: Chatto & Windus, 2010).

Tomlinson, Jim, *Government and the Enterprise since 1900: The Changing Problem of Efficiency* (Oxford: Oxford University Press, 1994).

——, *The Politics of Decline: Understanding Post-War Britain* (Harlow: Longman, 2000).

——, *The Labour Governments 1964–1970, Volume 3: Economic Policy* (Manchester: Manchester University Press, 2003).

Toye, Richard, *The Labour Party and the Planned Economy, 1931–1951* (Woodbridge: RHS, 2003).

Tratt, Jacqueline, *The Macmillan Government and Europe: A Study in the Process of Policy Development* (Basingstoke: Macmillan, 1996).

Turner, John, *The Tories and Europe* (Manchester, Manchester University Press, 2000).

Wall, Stephen, *The Official History of Britain and the European Community, Volume II: From Rejection to Referendum, 1963–1975* (London: Routledge, 2013).

Wass, Douglas, *Decline to Fall* (Oxford: Oxford University Press, 2008).

Weeks, Jeffrey, *Sex, Politics and Society: The Regulation of Sexuality since 1800* (3rd edn, Harlow: Pearson, 2012).

Wickham-Jones, Mark, 'The Debate about Wages: The New Left, the Labour Party and Incomes Policy', *Journal of Political Ideologies*, vol. 18, no. 1 (2013), pp. 83–105.

Wilkes, George and Dominic Wring, 'The British Press and European

Integration, 1948 to 1996', pp. 185–205, in David Baker and David Seawright (eds), *Britain For and Against Europe: British Politics and the Question of European Integration* (Oxford: Clarendon Press, 1998).

Williams, Philip, *Hugh Gaitskell* (London: Cape, 1979).

Wrigley, Chris, *British Trade Unions since 1933* (Cambridge: Cambridge University Press, 2002).

Young, Hugo, *This Blessed Plot: Britain and Europe from Churchill to Blair* (London: Macmillan, 1998).

Ziegler, Philip, *Edward Heath: The Authorised Biography* (London: HarperPress, 2010).

Online sources

Oxford Dictionary of National Biography (ODNB): various.

Levy, David et al., *UK Press Coverage of the EU Referendum*, p. 5, http:// reutersinstitute.politics.ox.ac.uk/sites/default/files/2017-06/UK%20Press%20 Coverage%20of%20the%20EU%20Referendum_0.pdf, accessed 28 June 2018.

www.bankofengland.co.uk/-/media/boe/files/quarterly-bulletin/2010/the- uk-recession-in-context-what-do-three-centuries-of-data-tell-us.pdf; researchbriefings.files.parliament.uk/documents/SN06167/SN06167.pdf, both accessed 30 June 2018.

www.ifs.org.uk/tools_and_resources/fiscal_facts/public_spending_survey/ total_public_spending, figure 1a, accessed 17 November.2016.

www.ons.gov.uk/ons/rel/.../unemployment--trends-since-the-1970s.pdf, accessed 24 August 2018.

www.statista.com/statistics/287232/trade-union-density-united-kingdom-uk-y- on-y/, accessed 18 August 2018.

Piketty, Thomas, *Brahmin Left vs Merchant Right: Rising Inequality & the Changing Structure of Political Conflict (Evidence from France, Britain and the US, 1948–2017)*, http://piketty.pse.ens.fr/files/Piketty2018.pdf, accessed 18 September 2018.

www.ons.gov.uk/ons/rel/lms/labour.../unemployment-since-1881.pdf.Table 1 and statswales.wales.gov.uk/Catalogue/Business-Economy-and-Labour- Market/People-and-Work/Unemployment/ILO-Unemployment/CHART- ILOUnemploymentRates-by-UKCountry-Quarter, both accessed 9 July 2013.

Index